OPIUM LORDS
China 1832 - 42

by
AMY Mc GRATH

*Opium was the immediate, but not
the ultimate cause of the war
Hsu Emmanuel: The Rise of Modern China
(New York 1970)*

*It might have been the Molasses War
if molasses had happened to be the commodity the
British merchants had been determined to sell.
Chang Hsin-Pao: Commissioner Lin and the Opium War
(Harvard 1964)*

Published by Tower House Publications
Box 737 PO Kensington, Sydney Australia NSW 2033
Tel (02) 9962 2282

Distributed by
Tower Books Wholesalers Pty.Ltd.
19 Rodborough Road, Frenchs Forest 2033

First published 1997

Cover Design Wendy de Paauw

Typography & Typesetting John Frampton

Printed by Ligare

©Amy McGrath
National Library of Australia Card Number
IBSN No 0 9587 104 14

The Emperor holds an audience in the Forbidden City

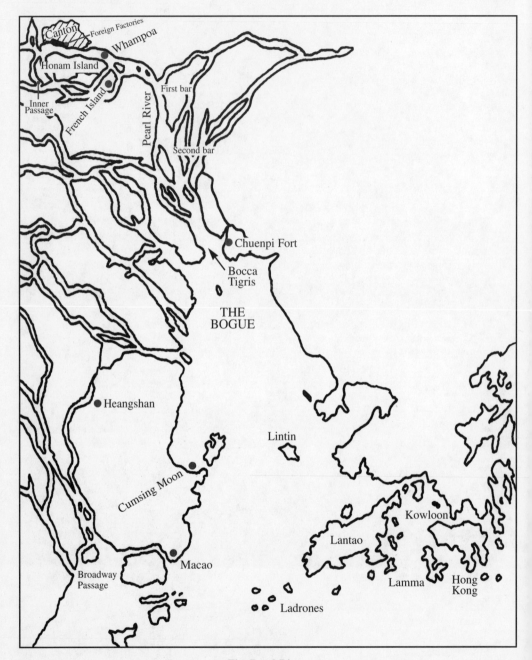

Canton
Foreign Factories
Whampoa
Honam Island
French Island
Inner Passage
Pearl River
First bar
Second bar
Chuenpi Fort
Bocca Tigris
THE BOGUE
Heangshan
Lintin
Cumsing Moon
Broadway Passage
Macao
Lantao
Kowloon
Lamma
Hong Kong
Ladrones

The Pearl River

CHAPTER 1

The Year of Our Lord 1832

Salem, Connecticut, USA.

In this fine spring of her twenty-first year, Holly Shay was about to take destiny into her own hands. She would up anchor from the port where she had always lived, and cast the ship of her life adrift with the same resolution as her forebears, those old whaling captains who, for three generations past, set sail for the open sea knowing they would not return from the Pacific Ocean for at least two or three years if at all. She would abandon this dying port where the cluster of sailing ships in the reaches of the river grew thinner every year, and leave America, possibly for ever.

Throughout the long-drawn out days of her father's last illness, she knew she was heir to their restless spirits, and longed to be free. Not to go to New York under the wing of her Aunt Jean, as her Uncle Bart, executor of her father's will, had urged, but to the place of her longing for independence. So she announced now the predictable will had been read that she and her brother were his sole heirs, 'I'm going to China'.

The shock of five of the six people in the room was palpable: not only of her uncle and aunt, but of her dearest friend, her cousin Abby, and Jim Peel, captain of the ship owned by her father, the Eugenia. But not of her brother, Lou, who already knew. Such a plan was simply scandalous, preposterous, beyond all bounds of propriety or custom they declared vying in their outrage as she stood defiantly before them, a slender delicate figure in her flowing sprigged muslin gown looking younger than her years.

Proper enough for her to be a teacher or governess, even to help Uncle Bart in the business they insisted. But she could not, in all seemliness, go to China, not unless well-chaperoned by a married woman. Her Aunt Jean wept hysterically, clutching Holly's sleeve as if to detain her from a voyage already begun.

'I often warned your father. A girl alone in a household of men! Live-in apprentices and all! Warned him where it would lead! Too much independence, I said!'

Holly rebuked her timid aunt impatiently. 'Tush, aunt. Salem women have always had to be independent. Who ran the shop but mother, for heaven's sake, while Dad was at sea months, years at a time, until he swallowed the anchor?' As he had after a fall from a yardarm in a hammering storm rounding the Cape, lucky to lose no more than a leg.

Abby, arm round Aunt Jean, said soothingly, 'Holly is right. She needs a change after her sad loss.'

Holly rejected this sop. 'I'm not going for a change.'

The perplexity on Uncle Bart's stolid face was almost comical, 'then why go at all?'

'I want to go into the China trade'.

Uncle Bart protested, 'if that's all you want to do, you can trade out of our Brooklyn warehouse. Your father did. Come and live with us if you will.'

Thinking nothing could be further from her wish than to live with her indolent, fatuous aunt, Holly replied tersely, 'and what happened Uncle? Too often goods bought for female taste by ignorant males in China. Ladies should buy for ladies.'

Uncle Bart hesitated. Holly talked sense. She knew the business and had helped her father with the books even before her mother's tragic death.

'You would gamble all the capital you have?'

'As my father did.'

'And nearly left you and your brother penniless at one time,' Aunt Jean interposed acidly.

'That's my risk. I'll hurt no one but myself.'

Uncle Bart perceived one last problem. 'Who will look after the shop while you're gone?'

He assumed it would not be her brother, Lou, already known to reject all connection with the sea. Those stories of tragedy at sea, whose whispers haunted every last corner of Salem, had always filled him with horror. It was Holly who seemed to borrow the inward strength of those grandfathers both lost at sea, although outwardly as delicate as the porcelain figures on the mantelshelf behind her; she who could face the sea with equanimity rather than Lou.

Holly explained, 'Lou and I have decided to sell the business.'

Her uncle's reaction was as sharp as she expected, 'the only security you both have.'

Lou, dear quiet Lou, spoke up at last, 'I need the money to buy a farm.'

Aunt Jean, acerbic now, spat out, 'your plan is sensible, Lou, Holly's the utmost folly.'

Holly curbed her anger with difficulty. 'Did anyone say it was folly for my father and my grandfather to abandon their wives and children to hunt whale and seal in the wastes of the Antarctic? You only say so now Aunt, because I'm a woman.' Aunt Jean evaded her eye. 'Blame their restless blood if you will, but I can't deny it.'

Uncle Bart, aware he was doomed to live with Aunt Jean's disapproval, tried one last plea. 'Salem is running down, as we all know. You'll find the business hard to sell.'

Holly disposed of that objection. 'Mr Pratt longs to buy it. He's come into a modest competence.' The little crippled assistant was devoted to the business and loved by all.

Uncle Bart threw up his hands, his protest done. But Aunt Jean's was not. 'Who will chaperone you in China?'

Holly dealt her last triumphant card. 'Why Mary Ann, of course.' Absurd though it was, her old school friend, Mary Ann, could, as a married woman, chaperone her although only a year older than herself.

But Aunt Jean had one more throw of her own. 'What about your mother's boast of an inheritance?'

Holly laughed, 'Oh that hoary old family legend that Dad was in line for a title and castle? Dreams we migrants carry in our baggage when we cross the sea, no more.'

Afternoon tea brought an uneasy truce. Argument hardly a propos to tea served on an embroidered Chinese lace cloth in shell-thin Chinese cups with slabs of moist chocolate cake on matching plates.

Holly seized the chance to enlist Abby, 'Why don't you come too, Abby? You always said you wished you could find a man to whisk you off to the magic of the East like Mary Ann.'

Abby gulped a scalding draught of the tea she had been gently sipping, and dabbed at her mouth with a minute lawn napkin in distress over both the tea and the idea.

'Why that was just romantic talk! I never seriously considered...'

'Now's your chance', Holly urged, hand persuasively on Abby's plump arm.

Uncle Bart now unexpectedly backed Holly up. Holly deserved a time span of light-hearted freedom growing up as she had in the shadow first of her mother's lingering death, and then of her father's last agonising months with his will to live undermined by his grief. Who better than the fun-loving Abby to guarantee that?

Abby had her own compelling reason to heed them both - a broken engagement to a childhood friend, one she had drifted into rather than thwart a father she adored. Her kindly fiance, unwilling to hurt her, had allowed it to drift. It was Holly, who had shocked her into the truth that a lifetime with Joad would not be the same as life with her father, a buoyant man, had been. In appalled appraisal, she realised Joad was opposite in every way, and broke the engagement, only to be dismayed at Joad's obvious relief.

Holly had even more reason than Abby to leave Salem - the heartbreak of first love for the wrong man, a wealthy young man of handsome negligence of manner amusing himself with her during the sailing season. She had allowed him to devastate her heart with his flirtatious expertise longing for the love she received neither from her quarrelsome brother, nor her father too withdrawn into his sorrow. But it had meant no more to him than idle dalliance, his true ambition being to loaf his way through Harvard and marry even more money.

Holly urged Abby, 'You will come, won't you Abby?'

Abby jumped up to throw her arms round Holly. 'I couldn't allow you to go alone. Besides, Captain Peel has just convinced me there are plenty of real gentlemen there, and a real polite society. The East India Company men live like princes. And when they come down from Canton to Macao for the summer, there's quite a season in Macao. Theatricals. Opera. Concerts. Boat races. And perfectly splendid parties.'

Aunt Jean asked, 'And in the winter, what then?'

Bewilderment on Captain Peel's candid young face, 'Ma'am? Whatever young ladies do. Read. Talk. Visit.' Then aware of the girls' alarm at this vista of boredom, he added, 'Ma'am, it's true the ships do go up the Pearl River to

Whampoa and the merchants to Canton, but they are back and forth all the time. When they're gone, there are always others - captains of the coastal and depot ships, or wanderers. Some call it the Naples of the East.'

Holly smiled affectionately at him. She had known him as long as she could remember, reappearing from vast ocean voyages as he grew from boy to man always at ease with himself in the good fortune of enjoying the one and only vocation he had ever wanted, that of first class seaman like his father before him. Dear Jim, whose adventures she had always longed to follow, adventures in which, as fate would have it, she was now destined to share.

Now Jim hastened to reassure Aunt Jean, clearly oblivious to his easy charm in her frowning disapproval now that his talk of Naples had reminded her that Macao's notorious opium trade made it no fit place for a lady.

'The East India Company forbids its captains to carry opium as cargo on their ships. They have to sign bonds to that effect when they reach Macao before they can enter Pearl River. And while some country traders out of India do smuggle it, they risk losing their licenses.'

His half-truth satisfied Aunt Jean, but not Holly. What of those traders who sailed under a foreign flag as many, including New Englanders, did?

'Does Mary Ann's husband deal in opium?' she asked Jim.

Uncle Bart answered for him. 'All American ships do. They need the ready cash to buy their tea, silk and other goods. The Chinese buy so little from us.'

'Where do we get the opium?'

'From Turkey chiefly. Can't get Company opium from Calcutta. Can't even get Malwa opium from Portuguese territories in India. That mostly goes through the Parsees of Bombay.'

Holly was horrified at this insight into Uncle Joshua's affairs. 'Does this mean I'll have to carry opium to make the turn around pay?'

Uncle Bart put his cup down with a rattle. 'You, Holly? Why ever should you be concerned with opium?'

'Because I'll own the Eugenia. I've bought Lou out so I can run her between China and New York.'

Aunt Jean cried, 'Your mother would turn in her grave'.

'My mother would have been the first to approve.'

Memory stirred in Uncle Bart. 'Holly won't be able to trade in Canton herself like the other traders, will she, Jim?'

Jim admitted reluctantly, 'no. Women are forbidden.'

Holly was appalled at this unforeseen piece of news. 'Women forbidden? Perhaps no one has wanted to try.'

'They've wanted to alright,' Jim admitted, 'but they know the price. All trade stopped in the port. All supplies of food and water cut off. All servants withdrawn. Everyone locked in like rats in a trap eighty miles up river from the sea.'

Her aunt voiced her distress. 'Holly, you'll be a woman in a man's world. You can't.'

'Stuff and nonsense, Aunt. Of course I can if I use Uncle Joshua's name, not my own.'

When they had left at last, Abby asked only, 'won't you find Macao very restricted, Holly? Just one small town and nowhere to go?'

Holly seized Abby to whirl her round the room, crying, 'and what would I do here in Salem but twirl in one small spot. The journey is always in the mind, and so it will be there. The world will come to us.' Abby left to wonder if Holly would maybe turn her life not merely into a whirl, but irrevocably upside down.

In the frenzy of packing, as if they were going to the North Pole not a civilised city as Jim Peel protested, she found time to insist to him, 'not a word to anyone out there that I'm the true owner of the ship. I'll play the part of a silly, simple girl the world expects.'

'You could never be that, Holly,' he smiled down at her, protective even now as he had been in childhood. 'No play actor will do better.'

She sighed. If only she could love a solid enduring man like Jim. Alas, she feared she needed a man with the dash, the intellectual play the sturdy Jim lacked, and wondered whether she would find her true match in the exotic world for which she was bound.

Jim tried to give Holly one last warning. 'Violence is always round every corner even in Macao.'

Holly brushed his concern aside. 'Jim, the reason I rejected moving to New York was the violence of Manhattan and Brooklyn. Roughs everywhere as fortune hunters drift into the city and take to the streets when they fail. What's the difference?'

'Then God keep you safe!' Jim said with a fervour Holly thought misplaced.

When the Eugenia called into New York to load, and the business of registering her at the Tontine was over, her uncle put it otherwise. 'I hope you haven't made a devil's bargain, girl.'

In the excitement of departure on a singing spring day, Holly felt no gloom could touch her. She chided him. 'Do I risk selling my soul to the devil, uncle?'

His eyes crinkled with fun, for once not the Sobersides he tried to be. 'I'll tell you a story. There was once an Irishman who loved to play cards. If there was a game, he would sit down to gamble. One day he had lost everything and was about to stagger home penniless and drunk, when a charming stranger sat down and said, 'would you like a game?' Thinking that even now he might redeem his fortune, he said 'sure'.

He played like a demon and had won a great pile of money when he chanced to look down as he stacked the cards, and saw the man had a cloven hoof. Frightened out of his wits, he swept the money into his cap and ran as fast as his feet would carry him to his house. As he staggered through the door, his wife accosted him, 'anyone would think the devil himself was after you'. He gasped 'the devil is'. In proof he opened his cap to show her his pile of gold but found nothing there but a pile of autumn leaves. 'For sure,' she said, 'the devil himself has taught you a lesson - the evils of gambling and drink.'

'And what is my lesson Uncle? Not to gamble too much or at all? But trade is always a gamble.'

'My dear, I hope you come back with the gold, not the autumn leaves.'

Holly dropped a kiss on his seamed brow. 'The only leaves I'll gather are the holly leaves, Uncle, for the elves to shelter under from the bitter cold of winter. They'll bring me luck.'

'There are no leaves in Macao, Holly,' he reminded her, but nevertheless cut her a clutch of holly branch for luck as she boarded the ship that would carry her on her perilous voyage into the future.

* * * * * *

Macao

Sean Jarman stared with astonishment at the pink three story building he was about to enter. So unadorned, so anonymous like all the rest along the Praya Grande, the waterfront promenade of Macao.

Yet this was the headquarters of the China Branch of the United East India Company, ruler of the three Presidencies of India. The Company of such great generals and statesmen as Clive and Hastings. The Company that possessed great warehouses, territories, its own army and vast fleet that doubled as a navy in time of war. The Company that had been king of the vast silk, china and tea trade of the Treaty Port of Canton for so many years.

Sean's uncle, Dr. William Jarman, was already waiting in the entrance hall to greet him with warm approval, a generous smile softening the imposing gravity of his strong face as he gripped Sean's hand in both his own. Sean was surprised to see his uncle physically more a mirror of himself than his own father even to their matching height but, as he realised to his horror, far more resplendent in full evening dress. As were those he could see in the grand reception room beyond, and to make matters worse wearing hats or caps except for the captains in their formal buff and blue. He, hatless, and in his green velvet jacket, hopelessly out of tune with etiquette in a sanctum obviously dominated by it. He felt an ignoramus, a fool.

'Uncle William you should have told me it was formal.'

'And embarrassed you without evening dress?'

'I might have borrowed one.'

He put a consoling hand on Sean's arm. 'Not so many men in port your size! Time to introduce you to the Honourable John.'

'Who is he?' Sean asked doubtfully, scarcely mollified.

'His uncle laughed, 'everyone in that room. The Company known as the Honourable John, the world's most exclusive club.' A club exclusive and awesome in the grandeur of the statement of wealth and power symbolised by the massive crystal chandelier and monstrous paintings, boastful of Indian occupation, that dominated the room.

'Dying throes of an age about to end,' his uncle said dismissively as he steered him through the throng. 'Remember titles are all naval here whether on ship or shore. That man over there, talking to the master attendant of shipping, is a purser. And this one on our right, talking to the surgeon, is a supercargo.'

'Supercargo?' Sean queried, mystified by the jargon of the trade.

'Merchandiser on board ship. Buys and sells. You must be a supercargo to serve on the Company's Select Committee which controls all Company trade in China. Like those four gentlemen there.' He pointed to four men clustered in front of the vast marble fireplace. 'And that is the President, the next thing to God in China always to be found in his rightful place below his lord and master'. He pointed to the great Ramsay portrait of King George over the fireplace. And then in turn introduced one of the four men of the Select as John Davies, Deputy to the President.

Whatever Sean had expected of one of the uncrowned kings of the Company, it was not this jovial short round man with a childlike face, deep in some hilarious anecdote. He seemed an unlikely adversary for his craggy uncle, every inch the descendant of fierce combative clan chiefs of Scotland, who now said reflectively, 'otherwise known as the Mad Davies'.

'Mad', it seemed, because he was not only preoccupied with the history, law and customs of China but was also fluent in their harsh and difficult language, more expert than anyone else except the Company interpreter, the missionary Dr. Norris.

'Ah Dr. Jarman, your nephew arrived at last!' John Davies shook hands with an effusion that belied his real feelings about the Jarman clan.

Trust William Jarman to find a young relative an exact replica of himself from thick dark wavy, hair, strong nose accentuated by the aggressive jaw under striking ginger sideburns, down to mighty 'thews' and outsized feet. An heir no doubt as tough and bloody-minded as himself. A breed, tempered in ancient feuds, here on the coast for one purpose - to make their fortunes without bending to any corporate will whatever the cost, as those in the Company had had to do these past two hundred years.

Belying his true feelings, John Davies' urbane civility was unexceptionable. 'Welcome to China! I trust it will fulfil your hopes. They will be different, of course, from those of the old Company men. For you are the new order, you free traders. I hope they will all be men of such high calibre as you. I fear they will not'. In fact he believed free trade would attract many men of the worst type - without principles, capital or ties. 'And no longer any Company to keep them under control. No law and order.'

Dr. Jarman could not resist baiting his old enemy. 'At least they will all be their own men.'

John Davies' smile did not falter. 'And not puppets dancing to the Emperor's tune as you say we have been?'

Dr. Jarman's smile did. 'Putting up with their insults of 'dogmen' or 'red-haired demons' as we have been obliged,' he declared harshly.

He had never become accustomed to the impudent shouts of the common herd of Cantonese encouraged by the humiliating language of port regulations posted by the mandarins for all to see, or to their scorn of Englishmen as barbarian slaves of a lower order than citizens of the world-ruling Chinese empire.

John Davies' smile was at odds with his barbed words. 'We never believed those insults worth the price of a war against this peaceful Empire, Dr. Jarman.'

'Peaceful since when? Swept by rebellions. Rotten to the core. Bankrupt. Its army worthless. It will collapse at the first push.'

'I don't mean the cost in money, Dr. Jarman, but the cost in reputation.'

'We differ on questions of honour, Mr. Vice-President.'

'The dishonour of making war on China would be a bitter price to pay.'

'If it gives us the equality that is our right, and opens the door to China?'

John Davies' voice fell to a whisper. 'If it opens the door to your trade in opium, our children will be blamed to untold generations.'

Dr. Jarman curtly offered his stock justification. 'May I remind you, we country traders do not sell the opium on land, Mr. President. The Chinese do that themselves.'

John Davies had no taste for that weary argument. 'Then have your war if you will. But I hope to God I am not here to see it.' He turned away to his burly fellow Committee member, Hugh Hodgson.

Sean had listened to this sharp exchange with growing dismay. All through the long voyage out, his only thought had been to survive the perils of the deep to reach the promised land as he imagined it to be, only to hear the shocking truth. It was nothing but a romantic illusion. He could see that now thanks to John Davies.

On the summons of the great bell in the hall, the crowd resolved itself into processional rank as his Uncle drew him aside, explaining 'we don't form up. We're outside the pale'.

'What about your rank as Danish consul?'

Dr. Jarman smiled wryly. 'Ignored for the subterfuge to trade without a Company licence that it is. I don't take offence. I can afford to be charitable. The dog has had his day.'

They moved slowly up the sumptuously carpeted stairs at last. 'Why do you hate John Davies, Uncle?' Sean enquired.

'Despise rather for unfriendly sentiments towards me.' They had conducted a duel by insult, either face to face or in the Canton Register for so long it had become second nature.

'Surely such differences are common here?'

'It's not common for them to be formally recorded in evidence before a Select Committee of the House of Commons, nor in the widely circulated Quarterly Review.' His voice was tense with remembered anger.

The Company men were already standing to attention in their places in solemn reverend brotherhood as they entered the dining hall. The setting of the great dining table was grand enough for a visiting monarch. Gold-rimmed Company plate. Elaborate silverware sporting the Company insignia. Waterford cut glass. Elegant candelabra.

On the President's signal, they doffed their hats as one, raised them in salute, handed them to the white-robed servants hovering behind their chairs, and reached eagerly for their glasses of steaming whisky toddy even as they sat. One of the swiftest, Captain MacDonald, was on Sean's right hand.

'Why they torture a man so long with one wee tot of sherry I'll never know,' he complained as he tossed his toddy down, handing his glass to his attendant for a refill. 'Nothing to beat a good Scotch! You'll be going up to Canton, the noo, I suppose?'

Sean nodded. 'On one of the fast boats next month.'

'Och Ay!' Captain Macdonald nodded, his mouth full of an excellent baron of beef from the providores of Macao. 'don't forget to look us up in Lintin.'

'Lintin?' No one had mentioned Lintin yet.

'Island off shore. Very thoughtful of the Good Lord to put it where it is, right where we need it.'

'Why live on an island when everyone else..'

Captain MacDonald chortled loudly as he slapped Sean on his back so forcefully he almost choked on his beef. 'Easy to see you're a new chum! Why indeed would I want to live on a semi-barren island inhabited by as sinister a bunch of cut-throats as you would ever hope to find in a day's march? Blood brothers to the ex-pirates in their caves on Cheung Kao next door. Not to mention the cut-throats of Hong Kong harbour. No, my lad, I live on the Apollo hard by, a floating go down.'

'A go-down sir?' How would he ever master local jargon?

'A go-down is a goddamned floating warehouse, boy.'

Why would the Captain need to live on a floating warehouse out near a barren island, Sean wondered, astonishment plain on his face?

Captain MacDonald felt sorry for the boy. Dr. Jarman had clearly told him little of the disagreeable truth of the firm's considerable smuggling trade, chiefly but not altogether in opium. Anything that could be smuggled, from rice to arms was grist to their mill as well as banking, insurance and the legitimate tea trade.

'Warehouse ships, boy, ships that became necessary when trade was driven out of the river ten years ago over the Topaze affair. Driven even from Macao later. Over the waterbearers. They now trade in all articles prohibited in China. Using the smug boats.'

'Smug boats?' Sean rose to toast the King and Company in dismay he would never learn.

The dinner seemed endless before the four members of the Company's Select Committee withdrew to their private drawing room at last, leaving the hoi-polloi as William Jarman described themselves, to go to the devil which was usually Dawson's Hotel on the Praya Grande.

'What have you done to annoy the Select Committee, uncle?' Sean demanded of his uncle as they walked the short distance to William Jarman's villa instead.

'Refused to let the Hong merchants range like milch cows on the pasture of my trade to the profit of a government which uses them like a sponge.'

'The Hong?' Sean asked, the name yet one more mystery.

'A guild of some twelve or so merchants assigned by the government to control the trade of the port of Canton under the direction of a Hoppo or Master of Imperial Customs. The Hong merchants are Chinese, but the Hoppo is always one of the ruling Manchu race, usually a member of the Imperial family but at the moment a nephew of the Emperor himself.'

'Surely rather an inferior post for such an exalted prince?'

'Where else could he amass a fortune so quickly except here? Even his closest colleagues, the Governor of Kwantung or the Viceroy of the two provinces of Kwantung and Kwangsi, pay a large sum for their posts here in the hope of making enough to retire on in three years.'

'Ah, I see. You are the milch cows, and they do the milking.'

'The Hoppo and his ilk squeeze every last drop from our udders and then more.'

'You will not be milked, Uncle?'

Dr. Jarman strode grimly through the baronial gates towards the mansion built long ago in the heyday of the Jesuit Black Treasure ships to Japan.

'I will not submit to their capricious and exorbitant levies - one day a flood, the next a drought, a rebellion or an Imperial birthday - until oppressed Hong merchants go bankrupt owing us money more often than not.' His doorkeeper swung the door open bowing low. 'The Chinese have a saying that it's better to be a dog in peace than a man in anarchy. The Company are dogs in peace. I would rather be a man in anarchy.'

In Sean's ignorance, he did not realise that his uncle Dr. Jarman meant a greater anarchy than mere freedom of trade, that of renouncing law and making war.

* * * * * *

Holly and Abby arrive in Macao

114 days out of New York, the Eugenia, battered but still in good trim, made landfall on the South China coast at last at first light; a steady trade wind sweeping her through the ruffled green sea towards Macao huddled on the southern shores of the wide mouth of the Pearl River delta.

Captain Jim Peel stood beside Abby and Holly as they hung excitedly over the rail, more than ready to give thanks in any one of the 13 churches of Macao the journey had come to an end at last. Not because of the fury of Cape storms, nor the menace of savages in the Spice Islands, nor onslaught of pirate junks off Hainan Island south of Macao, but because he had found Holly increasingly irresistible in the close intimacy of the ship all these months, and knew he must resist this emotion with all the discipline born of prolonged years at sea. She all too plainly saw him as he had always been, long-standing family friend and business partner, not the lover, the husband, he now longed to be. Solid, reliable, unexciting.

He suffered her proximity now, with the familiar torment of agony and pleasure he was doomed to endure so long as they remained partners, as he pointed out the sombre outline of the small peninsula on which Macao stood, scarcely visible against the higher land beyond.

'One of the only anchorages on this coast that gives reasonable shelter from the typhoons.'

Abby's expressive face registered disbelief. Shelter? The open sea seemed to beat to Macao's very doorstep.

'The headland is only narrow. An inner harbour, the Taipa, leads to another channel through the delta. A back door to Canton forbidden to us.'

He turned to face the eastern horizon where the sun's red crescent surged up like a gigantic firework, and swept his arm up as if in some dawn ceremony. His gesture embraced a procession of islands marching north to south in parallel with the coast. 'Lintin and Lantao islands to the north. Much larger than they look. The Grand Ladrones, scene of the great Ladrone pirate wars on the south. Achou and the Asses Ears over there.'

Holly felt neither dismay nor doubt, only exhilaration that here was China at last, the goal towards which the ship had driven so long, the reality instead of the vision - the reality of other ships like theirs already swinging at anchor. All manner of ships. Two bulkier Company ships, uncompromisingly chequerboard black and white. Junks like Spanish caravels or Roman galleys, images of another age. Sampans and eggboats, small fry ferries of the harbour. Brigs and brigantines of the coastal or American trade.

Beyond them the three forts on the three hills of Penha, Guia and Monte that cradled portentous public buildings, cathedral-sized churches and bulky villas. A symphony of colour- pink, purple, yellow and green - like a coloured drawing out of a child's imagination. A glimpse of paradise after the prolonged tedium of vast, monotonous sea.

So many questions sprang to mind. Who built Macao? The Jesuit Fathers with their Black Treasure ships? The burghers of the Portuguese Empire in the days of their glory before more aggressive empires threatened their trade?

Abby clutched Holly in sudden doubt, a troubled frown on her brow. 'It's small, isn't it Holly?'

Holly hugged Abby to her, each giving strength to each as they always had in the special alliance of their childhood; once against the awesome headmistress of their Academy, now against the unknown terrors Macao might hold.

'We can't turn back now, Abby.'

She swung down a rope ladder to spring into the waiting rounded eggboat manned by a smiling barefoot trousered oarswoman. Abby hung back, forcing Jim Peel to manhandle her shrieking into the bosun's chair, swing it out in its davit, and lower her into Holly's waiting arms. She shrieked again as the eggboat swirled around when the Tanka boatgirl thrust it away from the side.

'She'll tip us in the drink. We'll never reach land. I don't want to die after coming so far!'

Holly pointed to other eggboats flocking skilfully across the bay in a perfectly straight line. 'Look how they can row straight and true, Abby.' Which their own rower did, her strokes swift and skilled, towards their black beauty rose, Mary Ann, jumping with excitement on the stone quay. She swallowed them both in a prolonged embrace, crying and laughing. 'I thought you'd never come.'

'So did we,' Abby said fervently crying on her shoulder, 'the perils of the deep were nothing to those we faced in some of our landings.'

Joshua's house was a surprise. Not the modest dwelling they had expected but a handsome edifice high on the slope of Penha Hill with a wide marble verandah, and what Abby called 'a whole raft of servants' massed to meet them. Twenty in fact. Not merely the eight the Viceroy's regulations allowed each merchant, but twelve more, an excess ignored by their comprador in return for greasing his palm with silver.

'How do you fit them all in there?' Abby demanded as they vanished within.

Mary Ann laughed. 'I don't. The comprador does. All I have to remember is who does which job. Wife No. 1 clothes. No. 2 flowers. No. 3 laundry. Woe betide me if I make a mistake.'

The room they were to share was on a scale to match the house with a lofty ornate ceiling and baronial furniture. No sooner inside than Holly's first act was to garnish their massive dressing table with the sprig of holly.

'Not a horse-shoe for good luck?' Mary Ann jested.

Holly retorted, 'this is your home not mine.'

'But you must consider it as your home,' Mary Ann insisted, arm round Holly's waist as of old school days.

'Mary Ann I can't impose on you indefinitely. Abby and I want to rent a house after a time.'

Mary Ann reeled back in mock shock. 'Goodness gracious, you can't...'

Holly rushed on. 'We must not impose. You expecting a baby and all.'

Unwilling to distress Holly with the truth, Mary Ann prevaricated. 'No, Holly. There's plenty of room and servants. Not like home. No extra work for me. And I have so looked forward to your company. Besides you'll take a little while to become accustomed to the strange ways of this colony, and we'll be at hand to answer questions as they arise.'

Holly, overhot in the rising heat, took off her jacket and hung it on the wooden valet stand. 'What you're really saying is we need protection. Only more tactfully than Uncle Bart.'

Mary Ann perched on the bed beside her. 'What I am saying, Holly is that you cannot live alone without scandalising Macao. Only women of doubtful reputation live alone. Pensioners calling themselves 'widows', whose lovers have either abandoned them or gone home leaving a trust for their care. Others, of course, whose lovers are still here. '

Holly was disappointed. So much for her dream of independence. 'Are you sure we couldn't explain?'

Mary Ann grasped Holly's hand in commiseration as she delivered a further blow to her cheerful optimism. 'There's another complication. The Portuguese own all the houses and only let to Portuguese nationals. And if you even presumed to ask, we would both be blackballed.'

Holly was aghast. 'Why didn't Jim warn me?'

Abby rushed to Jim's defence. 'Holly, it wouldn't have occurred to him. You had already pacified your aunt by saying Mary Ann would chaperone you in Macao.'

Holly shrugged acceptance. After all it was trade that would decide her future in Macao not where she lived, and Joshua's readiness to help her. So she eagerly awaited his summons.

She scarcely remembered Joshua, having seen little of him during his swift, skilful courtship of Mary Ann three years before during a brief home visit; except that he had seemed unacceptably older then. But the enthusiastic warmth of his greeting dispelled her doubts as he rose to greet her when she entered his office in one of the spacious front rooms of the house.

'How marvellous to see Mary Ann's oldest and dearest friends here with us. The best cure for homesickness a man could possibly want.'

He looked younger than she remembered him, a man novelists were wont to describe 'as of cheerful mien'. A mild expression more apt to a bookkeeper than a competitive trader. Yet Uncle Bart had insisted she must not underestimate him. He was tough and quickwitted, capable of making decisions against the swing of price and tides of rumour rampant on the Coast and proving right time and again. So Law and Partners had sailed on in business from year to year when other eager newcomers to Macao ran too close to the wind and to shipwreck.

Joshua was already familiar with her plans thanks to a letter from Uncle Bart by a prior ship. He now cross-examined her as she sat, a slight figure lost in the excessive embrace of the ponderous leather couch.

All was plain sailing between them until she remarked casually. 'Jim has told me I can't go to Canton. But I must if I'm going to trade in my own right. You can see that.'

He objected as strongly as if he were the Viceroy of the two Kwangs himself. 'The Viceroy has just renewed the regulations once more after various breaches, Holly. Merchants must not take weapons, women or boys into the factories.'

She exploded at that. 'How dare he insult us so? Lumping us with weapons and boys.'

Joshua was thankful she had asked no questions about those 'boys'.

She added defiantly, 'I'll take the risk. Go anyway.'

Joshua's mildness changed to horror. 'If you do, my company will have to pay the price.'

Holly's confidence to confusion. 'Why should you pay any price for what I do?'

Joshua tried to explain the 'responsibility' system of Canton, indeed of all China. 'I'm responsible for the actions of anyone in my firm, whether I'm party to them or not. Smuggling, robbery, murder anything. In turn my security merchant, Howqua, is responsible for everything I do, to the Hoppo or Master of Customs and beyond him to the Governor and last the Viceroy.'

He explained the difference between the Governor, responsible only for the province of Kwangtung of which Canton was the capital, and the Viceroy for the two southern provinces of Kwangtung and Kiangsi. The Viceroy did not have overriding power over the Governor. Rather he was a colleague in a balance of power.

Holly sat with knitted brow. 'I don't follow why you should be responsible for me in the first place, since I am not a member of your firm.'

'You are under my roof. They will know that. And I understand you have nominated me as proxy. You clearly need to understand China better. I'll put you under Billy Howe's wing to see you do.'

He rang the bell, and sent his clerk to summon Billy, whom Holly imagined to be some grave ageing veteran of the coast. In fact Billy proved no older than herself with an irrepressible smile and self-assured air that belied his youth. He showed no undue surprise when Joshua explained he was to give Holly a helping hand, saying 'she's here on business to buy cargo.' Small shareholders in coastal traders were common enough.

He enquired politely. 'A small investor?'

'A large investor. She owns the Eugenia, not I.'

'She does?' Billy frowned then, all the implications as instantly clear to him as they had been to Joshua. 'I'll be delighted to act as her guide.'

So, Holly thought, a brash egotist to contend with, and was about to protest when Joshua explained. 'Billy can protect you better than anyone in Macao. Grew up here. Speaks both Cantonese and Mandarin.'

Billy saluted. 'If any trouble blows up, and it can at the drop of a hat, I'll be there to defend you with a respectable volley of Cantonese curses.'

Holly eyed him dubiously. 'You don't look that kind of man!'

He smiled wickedly, 'needs must when the devil drives.'

Joshua advised Holly not to take these problems lightly, but to discuss them further with Billy in his office, warning her 'you should take no one but Billy into your confidence, Holly. No one.'

In his tiny retreat overlooking an efflorescent courtyard, Billy eyed her critically. She was too slender, too frail by far for the task she set herself.

'You're going to have problems you know. No comprador will be allowed to work for you.'

'Why do I need a comprador?'

As soon as she was ensconced in his one spare chair, he stood before her for all the world like her old history teacher, faintly exasperated but patient. 'First because it's compulsory to have a comprador. What better reason? Second, because he is your go-between to any merchants you may need. Third, because he understands the money market.'

Holly was both puzzled and intrigued. 'Is there much to understand?' Money to her had always meant simple transactions - how much a dollar would buy and at what percentage of profit.

Billy threw up his hands in mock horror. 'What an innocent abroad you are, Miss Shay. Do you really think you can succeed in this market when you are such a greenhorn?

'Mr. Howard, I understand you were to see that I will,' she replied tartly.

'This market is a madhouse, particularly a Chinese madhouse.'

'How can there be a difference when it comes to money?'

'Prices are seldom fixed for more than a few hours at a time. Values fluctuate.'

'Nothing so Chinese about that. Sounds exactly like the New York Stock Exchange.'

'But there they don't trade in several currencies at once. Spanish, Mexican, and Peruvian silver dollars. Chinese taels and copper cash. The pound. Counterfeit coins. Or best of all, plain silver sycee.'

Abby's invasion was a relief to them both. 'Ran you to earth at last. Guess what Holly. There's going to be a fancy dress ball and we're invited. Just imagine. The social event of the season. We've just got time to have costumes made.'

Holly burst out laughing. How absurd it was that they should think of going to a masquerade in fancy dress here in China. At home yes, where such frolics were always high points in otherwise drab times. But here everyone seemed already to be in fancy dress or uniforms of one kind or other. How absurd to transport the social fancies of the west to the fringes of the east! Or was it an absurdity that was an essential antidote to the strains of six months of unnatural batchelor life in the one minute tiny patch of Canton permitted foreigners in all China outside Macao, or in Macao itself - at least for those, who belonged to the British East India Company, forbidden to marry.

Abby swept Holly upstairs, demanding, 'what will you go as, Holly? A court princess, an Egyptian priestess, a page boy? A Shakespearean heroine'

They found Mary Ann poring over a voluminous book on the history of costume with a man so scarred of face it was hard to dissemble the shock. Mary Ann introduced him as 'Adam Darion, the brilliant painter', with Billy adding, as Adam bowed low, 'also the brilliant journalist'.

Adam demurred, 'no better than you, Billy!'

Billy clapped him on the shoulder, 'Ah, but you are so much wittier.'

Adam groaned ruefully. 'The cost! Libel writs to burn.'

Abby was already flipping over the pages of the costume book until she settled on Queen Elizabeth 1 in grandiose panoply.

'Let's make a splash as a pair! I'll go as Elizabeth, you as Marie Antoinette.'

'And look a travesty of you. Never!'

Holly idled through the pages until she reached the Shakespearian era. Why of course, she thought, she must go as Portia. Masquerade as a man. Go not only to the ball but to Canton. No trouble to anyone but herself disguised as a man. Adam obligingly sketched her a simple open-necked velvet tunic and trousers with ribboned cap for the dressmaker.

Billy agreed to match her Portia with an odious Shylock despite Adam's protest that 'surely the cap would fit Dr. Jarman better than you. You don't own any ships and you're not tightfisted.'

Abby asked curiously, 'will Dr. Jarman be at the ball?

'He's giving the ball. Dressed as a Scottish Laird to be sure in full war paint of kilt and sporran, and piping us into dinner no doubt. But he should be wearing the Jolly Roger. Far more fitting.'

'And what about you, Adam?'

With a flourish, hand to chest, and a sweet smile grotesquely discordant with his grossly pitted face, 'I, dear lady, What else for one of my appearance, but as the Pirate King? I am as people imagine him not Dr. Jarman with his aristocratic airs.'

Holly made amends. 'What a magnificent voice you have.'

Adam struck a pose, 'born for the stage till nature betrayed me.'

Billy added, 'son of the great Yankee actor, Lucian Darion.'

'How terrible for you!' Abby cried, compassion always near the surface in her nature.

'To have him as my father? Or to have to renounce the stage? Why I have never renounced it. All the world is a stage. A drama unfolds on it every day - strange, curious, mad, funny, or tragic if you have eyes to see. A stage on which I am forever cast as the villain.' He waved his hand to embrace the peninsula of Macao on which they were all stranded.

Holly resisted the sadness of Adam's message. The strands of Macao were no different than those she had known in Salem; a port where life's victims were all too common, and the tragedy of other's lives could not be allowed to drown one's own survival. And survive she must as he so courageously had.

* * * * * *

Dr. Jarman's Fancy Dress Ball

Billy decreed that Holly's fancy dress for the ball should be made by the best tailor in Macao; not the man preferred by the British colony because of his unctuous manner and plausible pidgin English but a man deep in Chinatown.

When Holly heard this she refused to summon him to the house, insisting 'I won't turn down a chance to take a ride in a sedan chair and see Chinatown.'

She wanted to see for herself the bizarre sights Billy had described: the money changers with their portable scales and strings of copper cash, the dentists with their strings of pulled teeth, the water bearers with their double buckets on bamboo poles, even the beggars.

She did not realise she would be breaking the law as foreign devils were forbidden to use sedan chairs reserved exclusively for mandarins or ceremonial use. Billy said nothing because the law was seldom enforced and only when the mandarins wanted to remind foreign devils they were barbarians without rights, their rank no higher than the common people.

Holly was no sooner in the sedan chair with Billy walking alongside than she regretted her choice. The motion made her queasy, and the pitch obliged her to brace her feet against the footboard with her arms jammed against the sides. Forced to peer through curtains, she was only dimly aware of the sights she had hoped to see.

As her bearers trotted down a narrow street into the heart of Chinatown, Holly felt the chair lurch sideways then tip slowly forward. She swept the curtain aside to the appalling sight of her two forward bearers being driven to their knees, still clinging grimly to their poles, as attackers thrashed them with staves. And Billy beating them in turn with his walking stick as he shouted to her to get out. As she scrambled out of the tilting chair, a young Chinese boy flung him himself forward to cling desperately to her skirts screaming as a grimacing ruffian tried to prise his hands away. She battered the boy's attacker, shouting to Billy for help. Billy abandoned the bearers to seized the kidnapper by the long queue hanging down his back, cursing him fluently in his own language. The man hung there terrified, not so much because of the queue - he could have fought despite that - but because the red-haired demon cursed him so dangerously. His curses might work. But at last his terror galvanised him to twist free to melt away through a gathering crowd down a side alley.

The child's ayah clutched him tightly to her dark pyjama suit, sobbing hysterically as if he were dead not saved and bowing over and over to Billy until Holly protested with asperity. 'She should thank me. I saved the child.'

Billy assured her, 'she is! She only speaks to me because she heard me speak Cantonese. No time to argue.'

She bowed to the ayah. No time for regrets. They now faced a new, more hostile menace. The crowd around them was growing by the minute forming a cold, implacable wall of hatred for the she-foreign devil who pretended to be a mandarin's consort.

Billy urged her now. 'Let's get out of here fast. Show fear and we're lost.'

As he worked his way through with fluent chatter in their own language, larded with courtesies, he turned their hostility to astonishment even approval. Once safely well beyond their cordon, Holly complained angrily about the crowd acting 'as if we were criminals.'

'In fact in their eyes you were. You had broken the law by riding in a sedan chair. Therefore they could attack us with impunity knowing they could defend themselves by saying they were offended by the sight and would go free. We could even be accused of causing a riot. It's happened before.'

Subdued, she asked 'who do you think attacked us?'

'Robbers or runners of an angry mandarin.'

'Angry with us when he doesn't know us?'

'Angry with all Europeans! There's such bitterness about loss of trade these last few years to offshore traders.'

Holly marched on with no eyes for the curiosities she had hoped to see. The stares of the locals were not only disconcerting but disturbing.

She was thankful to find herself inside a tiny shop at last where two elderly Chinese tailors stood waiting, neat as wooden peg dolls in their long deep-sleeved gowns and black and white cloth shoes. They bowed deferentially until their wispy beards brushed their chests. Holly sat meekly on the offered chair while Billy engaged in a dialogue that involved much further nodding of heads and cries of 'Eiyah!' If Holly had but known, Billy had thrown in dire threats that he would skin them alive for supper like good Cantonese kittens if they failed to produce exactly what they saw in Adam's sketch, and indulged in any temptation to make the dress look Oriental.

Watching Billy's ease with the locals, Holly wondered if he had shrugged off the assault too quickly as a turbulence of the streets. She was certain the attack had not been on them at all but on the child. She taxed Billy once they were safely home.

'Possible, yes. Kidnap for ransom is common enough in these parts. Or for sale into slavery. Inland or overseas to places like Manila, Java or Penang.'

'How terrible! Don't the mandarins try to stop it?'

'Of course. But victims mostly simply disappear into thin air. Too many people want a son to look after them in their old age'.

She swore Abby and Mary Ann to secrecy. Joshua must never know, or as Mary Ann asserted he would be forever in a state if they walked further than the Praya Grande. All other thoughts banished but that of the grand party, their chance to meet 'the high society of Macao' as they unwisely told Adam, who growled his cynicism with 'if there is any'.

The day of the ball came at last, and the moment when they would take the short walk from Joshua's house to Dr. Jarman's much more grandiose residence. Once they had passed through his imposing gates, the skirts of Abby's Elizabethan costume were so voluminous that Adam Darian, a pirate king in full skull and crossbones, was forced to walk behind her up the flagged path that led between massed banks of potted plants to the great portico.

Behind them came Holly as a brilliant blue Portia slim as a spring sapling, her dark auburn curly hair springing from her velvet cap, arm in arm with Billy, his hilarity utterly out of his character as a lumpish old Shylock.

As their motley crew mounted the imposing steps in a gale of laughter, Adam declared 'we look a proper set of loons.'

'But having more fun than we ever imagined,' Holly responded.

Even the grandeur of the soaring entrance of the Jarman mansion did not prepare them for the sensational decorations the famous artist Chinnery had conjured up for the occasion. Although Billy and Adam had made all sorts of bad jokes about Chinnery's feats in wife-dodging, eating and storytelling, they had said nothing about his artistic brilliance. The elegant archway, surmounted by the flags of England, Portugal, France and Holland, led into a pavilion which boasted British trophies, where Dr. Jarman in full Scottish rig of plaid kilt and sporran welcomed them.

He took their hands simultaneously bowing in mock gallantry, 'my dear ladies, what ornaments you are to my ball. Your cards will most certainly be filled.'

'Ornaments! Is that all he thinks we are good for?' Holly muttered crossly as they entered the ballroom where a great gauzy tent flowed down from a huge central bronze carousel lamp, its drapes and the spokes of the carousel so heavily woven with flowers it seemed as if the garden had invaded the house. The whole was a frame for portraits marching round the wall with the names of English poets - Pope, Milton, Shakespeare, Chaucer - and round the flag-covered orchestra platform with the names of celebrated English generals - Clive, Ponsonby, Moore and Marlborough.

Adam growled, 'he doesn't mention the generals who lost the battles in good old USA.'

Billy reproved him, 'this evening honours the genius of the British Empire.'

'It reminds us of what we lost when we held the Boston Tea Party,' Abby said peevishly, her protest born of envy rather than opposition. She felt she could quite readily acquire a taste for the British haut ton and heroic tradition, as yet all too lacking in their own frontier society.

Holly exhorted Abby, 'when in Rome you must do as the Romans do. Admire their champions and heroes.'

Abby pointed to the blue and white pennant of the Jarman fleet. 'Does Jarman rate himself a British hero?'

'No, as a man of power,' Billy explained, 'He knows a mandarin out here is taken at face value. If he wants to be king of the coast, he must walk and talk like a king.'

'And I'll take this ball at face value, Billy,' Adam interposed, 'a time for fun and laughter.'

Laughter so unrestrained Abby begged Adam to stop his brilliant flow of satire on the local characters that passed them by. 'See how many dress up not down. Not many willing to be a wagoner or a mendicant like that chap. What they wear is a fantasy of their ambition not the truth. And their ambition seems to range through all the nations the British still hope to conquer - Syrians, Persians, Egyptians, Africans, Malay Chiefs and Circassians. Or to play the role of the conqueror as Hussars, Highlanders, Jolly Jack Tars and Red Cross Knights in armour. But there goes one who conquered them.' He pointed to one of Jarman Malleson's partners, the Laird, a real veteran of the Coast dressed as Julius Caesar in full laurel wreath.

Just then the sight of two Lintin warehouse East India Company captains dressed with wry irony as smugboat crewmen prompted Holly to ask, 'which are they? Conquering or conquered?'

Billy gave a wry grin. 'Depends on which razor gang they work for, this one or that.' He indicated Jarman just inside the main door first, then some of the smaller free traders at the other end of the room.

Just then the band struck up for a quadrille. Holly was swept off by a handsome Hussar, and Abby by James Malleson's nephew David, whose admiring eye had embraced the mammoth vision of Abby with enthusiasm when they arrived.

Many dances and suitors later, exhilarated and elated by the sparkle of good feeling that enveloped the room, Holly was at last captured by an exasperated Billy complaining he was the one who after all had brought her to the ball. Contrite, she swung into a fast waltz with him that landed them, short of breath and flushed, hard by William Jarman, James Malleson and their nephews Sean and David. All four deep in conversation, backs turned to their guests, in their full Scottish war dress for all the world like a group of generals debating a strategy of battle as they indeed were.

Dr. Jarman's question to his partner James Malleson caught Holly's attention. 'What ails thee man?'

Malleson struck a pose, one hand on his dress sword hilt as if the Battle of Culloden itself were lost. 'That creature of the Company, Davies, has sunk us in London. Our lobby has lost.' She could not know his lobby was one from the Midlands, Manchester, the North and friends in the Ministry of the British government itself.

David Malleson elaborated. 'We've just heard from London, Dr. Jarman. Uncle James will not be the new Trade superintendent after all.'

Dr. Jarman shrugged. 'I'm not surprised. The Court of St. James wants no more broils, not with those Maharajahs in India restive and Russia rattling the sabre in Afghanistan.' He clapped his partner on Malleson's shoulder. 'Is there no good news?'

'Only that the new Trade superintendent will not be a Company man.'

'There you are. We lost the war but won the peace. Now you're a lawyer. Can't you see you doctor his brief somehow? After all you don't have to wear the crown to exercise the power.'

Malleson assured Jarman. 'I'm working on it.'

Intrigued but appalled by what she was overhearing, Holly was oblivious to Billy's ribald comments as the dancers swept by.

Malleson's tone grew angrier. 'In the meantime the Parsees play merry hell from Bombay with our investments. You should pull them into line before their speculations, with us and against us, cause a serious crisis in India.'

Dr. Jarman was sceptical. 'Do you think they'd stay in line longer than it took for my boat to sail out of the harbour? They threw the opium trade at us, when they became discontented with the Portuguese, because we trade harder and better than anyone on the Coast. To do that we must stay in Macao I know. Tempted as I am to get away from the tedium of these idle frivolous women and their trivial gossip.'

Stirred by Dr. Jarman's remark faster than a Scot by the skirl of a bagpipe, Holly thrust her way between him and the two Malleson men like two Swiss guards at Emperor Napoleon's elbows to accost him angrily.

'If you scorn us so much, why condescend to invite us to your ball. So you can insult us by standing in a corner with superior Scottish airs trading politics? I can see you Scots have yet to learn the art of gracious manners.'

Dr. Jarman looked down on her with supercilious amusement. 'So you come to Macao to see how we barbarians behave? It would seem your worst forebodings are now realised.' He smiled unexpectedly. 'You must be one of our Yankee lassies.'

She spat out, 'I am not yours in any sense, Dr. Jarman.'

'You must forgive me. As a batchelor, I lack the refining touch of women. Gossip would tell you that.'

Holly rushed to the defence of her sex. 'Gossip? Do you really think that's how we pass our time? We do a great deal to entertain the lonely officers in port not to mention visitors passing through.'

Dr. Jarman goaded her, an amused glint in his eyes, 'You think that kindness makes your chatter any more significant than that of the birds in Tom Wells' aviary.'

Holly rose to the bait. 'At least they sing sweetly. You gentlemen would not know how, airing your quarrels in your petty newspapers, snapping at your rivals like snarling dogs. Perhaps you should encourage our civilising influence at Canton.'

It was Malleson who replied. 'Admit the fair sex to Canton? If we did the Viceroy would bring a trade worth millions of pounds to a standstill.'

All through this sparring Sean had stood enthralled by Holly's bravura. But he knew Dr. Jarman well enough to realise he must extricate Holly before she said anything more provocative to earn the enduring antagonism of a man with so much influence. For almost all free traders in the port were shackled in some relationship to him.

Seizing Holly's arm, Sean dragged her from the group with more than gentlemanly force not letting go until he swept her well away. Expecting her wrath, he did not dare the laughter he felt for fear of another outburst from her.

But she merely said primly. 'You are summary, Mr. Jarman, for so I presume you to be, since no one had the courtesy to introduce us.'

'You'll pardon me saying you didn't exactly wait for an introduction.'

'How dare Dr. Jarman say what he did?'

'I'm sure he wouldn't if he'd known you were eavesdropping.'

'That is outrageous.'

'Can you honestly say you women don't condemn my unfortunate sex?'

She retreated behind her fan then, looked up, caught his eyes so he felt a catch of his heart and dissolved in a splutter of laughter which caught him up in one long irrevocable moment of recognition that this was only a beginning for them both.

At last he demanded, 'why is it so important women should be in Canton that you insist on the last word?'

'Because I want to go there. Surely I could be smuggled in so the Viceroy won't know?'

Sean was serious now. 'No, because the Viceroy knows everything. Every man Jack that serves us is a spy. You would never get away with it.

He gazed down at her perplexed. Why did she want to go so much? She dropped her gaze, too acutely aware of his swift appraisal of her ivory white shoulders, velvet as the slashed bodice that framed them, the rise of her bosom and the slim elegance of her hands in emphasis of her remarks.

Time seemed to stand still between them, oblivious to the crowd surging past them. She heard him speak as if distantly. 'A penny for your thoughts.'

'If I can't go to Canton as a woman, I can as a man.'

'I beg your pardon.'

'Yes, dressed as a man'.

'All hell would break loose if you were discovered.'

'You could smuggle me in.'

'And what if we fail? Who pays the price? Not you.'

'How does your opium get through then, I ask? But then I am only an empty-headed woman.'

He was amused not angry. 'Why not your Uncle Law?'

'Because I would not get him into trouble.'

'Yet you would get me into trouble?'

'You are already in so much trouble, the trouble I would cause would make little difference.'

'Not such an emptyheaded woman after all,' he exclaimed.

Holly had no retort. She was truly emptyheaded now of all further thought except his towering strength, compelling good looks, a physique and style built for a cavalry officer's uniform, a glory of red and golds rather than the dark green and black of his ancestral clan.

Abby broke the spell by sailing up to be introduced. 'I was telling Miss Shay it is a man's world on the China Coast. A woman is out of place.'

Abby took up the cudgels manfully. 'What about Mrs. MacDonald on your warehouse ship, the Apollo? Out there in a man's world all year round.'

As Sean Jarman began to wonder whether he would prove equal to these fiery Yankee ladies, he was extricated by what Billy and Adam saw as their rescue effort to snatch the ladies from what they supposed to be unwanted attention. Yet they were wrong.

As the evening wore on, Holly was all too aware of Sean's watchful eyes always on her, and the magnetism of the man for herself. She was outraged at the thought she could be so instantly attracted to one of that band of ruthless smugglers and plotters of war despite her determination to remain fancy free in China.

Sean himself was quick to note Holly's hesitation and panic when he headed the usual rush to ask her for a dance, her relief when the band played an abrasive fanfare to announce time for supper, and her summons to Billy to escort her into the grand dining room. She was avoiding him. That was obvious. It seemed so out of character with her brash manner, her easy open ways with her Yankee friends. Could it be that she was as disconcerted by their meeting as he himself was? Could she feel as irresistibly drawn to him, as he to her, in an attraction clouded with misgiving? Misgiving at least on his side. For how could he circumvent her diligent squires or her inseparable friend Abby, or the fact the Jarmans were not on visiting terms with the Laws.

Holly felt a wild sense of relief as she escaped into the supper room, then astonishment at the vista within - a superb pastoral panorama of a ruined city, lake, mountains and cascades as decor for a sumptuous banquet on what Billy declared to be 'a groaning board' while Abby rejoiced that there were 'no more British heroes to make me groan.' So far every room, including several 'sitting-out rooms' had had a roll call of Britain's 'greats'.

'Just stand a moment and admire this pearl our genius Chinerry has put before these swine,' Adam declared as an onrush of guests swept past towards the loaded tables without a second glance. 'That superlative painting all in three hours. If I had so much talent in my whole body as he has in one finger, it would be enough.'

Adam introduced them to the capacious man in question, who had led the onslaught on the banquet table and now attacked his heaped plate with gusto. Chinnery's deepset eyes under heavy unruly eyebrows and thatch of white curly hair, beamed with lively good nature as he studied them both approvingly. 'You must allow me the honour of painting you.'

Holly rejoined, 'The honour would be ours, Mr. Chinnery. You are a great master.'

Ah, Miss Shay you will get on in Macao,' Chinnery cried, grasping her hand and kissing it with a flourish.

'Not so, sir. I only praise where there is cause for praise.'

'Beware of gossip in this town, Miss,' he warned.

Adam chuckled. 'Look who's talking. The arch-villain himself.'

'Only to you, my friend,' Chinnery responded unperturbed. 'the man who stole my crown of the ugliest man in Macao.'

Affection obvious between them despite their jocular trade of insults. How could that be, Holly wondered? But of course, Adam could only be at ease with a man as ill-favoured as himself, a man whose irony could help him face the world without bitterness as Chinnery did without the churlishness that still clung to Adam.

The young man who joined them now was as Chinnery would have wished to be; with the same smiling face as if continuously in touch with the benevolence and yet cosmic joke of human love, with the same colouring of dark hair and fair skin but without any of the excess of every feature that robbed Chinnery of any pretension of looks and turned him into a caricature.

Chinnery chuckled as he introduced Dr. Collins as the Company doctor. 'He's got a better bedside manner than Dr. Jarman.'

'Does Dr. Jarman practice medicine?' Abby asked in surprise. The cap did not fit the wearer.

Chinnery's smile vanished. 'Only trade with the devil.'

No love lost there despite the elaborate artistry of the decorations he had conjured up for Jarman to outshine everyone else in Macao.

Tom Collins shook hands with them both with a strength surprising in a man of so relaxed a manner. Abby warmed to him at once, but felt no touch of the hand of destiny on her shoulder as Holly had with Sean. Or as Tom now did with her, an overwhelming touch he had never expected to experience in this remote corner of the world. He hoped against hope she had felt as profoundly moved as he, even while acknowledging a truth he had come to terms with long ago that he was not the kind of man with whom girls flirted, let alone fell in love with at first sight.

As for Sean watching Holly from afar, he had no more hope than Dr. Tom that Holly would respond with the same extreme attraction he had felt for her. He could read only a disquiet and foreboding.

* * * * * *

Sean sails north to the Fukien Coast

Sean braced himself in the stern of the little opium-running brig, the Mercury, as she headed across the fretting dark green sea towards the low shoreline of the Fukienese coast north of Macao, a trade wind steady in her sails.

He fluctuated between elation and terror to think they were running inshore towards a totally unknown, and possibly dangerous, beach. Certainly one that did not exist on any current map in Europe. At last he was embarked on the adventure, the danger he had longed for but at the same time dreaded. After all, they were flouting an often repeated decree that trade must take place only through the port of Canton, and its monopoly guild, the Co-Hong. And he had heard many horror stories of what happened to shipwrecked sailors.

The closer they came, the more he began to regret that his uncle had thought it vital he should be blooded in the harsher realities of their offshore trade before he went upriver to the Jarman Malleson Factory in Canton, stating, 'you're not here to pen-push, Sean. We've got a comprador to run that side of the business. You have to know what the trade's about. The hands may be theirs, but the backbone is ours.'

No sooner had the captain anchored off shore than a small flotilla of junks emerged in a stately array from a small estuary nearby. Two of the three largest bristled with swords and cannon. As they approached, fanning out in a crescent, Dr. Jarman stood watching them uneasily, his craggy jaw jutting out even more than usual.

'They don't look like mandarin junks,' he said irritably as if in rebuke to the squat, rumpled missionary interpreter, the Reverend Dr. Grusson, beside him.

'Arms can be a sign of rank as well as hostility,' Dr. Grusson replied mildly, ignoring the surly scowl on the face of his towering employer. He had never shared the terror of others for Dr. Jarman's brooding gravity, knowing it signified merely the intensity of his Calvinist nature and its drive for a mission in life albeit for power, whereas his own was for disciples.

'Arms can also mean he means to seize rather than buy.'

'He's not one of your rebel pirates like the Beggar King,' Grusson objected, his misshapen face in a grimace, 'He's an official who has to answer to the Emperor for his actions.'

Dr. Jarman's tone was scornful. 'Do you think the Emperor would fine him one tael if he played the pirate towards us? Fed us to the sharks? Snatched our opium? Scuttled our ship? Our very presence here is grossly illegal as you well know. Just as welcome as your evangelising.'

Dr. Grusson pulled a wry face at Dr. Jarman's cynical reference to his incongruous and opportunistic effort to spread the gospel from the deck of an opium ship. He was barely able to restrain the angry retort he longed to make that Dr. Jarman's daring ambition would make him the power of the future as the East India Company had been in the past, king of them all. And look like a king he did, astride his deck.

Dr. Jarman surveyed the junks grimly. He and his crew were outnumbered at least three to one. Should he order his captains to break out the weapons' chest now? Greet them with a show of strength? Could he make a run for it, if it came to a showdown? He wet his forefinger in his mouth and raised it to the even breath of the monsoon. The message of his forefinger was that this day's wind would be too slight to let him outrun any Chinese junk on the coast.

'Curse this miserable specimen of the shipwright's trade,' he swore.

'Why, sir, surely we've got nothing to fear from those junks!' Sean asked in surprise. They seemed too cumbersome and archaic to be any match for their swift modern vessel.

Dr. Jarman's tone was withering. 'Let this be your first lesson in China, laddie. Those junks you are pleased to scorn, could outsail me any day in a light wind. They run closer to the wind than I can.'

The mandarin's junk, plainly used to the process, hauled in close to the waiting bosun's chair while the rest laid back on their oars. The bulky official was hoisted aboard. The bosun's pipe shrilled. Dr. Jarman bowed low as his visitor struggled to his feet. They stood bowing and nodding a moment like puppets on a string, yet no two men could be less like puppets. Both were equally their own masters, far enough from the reach of their remote monarchs to be free to equivocate, to bargain, to dodge any retribution for any transgressions from the customary law of their countries.

None the less appearances had to be observed. The magistrate went through the prescribed Imperial ritual. He read the Imperial decree in stilted tones as his bodyguard soldiers flourished their spears and glared at the foreign devils. No one might trade with any ocean barbarians outside Canton, least of all in opium.

A whispered warning from Dr. Grusson caused Dr. Jarman to hesitate. Could he risk inviting him into the Great Cabin? If so, would he dismiss his glowering secretaries and sit down to the business the Beggar King, as his go-between, had promised in Canton. An order so large it had roused suspicion when first made, no less than the sale of his entire shipload of opium in one place?

'No,' the Beggar King had sworn, his damaged lip twitching, 'you're dealing with us now, a bigger organisation than before, much more powerful.'

Dr. Jarman, finding it hard to believe the Cantonese mandarins would see their own organisation thrust aside, had asked, 'would they tolerate you?'

The Beggar King had shrugged, refusing the opium pipe Dr. Jarman had offered. 'You can't deal and smoke at the same time.' They'll get their percentage. What matter from whom? Us or the Elder Brothers?'

Dr. Jarman had rejoined, 'you are more dangerous.'

'They're too innocent to see that yet. Too naive to know who we are, not just another gang of bandits.'

Now Dr. Jarman surveyed the fat belly of the mandarin before him. It had not been fed by honest means, nor that smug air of sly self-satisfaction. He gave Dr. Grusson the nod.

The mandarin's answer to Dr. Grusson's brief volley of staccato Fukienese, rolling with brilliant ease from his nimble tongue, was to turn to his secretaries with peremptory dismissal, and accept Dr. Jarman's ushering wave of a hand through the bulkhead and down the ladder into the Grand Cabin, where he settled himself into the only comfortable chair. He took a stiff gulp of the offered mao ti wine, a good pinch of snuff from a stoppered bottle he whisked from his reticule, and a generous helping of the sweetmeats Dr. Gustav offered, before he reached down and plucked a folded sheet of paper from his long black cloth boots, smacking his lips greedily as he said 'now we get down to business.'

Shrewd and tenacious bargaining on the price per chest. Earnest questions on how often they would come again, and how much they would bring. More questions about all the objects around him - pictures, lamps, books, instruments. Then departure at last in a flurry of polite sentiments.

As Dr. Jarman watched the flotilla dwindle into the westering sun, he wondered if his dream of a fleet of ships prowling up and down the coast with immunity, and of the five Treaty Ports of old restored, would ever come true. Ships that would sell not only opium but cotton and much more from the exploding industry of England into this infinite market that stretched beyond the dimly visible shore.

Dr. Grusson's troubled whisper dispelled his dream. 'Something's not quite right sir. One of them joked "the dog will catch the rat". Pirate talk, sir. Something for nothing. We should up anchor and clear out at once, sir.'

'Be first to break a deal that we brokered, Reverend? We can't take that risk.'

Sensing their unease, Sean could not sleep. At last irritated by the slow roll of the brig and slap of waves on her hull, he went on deck to find his uncle already in the fore gazing down into the dim circle of light thrown on the water by the lamp on the bowsprit.

'Ah, young Sean!' His uncle spoke low as if he might be overheard. 'I was just indulging myself with memories of the years I sailed as ship's surgeon in Company ships. Learnt how to run a ship then. Damned if I couldn't captain any tub on this coast if I'd a mind to. How many merchants in Canton could boast of that?'

He paused with a sudden lift of his head like a pointer dog that has caught the scent of prey. Sean stiffened. Now he could hear what his uncle had heard - a stealthy rustle of oars, a faintest chink of weapons.

His uncle bent to whisper, 'we're being attacked. Move slowly back towards the bulkhead. Rouse the crew.'

Sean glided back as if to gaze up at the stars, the only visible thing in this great black circle of night, shivering to think what a clear target he made in the glow of the ship's riding lights. Once down the ladder, he rushed through the ship, shaking officers and sailors awake with a fierce low call to arms. In his wake stifled oaths as men struggled to throw on clothes and seize weapons hastily handed out in grim silence.

Sean fumbled in the box under his hammock for his own sword, and buckled it on with numb, shaking fingers, cursing his uncle silently for not having been more on his guard. No extra watch on deck this night. Surely he could have guessed that anyone unscrupulous enough to engage in a highly dangerous trade might be tempted to seize such a prize for nothing rather than pay his heavy price.

Even as he pushed the end of the belt home through the heavy buckle, a high-pitched screaming launched the first dreadful sounds of a wild pitched battle. As Sean reached the swirling uproar of the deck, yelling the warcry of his clan, a thrill of fear seized him. The invaders, rattan shields across their chest and red cords knotted on their heads, were wielding their sinister weapons - two-bladed swords and long curved serrated-edged rapiers - with terrifying skill and ferocity. Two rough battle lines had already been drawn - one before the mainmast and the other before the quarterdeck ladder which Dr. Jarman was desperately defending against an opponent, white knotted cord round his head, leaping and twirling in a dazzling display of acrobatics, his moves almost faster than the eye could follow. Mocking him. Tormenting him. Tiring him in a terrible game of death.

Sean ducked and weaved his way towards the quarterdeck across the blood-drenched deck wielding his sword low like a scythe, until he could clamber up behind his uncle. His sword too short in reach now to save his uncle from his attacker's lethal sword play. What would serve? Something that could not be turned. He looked wildly around. Ah there it was right at his feet, a coil of stout British rope strong enough to hold a heavy wet canvas sail, thrashing in a high wind, a cruel gale. Rope thick enough to strangle a man in seconds.

He seized it up with a whoop of joy, swiftly made a loop of its free end, and began to swing it with ever increasing speed feeling the weight lift like a sail filling with wind as he had so often done on his family's farm as a child. What courage its motion leant him! He was unconquerable. Now was the time. His uncle driven against the mast, his sword tiring, his cuts a fraction too slow, sweat standing on his brow. His enemy closing in for the kill. He moved forward, swinging the rope in a deadly hissing circle faster and faster. In the brief moment his enemy paused in his frantic dance of death to take aim for the death blow, Sean swung the hideous whip of rope over the man's head whipping it tight as it dropped round his neck. He fell writhing, tearing at the rope's grip, sword clattering to the deck.

His uncle, seizing his chance, lunged forward to plunge his sword in the man's chest, then to withdraw it as blood poured from the fatal blow, to lift it on high for momentum enough to strike the dead man's head from his body in one swift blow. With the head impaled on his sword point he climbed to the quarterdeck where he could be seen above the commotion below him, where he raised it on high with a mighty yell. The first man to see it uttered a desolate long wail for his dead leader in summons to the rest to abandon the fight and leap overboard.

Last his uncle wiped his sword contemptuously on the rough cotton trousers of the wrack of his deadly assailant, stooped to put the white bandeau back on the man's head, sheathed his sword, then held out his hand to Sean with a ghostly smile of approbation.

'Our saviour and mine. You've a quick wit, young man. It won't be the last time you'll need it to survive in China.'

Then he ordered the crew to throw all wounded overboard. Sean started forward to protest a true Christian would have more mercy but Dr. Grusson restrained him. 'Don't interfere! The mandarin can hardly admit he sent them to murder us when he comes tomorrow. He'll disown them. Who'll take them then?'

'We could land them onshore.'

'For those waiting to massacre them in case they talk?' Dr. Grusson chided him gently.

Sean turned gloomily away. How naive he was! His uncle had sent him north to be blooded in the brutal realities of life on the China coast; the latent violence behind the excursions to pleasure gardens or Honam Island, the flower boats, the endless enjoyment of good European liquor and food, and the petty quarrels of the cloistered life of the factories. Well, he had been blooded, blooded more literally than his uncle intended. He was proud he had not only acquitted himself, but excelled. He could enter Canton as nobly as his uncle could have wished; not just a relative with no prospects back home being given the chance so many British men of no fortune had taken in the East over the years, but as a young sprig of the family who had proved his mettle, who had been tried in action and found not wanting.

CHAPTER 2

1833
The Unholy Alliance

*A*fter Sean's ferocious introduction to the naked conflict festering under the ritual skirmishing of the China trade, Sean was more prepared to tolerate the less exciting routines of daily trading and ship insurance in Jarman Malleson's Canton headquarters in Number 1 Creek Factory lying at the upriver western end of the 13 Factories that comprised the foreign settlement. But he was not prepared for James Malleson's opening words to the inner council of the firm of Jarman Malleson, known by its critics as the Unholy Alliance.

'The temper of the British government must be provoked. The Lion must be made to roar.'

Nor was he prepared for the consternation among the rest of the Alliance - his own uncle, James Malleson's younger cousin David, and their lesser allies Rod Ince, known as the Laird, and Kier MacKeane, known as Paddy.

Dr. Jarman's the most imperative of all. 'The last time we tried, Jarman, the lion refused even to whimper.'

'Times have changed,' James Malleson insisted.

Dr. Jarman rose, towering above his partner the better to make his point. 'Have you forgotten we tried two years ago? Hounded the Company Select into asking for a naval force from India. The result? The Governor-General reminded us Company policy demanded no force be used to protect or forward British interests in China. Three of the Select recalled home for listening to us?'

James Malleson brushed aside the objection, his manner relaxed and persuasive, 'we were too crude then demanding a blockade of Canton. This time we'll be more discreet.'

The Laird, looking more ruffian than merchant with the slash of a duelling scar disfiguring his scarred weather-beaten face, wagged his finger in reproof. 'That was the strategy of a real boneheaded John Bull not your canny Scot.'

Paddy, looking more rogue than respectable trader, agreed. 'We had to come crawling back into port on the Hoppo's terms. Worse loss of face than before.' The Hoppo, as Sean had just been reminded being the supreme Manchu head of the port.

The Laird applauded by overturning his cane and knocking its dog's head on the floor to symbolise the shameful kowtow of an obedient subject's submission, a sneer on his pirate's face in memory of their subservience on that occasion.

James Malleson continued, 'if we go on kow-towing as we do now we only lose more and more face.'

Dr. Jarman studied his partner's face quizzically. 'What do you want us to do about it short of persuading His Majesty's Government to declare war?'

James Malleson, mollified, sat down again. 'Contrive an insult to the British flag.'

Dr. Jarman protested 'this port is calm as a baby's bath right now.'

'Well it won't be tomorrow,' James Malleson announced gleefully.

He kept them waiting before his answer, reaching for his inseparable pipe, badge of the 'fire-eating' barbarian, extracting tobacco slowly from his pouch, tamping it meticulously into the bowl. Sean studied him in bewilderment that he, son of a chief, graduate in law of the venerable University of Edinburgh, should have all the instincts of an outlaw - to mystify, to intrigue, to rebel, to flout the law. The soul of some ancient transgressor lurked in that powerful frame.

The Laird and Paddy fumed with impatience as he fussed into life before explaining 'the Viceroy will send troops and coolies to demolish the wall around the Company's garden and quay.'

Dr. Jarman shook with laughter. 'And well within his rights. The Company flouted him twice with that wall.' He ticked off the adverse points on his fingers. 'Built it without permission on Imperial land. Refused to remove it when requested. Rebuilt it when demolished. All so petty. All so typical. But I fail to see how such an episode can be either incident or insult enough to provoke the temper of the British government.' He blew smoke rings to emphasise his cynicism.

James Malleson smiled smugly. 'It can if the King's portrait is defiled.'

Dr. Jarman stopped blowing smoke rings. 'Who's going to force their way into the New English to do that?'

'The Triads will,' he replied waving towards the northern hills as Paddy leapt up in a wardance of approval.

Not so Dr. Jarman who regarded his partner with barely controlled anger. He should have known better than to invoke the Beggar King and his Triads. Was Malleson going to turn out a dangerous partner, too likely to go off half-cocked on his own account? He enquired tersely, 'your plan?'

'Coolies will rush the factory. Triads on their heels up the stairs in a flash and Bob's your uncle. The picture slashed, our King grievously insulted. The Viceroy will refuse to apologise.' He sketched the route on a copy of their newspaper, the Canton Register.

'What's the pay-off?'

'Opium naturally. Do you think it will work?'

The Laird interjected. 'I don't like it. You trust the Triads too much. What if one of these is caught and betrays you to the Viceroy?'

Malleson shrugged. 'Who wouldn't care a fig, old boy, if he can turn them against us rather than himself.'

'Until he learns our alliance with them extends a lot further than one small riot.' Minor riots caused little panic in a city where they blew up as fast and frequently as thunderstorms.

'The Triads won't betray us,' Dr. Jarman said easily, 'they can't afford to. Our smuggling trade finances their rebellion. The more we make, so do they.'

'One more question James.' The Laird stood to address him, 'what use are all your plans - the anger of the government, gunboats, humiliation of the

Company, if the government appoints a Company officer to be the new Taipan of the China trade when the Company folds up next year after all.'

'Why do you think I'm going to London?'

'To canvass for the right man?' The Laird ventured.

Dr. Jarman announced, 'And who better than himself?'

Paddy echoed, 'Its plain as the nose on your face, Laird, he's the man.'

The Laird demurred. 'You'll never match the Company Court of Directors in clout with the government, James.'

'I have clout with the court of the King,' James Malleson boasted, 'against which no company director will be worth a tinker.'

The Laird raised his glass to toast Malleson and the coming Taipan with the old jocular Company toast of 'a bloody war and a sickly season' - the two things Company officials least desired. As Sean raised his glass, he thought these coming kings of the coast wanted only bloody war and certainly not the sickly season.

He had listened in troubled belief to the profoundly manipulative politics of James Malleson - his short-term plan to become Trade Superintendent on the coast, his long-term plan to provoke war in China to secure concessions from the Imperial Government so long refused, and his sinister association with the Triads. But he preferred not to believe his absurd plot of attack on the Company factory next door until, as he sat with his uncle on the upper verandah of their own factory, it unfolded below exactly to James Malleson's description and obvious glee.

Troops in ragbag uniforms, and coolies, came marching from the guardhouse on the left of them to the New English Factory to the right, then divided in two, one to begin demolishing the mudbrick wall and fence of the garden and the other the quay. At the first thud of crowbars and spades, members of the Select Committee, led by the Mad Davies cursing them in fluent Cantonese, and several of their pursers rushed out to do battle. Their brief fierce scuffle with the soldiers ended when a fresh rabble, flooding in from the Common, drove them back towards the American factory, helpless to stop their marauders pouring into the building they had abandoned.

How could James Malleson sit watching from his upstairs balcony with glee without a shred of conscience as if a mere spectator not the guilty author, Sean wondered? Was this the sort of man he himself must become to survive in the House of Jarman Malleson?

When the mob had vanished as swiftly as they had come, his uncle dragged him in his wake to visit the President in the New English factory to make capital out of the incident, all unaware the Triad leadership had been unable to decide which of the two giant portraits - King George 111 in his coronation robes or the ambassador, Lord Amherst, in the official dress he had worn in his unsuccessful presentation to the Son of Heaven in 1795, was truly the King and had made doubly sure by slashing both.

He condemned the assault as an outrage so vociferously he panicked the President of the Select Committee into a petition to the Governor-General of India asking for the flagship of the Eastern Squadron under the command of the Admiral himself with a warfleet large enough to carry a thousand troops; and to rushing it downstream to Whampoa to catch a ship due to sail on the next flood before the panic wore off or saner counsels prevailed.

The President's trio of fellow Committee members - John Davies, Ross Newman and Hugh Hodgson - were appalled. Though the three big men were utterly unlike, the restless John Davies in intellect, the genial Ross Newman in his caution, and the astute Hugh Hodgson in his shrewd diplomacy, they were as one in condemning their President for his stupidity.

'The Company Court's rule of 1822 is quite explicit,' John Davies, now President elect, stormed as he waved a fan energetically over his wrists Chinese-style, 'Request no force except in dire emergency. Is this such a dire emergency Mr. President? A fracas in the garden? A pettifogging skirmish? Start a war over that, I ask you? Has he gone mad?'

Ross Newman held up a hand to be heard, 'I think I have the answer.'

John Davies stopped waving his fan. Ross Newman only committed himself when he had evidence too certain to be denied. 'Well out with it man what is your answer?'

'To impress the new Triads rumour has it are taking over the old by any means short of outright war.'

'The Triads?' John Davies and Ross Newman chorused.

'Their new allies.'

'Allies in what?'

'Taking over the smuggling trade.'

'The implications of what you say are frightening.'

'I know. You should be warned.'

John Davies demanded, 'are you alleging the Triads will divert the smuggling trade away from the Co-Hong who control it at present into their own hands?'

Hugh Hodgson nodded fervently. 'They need the opium to buy guns to finance rebellion against the Manchu.'

'If what you say is true, the purpose of the Triads is no longer secret whatever pretence they have to be a secret society,' Davies raged slamming the now closed fan down on his palm. 'Opium to finance rebellion, guns to carry it out.'

As the Mad Davies slumped back into his chair to brood on this threat to their future, Maxwell Raine, free trader head of Thomas Raine's, burst through the French doors with the jerky angularity of a puppet in a Punch and Judy show and coiled his lanky body into a spare cane chair, anguish on his face.

'Sign their wretched petition for extreme measures of resistance. No! Sign and brand myself a trouble-maker in the eyes of the Viceroy, worse a potential rebel? No! Its one thing, Day, to flirt with the Co-Hong here in Canton and sail the Coast to find Co-Hong trade where it's willing, another to plot to break the monopoly wide open. They'll give us a bad name, same as themselves.'

Ross Newman smiled at the irony of Maxwell Raine's concern, a man who would already be branded a smuggler in any other country but this. For Raine was in the same business as Jarman Malleson, indeed their chief rival. However although as aggressive a trader, he had none of their instinct for political intrigue.

A soothing hand from Davies on his arm. 'Never fear! The Court of Directors in London will have his neck.' He drew his fan across the throat in an ear-to-ear cutting motion. 'They will recall him. I'll succeed as President. A very different cup of tea.'

Raine was not assuaged. 'That's not the worst of it. They want me to sign another petition to Viceroy Lu threatening to bring armed men from Whampoa if he doesn't amend the eight regulations for trade at once. Calls them unjust and offensive, which is to say not just the Viceroy but the Emperor himself.

Davies swore. 'Blundering fools! Crass clowns! Will they never learn? Has the Hoppo heard yet?'

Raine threw up his hands in despair. 'Has he ever! Threatened Howqua with death and put his senior linguist in prison for letting a riot get out of hand.' This was grave news. Howqua as head of the Co-Hong was responsible for any breach committed by foreign devils. Howqua, who had dodged trouble this last ten years. All in the cause of their ambitions to monopolise trade as the uncrowned kings of Canton.

'With all their talk of free trade!' Hodgson spat his contempt into the spittoon.

'They want to be the banyan tree under whose shade everyone else will grow,' Raine declared angrily.

Davies threw down his fan in lieu of a gauntlet. 'Let them just try!'

'No holds will be barred,' Raine warned them.

'If its war they'll find me ready.'

* * * * * *

Viceroy Lu's Fears of the Fanqui

Viceroy Lu was as disgruntled and dissatisfied as the Select Committee rebels feared, despite the fact he had climbed the 'ladder to the clouds' to the very top. Although he was the highest of all nine ranks of mandarins as member of the tribunal of war, secondary guardian of the heir apparent, wearer of the double-eyed peacock feather for service in two major rebellions and one of only nine Viceroys for the eighteen provinces of China, and therefore the envy of all thrusting up the ladder below him, he did not envy himself as he turned to his hobby for distraction.

This was his stable of fighting crickets in stacked golden cages along one wall of his intimate private sitting room. He stood gloomy and irritated before the cages, took up a small ivory prod, chose a cricket and tickled it to stir up its fighting instincts. It lashed out at once as it should considering the good money he paid hunters to cull excellent fighting crickets for him. He tempted another one even as he thought this a suitable sport to pursue in a province like Kwantung\where the people themselves were like fighting crickets - aggressive, combative and persistently intractable. Men who had fought the Manchu invader until the streets ran with blood.

A short broad man, eyes almost eclipsed in fat, a state much admired by Chinese standards of male elegance, he turned to his equally solid, slow but cheerful friend, the Co-Hong merchant Mowqua. 'I have asked Howqua to come.' He valued his friendship with Mowqua, a straightforward man not given to speculation and subtlety like Howqua and therefore not susceptible to see the other person's point of view like Howqua. Howqua he feared was too amenable to the foreign devils, whereas Mowqua was comfortingly inflexible like himself, believing as he did that the Emperor should never extend rights to these presumptuous barbarians but should insist on their rigid conformity to the law.

He sat down in an elaborately carved blackwood chair, picked up the rounded piece of jade he kept by him to roll between his fingers and thus calm his nerves, and sought Mowqua's opinion. 'The fanqui have written to say they need protection after my soldiers went to their factories. They lie to me. No one was hurt. Nothing was taken from the buildings.'

Mowqua gave the answer he expected. 'They don't need protection.'

'Then why do they lie?'

'As an excuse to bring their fighting ships.'

'When it will be our turn to need protection,' he said glumly.

Mowqua nodded. 'Their fighting ships and weapons are so clearly superior in every way.' He longed for an opium pipe at the very thought of the taxes he would face to rebuild any forts those fighting ships might destroy.'

Viceroy Lu had much the same thought. 'Our navy is nothing.' He would not have dared utter such an alarming truth beyond the privacy of this room, and only did so now because he utterly respected Mowqua's discretion. He added doubtfully. 'Perhaps Howqua has some answer.'

Howqua glided in, a thin vulnerable figure compared to his two fellows. His rounded cap bore the blue button, his rich robe a peacock emblazoned on the chest. He bowed reverently. He took the proffered seat on the required level below his Viceroy. He glided through the courteous formalities of enquiries after health and fortune, wished Viceroy Lu prosperity everflowing like the Pearl River, then discoursed for a time on the matches his champion cricket, Bright Moon on the Water, had fought the day before then took a seat below his Viceroy.

The Viceroy began gently enough. 'You know the fanqui have not kept their respectful and submissive place lately? They plot to bring ships of war here'.

Howqua dared to correct him. 'Some of them do.'

'Do they plan to eat us up as they are doing in India?'

'They deny this.'

Viceroy Lu said curtly, 'if they don't want land why make war?'

Howqua ventured 'for power!'

The Viceroy flashed in anger, 'like the black ships of the Portuguese Jesuits in Japan? Look what they led to!' The history was well known. The Jesuit intrigues had threatened the very court of the Emperor of the Sun. Japan had expelled them, and the Portuguese government in Macao had followed suit.

Viceroy Lu peeled a watermelon seed with practised fingers to soothe his temper. Indignation did not become a mandarin of his rank, most of all before inferiors in rank. He went on, 'these red-haired devils are just like the Portuguese, greedy for treasure. And just as ruthless in the means they will use.'

Howqua asserted quietly, 'more ruthless, Your Excellency, despite all the lessons we have taught the Company. They are raiders like the foam of the sea.'

Viceroy Lu sighed, reaching for the cloisonne snuff bottle. 'Bandits of the sea again.'

Who could ever forget the White Lotus rebellion that engulfed four southern provinces, or the more recent revolt in the highlands that had sent his immediate predecessor as Viceroy stripped of all his honours and consigned in chains to

Dzungaria? Viceroy Lu used the tiny ladle attached to the stopper of his snuff bottle to spoon a little onto his bent thumb, breathed it deeply into either nostril and then addressed Howqua by his family name striking terror in Howqua's heart.

'Old Wu, were those men people of the city who poured into the square yesterday after their leaders like ducks from a duckboat?'

'Our people run like seagulls in a squawking frenzy.'

'Who would run in such a flock, Old Wu?'

'Foam of the land, Your Excellency.'

'Who is their leader? I must find their leader!' he declared angrily as he took another pinch of snuff.

Mowqua muttered, 'their many leaders.' The foam of the land did not need one leader for strength of a fleet like the pirates. Their strength lay in their many branches strewn across the land, their numerous leaders.

Viceroy Lu's piercing gaze was implacable. 'Names, Old Wu. I must have names. You must get them for me.' He must have a victim before wind of this ultimatum from the Select Committee reached the Emperor.

Howqua trembled before the harsh wind of the Viceroy's justice. 'I, Excellency?'

'Yes names. You know all the shroffs.' The Viceroy was right. He did know all the money changers in the lanes behind Thirteen Factories Street, indeed owned some of the shops himself. 'Make enquiries. Find out who has formed treacherous connections with the foreign devils.'

Howqua shivered. A Co-Hong merchant had been executed for such treacherous connections not so long ago. Was Viceroy Lu hinting that he, too, would meet such a fate? In fact Viceroy Lu had no intention of sacrificing Old Wu. He was irreplaceable as the most astute financier in China. Had he not amassed a vast fortune of some thirty million taels despite paying at least ten million more in cumshaw or 'squeeze' during his career?

Old Wu pleaded. 'Your Excellency, this will not be easy. We are faced with new dealers. We do not know them. They do not belong in Canton. They are on the move - pedlars, beggars, boatmen.

But the Viceroy knew perfectly well that Howqua, as head of the Co-Hong, had his finger on the pulse of all the highways of this province. Very well he would have to use the only weapon that would move Howqua, not cajolery nor threats, but blackmail.

'Old Wu, you stand twice accused of dealing in opium.'

Howqua blanched. Viceroy Lu had struck at his very mortality. Yes, he had paid a fortune to save his hide both times. The second affair of Asee, chief bribe collector or 'water-bearer' of Macao, had almost sent him bankrupt and terrified him into renouncing opium-dealing for ever. Asee had denounced not only those who arrested him so rashly on a criminal charge, but everyone from the Viceroy down including Howqua.

'Sir, I have not touched the opium trade in ten years.'

'You are friendly to those who do,' Viceroy Lu was stern.

'Excellency, I am the only bridge prescribed by the Emperor to your most high and mighty office. To the Governor. To the Prefect. The foreign devils are forbidden to do any business except through me. That is well known. Courtesy is proper.'

'Can you prove your courtesy was nothing more?' Viceroy Lu's gentle tone belied the threat behind the words. Howqua felt cold and ill as if the shadow of death already hovered over him. Viceroy Lu could all too easily torture him into confessing courtesy was conspiracy if need be to save himself. 'I want a name, just one name of a leader who runs with the men who abused the English Hong, the men of James Malleson.'

Howqua dared not refuse. Very well, he would make an evil bargain with the Viceroy once but no more, not to please him or even to save his own neck but to buy time till his own ten year old grandson and heir could inherit as his son had rejected trade in contempt. He dared not refuse even knowing that the vengeance from Jarman's new allies would be far worse if he were found out than any disgrace of exile to which the Emperor could condemn him.

Grumbling that 'the Viceroy is catching hares to pacify Pekin when he should be chasing stags,' he assigned his most trusted servant to follow Dr Jarman's new comprador, day and night, swearing before his ancestral tablets that he would never again be so dangerously compromised. He would do everything in his power to help the forces of conciliation against the encroachment of the new Triads, use every wile to dodge the potential for destruction in his compulsory role as bridge between the foreign devils and the Viceroy.

Viceroy Lu grew impatient before Howqua's man led them to the owner of one of the new well-hidden 'small furnaces', 'furnaces' that had sprung up in the twilight trade of the back lanes to melt silver into illegal silver 'sycee' cakes to pay for illegal opium and were the meanest in the chain of command as Howqua well knew.

In the prison of the Viceroy's yamen, the lictors beat the unfortunate victim cruelly until the wire of the bamboo rattans stripped the flesh off his back and buttocks and bruised his face until he could scarcely eat or speak. Only then did he name others, all borne together in bamboo cages three feet high, with names and legends bold for all to see and 'tremble' to the execution ground east of the foreign factories on the bank of the river, where they were beheaded with chill efficiency in awful example to all.

Not content with this sacrifice to the Gods of Beijing, Viceroy Lu exhorted the Co-Hong to persuade the East India Company in India to act against the smuggling of the 'foreign mud' as much to impress Beijing as out of any real hope of action from the Company. The President of the Select Committee snorted when he read this command. 'Viceroy Lu tells us we are to cut off the smuggling trade! Why it wouldn't exist if it weren't for the Co-Hong's own imbecility and the corruption of its officers.' And said as much in his autumn despatches to Lord Bentick, Governor-General of India.

* * * * * *

Holly meets Kaida Hung

Siesta time. Everyone asleep in the soporific heat but Holly, driven downstairs by the noisy chorus of snores from the domestic staff drifting up from their quarters across the rear courtyard. She took refuge on a stone seat in the front garden overlooking the dreaming bay. There, hidden within a vine entwined arch, she could see her Eugenia like a toy ship below. It was her one tangible link between the solid past she had abdicated and the vague future she hoped for here in Macao.

But now she was here nothing was as simple as it had seemed in Salem. Uncle Bart had not told her the market was eighty miles away upriver in Canton. Nor had he made it clear all the goods were loaded seventy miles up river at Whampoa. Moreover trade was not merely a matter of selecting the goods and paying the right price, as she had fondly imagined. It was a battle to make deliveries match orders, and to deal with wildly fluctuating prices; a battle likely to be far worse when the East India Company pulled out of China for good soon and there was no longer any guarantee of standards.

Suddenly a Chinese appeared before her - a tall, bright-eyed, high-cheekboned man dressed as all lesser ranks in casual dark nankeen tunic, white large loose hose and black and white slipper shoes. She took him for a servant until he bowed low, hands pointed together as none of the houseboys did. She was perplexed as he stood waiting before her. How could she speak to him? She had only a few words of that idiotic pidgin English yet.

So she spoke sternly relying on her tone and frown to convey her disapproval. 'What do you want young man?'

To her obvious astonishment, he replied in fluent, if oddly precise, English. 'I apologise if I frightened you, Madam, but I had to speak to you alone.'

'Who are you? Why do you want to speak to me?'

'My brother works here. Today I take his place.'

'Does this authorise you to accost me when I am alone?' He bowed again at this reproof. 'I apologise! But I must speak to you alone. You saved a child. He has a grandmother. She would thank you for the child's life.'

'She doesn't need to thank me. I did nothing.'

He insisted. 'A life is owed for a life. The child is too young to meet his debt. She will meet it for him.'

Holly, bemused now, felt she could not deny this commitment of honour. 'Yes, of course. I would like to meet her. Can you bring her here?'

He shook his head. 'No, that is impossible. I must take you to her. But first you may need approval.'

She asked tartly. 'Why should I need approval?'

'She runs a gambling casino.'

'Object to that when so many foreigners gamble?'

'One favour please.' Tension and fear in his taut face.

'That depends on the favour.'

'I would request you tell no one I speak the King's English. No one must know or I am in grave danger of my life.'

She scoffed at the thought. 'Kill you? Ridiculous.'

Terror on his face for answer. 'We are forbidden to learn or to teach. You ask Dr. Norris, interpreter to the Company. He had to learn English in secret.'

'And you? How did you learn?'

'From the doctor. My mother was nurse to his first wife and children. I went to England with them on leave. His son John and I are like brothers. Ask him. He will speak for me.'

'Your name?' Let him declare that at least.

'Kaida Hung. Please respect our secret or you are in danger. Then so are we.' He vanished on that enigma silently as he had come, symbol of a country that every moment seemed to offer her new mystery.

She wandered back to the wide verandah stretching out on a cane chaise longue to ponder these riddles, ending up baffled and disturbed. Abby and Mary Ann more hindrance than help. Full of mock horror and wild ideas. Kidnap for ransom or worse! Hostage to the Viceroy! Until she protested they alarmed her more than the stranger.

Joshua was no better, supposing 'it might be a trap to inveigle you into an awkward situation and then accuse you of smuggling.'

'How could they do that if I'm not carrying it on me?'

'Send runners to arrest you, and plant it on you.'

Naively she asked, 'where would they get it?'

'Produce what they carry themselves for their own use.'

'Why me? Why would they want me?'

'To trump up a charge because of that street affray.'

'Charge me? Put me on trial? They can't do that.'

'Oh yes they can. Chinese law prevails here.'

Holly's bewilderment grew. 'On Portuguese territory?'

'Unless the Portuguese Governor asks for exemption. He may not agree. No love is lost between us at the moment,' he warned her flatly, knocking the ash out of his pipe to close the debate, and replacing it on an elegant Spanish pipe rack with a flourish.

'Uncle, you're being beastly because you don't want Holly to go,' Abby protested.

'I would be delinquent to my duty if I glossed over the dangers facing unattached young females in this port,' he said pompously.

'Duty, my foot.' Mary Ann rebuked her husband, 'Holly is free, white and twenty one. She has every right to go if she wants, provided she's protected. John can go with her. Interpret what is said. My only objection against her going into the Chinese quarter again is to be seen either in a sedan chair or European dress.'

Joshua, unrepentant, guffawed at that. 'Have her dressed like a Chinese lady and break that law too?'

Mary Ann was not amused. 'No, as a nun.' They all joined Joshua in laughter then until she explained 'nuns like the Little Sisters of the Poor go anywhere without comment in Macao. They owe me some favours. They will loan me a habit.'

Joshua mopped his brow in mock irony. 'A nun in a gambling casino! And I thought I'd heard everything.' He did not voice his fears whether they would all be caught up in the wake of Holly's chariot. He hoped in his kinder moments not at all, being at heart a man who liked an untroubled life. In his more apprehensive moments as now, he knew they inescapably would be.

* * * * * *

Holly meets Chung Tai Tai

'You make a splendid nun,' Abby exclaimed to the demure pensive figure reflected in the long cheval mirror.

Holly nodded. The nun's habit diminished all personality and swallowed up all sexuality. It endowed protection as secure as any armour from the eyes and demands of men.

'With my tolerance for discipline, I'd last five minutes.' She picked up her skirts and twirled in a gavotte.

Abby agreed. 'You were never the headmistress's favourite.'

'This dress is so comfortable. We should all wear it.'

'Go round like shapeless sacks? I'm big enough now.'

'Why do we bind our bosoms? Cramp our waists?'

Abby had no doubts. 'To please men.'

To please our silly selves. Come on, we can't keep John Norris waiting.'

She danced singing out the door and down the stairs to waltz time landing with a flying leap at John Norris' feet and seizing his hand with an enthusiasm that left him staring at her in awkward silence until she demanded 'You are the right man aren't you? You are the one who's taking me to Chinatown?'

'Yes, yes, I'm sorry. How gauche of me. I expected- '

'Someone who behaved like a nun,' Holly added.

'Yes of course,' he assured her hastily, furious that Billy had not warned him that Holly would not be quite what he was used to with his discreet, gentle oh-so-correct sister, Rebecca.

Would the young man never stop staring transfixed at Holly, Abby wondered as she interrupted. 'Who are you going to visit?'

'You don't know?' They shook their heads vehemently. He surprised them by a ribald burst of laughter at odds with the habitual aura of gravity ingrained from the sorrows endured by his missionary father. 'It is the funniest thing in years. You're going to visit Chung Tai Tai.'

'What's so funny about that.'

'First of all the lady runs a gambling casino, then..' He stopped short. He could not tell Holly the truth about Chung Tai Tai yet. If he did she would refuse to go. Then what would Chung Tai Tai say? He improvised an answer. 'She works in various charities.'

Holly flounced out the door in a most unnunlike manner. 'It seems to me your sense of humour is just as misplaced as Adam's or Billy's. What right would I have to criticise her? Our men gamble notoriously over their card tables. And what is trade but a perpetual gamble?'

She marched down the street besides a desolated John Norris, her reproachful silence befitting her role as a nun. At first she scarcely acknowledged his entertaining comments, but gradually her own irrepressible sense of fun asserted itself. She arrived at last at the Almada de Rebiero, Street of Fan Tan Houses, in a state of gleeful fun most unbecoming to a nun.

She was astonished to find that Chung Tai Tai's gambling house, the House of Trusting Profit, had such a small unassuming facade, and that its patrons were not at all as she had expected. The crowd around the croupiers on the ground floor were quiet and orderly. The wealthier gamblers, overlooking them from a circular balcony above, looked more like the patrons of a tea house than obsessive gamblers as they accepted tea, sweetmeats and melon seeds from attentive waiters while they sent their bets down in baskets to the croupiers below.

So this was a gambling den, a place of dangerous rapture, where the rhythmic count of the croupier held a ring of half-shaven heads in thrall.

John Norris explained the point of the game - to work out how many coppers would be left from a gallon of cash after the croupier had raked in the coins by fours.

'But there's no skill in that,' Holly exclaimed as John explained the gaming to her.

'No,' John agreed, 'the game is simplicity itself. But remember it's a simple game for ordinary folk. For small bettors mostly, although not always. Fortunes can be won or lost too.'

Holly found the room where Chung Tai Tai waited for them on the second level, though small and unpretentious, exuded a subtle magnificence that matched the luxury of her white satin robe, jade jewellery and embroidered green satin slippers.

Holly bowed before the tiny imperious figure, seeming at first glance as fragile as fine porcelain on her carved cherrywood throne. But Holly was wrong. This slim lady, so tautly erect before her, was the toughest woman in all South China, tougher than the famous Tartar General presently in Canton.

Chung Tai Tai's opening remark was unexpected. 'You are born of a line of sailors as I was.'

How the devil could she know, Holly marvelled, as she answered, 'my father until he was injured at sea, and both my grandfathers. They died at sea.'

'Heiyah!' the old lady sighed. 'A typhoon?'

'No typhoons in our seas. One lost in a whale fight. One drowned when a stay whipped loose from a mast, and dragged him overboard.'

'Heiyah!' she cried again. She knew about such tragedies of the ocean. All her life she had known. 'And your father?' She had never left her own husband's side all those years at sea through all the hardship and battles of the Ladrones war.

'He fell from a yard in a storm.' 'Heiyah!' she cried again. She knew those masts, so much taller than the masts of her junks. 'Like our women you are not afraid of the sea.' Four long months at sea from their strange countries, she knew.

Holly turned to John Norris, whose unhesitating interpretation had more than restored him in her eyes. 'What does she mean by our women?"

'Tanka women. Women who are foam of the sea.'

As a maid served tea in thin translucent cups, the old lady got down to business. 'I owe you a debt I must repay. You saved my grandson.'

'Please, you must not feel you should repay me.'

Chung Tai Tai brooked no argument. 'A life owes a life. That child is my husband reborn.'

'Surely his life wasn't in any danger.'

Chung Tai raised a hand to command her silence. 'Miss Shay, these people are not of your world. They would have killed if necessary. They wanted to use my grandson to demand what I could not give. Therefore he would have died. Only after weeks in their bamboo cages while the haggling went on. Perhaps a lid through which to thrust his head. Perhaps not. Forced to rest his head on his knees.'

And this is the nation that dares to call us barbaric, Holly thought angrily. These new Triads of the King of the Beggars want to force me to become their ally. They are not honest men like the old Triads who took money from the boatmen and fisherfolk to build funds to help them when poor, sick or old. These new Triads force money from them under threats for 'protection' so they say. From whom but themselves? Wicked men who wanted to force me to join them by kidnapping my grandson. Would I make an alliance with men who know nothing but war on their own; I who grew tired of war twenty years ago and made my peace with the government?'

Holly only dimly understood what Chung Tai Tai was saying, that dangerous criminals were so anxious for her co-operation they would seize her grandson? Could this lady, seemingly as gentle and inoffensive as a benign Buddha, be so important?

Explanations over, Chung Tai Tai offered Holly a curious flat carved plaque of jade on a gold silk cord, urging her to 'show this if you are ever in trouble, and you will be safe. You women are in Macao alone half the year, your men in Canton. They cannot protect you. Nor can the law. You have less rights in Macao than the seagulls do. That is your danger.'

Holly hesitated before stowing the precious plaque in her reticule. But looking up into those watchful eyes again, she felt an inexplicable trust for this woman she had known such a brief time. They had a strange affinity that transcended race and history.

Chung Tai Tai now made it clear she offered more than a talisman. 'I will help you buy cargo for your ship. I can smooth the way. Unless I help, you will have trouble.'

'Is my connection with Law's not good enough?'

'Not to get first preference for the best samples, goods true to sample, price correct. We can do that.'

'I thought this was controlled by the Co-Hong.'

'We have our backdoor which is a front door,' she said enigmatically, 'I speak not only of goods but money. Capital to survive in a market where there are no banks. If you need money and you will, you must not turn to Jarman Malleson. Come to me.'

Under the command of those dark eyes, Holly promised, but was hardly out in the narrow, clamorous street before she begged John to explain who Chung Tai Tai really was. He insisted on consulting Billy first. She reproved him angrily.

'Billy is not my keeper.'

John would not budge even though he hated to oppose Holly when his whole instinct was to please her. 'He knows the Coast as well as I do. He can judge how much you should know.'

'I feel like a small child,' she said petulantly.'

'It's just knowing what Mr. Law might not want you to know.'

John, already half in love with her, grew more unhappy by the minute as

Holly stalked grimly ahead in disapproval, her skirts hitched a shade higher than was seemly.'

Once home, Billy bless his heart, urged caution to the winds saying scornfully, 'whose reputation would we defend, John? We hold no brief for the Scottish buccaneers or their allies. She's bound to find out sooner or later.' He turned to Holly. 'That lady with whom you sipped tea is none other than one of China's most notorious ladies, the famous ex-pirate queen.'

She gasped, 'you're taking me for a ride, Billy.'

'Make no mistake. That little lady is tough as the teak decks she rode on.'

'She did say she sailed with her husband.'

'And became Admiral of the fleet when he was killed?'

'She, the Admiral of a fleet? I can't believe...'

'And a brilliant one.'

Abby said, 'I can just see her mistress of a fleet, small and neat as herself.'

'Little fleet? Good Lord, no!' Billy cried.

John elaborated, 'At first it was the biggest fleet on the coast in centuries. Legend says some two thousand ships with twenty thousand men, more than half of them large junks. They commanded where they pleased on land and sea. Their chief, Apotsae, was ruler of all from Macao to Heangshan. Up to twelve guns on each - six eighteen pounders. Some of them Imperial ships that went over to them. They were not the usual part-time pirates endemic on the coast, although they were too were sprung from fishermen in the coastal villages of the boat people but well-organised with profit-sharing of booty and provisions, and welfare schemes for those hurt or killed in battle. They prohibited promiscuity or violence to women. They were cruel only to those they captured in Government vessels. From what I've heard, a great fleet at the time of the Ladrone wars.'

Holly asked startled, 'Our Ladrones?'

'Yes!' Billy confirmed. 'That battleground was right here. Apotsae captured many Government forces, and laid the whole land under contribution from here to Canton until he was betrayed to die the death of a thousand cuts. Chung Tai Tai's husband, Chung Pao, commanded next until killed in battle, then Chung Tai Tai herself after him. Eventually some of her captains, tired of being hunted, turned against her and joined the government fleet, and painted their junks black in imitation of ours as if to copy us would give them the magic we seemed to possess. Only the Portuguese warships could give them that. Then they cut off her supplies, bottled her up in the Ladrones and outgunned her.'

'She lived to tell the tale?' Abby enquired mystified. 'Why in the days of the Spanish Main she would have walked the plank or been strung from the yardarm.'

'Ah, but this is China,' John told them, 'a very, very practical country. Generals make deals. Generals change sides. Not only in the middle of wars but even in battles. Surrender cities, fleets, on the understanding no one will be punished.'

Abby shrieked, hand at her throat. 'With those cutthroats after they've massacred poor innocent villagers! How dreadful of the government.'

Billy was unsympathetic. 'Very sensible of them. Stopped all the killing. Put the pirates to work for them rather than against them.'

Holly laughed. 'What work is there for ex-pirates apart from casinos?'

'Traditional work of pirates when not in open rebellion - to protect the fishing fleet from those who still are.'

'Chung Tai Tai does that? Then who are the new rebels?'

'Why their allies, Jarman Malleson, of course.'

'But they don't hold villagers to ransom.'

'Do they not? Villagers pay them silver just the same. Money given for opium is like money given for nothing, less than nothing. In fact these new pirates are worse than the old. Once the villagers paid to live. Now they pay to be destroyed.'

Holly felt she no longer lived in reality as she heard these shocking truths. Here they were conducting their western tea ceremony with the full silver service and three tiered cake platters as if still in New England, while conducting a polite debate about the savage ways of pirates as if they were the peccadilloes of her next door neighbours. She caught a glimpse of her distorted reflection in the mirror of the bulging teapot like a gross gargoyle. It was as though her mental image of the protagonists in this villainous drama had become as distorted as her own face in the teapot.

Abby, true daughter of her Calvanist forefathers, pursed her lips in disapproval. 'I can't understand their passion for that horrid opium.'

John said dryly. 'They can't understand our passion for firewater.'

To which she retorted. 'I hardly think that is the proper viewpoint for the son of a missionary.'

'It's the proper viewpoint of a realist, which is why I can't be the missionary my father wanted me to be. From what I have seen probably far fewer people suffer from true addiction than is the case with the ginshops of England, taprooms of Manhattan, or the laudanum takers of either country.'

Abby protested. 'You sound as if they'd given you cumshaw.'

'I wish they had so Dad could live in luxury. The Chinese would respect him more then. But you're wrong if you think opium is the most valuable article in the smuggling trade. In fact salt is, and actually more dangerous to smuggle than opium because it involves tax evasion as well. Not forgetting rice and silk. They are smuggled too - in fact anything that can be bartered.'

'The Customs can't prevent it?'

'My dear Holly, they would have to examine every boat that moves on the water. You've seen how many there are of those.'

'Including Chung Tai Tai's?' Holly teased Billy.

'How do you think the Portuguese smugglers in Macao would manage without her?'

'Which means that Jarman Malleson don't work with her,' Holly concluded.

She trifled with her cake much too distracted to notice John had eyes for no one but herself; John consumed by extremes of emotions he had never known before. Elation that these feelings that swept over him must be at last the intimations of being in love he believed forever alien to him, his nature too cool, too contained, as his sister Rebecca kept chiding him. Despair that he without prospects, a child of China alien to the land of his original Britain, could ever hope to win Holly.

As Joshua Law swept in with a group of visiting officers only interested in the kind of giddy anecdotal diversion they expected of lightheaded young ladies in port, he took his leave. Not before Holly bound him to silence in a hurried whisper. No one, not even Joshua, must know. The intimacy of that moment, made with a handclasp to the incense of her perfume and the pounding drumbeat of his heart as she bent towards him, left him drained of energy.

Back at the simple home his father could afford, he slumped into a chair, oblivious to Rebecca's recital of her day's work helping the missionary, Dr. Sanders, print forbidden Chinese language dictionaries and Bibles. Like their father, the serious intensity of her nature was entirely focussed on the vision of China as a glorious mission field where the shining gospel would save the heathen from damnation.

She challenged him at last, 'John you're in a trance. What's wrong? Are you sick? Tired then?' He shook his head to both. How could he tell his sister that his vision was far more worldly than hers of winning China to God, of winning Holly to himself.

* * * * * *

Kaida Hung Learns his True Fate

The border guards passed Kaida Hung through the Waterlily Gate that led from the Portuguese enclave on the small jutting peninsula of Macao to China proper without question. He was a familiar figure from his visits to his clan village inland. Soon he turned from the main road to Heangshan to follow the windings of the foreshore of the Taipa Harbour inland.

As he threaded his way through the meticulously planned changing levels of rice paddies and gardens, his thoughts turned to the mystery of his mother. The choice she had made to take work with a 'foreign devil' like Dr. Norris rather than remain a matriarch in her home village like her sisters. Her risk in teaching Cantonese to Dr. Norris under cover of that work. Her strange concerns far beyond the role of a modest servant. Unexplained visitors. Conferences with relatives that appeared to extend beyond mere clan matters of weddings, deaths and legacies. Respect not usually accorded a humble widow. Most curious of all was that she, a humble denizen of an insignificant village, believed Howqua, the most powerful and richest of all Co-Hong merchants, would grant her an interview and arrange an appointment for him to the Viceroy's yamen. Why should Howqua perform favours for his poor mother? He couldn't even begin to answer that question.

After the alien transformation of Macao, Kaida loved to walk across the crumpled landscape where the great range of mountains, that had marched all the way across the south of China, petered out in a thousand shapes like a child's box of toys strewn across the floor of the world. Up and round and down the slopes farmers had manipulated with terraces, waterlevels, groves of trees and wandering paths through the ages- farmers who lived out their entire lives in the radius of their region. Never strayed as he had done. Never imagined such a journey as he had made to England, a journey which had not estranged him from his motherland but rather made him more content with it. For he had learnt by going so far that the freedom of the world, the majesty of London, was nothing if love and family were not there.

As he saw the watchtower of his grey and white village loom through the trees he felt the usual peace of homecoming descend on him, marred only by regret his first love was not for any girl to be found there as it should be but for a girl back in Macao, a mestizo half-British, half-Chinese - a creature in limbo of neither country. Beautiful. Haunted by her past. Haunting. An orphan from the Home for the Innocents and hence without family or dowry. Without any possible place in his village. This problem made more poignant for him by his best friend's entirely suitable wedding to the daughter of the richest man in the adjoining village that very day, a match that was proper in every respect.

He entered the miscellany of buildings of his clan village at last, where families, dogs, chickens, pigs intermingled apparently at random. In reality, it was a tight hierarchy of family units in strict harmony, every history of every person known to him; the whole spectrum of foolish, wise, idle or brilliant individuals, who hated, loved and exasperated each other all year round, yet escaped each other with difficulty.

At the far end of the village in the most capacious house, he found his uncle, a robust and jovial man, gloomy for the first time in his experience.

Bowing low, he asked anxiously 'What's wrong, Uncle?'

'Bad news today, nephew. Grave robberies.' He rocked back and forth in anguish over this violation of sacred ancestral tombs.

'Why would anyone rob graves, Uncle?'

'Ransom, nephew. I cannot afford the ransom they want. Heiyah! They will chop the coffins up for firewood.' A crime not too uncommon, as coffins, being ten feet long and deep to match, yielded a handsome quantity of firewood. 'They will throw the bones to the dogs! Oh your poor grandfather!.'

Kaida was incredulous. 'Stole my grandfather's coffin?'

'His soul won't rest now. It will return to haunt us..'

'Why would anyone think grandfather's coffin worth a ransom?'

His uncle suddenly became abstracted and vague. 'Old stories! Foolish stories, nephew! Of money hidden away!' This tale of ransom seemed too commonplace, too unlikely to account for his uncle's torment. His uncle was a rich man from both legitimate business and respectable smuggling. But he had no time to dally for the wedding was due to start.

The elaborate feast that followed ended far into the night. Well past midnight found Kaida hastening along a short cut across the plunging hillside above the Waterlily Neck through a graveyard of great omega-shaped stone armchairs in a thick shroud of darkness. He had just stooped to fumble his way round one particularly large tomb when a flickering light pierced the black below. Seized with terror, he crouched low. Who but criminals would choose to come to such a place where ghosts and evil spirits were said to walk at night? He lifted his head a fraction above the curve of the low wall of the tomb, dismayed to see many men with knotted red or black head scarves assembling below him. Were they members of one of those secret societies, whose names he had so often heard in frightened whispers among the Chinese of Macao? Names like the Green Dragon, the White Lotus or perhaps the Golden Dragon, which only a year or two ago had seen Viceroy Lu consigned to the outermost province of Ili in penniless disgrace because of their discreditable rout of the Emperor's army?

He lay still as a snake in winter, sweating with fear. Fortunately he was higher on the hillside than they, their attention riveted on a man sitting enthroned on a gravestone, knife in hand, guarded by four men with crossed swords on either side. A multiple-knotted red scarf was twisted around his head, a red riband draped round his neck, a straw sandal worn on one foot only.

A sacred book of rules lay open before him as his followers reiterated the vows of allegiance inscribed therein - to their Great Elder Brother, and the laws of the Heaven and Earth Society. Triads, Kaida thought aghast. Outlawed by the Viceroy. Forced to meet in places like this. Certain to treat him without mercy as a Viceroy's spy if they found him, to behead him on the spot as they would the trussed chicken awaiting its ritual sacrifice.

Now a novice came forward trembling, knelt in a posture of reverence, begged to become a member, answered the Great Elder Brother's questions, took a yellow paper effigy of the Emperor from him and set it on fire, kowtowed three times, recited the Triad credo - 'People of the top class owe us money. People of the middle class should wake up. People of the lower class come with us.' - and declared the Triad oath of brotherhood as Great Elder Brother held a knife poised over his head - 'Justice, the Way, the Will of Heaven.'

Next Great Elder Brother cut the wrists of the novice over a cup of wine, squeezed three drops of blood from each into a chalice, then passed the chalice round for all to drink the oath of blood brotherhood. And last to remind him that the price of breaking that oath was death, a candle was blow out, a bowl broken, and the chicken's head struck off.

But even now the weary ritual was not yet over. The novice must learn the secret forms of greeting. Kaida fought against fatigue to learn them, all too chillingly aware they would save his life if he were ever to find himself in such terrible danger again. The gestures first. The right arm through the opening of a vest. The lifting of a teacup with three fingers. The passwords. 'Have you come from the East?' 'Yes' 'How heavy is your load?' 'Two catties or thirteen taels.' 'When do you pray?' 'On the fifteenth, nineteenth or twenty-fifth'.

Then at last the final muted two hundred year old battle-cry of rebellion against the Manchu 'Restore the Ming' before the Triads abandoned their dangerous meeting in the eerie graveyard to vanish into the fading dark of threatening dawn.

Those final words 'Restore the Ming!' still echoed in Kaida's mind, as he stumbled from his refuge, numb with cold, long after the Triad rebels had left. How could they swear to bring about any restoration of the Ming dynasty? He had been taught the Ming rulers were dead and gone these two centuries past of alien Manchu Tartar rule. Yet could that teaching be wrong, merely imposed by their foreign rulers? Could an heir or heirs still exist? Was there not just such an heir to the thirteenth century Sung Dynasty, even older than the Ming, living even now on French's Island in this very Pearl River delta.

The Ming! The cry still a refrain in his head when, damp and exhausted, he stumbled into the Norris kitchen to find his mother already stoking the breakfast fire, her beauty undiminished by her drab dress, her severe hair drawn back into a tight bun.

She was horrified to hear of his narrow escape, seizing him in her arms and hugging him with a passion she rarely displayed, crying a grief out of character. 'My dear son, how could I have exposed you to such danger from the

Righteous Rising Society? I have left you ignorant too long. Both you and your brother. I have left it too late. I wanted to protect you. I should have told you.'

'Told me what? What should I know' What dire family secret could have been hidden from him?

'A secret more powerful than any of the Triads would have known.'

'No secret would have been powerful enough to have saved me last night if they had found me.' He shivered, partly from the chill still upon him, partly with dread at the thought.

'Oh yes, if they had known who you were.' She pulled a small stool across to the fire, and persuaded him to warm himself there saying, 'It is time you knew the truth of your origins. But first you must promise never to disclose the secret I am about to tell you to any fanqui except one, John Norris.' She turned to the small shrine of Kwanying, Goddess of Mercy, patron saint of Macao, which stood on a dresser, lit an incense stick in the neat brass bowl of sand between the fresh offerings of fruit and flowers, and bowed before crouching down on a second stool close too him. 'Did you never wonder why I defied the mandarins to send you to the school on the hill and Chinese tutors?'

'I thought you saw a future for me as an interpreter for the merchants, even the Viceroy himself.' 'A dangerous future you'll agree, since linguists are the first to suffer in any argument between the Manchus and the foreign devils. Particularly one like you with Christian contact and education.'

'Then why, mother, why?

'Because you might be forced to leave China one day.' Tears ran softly from her eyes to see his horrified dismay. 'Because of who you are, a man of the highest destiny. That is the danger with which you live, the danger for which I must prepare you now.'

She knelt beside him gabbling close to his ear as if in fear someone might overhear them. 'Some hot heads could brew discontent to rebellion before there is any chance of success. Many people die for nothing. And you, too. That is my fear. They cry Heaven, Earth and Man. But Heaven has too long seemed deaf to both Earth and Man.'

She gripped his hands, her fiercely troubled gaze locking his own. 'I have dreaded for many years the moment when I must tell you who you are. But last night you heard that cry of the Triad to restore the Ming. You wondered who that man was who might be hailed as leader, the man for whom the bowstring is now drawn so violently it will at last be broken. You wondered if he existed.'

A violence in her grip now as if she could transmit her own boundless courage to face what she had to tell him. 'You are that man. You are now the most direct living heir of the last Ming Emperor. You are the Pretender to their throne in Pekin.'

His sight blurred with shock. None of the stories of legends he loved could match this story she told him now; a story of Ming rebels hunted by the Manchu through the generations into the furthest corners of the empire they had once ruled.

'So that is my danger? To be sought as the hope, the leader of yet another rebellion against the Manchu? That is my inheritance as your eldest son?'

The enormity of the truth left him rocking on his stool, head in his hands, thinking of course his mother was right to prepare him either to fulfil his terrible destiny or to escape from it if he chose. She was right to have given him that choice.

'So that was why you had us both educated with the foreign devils. How wrong I have been!'

'And to give you a choice none of your forebears had before, not even your father. They had to live with the dread of battle to the bitter end.'

'Is that how my father died?'

'Yes, in Apotsae's pirate fleet.'

So she had hidden that distasteful truth from him too, he thought, protesting 'as a pirate!'

She rebuked him sharply. 'Is that worse than to persist as a tame peasant under the yoke of the Tartars, shaving half your head because they decree it, wearing their hated queue, badge of the defeated Sons of Han, badge of shame? Unable to carry arms. Less than half a man. At least he died a man, a free man on the free sea.'

He stared into the glowing coals of the fire, his brain in turmoil. Surely what she was saying could not be true, for there were other versions of this legend.

'What about Pao Shan who studied with Billy Howe at the Anglo-Chinese College in Malacca? He boasts he's the most direct living heir.'

'Absolute nonsense, son,' she responded tartly.

'Going to Beijing on Howqua's recommendation to interpret for the Emperor in Latin and English,' he added.

His mother laughed for the first time at that. 'How many Latin and English documents do you imagine are in Pekin for Pao Shan to translate apart from ancient writings of the Jesuit fathers and the few petitions the Viceroy sees fit to forward to Pekin?'

'Then why bother to encourage him?' Kaida asked. 'If they officially recognise him as legal by attaching him to their Court in Pekin, it follows nobody who makes the same claim can be. Thus they can denounce any leader of a new Triad rebellion. Then surely that would protect me from danger.'

'Never. Because they know the ruse will not be enough to prevent any rebellion while the true heir does exist and, so long as he does, another rebellion might break out as the White Lotus rebellion did a generation ago.'

She regarded him sadly as she revealed that his father had been one of the leaders before he was born, grieving even now to think how it had failed after an upheaval that convulsed at least four great provinces. She had no wish to see him relive those terrible days again.

'Was that the time you fled to Macao?'

'No, some years later when the Viceroy arrested and tortured three thousand of our people. No one betrayed us.' They had escaped as 'foam of the land' had so often done through the myriad channels of the Pearl River delta where the Manchu soldiers did not dare follow. Escaped to the protection of Chung Tai Tai and her smuggling fleet of village fishermen. Escaped to become 'foam of the sea' if they must.

He blurted out, 'so that is why you never had your feet bound? A disguise to appear as peasant or Tanka. To run when hunted, run to save me and my brother. You, who are a victim of your own destiny.'

He knotted his elegant fingers in a fold of his long dark tunic. The enormity of his mother's revelation weighed on him. He would no longer be able to move without thought of the consequence, knowing his actions no longer accountable merely to himself but to all those people waiting in the shadows with such hope. What did they expect of him? To lead a peasant army like his original ancestor, a peasant general? To found a new dynasty on a high road of untold bloodshed as he had done? No, he could never see himself at the head of a wild and wasteful army on the march. He quailed at the thought.

'I am not the man for their destiny,' he declared, 'These Triads live in the past, mother. The time for a Ming restoration has long gone.'

'You can't undo your destiny'.

'To plot to overthrow the Manchu?' Exasperation in his tone. Had she seen her whole life as moving towards the hour when he would catch the tide of his destiny?

For answer, she led him to the window to point to the foreign ships riding at anchor in the roadstead. 'No, it will happen without us. They will conquer the Manchu.'

'So few of them?'

'Their knock at the door will force the Manchu to open it to the winds of their change. Winds that will fan the embers of rebellion.'

Late into that night she debated with her son to ease his shock, to soothe his fears and prepare him for action. He must accept the double life with the foreigners and the provincial government she intended for him. He must learn to distinguish between the willing and unwilling tools of the Manchu Tartars in government. He must also enlist young John Norris as another means of escape should Chung Tai Tai by some mischance fail him.

When he rested his head at last on his bamboo pillow, he lay awake far into the night wondering whether there would ever be escape from his destiny. Would he be doomed to linger in the shadows as his father had done, the great hope of the Triads, to risk terrible reprisal every time they gathered in the dark to swear an allegiance to him even to the death as they cried 'Restore the Ming!'?

* * * * * *

The Merchants Return to Canton
for the Trading Season

Holly stood gloomily in the excited crowd gathered on Penha Hill to cheer the East India Company merchants on their way to Canton for the trading season aboard an armada of two hundred Chinese junks. Junks because they were taking the shorter route of the Broadway Passage through the Pearl River delta than the more roundabout route of the mainstream via Whampoa Island where the Company fleet was now anchored. How she longed to be standing on those gaily bedecked primeval vessels amid an uproar of gongs and firecrackers to chase away all that might bedevil them.

Yet she felt overwhelmed with self-criticism that she should be so discontented, demanding more than this country chose to offer her compared to the Nuns of Toledo in the Convent of St. Clare behind her. She was driven to self-fulfilment as they to self-renunciation. Witness their procession now leading the orphans in their charge down to the Church of San Antonio to celebrate his Feast Day- San Antonio, Portuguese patron saint of Macao, because he routed the Dutch invaders generations before.

Why couldn't she be as content as Tim Bird in the sanctuary of his old Portuguese house with its view far and wide over the glittering bay and mist-laden islands? A domain wholly persuasive an instant of paradise was possible on earth, his garden and aviary famous throughout Asia.

But she forgot her discontent when tiny Tim Bird, stately and formal, greeted Abby and herself all smiles and deprecation. 'Welcome to my poor garden, no match for such beauties.'

She was lost for words at the sight of his 'poor garden'. It was a magical realm with a surprise at every level of the terraces marching up the hillside. Camellia trees exploding with giant blooms of every colour. Fruit trees of every variety - lychees, oranges, mandarins, and a Bombay mango tree. Rank upon rank of Bonsai trees shrunk into containers as if, like Aladdin's genii, they were about to disappear altogether. And beyond the house his most cherished creation, a giant aviary of bamboo and wire filled with legendary birds. Birds of paradise from the Moluccas, peacocks from Damaun in India, Nicobar ground pigeons. Nearly two hundred exotics from all over the Orient and Pacific. Holly could only guess at the intricate wanderings of the captains Tim Bird had bartered with, or befriended, in his lifetime.

Time for introductions to some of these wanderers gathered on the verandah. 'Falling over themselves with excitement,' Abby whispered to Holly.

'No wonder with the shortage of eligible females,' Holly retorted with a mischievous giggle.

Tim Bird motioned Holly to a chair beside a tall young officer, 'name of Wagoner', with an engulfing smile that gave promise of restoring her to her habitual high spirits. Promise that vanished as he launched on his latest saga of disaster at sea. The cook, it seemed, had gone mad and jumped overboard saying they could go to Hell, he was going to Timbuctoo. Then their captain was lost overboard as dark fell. He, first voyage out as lieutenant, had had to take over. Not that he was new to the country trade to China from India, so he could step into the captain's shoes and find they fitted well enough.

Country trade? Often officered by Americans like this one or Parsees. Many Parsees no darker than Wagoner. Could there have been a miscegenation there? He flushed under her scrutiny, 'Terry's my name. Otherwise known as 'Tough'.'

'Is it because you are the terror of the Chinese main?' she teased him.

'Because I am not. One of the first to stop flogging Lascars before the new law to forbid it. How could I when they hardly understood a word of English and wouldn't admit they couldn't? No captain can afford enemies at sea. He never knows when he might need spare sailors, a tow, or rescue in a typhoon.'

Suddenly Holly was aware of Sean Dare bearing down on them. She was exasperated to feel a catch of breath and heart at the sight. She had been determined to scorn him if they met again, yet here she was fluttering like an infatuated debutante.

Sean intruded politely, saying there was no need of introductions as 'Tough' was one of Jarman Malleson's captains. Equally politely, Tough bowed himself out of competition with his employer.

Holly, too unnerved for social niceties, said tersely, 'I thought you sailed for Canton today.'

He began more graciously than she, yet struggled to hide how she disconcerted him, his response to her as out of character in himself as hers obviously was to him. 'In the next day or two I..'

At that instant he forgot all about her or any introductions to swing round to pump the hand of a giant of a man at his elbow crying 'congratulations, Bill. You knocked us all into a cocked hat with the Red Rover.'

Infuriated, Holly turned to Tim Bird for enlightenment.

'One of Bill Clifton's new ships. Hauls close to the wind and tacks fast. Capable of three trips to every one of the old ladies of the Company.'

'Why our Baltimore clippers..'

'Exactly, Miss Holly. The Red Rover is a Baltimore clipper, but built in the Hooghly River Docks in Calcutta where such ships have been built since time immemorial as ideal for running these pirate-ridden waters. All you Yankees did was discover how useful they could be to outrun the British blockade in the Napoleonic wars.'

'When they were under the noses of the British all the time,' she said disparagingly.

'You can't call the British stupid for their lack of interest. The tea trade demanded ships that were sturdy, full-bellied and watertight; ships that could double as warships if necessary.'

'Whereas your opium traders needed greyhounds of the sea.'

'Quite, Miss Holly. Sprinting greyhounds for the perpetual race of this gambler's trade.'

'I thought everyone made fortunes.'

'Oh no, my dear. Whoever told you that? Why look at me.' He grimaced sadly. 'But you won't want to bother your pretty little head with all this talk of ships and the men who sail them.'

Her eyes fell on Sean Jarman, obviously as elated as Bill Clifton over this impending revolution in the China coastal trade. Did they have no scruples knowing their three voyages a year, in place of one, would almost certainly triple the opium traffic on the coast if they could sell it all? An ever more disturbing thought - were these traders of Jarman Malleson any better than the smugglers who did their dirtier work for them?

Tim Bird read Holly's face like the map of Macao. No question the girl was attracted to Sean Jarman nor that it would be a recipe for trouble. All he could do was whisk her out of range.

'Come you must see a few objets d'art I have.' He led her inside to his parlour, as crowded as his garden with specimens that were a collector's dream. In pride of place a small bejewelled inlaid clock so beautiful Holly was astonished to see such a piece outside a great museum. 'My father sold one like this to a high mandarin as a gift for the Emperor.'

'He made them?' She asked in awe.

'His partner did. And others he hoped to sell to the crowned heads of Europe. When he failed in this ambition, he turned to the Orient with more success. Fell in love with Macao and stayed to fund a company. Partners came and went. So here I am.'

'What happened to his company in the end?'

'Why I thought you knew. It's now known as Jarman Malleson. Such are the fortunes of the East.' A sadness in his eyes. 'Today I specialise in the exquisite things of nature. They won't, alas, live on as things of beauty forever like Cox's clocks.'

'Do you still belong to that company?' she asked carelessly, her eyes on the jewel-coloured wings flashing in the boughs that bowered them.

'Young ladies are not supposed to ask such direct questions.'

'People here do not think I'm an average young lady.'

'Any gossip would have told you. I gave my money to the Chief Justice of Macao to invest in the Portuguese India ports of Damaun and Goa. He embezzled it and flew the coop, leaving me bankrupt as I had no indemnity. The moral of that story, young lady, is that I trusted not wisely but too well in a trade where there's no insurance.' He failed to explain the trade was opium.

'Somehow I think there's even more to the story than you care to admit,' she mused, her eyes on Sean Jarman.

'Sometimes, young lady, questions ask for trouble.'

'Such as when you left the partnership?'

'Well I can tell you that, my dear. In the years when the trade changed just before the Pirate War came to an end. The one they call the Ladrones War.'

She leaned over the balustrade. How could he, a bankrupt, afford the wonders of this vast remarkable garden and its aviary? To buy and feed the birds? To keep the gardeners? Did the answer lie in the hutches of the homing pigeons she could see at the end of the long birdwalk where few people, decoyed by all the fancy birds, would notice?

Sean Dare was at her elbow. 'I came to offer my services.'

'For what?' she asked, overwhelmed by his proximity.

'To offer the services of the most superior firm of smugglers to smuggle you into Canton!' He bowed smiling.

Holly was stupefied rather than angry. 'You mean - ?'

'I'll escort you and Miss Abby to Canton.' Sean sounded calmer than he felt so close to her.

'You would? Oh dear that is very gallant of you. But why should you do this for me.'

'Isn't it time the War of Independence was over?'

She hesitated. How could she travel with a man who provoked her into a temper every five minutes; she who was normally of the most equable temperament?

'I promise to be on my best behaviour.'

'What does that mean? You'll not be a tease?'

Her smile challenged him to please rather than tease. 'It means I'll be a very perfect knight and protect you from evils of the deep - goblins, demons, dragons, customs officers and mandarin runners. Even other foreign devils. And, if you'll wear my favour for the journey, fight all your battles.'

Her eyes dropped before the intensity of his gaze, as she protested, 'you must have kissed the Blarney Stone.'

She felt herself torn two ways - between the calvanist conscience of her ancestors that made her answerable for the morality of her every action, and the pragmatic realism that those same ancestors had developed in their struggle to survive in the harsh regions to which their wanderlust had driven them. For the moment the latter won. How could she sustain her scruples about Sean's involvement in the darker side of the China Trade, when her Uncle Joshua was in the black trade too? She would be as prissy, pompous and self-righteous as some of the missionaries were if she passed judgment on him for that. And who better than he to act as escort? He had no reputation to lose, so her presence could hardly blacken a reputation he did not have.

As she hesitated, he pleaded, 'say you will and save me from the awful boredom of that journey once again.'

She blushed as he went down on one knee. 'you look as if you were proposing. What will the gossips of Macao say?'

'That I have picked the prettiest girl in Macao.' He begged again, 'then say yes.'

She felt eager but reluctant, flustered but calm. She understood nothing of this paradox of her emotions other than that she was a 'prey' to them as the romantic novels were fond of saying. All discipline simply flew out of the window before the gaze of those jade green eyes, which the Chinese said were the true hallmark of the devil.

She demurred, 'I must not get Uncle into trouble.'

He took her hand in his own, moving distractingly close, 'if it were your choice would you come?'

She cried 'yes!' almost too quickly. But, for fear of seeming putty in his hands, added as she disengaged her hand, 'some like to ride tigers.'

'Should you rather say 'some like to ride dragons'. They are both benevolent and lucky in China ?'

Dragon or tiger, Joshua would have none of it when Holly confronted him with Sean's proposal over lunch. In a rare expression of anger, he banged the vinegar bottle back in its cruet stand angrily.

'Typical of Jarman arrogance not to give the slightest thought to the fact that it would be my responsibility, not his, if you were arrested.'

Holly was disconcerted. Sean had intimated the risk was his, and allowed her to admire him for it as a token of gallantry on his part.

Joshua continued. 'My responsibility is Howqua's as he's my security merchant with the Co-Hong. Therefore he would be arrested for your breach of the law, not me. Is that clear, Holly?'

'Howqua arrested for my crime?' Holly asked perplexed.

'He certainly would be,' Joshua emphasised, 'and that is not just a guess on my part for that is exactly what happened when three of our merchants took it upon themselves to take their wives up to Canton in defiance of the regulations. The merchants concerned were denounced for breaking the law. The Prefect of Canton took drastic measures to drive them back to Macao. He authorised a raid on the Factory where they were. The covering was torn down from His Majesty's picture. The outer gates were pulled down and broken to pieces, and the garden laid waste- the trees uprooted and the ground dug up and thrown into the river. The quay, on which they had landed was destroyed. The senior Hong merchant was summoned into the Hall and compelled to remain for over an hour on his knees while he was threatened with immediate imprisonment and death on account of his connection with the English. The senior linguist was thrown into prison in chains, condemned to death and only saved by the Hoppo's intervention. Several brokers were arrested and tortured.'

'But I've been told the authorities were conniving at the traffic themselves.'

'The authorities, my dear, bend to the winds that blow from the Emperor in Beijing. At that very time the Emperor Tao-Kuang was mourning the death of his opium-addicted son and heir. They believed a cold wind denouncing the opium trade was certain to reach them from the Forbidden City.

He allowed Holly to indulge her fear and horror with Mary Ann and Abby for a spell before he reassured her.

'Spare your tears, my dear. Howqua would be too smart to get his head into such a noose for such a person of no account as you. He'll shift the blame onto me at once by stopping all my trade knowing that it would send me bankrupt at this time of the year.

Holly cast her last throw. 'I must go to check the range, quality and prices of goods for myself against anything Chung Tai Tai might offer me.'

He dropped his fork at that. 'You wily bird. How did you manage that. Chung Tai Tai as your agent. Well, well, you do like to get into the firing line, Holly!'

He sized her up with new eyes. If only she had been a man, he could have made her a junior partner like Billy Howe. He touched her regretfully on the shoulder.

'I suppose that's a good argument for going. But you would have to be careful. Our Western ways shock the Chinese. They think we behave no better than animals. Don't give them any reason to think so.'

Abby protested curtly, 'the sailors perhaps, not us.'

'They are shocked that we give way to you, hand you into chairs, carry things for you, eat with you, even dance in public with you. They see this mixing of the sexes as a sign of our lack of civilisation, our profound ignorance. They say we don't know the five great relations, or the three hundred rules of ceremony. Above all they are shocked by your tight dresses and low cut bodices.'

It was Mary Ann who won the debate for Holly in the end by telling him Holly and Abby would make themselves as inconspicuous as possibly by going disguised as men, hiding themselves as best they could.

'You can't say you didn't warn the girls so your conscience will be clear,' she concluded hugging and kissing him as she praised him for being such a wonderful understanding husband.

'As long as they promise to hotfoot it out of there at the first hint of trouble,' he agreed at last, commanding her to take her siesta. 'You mustn't exert yourself too much now.'

'Why should exercise be considered good for a girl when she's not expecting, yet suddenly be bad when she's in the family way?'

He swept her out the door, arm tight around her, muttering 'China will be the death of me yet.' But it was the death of her he had in mind. What if she were taken in labour before her time with both the English doctors away at Lintin or Macao?

* * * * * *

Sean Smuggles Holly and Abby into Canton

Holly studied herself in the long mirror. Her slim legs were housed in the stovepipe trousers Chinese thought so ludicrous a fashion. Her small, neat bosom was hidden under a tight wide-lapelled cutaway jacket. Her neckline was swamped by a flowing stock high under her chin. Her now cropped curly hair was thrust under a cap made from an amputated stocking top, and then under a stiff quasi-naval hat.

'Will I pass for a man?' she asked anxiously.

Abby tittered at the improbable soft cheek of her friend. 'You'll pass for a boy.'

Abby presented a different problem. Her all too ample bosom refused to be disposed of by flattening with bandages, and could only be disguised in the far too neatly fitting jacket by making the stock billow in a waterfall of cloth contained only by a vulgar outsized pin.

Holly surveyed her in despair. 'You'll have to shroud yourself in a cloak the whole time.'

They both practiced the art of sitting like men on ornately carved upright Macanese chairs, only to end in gusts of laughter at the sight of their immodest postures.

'Why worry? You'll pass as you are.' Mary Ann assured them. 'The Chinese won't tell the difference any more than we do with them. But they can distinguish between a soprano and a tenor. So keep your mouths shut. Oh, I'm so jealous. I wish I were coming with you, but with the baby coming!' She threw up her hands in renunciation. The dangers were enhanced once you penetrated the Pearl River estuary. Men died every week among the fleet at Whampoa. Only the Old China hands seemed to have acquired an immunity.

Mary Ann was still waving wistfully long after their eggboat had drawn away from the stone quay on the Praya Grande, until she had dwindled to a toy figure in a painted toy town, so like a medieval town with its walls marching up and down its three hills. But so unlike a medieval town, Holly thought, because it had no real heart such as a fortress or castle. Its real heart was in Canton eighty miles away.

Abby squealed in a most unmanly fashion as their eggboat swirled to avoid a cumbersome junk. 'We'll be run down. We'll drown. Why didn't your Sean come and fetch us in his boat?'

'He's not my Sean,' Holly objected, 'and it would give the game away. Macao has eyes in the back of its head.'

Abby still grumbled, 'so we risk our necks.'

'We're doing that any way by going to Canton.'

'You make it sound as if we're crossing the River Styx to Hades.'

'But no hideous Charon at the oars.' Only striking oarsmen, shining plaits swinging rhythmically under their cane hats.

'No hideous Charon captaining the Bonnie Lassie either,' Abby declared approvingly at the sight of Sean coming forward to welcome them at the Jacob's ladder as they approached.

Holly's attention was elsewhere on the lovely lines of the Bonnie Lassie with her three masts soaring high above the long sweep of her hull broken only by a single line of portholes. A vessel built to ride a good Atlantic howler as easy as a storm bird.

At first Abby jibbed at climbing the ladder until Abby urged her they must as they were supposed to be men. She went up and over the side first to show Abby how easy it was to climb in trousers.

Sean shook her hand man to man, but his gaze was as man to woman sweeping over the flowing line of her figure as he said softly, 'never has such beauty passed across my threshold.'

She felt annoyed with herself to think his glance of possessive challenge could cause her lips to tremble, her pulse to leap, her gaze to lock in his as David Malleson was welcoming Abby over the side with equally eager enthusiasm.

He pointed to the grave, portentous man following them on board. 'Our pilot. Steer clear of him. He just might speak English.'

'A pilot already out here in the open ocean?'

He explained with a glint of amusement, 'in case we have the bad luck to collide with any mandarin junks.'

'And 'makee topsail sick, makee die',' David mocked.

'Watch out for two danger points,' Sean continued. 'First the passport control at the Bogue twenty miles upriver, where we present our port clearance from Macao, pay our dues and collect our 'chops' to proceed up river after we swear we have no opium aboard. Second, the Whampoa anchorage sixty-nine miles upstream where our comprador will come on board to take charge of all the business of a ship at anchor. Fearful work, day and night, for the poor fellows. All the worry of going bail for our good behaviour. From there, eleven miles by gig to the landing stage at the factories in Canton where the Hoppo's minions lie in wait to watch if we smuggle good in or evade customs duty on the way out.'

As they got under way, Abby asked David anxiously, 'What happens to us if they find out?'

He leaned towards her, gently taking her hand to trace his fingers caressingly across it as he reassured her, 'I'll cross their palms with silver.'

'A bribe?' Abby feigned horror, snatching her hand away to calm the turbulence his touch evoked in her.

'Let's call it by its local name cumshaw. A sweetener to trade as sugar to tea,' he answered his thoughts plainly on Abby not trade.

'Cumshaw greases the wheels of China at all times,' Sean added.

'And buys us out of trouble?' Holly asked thankfully.

Sean whispered close to her ear, 'if smuggled goods can pass all these points surely smuggled ladies can.'

The sense of intimacy flowing between them spoke of other things than cumshaw, an awareness one of the other as if no other existed.

It was broken by the reality of getting under way at last. A swarm of sailors suddenly everywhere. Up the ratlines to unfurl the sails in a discipline of movement like an aerial ballet. Down on the deck to man the windlass to the cry of 'up anchor' and the beat of a drum. A cloud of canvas broke out on the lofty masts towering above them. They got under way to a symphony of sound which prompted a rising excitement of the blood - creak of canvas, slap of waves, whistle of wind.

Holly braced herself against the rail as the boat heeled to tack provoking another flurry of action of the crew. How she envied the men who could spend their lives at sea as these did, catching the wind on the shoulder of their sails to cleave through the endless freedom of sparkling water. As she stared out to sea, Sean watched her with fascination tinged with terror. To fall in love with his high-spirited Yankee visitor would be utmost folly. It could only lead to a dishonourable pursuit of a passion he could not honour unless he disengaged himself from the love of his youth, Jean MacArthur, still waiting back home while he amassed a quick fortune in the east. Yet he already knew in his inner heart that that pursuit would be all too hard to resist if he were to see too much of Holly.

As the Bonnie Lassie made its way north across the wide mouth of the Pearl River towards Lintin Island before turning west into the river itself, Sean and David were kept busy identifying the vast number and variety of boats in the incessant traffic passing them by.

'Where do they all come from?' Holly asked, entranced by the endless procession. David answered indifferently, his eyes only on Abby. 'Oh, from absolutely everywhere.' As indeed they had. Battered dhows from Africa or Arabia. Long lean craft from Java. Junks with short ugly masts from South-East Asia. Fat-bellied boats from Manila. Lowlying coast trade brigs from India. Arklike salt junks from Hainan Island. Brisk fast schooners from Macao. China coastal junks like carnival boats with painted eyes and coloured flags. And surely king of all this motley fleet, a black and white double-portholed stately East Indiaman under a panoply of canvas.

Holly scarcely listened to his recitation, baffled by such a disturbing and confusing exultation of her heart only one fact was clear to her - that this was the moment towards which her life had always moved, to be with a man who could match herself. Therefore she could not understand why she felt provoked to bait, to argue, even to best him as she did now, when he pointed to an aggressive ocean-going junk forcing their pilot to shift to windward.

'They paint those grotesque faces with tusked mouths on their bows out of superstition.'

'Actually to frighten away large fish and demons of the deep just like the eye of the Egyptian god, Osiris.'

Sean frowned. This was no compliant young lady. 'You have become an expert in your short time in China?'

'No, but Billy Howe has in his long time in China.'

Fierce jealousy swept over Sean, knowing Howe's famous intimacy with the language and laws of China. 'The universal expert,' he said scornfully.

Abby grimaced. 'I declare I wouldn't like to go to sea in one of those junks. They look as though nothing has changed since Noah.'

David contrived to lean closer to her on the rail. 'But don't forget Noah's Ark could beach anywhere after the Flood. So can the junk. No doubt Noah had bulkheads too, just like the junks.'

'So they don't envy us our ships,' Holly conceded

Sean disagreed too sharply for his own comfort. 'Oh yes they do. But if they dared to copy us they would be classed as owners of foreign ships and pay much higher dues.'

He was saved from his own chagrin by Tiger Island looming ahead, 'Tiger' being short for Bocca Tigris, meaning Mouth of the Tiger, for its big bluff rock looked like a crouching tiger. Here was the first of the five fortresses that guarded the first five mile reach of the river that had, since time immemorial, been the southern gateway into China; here the point at which they must receive their 'chop' or passport; and here the moment when Sean commanded the girls to hide below decks until they had passed out of the danger zone of discovery beyond them all.

Beyond the bare, black bluffs of Tiger Island, the river grew wider and the incessant parade of boats of all shapes and sizes increased. Flat plains, now emerald with springtime rice, stretched to the far-distant hills. Villages nestled in bamboo groves and orchards. The scene must have remained unchanged throughout history: of peasants in the paddies, buffalo at the water treadmills, gossipers idling among the dogs and chickens, slender pagodas.

The serene progress of the Bonnie Lassie had a timeless, dreamlike quality; serene however only until an imposing green and yellow mandarin boat charged down the river towards them under sail, forcing Sean's pilot to alter course sharply so their ship heeled dangerously.

Holly protested 'you had right of way.'

He smiled indulgently. 'We're not lords of the ocean here, Holly, commanding all to our rules of the sea. In China, we must observe the rules of rank, and my rank is little better than that of a slave.'

'Then perhaps you should look as though it is better,' Abby interjected pointing at the grave mandarin enthroned on a scarlet velvet couch under an elaborate gilded and painted canopy festooned with red silk on the stern deck.

'Can you see me putting on such airs?'

Holly studied him thoughtfully. She could in fact. An authority, no more subtle than the mandarin's, oozed out of every pore of him enhanced by the gravity native to those craggy Scottish features of his. But truth was never wise. She changed the subject. 'Smoking opium no doubt.'

To her surprise Sean agreed. 'No question of it with a pipe that length, though often mixed with tobacco. That's how the habit began in China according to my uncle. A dash of opium to give the tobacco a lift. Began with the Dutch in the East Indies so they say.'

But Abby, still piqued, exclaimed, 'You allow yourself to be pushed aside? Isn't that a recipe for future trouble?'

'I allow myself to be sensible to avoid present trouble. Take a good look at those oars laid back against the side of the boat. Thirty of them at least. Each one stands for a soldier. Thirty more on the other side. Sixty soldiers.'

Abby stared in disbelief at the men lounging on board with painted flowers and figures on their caps. 'They are soldiers?'

'More colourful than our own, I agree. But still soldiers and very experienced ones. Don't run away with the idea the shields and spears along the sides are for decoration. And see those objects smothered in little bright flags. They happen to be guns, guns that work. And soldiers who know how to use them. They practice often enough. I'm hardly in a position to fight a one man-war with the fighting force I've got.'

Holly turned away annoyed at the conflict of emotions he provoked in her. Anxious to please him as a woman but urged to dispute with him like a man.

Worse, she, who had spent all her life among men, willing to play the foolish naive despite herself.

At the Second Bar, they joined a queue of large ships waiting for barboats to tow them across a large shoal, fuming at the delay when already within sight of the grey tower of the Great Whampoa Pagoda on Whampoa Island just seven miles away and the masts and riggings of the semi-circle of ships already anchored there. Once across themselves, in no time at all they reached the merchant fleet, the first ships in the two mile long line those flying the scarlet and white pennant of Jarman Malleson, and drifted into anchor to the cry of 'Top men aloft! Sheet home! Heave round.'

Holly and Abby hung over the rail as a cluster of 'bumboats' of all sizes selling all kinds of wares swarmed towards them; and the comprador, without whose services David said Sean would be as impotent as a ship without wind, came aboard. A clamour and commotion that was not as romantic as it looked, according to David, after living with it for weeks at a time. For the crews, whether officers or sailors, could not land on Dane's Island without fear of robbery or assault, while they were only allowed up to Canton a few at a time.

'Why? Because they go berserk on that devil's brew, samshu, and end up brawling in Hog Lane.'

The moment Sean was free, he hurried them into a gig for fear the tide would turn against them and give them a hard pull to Canton. The crew bent to the oars as they passed the spectacular and formidable grand parade of power and high craft represented by the ponderous magnificence of the black and white East Indiamen with their lofty decks and even higher poops abaft, as large as 74 gun warships of the navy armed with no less than 18 visible guns apiece. The last flew the Commodore's flag denoting the most senior captain in port and therefore the man responsible for law and order at Whampoa. On board a brass band practiced martial airs in the chill sunshine in comic incongruity with the distinctively Oriental landscape. Beyond them the French tricolour, the Spanish yellow, and the Yankee stars and stripes.

Holly's heart lifted at the sight of the familiar brown and yellow American vessels. Among them her own Eugenia snug at anchor with the rest. She wanted to shout, 'look there's my ship, Sean, my very own ship.' Instead she stood proudly mute, gazing at the ship that earned her the right to be on the list of merchants trading with the Co-Hong.

'A penny for your thoughts!' Sean startled her.

'I was wondering why Jim Peel has not shipped the Eugenia's upper standing gear yet, unbent the sails or unrove the running rigging. She should be cropped of her upper masts and yards already like her neighbour. Obviously he hasn't unloaded any cargo yet or she would be topheavy.'

Sean's astonishment brought her back to reality. 'Where did you learn such things?'

She covered herself hastily, annoyed she had nearly betrayed her own secret, 'why my father was a sailmaker.'

'You learnt all that from him?'

She shrugged. 'Are women meant to be stupid?'

'No, but they are seldom knowledgeable about ships.'

She changed the subject. 'Why is this reach called Whampoa?

'From this island of Wang-po. They all live there.'

His gesture embraced the satellite population of stevedores, blacksmiths and other tradesmen, their shouts and cries a strange counterpoint to the bizarre sound of the brass band still faintly drifting across the scene.

'And now we turn into Junk River.'

'Why don't you go on up the Pearl River?'

'Because I don't like physical and verbal abuse from the villagers on shore, or getting impaled on their fishing stakes as a sitting target for physical assaults.'

But the villagers along Junk River were no better. Jeering with the chirping noises devils were supposed to make. Pelting them with garbage. Encouraging their children to a pantomime of chopping off heads, using their miniature pigtails for a 'knife' while shouting 'Fanqui! Fanqui!' Hostile and contemptuous. No doubt of that. So why had she been told only the officials hated the foreigners not the people? These people certainly did. John Davies must be right when he said they considered foreigners as wandering spirits and therefore creatures of the dark, seeking endless harm to humans from their haunted world.

When the crew of the gig stopped for a 'snort' at the Great Halfway Pagoda before the worst of the pull onwards towards Canton, Sean pointed out a cluster of masts visible in the distance as if stranded in a sea of rice paddies. Masts of crab boats or smuggling vessels lurking at anchor at the hub of a network of small creeks which served them as private backdoor roads through the delta to Canton. Not from fear of discovery - for they paid their dues to the mandarins, navy and police as regularly as any merchant ships - but for necessary means of escape using familiarity with all the intricacies of the delta should any of these officials turn against them in quixotic campaigns of reform ordered by Beijing now and then, and should it prove expedient to go underground so they would not compromise such officials too far.

Beyond the Pagoda, the gig struggled onward through the ever increasing congestion of the river. Forty foot junks moored in rows midstream. Streets of smaller boats strung outwards from the shore. Sean now silent and watchful to shift the rudder swiftly, here to avoid being overturned by the cable of a junk, there to avoid being run down by larger vessels.

David, ever solicitous of Abby, gripping her elbow. Abby, exasperated with the constant spin and lurch of the gig, asking David angrily at last, 'why do the mandarins allow so many people to live on the water?'

'Because they won't allow them to live on the land,' he replied unexpectedly. 'It goes back a long way, some say to the Sung dynasty. A certain Emperor went to war, leaving his two most trusted Ministers in charge, only to find, when he returned, they had betrayed him. He banished all their clan forever from his land - wives, children, relatives, servants - as if they were dead. And So they remain to this day.'

Holly gasped aghast, 'and no one has ever forgiven them, not even seven hundred years later?'

'Others say they are Mongol descendants of the Yuan dynasty, driven onto the water by the Ming when they lost the war.'

'Who knows what to believe in China?' Holly groaned.

Sean had difficulty finding the one ingress possible to the stone quay at

Jackass Point that served the row of thirteen Canton Factories strung along the shore. When at last they found the way in, his four Lascars shipped their oars in favour of native spade-shaped paddles and began to shove their way along the narrow-gutted waterway of floating homes of boat people, moored deck to deck, Sean warded off the barge-poles of abusive owners with a boathook as he screamed Cantonese curses back at them.

When at last they had battled through, Sean picked a fight with the keeper of the stairs Old Head to distract the Hoppo's long-eyes from taking too sharp a look at his 'gentlemen' while David bundled them hastily across the common in front of the Factories to the Sui Hong to the far left of the Company's Factory, announcing 'Here we are, Little Jerusalem, home of the holier than thou, Colin Kingsman. We're the devil's brood as far as he's concerned.' Holy because he was the only merchant who flatly refused ever to trade in opium.

He commanded the gatekeeper in pidgin English, 'Chin chin you come down, Lawqua.' And when Joshua loomed at the gate, he cried, 'please take delivery of two flowery flag devils.'

Joshua rushed them through a long, gloomy labyrinth of passages linking the series of buildings comprising their factory and up a flight of stairs to a secluded room overlooking a small courtyard, warning them 'be careful at all times. Remember every servant, every hawker in this building is a spy. They don't knock on doors before they walk in.'

The chest Holly shoved across the door seemed to her the truest symbol of the China she had now entered, a country where the door was always shut to foreigners - the rules implacable, the etiquette, old as time, utterly rigid. She wondered if it could, or ever would, change to the clamour of the Jarman Mallesons of this world. She doubted it. If not, how could there ever be a future for her here?

Billy Howe was both unhappy and uneasy, the two emotions most foreign to him, when Joshua appointed him their guardian.

'Show the girls the ropes? Take them down to the Common? Outside the Factories? Too dangerous,' he protested.

He persuaded them to see the sights of the Common from the roof instead, where they found Adam already sketching quick roughs for future paintings of the scene below. It was a colourful commotion of market stalls of every conceivable kind packed along the river edge. Sellers of ground nuts, pickled olives, hot rice, congee water, dogs, cats, fowls, fruit, shoes and what Billy called 'the most horrible hats.'

Billy explained, as they leaned excitedly over the rail that it had not always been so. The local Chinese had been excluded until ten years before.

Abby, a true Yankee in her espousal of the Rights of Man, was outraged. 'How arrogant of the traders to exclude the Chinese like that. I don't suppose they liked mixing with the common herd.'

Billy corrected her dryly, 'We didn't exclude the Chinese, Abby. The Viceroy did because he knows their dislike, even hatred, of foreigners can erupt out of a clear blue sky any time and cause big trouble.'

'More often than not encouraged by the Viceroy,' Adam elaborated, pencil swift across his sketching pad.

Directly below a 'seeing-eye' beggar with dirty matted hair and tattered verminous clothes led a chain of blind men, each linked to the one before by left hand on the shoulder as they tapped their canes along the stone paving to the rhythm of doleful, remorseless grunting of 'Cash! Cash!'

The prospect was enough to stop Adam's unwearying pencil. 'God preserve us! The Heavenly Flower Society of Beggars in person. Loathsome, miserable, offal-eating refuse of society.' He began to immortalise them with quick strokes of his charcoal.

'Dangerous refuse,' Billy asserted as the terrified owner of a tea stall paid the hideous column a due.

'And if he didn't pay up?' Holly demanded.

'The beggars would set up a terrible clamour until he did. All day long if necessary.'

'That's blatant blackmail,' Holly declared, an angry frown on her face as she watched their vicious progress, 'why don't the police arrest them?'

'Better this than - '.

They all swung round at a shout from the rotund figure of Paddy Keane as he hurtled towards Adam, a folded copy of the Courier that Adam edited in hand. 'You villain. I demand an apology for your libel of my paper in your despicable rag. How dare you say it is 'a paper principally distinguished for its disgusting details of Chinese depravity' indeed?'

A villainous sneer on Adam's pockmarked face betrayed his hatred of this lickspittle lackey of James Malleson. 'It's fair comment.'

Paddy knocked his sketch pad out of his hand. 'Do you deny the facts I print about Chinese society are true?'

'No, but I deny the wisdom of showing we have neither tact nor restraint in our public comment, and are therefore as uncivilised as they think we are.'

Paddy's fair boyish face flushed in a new access of rage. 'I demand an apology, or I'll call you out.'

'And you shall have it if you apologise for the anonymous abuse you tender me in your newspaper which everyone knows is meant for me.'

Paddy bowed stiffly. 'You shall hear from my seconds.'

Holly thought she had not heard correctly. 'Seconds? Is Paddy honestly going to fight a duel with you?'

Adam shuddered, 'I hope not. He cherishes the most handsome set of duelling pistols in the port. Engraved butts. Real heirloom. He just wants to show them off.'

Holly wondered if the casual flippancy of Adam's manner was because he saw life as theatrical conflict, hence why he could deliver the broadsides of his newspaper with such abandoned felicity and wind up his diatribes with such sharp derision as if everyone played by the rules of melodrama or farce. Yet in a moment of insight, she knew that comedy was perhaps the best spyglass through which to see China.

'You'll be my second, won't you Billy?' Adam enquired, 'five in the morning on the Common then.'

They clasped each other in mutual hilarity jumping a wardance until Holly demanded angrily, 'how can you two treat this duel as such a joke?'

'Oh but Adam wouldn't be so stupid as to fight any duel,' Billy assured her, 'Paddy's a splendid shot even at 200 paces let alone 20.'

'I heard you offer,' Holly reminded them indignantly.

Adam laughed as he took up his sketch pad again. 'It's an old game of huff and puff. He knows as well as I do the penalty for manslaughter in China is death. Stops us all dying of boredom in this hole. The only duel we'll fight will be the same old war of words.'

* * * * * *

Chung Tai Tai Visits Howqua

Howqua's park-sized Ten Thousand Pines Garden was famous in all Kwangtung province. It opened up vista after vista down wandering flagged paths, over crescent bridges and past reflective lakes hosting ibis, swans and golden carp among the sacred lotus, and viewing pavilions for the various seasons joined by covered decorated walkways. It was a world so orderly every rock and leaf was in place, and dead leaves had barely time to rest before some servant's diligent hand swept them away lest they mar the perfection of garden or goldfish-laden waters. The swooping rooves of the buildings mimicked the drooping sweep of the graceful pines in a miracle of harmonised formality.

Kaida was astonished at the transformation of his mother when she landed with Chung Tai Tai from the ornate barge that had brought them from the city opposite. She was now indistinguishable from any highborn lady in the expense and elaboration of her embroidered satin cheong sam and jewellery except in one respect - the phoenix hair ornament that denoted her royal style.

Howqua himself belied the imperial scale and style of his domain. The room where he held audience proved no larger than the tiny garden beyond its moon-shaped window. His deep-sleeved blue robe was as austere and unadorned as that of any Taoist monk. Nothing monk-like, however, about his effusive welcome of Chung Tai Tai as she bowed before him with clasped hands.

'Old Wu, you grow more like that wisp of your beard every day. Frail as a bamboo leaf I swear.'

'Tough as a bamboo stalk, Old Chung. We'll see them out, you and I.'

Chung Tai Tai envied his optimism as his servant offered them steaming towels and green tea. 'Don't lie to yourself, Old Wu. We'll die young of worry and trouble.'

'What worry, Old Chung?'

'I worry about the changing wind. A new monsoon blows.'

He let out a long sigh, accepting a lighted pipe from his hovering servant to sustain him. Chung Tai Tai must fear serious trouble if she came so far to see him.

'The red-haired demons, Old Wu. Not the old John Company, Old Wu, but the Red Beards.'

'The Iron-headed Old Rat?' Old Wu ventured, using the Chinese nickname for Dr. William Jarman with a tinge of admiration earned when he had been struck on the back of his head by an old iron pot as he waited before the closed Petition Gate, and he had neither flinched at the blow nor turned around.

'And the Old Snake,' she said with distaste, using their private name for his partner, James Malleson. 'They corrupt the old members of the Triads by bringing in new ones. Water rats. Bad characters. They pay them to grow bold and run wild on our waterways showing their teeth.'

He sucked thoughtfully on his pipe. This was dangerous news. 'Where do they get the teeth?'

'From foreign devils. Goods, weapons and now boats.'

'Do you know which members are still ours?'

Chung Tai Tai shook her head. 'That is not easy. As you know the Second Lodge has always attracted many sorts of men. Not just ours of the boats on the rivers, canals and ocean, but pedlars, itinerants, men of no fortune or future. Rebel philosophers, failed intellectuals, criminals and bandits who are not true patriots.

'Eiyah!' Howqua exclaimed. These were the men they had always been least able to trust. Too many of them joined the lodge for their own ends. For greed, shelter from crime, crime itself. But, except in times of truly disruptive rebellion they had been able to control them by the law of the lodge.

'This evil is just beginning. It can be stopped.'

Chung Tai Tai tapped her fan impatiently on the square arm of the ponderous chair, in which she was perched like a small bright bird in a solid old tree.

'Old Wu, you must not be tempted to persuade yourself this trouble is only a small cloud on the horizon bound to turn into a small storm which will blow itself out. These men are not like the malcontents that surged up in the past, criminals without plans or money. They are well-organised by the Red Beards, and therefore have a strength which will swallow us all if we ignore it.'

Howqua conceded, 'I'm listening now, Old Chung.'

'These men use our name and are organised. They have a name, the Red Circle, and enforcers of their own, the Red Rods. They want to rule the delta. They blackmail everyone. They make the stallholder pay for his pitch, the shopkeeper for peace and quiet in his shop, the peasant to preserve his rice crop from robbery or destruction. If they don't pay up the Red Rods threaten them with reprisal.'

Howqua said heavily. 'They copy the Beggar King.'

'They are worse than the Beggar King, Old Wu, whose blind beggars only practice extortion on the hawkers and little shopkeepers. These make slaves of them all, even the blind beggars themselves. They're worse than the Manchu in their violence to those who oppose them - flogging to death, burning of buildings, kidnap of wives and daughters. And now they have begun to impose their terror on our boatmen.'

For a moment, Howqua felt overwhelmed with a despair he had not felt these many years since that Macao affair. The implications of Chung Tai Tai's news were awesome. Two rival networks in the smuggling trade, one so much more ruthless than the other, could only mean that the latter, backed with the tremendous resources of the ocean barbarians, would win out. If so, two things would follow. The Red Society under its five colour standard would no longer be content to barter in opium, salt, silk and the rest, but would want to be paid in silver sycee. They needed silver to buy arms, while Jarman Malleson needed silver for ready cash to finance the short term money market they played for opium, and to act as bankers loaning ready money to pay for their tea when

John Company closed its doors.

The delicate financial balance of the port that ensured the acquiescence of the pyramid of mandarins in smuggling would be so distorted political disturbance must follow. This would not only impoverish the Co-Hong itself, but flow upwards all the way to the Son of Heaven himself. With what consequences, he shuddered to think. No Emperor could ignore local affairs, however distant, once the copper cash of the people became too dear in relation to silver as it would if silver drained into those nefarious Lintin go-down ships. Inflation in value of the peasants' money could have only one end - hardship and then rebellion.

As Howqua's servants offered his disturbing visitors lychees and dates, he rose in rare agitation to gaze out the moon window at the weeping elm's graceful umbrella shape beyond. The Pearl River delta had been like an umbrella to the trade of Canton once, its ebb and flow regulated under that shade as easily as the shallow tides within the river. No more. The Red Beard foreign devils had overturned the balance of traffic, of money, and finally of power with their diabolical pact with the Red Circle. Would they pay the percentage expected by mandarins and officials as imperative supplement to their paupers' salary? He was as certain they would not, as he was that the backwash of those who were deprived would fall on him and all the Co-Hong rather than on those beyond the 'pale' offshore, unless he found some unforeseen allies or could yet discipline the Reds.

'Will your members help you purge the brotherhood of the straw sandal?' he asked with a wild hope.

'No, they are too afraid of the Red Rods.'

He turned to Kaida's mother, 'What do you say, my lady?' Her manner was authoritative, her voice firm, as she gave judgment in a way Kaida had never seen before. 'Chung Tai Tai has reason to fear. These pirates are more ruthless with mens' greed than John Company and will end up more powerful. They gamble with opium as the old Company never gambled. Operate outside the law as the Company never did. They keep half their fleet outside the port like the pirate ships they are, ships that can outgun, outrun any pirate or other ship in China. Demon ships run by demons. How can you fight that, Old Wu?'

Howqua tucked his hands in his deep fur-lined sleeves defensively. 'Catch them when they come on shore?'

'And become criminals ourselves, Old Wu? No, you can't start a new pirate war against these new pirates.'

'At least to harass them?'

Chung Tai Tai stood up then, seeming more than life size, and Kaida could understand the awe in which men had once held her. Her voice brooked no rejection.

'You ask me to command in battle once again, Old Wu. I fought in those days because I had no other life open to me. Now I am a friend of the law. You ask me to lose all that to help you keep your ancient monopoly of the trade?'

She warned him that the barbarian gweilo had begun trade illegally further up the coast.

'And we, the Emperor's guardians of his legal trade will suffer. How can we protect ourselves. What do you say my lady?'

She answered without hesitation. 'Forget the delta. Shift your focus to Heung Lo To, the island the Red Beards with clumsy tongues call Hong Kong, where pirate haunts have always been.'

Chung Tai Tai considered her sharply. No one knew this island better than she, a place sacred to the Triads because one of their first five ancestors, Fong Tai Hung, had gone there of old to recruit the lady pirate, Cheng Yat So.

Howqua tapped Chung Tai Tai with his fan in rebuke. She could not hope to avoid the Red Circle by retreating from them, valuable though this plan might prove.

'Rebellions are only as good as their leader. We have no alternative. We must kill him.'

'But how to find out who that leader is?' she threw back at him.

'Kaida will be our eyes and ears,' Howqua declared.

'A spy?' his mother cried out in protest, 'And if he's caught you know what will happen to him then, Old Wu!' He would be lucky to escape the death of a thousand cuts.

'He will be in the safest place in the world for him. I will make him disappear into the Viceroy's yamen like a magician's duck. Not simply to spy for us, but to learn the law, and to learn who is enemy, who friend.'

Kaida could find comfort in only one thought that he would be out of the way when the Triad battles began.

* * * * * *

Fortunes of Holly and Abby in Canton

Holly drowsed in the stifling heat of the minute chapel of 'Little Jerusalem' as she listened to Dr. Norris' sermon, his eager evangelism undiminished despite his tiny congregation and years of suffering in the East.

What drove men like Norris to take the Word of the Lord like a sword among the indifferent heathen, she wondered? Or Elijah Sanders and Peter Penn? Why did that Word fall on such stony ground in China compared to Africa or the Pacific islands? Even the one grave 'convert' at the back of the chapel - a 'rice Christian' it was said, grateful for promotion from ship's cook to owner of a shop trading in congee silk because of his conversion.

She put the question to Maxwell Raine and his partner, Jeremy Russell, over lunch in their modest quarters in the Pao Shan factory next door.

Jeremy, erudite ex-patriate of Paris and Boston salons, laughed. 'So you want to know what they think of 'story-telling devils' like Dr. Norris? Let me tell you what happened when Dr. Norris gave an old tea merchant, Quan Shing, a translation of the parable of the loaves and fishes convinced Quan Shing only had to read the truth of the divine character of Our Saviour to believe. When the old fellow returned the tract several days later, he agreed it was 'Truly powerful Joss! No. 1 curious! Only my country has got very much more curious.'

'To prove it, he embarked on a rather long-winded story about the great Joss of an ancient Emperor only to be interrupted by Colin Kingsman saying 'How can talkee so fashion, such foolo pigeon?'

'The old man was highly incensed. 'I read your story and said it was remarkable. I tell you my story. You say it is nonsense, not worthy of belief, yet millions of people have believed my story for thousands of years. Should I deny it because you say I'm a fool for believing it?'

'Now I comprehend why they say East is East and West is West and the two will never meet,' Holly said gravely. Jeremy was right. The story made it so much clearer than Joshua's convoluted explanation about how the Confucian Five levels of filial piety, and the Emperor's Divine Right of Kings, made equality a concept impossible for the Chinese to understand.'

Maxwell Raine counted the number of heads at the table, then sliced the rich plum pudding into as many generous slices. Abby hesitated over her outsized portion, concerned she showed signs of bursting out of her suit already. She not only succumbed but drenched it with brandy sauce after Maxwell Raine announced, 'We could do with a miracle of loaves and fishes right now. But I doubt if that would be enough to feed the many thousands that starve in the province.'

'Starve?' Abby put down her spoon guiltily.

Holly voiced her disbelief. 'Why there's food everywhere we look. And don't the Cantonese boast their city was founded by five genii riding five rams bearing the five grains so the city would never starve?'

'The genii have let them down. Or rather the Rain God has. No rain for eight months to back up what rivers bring from distant mountains to keep their irrigation systems going.'

Abby demanded, 'what are the authorities doing about it?' adding petulantly, when Maxwell Raine's shock of grey hair shook with laughter for answer, 'starvation is hardly a laughing matter.'

'When Viceroy Lu is involved it is. After visiting the Temple of the God of Rain daily with the Governor and other high officers without their prayers producing any rain, he decided something was wrong with the Temple. Perhaps noxious vapours. Or perhaps they hadn't given the God sufficient importance. So he had the God re-decorated and gilded, then taken on parade through the streets led by trumpets, drums and gongs followed by an immense crowd with lighted sticks of incense whose smoke would gratify its nostrils.'

'A wonderful show. I saw it from the wall,' Jeremy Russell interposed.

'And you didn't get lynched?' Joshua asked, amazed by his audacity.

'But nothing worked. A sing song. A sorcerer. A day of prayers and fasting. Still the cantankerous God of Rain ignored the plight of his human subjects. Finally they lost all patience. They punished him by marching him round the city, abusing and whipping him with each blast of the trumpet or clash of the gongs, then demoting him to a lower pedestal and altar.'

'Surely the Viceroy must lose face in the end.'

'Of course! If the God sulks long enough they do blame the Viceroy. They say he has been an unjust ruler, which was closer to the truth all the time.' He paused to put another light to his sulky pipe. 'You see the shortage of grain would not matter if the Viceroy had built up a surplus in the public granaries against this emergency. That's the purpose of allowing us to bring rice tax-free from Manila.'

Holly made a mental note to investigate the possibility of engaging in the rice trade herself.

Raine worked on his pipe once more until at last it yielded a satisfying puff, gazing contentedly over Holly's head like the lofty Rain God himself as he went on, 'the truth is that the Viceroy and his minions have been buying up rice cheaply to sell to those who can afford it most instead of hoarding it for those who can afford it least.'

They were spared further enormities of the Viceroy by the arrival of Chinnery to a gust of chaffing as to why he was in Canton. 'Fleeing from my wife. Thank God, women are prohibited in Canton.'

In fact Chinnery had come to paint Howqua and Mowqua as he admitted over one of the outsize cups of tea he preferred to the 'white man's curse'. 'Ruins your stomach,' he opined, oblivious to the fact he might be wrecking his own stomach with his gargantuan appetite as effectively as they with their whisky, rum, Madeira sherry or fine Portugal wines.

His badinage with Jeremy Russell amused Holly to think how 'Number 1 Curio Pigeon' it was that they should sit calmly swopping anecdotes of salons of Europe or America, their hearts with the only civilisation they really understood. No heart at all for the exotic ceremonial society of China such a short distance away. Their host, Maxwell Raine, far more like a gracious English squire in a county manor than a sharp China Coast trader.

Yet Maxwell Raine was the first to hear an angry chant of 'Fanqui! Fanqui! rising from the Common, to rush out on the balcony and to shout as he rushed back into the room, 'We're being attacked. Men to the stairs. Ladies to the back rooms.'

Raine and Russell knew the drill. Wooden bars, from a pile kept ready for such an emergency, jammed in the newel posts of the stair-rail. Padded cloths thrown over them. Muskets from a cupboard at the head of the stair. Armed men two by two up the stairs behind the barricade. All in place by the time the frenzied mob broke through the door and flooded in with blood-chilling yells to grind to a halt at the chilling sight of men armed with rifles on the stairs above. Unwilling for death, when looking for food to give them life, they surged away down the ground floor corridor in an endless gesticulating stream to find the kitchens at the back of the building and disappear when avenging lictors of the Governor arrived from the Petition Gate wielding their formidable wire-knotted whips. The 'foreign devils' left to clean up the shambles left behind.

They had scarcely returned to 'Little Jerusalem' next door when Dr. Tom Collins was on the doorstep. Dismay and agitation on his genial and kindly face as he seized Abby's hand too long, too affectionately for Holly's peace of mind, terrified a servant would see them and report that foreign devils from the 'Flowery Land' smuggled young boys in after all. Abby's reply, however, was anything but flirtatious when Dr. Tom asked if she were upset by her dreadful experience.

'Dr. Collins, I've been out sailing with my father in an Atlantic storm when he refused to turn back to port. I assure you that was a much more alarming experience.'

Hard on Dr. Tom's heels, their erstwhile escorts, Sean and David, arrived full of alarm and concern. Ignoring Holly's cool welcome, Sean gripped her unwilling hand fervently in both his own saying 'we feared the worst.' Her answer belied the storm of her inward response to his touch.

'Most kind of you to take an interest now, considering its conspicuous absence since we arrived.' For the two young men had been invisible from the moment they had landed, their neglect more marked as every other batchelor in sight seemed to have called at least once.

The stricken look on Sean's face, as he dropped Holly's hand, provoked a sharp reply from Dr. Tom. 'Holly, you obviously do not know they can't be on visiting terms to 'Little Jerusalem.'

Abby came to Holly's rescue. 'Why ever not?'

'Because the Viceroy would soon be told. That would do you no good nor Joshua. No good at all.'

Holly turned in astonishment to Joshua. 'Do you see it that way, Uncle?

He admitted tactfully. 'We would be fools to tangle with their reputation.'

'Do you mean theirs is better or worse than ours?' she asked ingenuously.

Everyone roared so much at that, Joshua was spared giving the self-evident answer that Jarman Malleson's reputation of course was worse in the Viceroy's eyes.

After Dr. Tom had ministered a 'reviving drop' of sherry, the men retreated into the usual cheerful gossip of port trading with a camaraderie that reminded Holly once again she was an outsider despite her ambition to share their life as a trader; an ambition which could only sit on her as unsuitably and uncomfortably as the mens' clothes she still wore. She must face the fact that Canton was no place for women as the Chinese truly insisted. It would take a war to change it. She must leave Canton as soon as possible, before the winter now drawing in became the winter of her discontent.

* * * * * *

Abby and Holly visit 13 Factories Street

It took Billy's introduction of her new comprador, Pu Ping Pang, to lift her from her depression. She took an instant liking to him. His tremendous smile was not simply the polite facade of proper courtesy as he stood before her, hands folded neatly into the long drooping sleeve of his neat blue robe, head bobbing low in respect. He exuded a cheerful radiance that reflected the incorruptible and sunny nature of the man. His one drawback that he spoke only pidgin English.

'Don't be too critical of that,' Billy warned her, 'pidgin may only include a few hundred words, but those few leave no room for mistakes in contracts. What can be clearer than 'can do' or 'no can do'?

What Pu Ping Pang 'can do' apparently was to relieve her of all problems in the China trade. She would simply hand him her orders of purchase. He would break them down into innumerable smaller orders to be lodged in a myriad unknown sources in the byways of the city. And when she had goods to sell, he would reverse the process. She would merely pay him a percentage to cover costs.

'A Chinese magician of commerce,' she joked, when Billy explained, failing to mention that magic would conjure up a host of satellite staff forever scurrying in and out of his office. Horrified, she taxed Billy who reproached her for doubting Pu Ping Pang's honesty.

'You're in China now, Holly. Many of that horde of hangers-on, as you call them, are relatives who work for no more than their keep. Don't give them a second thought as long as they don't sleep on the premises, and he doesn't demand more money.'

Strangely enough it was Pu Ping Pang, who urged her to go into Thirteen Factories Street behind the factories. Joshua did his utmost to deter her.

'The streets are narrow and filthy, the scene of many frightful affrays over the years. Jack Tars get high on their atrocious samshu firewater and go on the rampage. Droves of Chinese join in. Charges and recharges follow. Bloody scalps. 'Foreign devils' definitely not welcome. No place for a lady.'

Holly looked anything but a lady as she stood slim and defiant before him, arms akimbo. 'You may be my dear host, Uncle, but you are not my keeper. With due respect it's been a total waste of time for me to come to Canton so far. Both you and Billy have shown the utterly male imagination I feared before I came to China. Worse, you simply pander to me just enough to pacify me. Pu Ping Pang tells me 13 Factories Street will give me some idea why Canton is famous in all China for its varieties of goods,' adding with a frail confidence, 'Pu Ping Pang will see I don't get into trouble.'

He washed his hands of the affair. 'And if you do, we'll throw you into the boats like the drunken sailors and send you down the river.'

Holly was not fearful as she and Abby headed down Hog Lane, the narrow pinchgut street than ran the length of the New English Factory to end in Thirteen Factories Street. After all they had two fluent Cantonese-speaking Old China Hands with them in Adam and Billy as well as Pu Ping Pang himself. Not even when Billy teased them saying the Hog Lane shops were run 'by the greatest ruffians imaginable who would fleece their own mothers,' their samshu 'unadulterated gutrot' to unwary Jack Tars. The blandishments of Old Jemmy brandishing a bottle of 'No.1 Chop No.1 rum you like? Olo flen, my savee you last voyage' bore him out.

Holly was thankful when they turned out of the squalid congestion of Hog Lane into the much broader Thirteen Factories Street, the street where the sailors stocked up with yellow nankin trousers, shawls, handkerchieves, canvas shoes, rice-paper paintings, lacquered boxes, bamboo knicknacks, porcelain and much more.

She was overwhelmed. 'Macao doesn't offer a fraction of this merchandise.' Indeed little but an abundance of incense sticks and firecrackers.

Abby was like a child in a sweetshop at the sight of so much exotic feminine frippery. She hardly knew which way to turn for the temptations glimpsed on every stall in Thirteen Factories Street or the branching Curiosity China Streets. Exquisitely fragrant beads, scented amulets, coral strings, perfumed Hangchow hair oil, incense, shawls, scarves and bedroom hangings. Holly lingered before fabric stalls, absorbed by the bewildering variety and immaculate quality of bolts of silk and cotton, Nankin crepe and embroidered Nankin cloth.

Billy hustled them by a meat market hoping they would not notice the live meat on sale- snakes, cats, dogs, mice and rats, hung by their tails and snapping at any who came too close. No one was likely to have told them the Cantonese prized roast dog, casserole of stewed cat, or rats garlanded with stewed mice.

He distracted their attention to the placard on the chest of an old man, whose eyes were covered with patches. 'He's selling a divine drug from a Taoist priest of the Mountain of Nine Blossoms which will cure everything from cancer to leprosy but obviously not his own blindness.'

Holly found the curious and eager faces of the crowd that swirled past or paused around them strangely fascinating. Fascination too in the exotic customs, florid language and naive candour evident all along the street with occasional glimpses of tragedy as on the advertisements of parading sandwich-board men for kidnapped children or absconding apprentices.

Further along they came to Consoo House, imposing headquarters of the Co-Hong rulers of all Cantonese trade and resort of merchants for all their problems or simply to drink tea. Beyond lay Carpenter's Square. Here Old Ashoe's shop of Perpetual Concord shamelessly boasted 'Rich Customers Perpetually Welcome', Old Ashoe himself at the door reciting his stock greeting for gullible 'foreign devils', 'How fashion you wanchee? Got No. 1 First chop, too muchee handsome.' Even Billy's expert Cantonese could not stop him from lapsing into the cobbled jargon of pidgin such as 'No.1 Proper can do' and a positive eruption of further bows as Holly made a liberal purchase of carved and inlaid boxes of all sizes from trousseau chests to jewel boxes through Pu Ping Pang.

Emerging at last, they were shocked to see all the pedestrians in the tiny square were stock still, pressing back against the buildings eyes riveted on the ground, clearly in arrant terror of a weird howling coming towards them down Thirteen Factories Street.

'A high mandarin. Head down likewise, girls. Eyes down,' Billy fearfully ordered Holly and Abby, thrusting them back just in time as an advance guard of uniformed servants under red umbrellas burst into view bearing red boards announcing the titles of the hated Prefect of the city. Holly, eyes obediently downcast, was amused to see they wore ragged trousers under their smart hip-length tunics as if beggars recruited for a jester's romp on festival day. But this was no romp. Four menacing lictors in combat vests and high wire hats followed, swinging chains or bamboo bastinados ready to punish anyone who dared show disrespect. Dangerous hate in their eyes as they briefly met her own.

At last the Prefect himself, borne in a chair manned by no less than six bearers, swept into view too fast and too tight round the corner. The low, blunt handles of the forward poles caught and toppled a large wooden tub. A torrent of slippery fish slithered under the feet of the rear bearers. The chair lurched violently. Even the bearers might have fought their way over the flopping silver carpet if the crowd had not surged forward in a concerted roaring rage of protest. Suddenly obedient citizens become violent thugs beating innocent bearers, who disappeared from view beneath their blows, then turned their fury on the sedan chair smashing it into a thousand matchstick pieces.

Somehow the prefect escaped through the boiling circle, chiefly because no one actually dared lay a finger on his august person. He jogged briskly out of sight down a lane at a surprising pace for such an eternally sedentary man.

'Let's clear out,' Billy urged them now in terror. The crowd that was swarming into the square from every nook and cranny might well want a second act, and turn on the equally hated fanqui. He hurried them down the side street leading to the Hoppo's warehouse on one side and Jarman Malleson's No. I Creek Factory on the other, urging them into a run as he stopped to seize logs of wood from a great pile lying against Number 1 Creek Factory and hurl them in a rearguard action to slow the rabble giving chase until the girls reached haven there.

Not that they received a gracious welcome from Dr. Jarman. He kept them standing, as he did all visitors to his office in case they lingered on to gossip and interfered with his work, while he castigated Holly and the others for being in 13 Factories Street in such a foolhardy disguise they were found out, and thus endangered not just themselves, but everyone in all 13 Factories.

As to Billy's complaint to Dr. Jarman the woodheap against the wall of the Jarman Malleson factory was a danger, he was curt in the extreme. The kitchen coolies in the Hoppo's Customs House found it handy to put it there. They had refused to remove it despite all pleas and all reminders about the fire of 1822 when half the western city, all the factories and a massive quantity of uninsured goods in the godowns, had been destroyed in that terrifying inferno. And one of the kitchen hands in the chophouse had attacked the Laird savagely, wounding him in the arm, when he had tried to force his way in to petition the Hoppo in person.

'Let me assure you that danger is about to disappear. As I hope the danger you represent will too,' he concluded, staring at Holly, 'for the longer you stay here, that danger to us all will grow. In short, the sooner you leave the better.'

His words were prophetic. Howqua summoned Joshua Law to Consoo House the next day. Wearing his richest robe, he sat enthroned in the carved magnificence of the audience hall surrounded by grave minions and fellow Hong merchants, no longer the friendly partner but leader of the almighty Co-Hong, dictator of all Canton trade.

He announced sternly. 'You break the law! You have women in your Hong.'

So that was it. Howqua would of course have known there were women there all along and that they were not 'fancy women', but he could no longer tolerate the transgression of official rules of residence in the factories after their public exposure.

Joshua dissembled. 'Who dress as women do?'

Howqua's voice no longer gentle. 'You break the law. It forbids smuggling women into Canton.'

Joshua objected. 'I smuggled no women into Canton.'

Howqua pointed at him imperiously. 'You split straws, Mr. Law. You took them into your factory after the young heirs of the No.1 Creek Hong brought them up river when the dark spirits walk, as they do their foreign mud.'

Joshua still prevaricated. To be too obsequious would only invite a harsher penalty. 'Howqua, beautiful ladies are hardly as dangerous as opium.'

Howqua shook his head angrily. 'Women are more dangerous than opium. As it is now, men come but do not stay. If women come the men will stay. Much worse for the Middle Kingdom.'

'You should accuse Sean Jarman and David Malleson.'

'They are your women. They came by your leave.'

Joshua abandoned pretence. 'They came by their own strong will. Don't you have pigheaded women in China?'

Howqua sighed. He had one such himself among his junior wives. But she did not put him at risk of a huge fine from the Viceroy as these pigheaded women surely would if it came to his ears. He could not afford to allow Law's little game of hide and seek to continue a moment longer. Time for threats now.

'If they have not embarked to go down river in 24 hours, we will stop all trade. You know what to expect.'

Indeed he did. When the Prefect issued such a command they would be isolated in less than an hour. No water, no food, no servants. Not just his own Factory but the other twelve at the busiest time of the trading season. He shuddered at the thought of the uproar it would cause. On the thought he bowed his way humbly out.

Holly started packing at once with relief not dismay. She had to concede Howqua was right. This was no place for women among men pursuing a long tradition of making a quick fortune in the east then going home to marry. Their social life was attuned to the camaraderie or feuding of a batchelor life incomprehensible to women. Or taking the law into their own hands, as the Laird had done when his deputation to Howqua of what he called his 'Prussian Guard' everyone of them over six feet like himself - Paddy MacKean, Jarman, Malleson and their nephews - failed to secure either the arrest of the kitchen coolie, who had attacked him 'so barbarously and without provocation', or the removal of the woodheap. If neither occurred before sunset, he stormed at the politely evasive evasive Howqua he would set fire to the Customs House over the Hoppo's head.

No one took him seriously. The keepers were not useless, although card-playing rogues. Abby was the first among those in 'Little Jerusalem' to see the flare of a blue light, to say tentatively 'Fireworks?' as the light lingered casting a weird glare briefly over the Common exposing the many wayfarers in transit between boats and city like so many fireflies with their bamboo lights.

Holly guessed correctly. 'No Abby! That's a ship's distress flare!' A rocket hissed like a flaming torch from No. 1 Creek Factory towards the chophouse on the river bank to lob on the roof. Its fire flickered briefly. Another and yet another, and the fire took hold at last.

Billy exclaimed behind them. 'The Laird's revenge. Why I do believe the maniac is setting the chophouse on fire.'

Joshua observed gloomily. 'The Laird will bring a hornet's nest down on all our heads.'

For the moment, it stirred a hornet's next among the long-eyes who had formed frantic bucket brigades, summoned Howqua's English fire engine from his warehouse and attracted a gawping crowd of useless onlookers. More flare lights. More rockets. More rousing cheers from No.1 Creek Factory, and a crowd of merchants, officers, and sailors flushed out of the rabbit warrens of the Factories and Standfords Hotel. Both Jarman and Malleson clearly visible outside the New English Factory in fierce argument with the President of the Select.

Whether it was Howqua's intervention - for Howqua's elegant barge had carried him across from Honam Island almost at once - or the Laird's one-man war, or both, no one knew. But the woodheap was whisked away, the man who wounded the Laird was arrested within the hour to be exposed in a heavy wooden collar cangue, and Viceroy Lu sent him a letter of apology. Only the Governor rebuked him through Howqua, for acting outside the standing arrangements that everyone must deal through the Honourable John Company.

A rebuke echoed by the President of its Select.

To which the Laird commented rudely. 'Do they expect me to maintain the same submissive attitude as you do? A permanent kowtow to the Son of Heaven? The very reason why they took me for the fool they know you to be until I proved otherwise.'

Meanwhile Joshua was less successful, unable to find a commodious passage boat to take them downriver with a willing escort too long. Howqua, fearful of the Viceroy, struck. Every servant in the Factories, and on the Common, vanished like swallows in spring. He appealed to John Davies of the Select Committee, who wasted no time in demanding help from the Commodore of the Whampoa fleet. Before the day was out a hundred blue and white Jack Tars were performing a few sharp manoeuvres on the empty Common, as a warning to the watching police, with the comforting support of four quarterdeck cannon they had manhandled on shore.

Holly watched with more amusement than the gravity of the crisis justified, declaring 'shame on the Boston Tea Party' to a mystified Abby.

'What on earth are you getting at?' she asked.

'Why to think we threw the British redcoats out of America. Look what we lost!'

Billy said slyly, 'Now we get them for nothing free of tax!' The joke was not lost on Holly for all of the Factories knew the British tax on the import of tea into Great Britain paid half the cost of the British navy as it had done in the days of the Boston Tea Party less than sixty years before.

All hundred sailors formed up in a guard of honour that would have gratified a four star general when Holly and Abby left next morning, their disguise abandoned in favour of billowing dresses and bonnets. But when the Sergeant at Arms bellowed 'Eyes Front!' after they had presented and soldiered arms, as one man their eyes followed the girls all the way down to the Jackass Point quay where every available American and young man in the settlement waited to join the sailors in their three rounds of Huzzahs to the crack of their rifles.

No sign of Sean Jarman among them, already sent down river by his uncle anxious to separate him from Holly before his obvious interest in her could go further. If only he had known, Holly was so convinced Sean returned no fraction of her unsettling interest in him, she had every intention of distancing herself from him as far as possible.

They revelled their liberation from the discomfort of male garb as their boat threaded its way through the tumultuous traffic of the river, even as Viceroy Lu posted up a notice: 'The presence of foreign women is a great and wicked innovation. If the foreign boats again bring up foreign women, I have ordered naval officers immediately to stop, seize and conduct them back to Macao and to open their guns up instantly, and make a thundering attack on them if they should oppose their presumptuous barbarism to our authority.'

* * * * * *

Captain Peel Takes Holly to Lintin Island

As Captain Jim Peel strolled along the Praya Grande of Macao arm in arm with Holly, he plucked up courage to remind her he would soon be too late to catch the trade winds south for home. For weeks since her return to Macao, she had drifted. Her old sense of purpose lost. No one could explain why.

Buoyed by the rare intimacy of the moment, he declared he intended to sail for New York willy nilly, so it was best she gave orders. 'Deliveries are running late. If there's a shortfall I'll still have to sail. And where will that leave us? Strapped for cash?'

'I'll have to borrow of course, Jim. You know all my savings are in that cargo. I don't like to run to Chung Tai Tai.'

'We run close to the wind then?'

'We do indeed.' Her piquant face was unusually grave.

He had recourse to a metaphor of the sea. 'We could turn turtle?'

'I could, Jim. I would go bankrupt, not you.'

He reminded her, 'if you lose your ship, I lose my command. Therefore, you must decide for both of us.'

Holly knew Jim was right. She had suffered from what Billy Howe asserted was China Watcher's disease, a failure of will.

'Where should I borrow short-term funds? From one of the three big 'W' banks in New York?

'No,' Jim advised her, hand under her elbow to steer her along the rough pavement towards the pavilion where the band had already started its concert. 'I've got an uneasy feeling about the boom in New York at the moment. My Dad used to say where there's a boom, there's always a bust.'

Typical weatherman of the sea, she thought as she smiled at him affectionately, always to see a storm beyond a calm.

She stopped to face him. 'What do you suggest then? That I borrow short term-money from Jarman Malleson like everyone else? Use their ill-gotten gains, their sycee silver, to buy my next season's cargo?

Jim, the realist, was not averse to that program. 'If we sell we recycle the money back into Canton quickly like everyone else.'

'Borrow from Jarman Malleson! Over my dead body.'

She would not give her reasons because she was too confused about them herself. She did not yet condemn their opium traffic out of hand as missionaries like the Rev. Sanders and Dr. Norris did. She could see too little evidence in Macao of the evils they fulminated against. Nor did she even inherently object to smuggling which seemed as ancient a practice in Macao as in Cornwall. Rather she sensed the danger of allowing their tentacles to become too pervasive, or the domination they sought in the market a monopoly.

'The new Company Agency could finance you and exchange your silver for long term credit with bills in London or New York,' Jim suggested.

'I have one problem, Jim, as well you know. They would learn the Eugenia is not one of Joshua Law's ships. My story would leak out and that would be the end of me here. The Hoppo would never allow me to have a comprador. No comprador, no trade.'

Jim dared to ask, 'How does Mr. Law keep afloat then?. Her answer confirmed his fears, 'Turkish opium.'

'No opium, even if I'm desperate.' She wanted none of that 'foreign mud' flowing in reverse up the river, not because of moral objections so much as a growing instinct that the rival simmering underground factions must inevitably boil up into pitched battles. Her own secret was too precarious to take the risk of being identified with any party.

'There must be other ways,' she pondered, holding Jim's arm tight as if to force inspiration from him, but in fact destroying all coherent thought in him in his devastating awareness of her slim, lithe body so disturbingly close.

Unwarily he proposed, 'unload your cargo at Lintin and load with rice at Manila. No port duties to pay then,' expecting her wrath at any thought of trading at that hub of all smuggling.

But far from it. She was intrigued, asking, 'how and where does the cargo go from there?

'Through Chinese smug boats to Whampoa or Canton.'

'And become as bad as the rest?'

He shrugged. 'You should go to Lintin and see for yourself.' He would to take her there himself if she would.

Of course, why hadn't she followed her own inclination, to see this extraordinary fleet of floating 'godowns' or warehouses for herself, before? Because she was a stiff-necked holier-than-thou New Englander too ready to condemn others who lapsed from moral virtue?

'Must you two be so deadly serious?' Abby cried as she came abreast of them.

She and Billy had been strolling full of ribald mirth over the racial patchwork on promenade in the evening air, a blend unique to this crossroads of the East where travellers from so many nations had left their calling cards.

'I'm taking a look at Lintin, Abby. Want to join me?'

Abby surprised her by arguing passionately against it. Holly would be tarred with the same brush if she went.

'Not if I said I was visiting the wives and families of the Captains out there.'

'They might talk you into their game of quick profits.'

Holly had never argued with Abby in their many years of friendship. She was not going to start now.

'I promise you I'll not be seduced by the opium trade.'

Then why was Holly going, Abby puzzled as she studied her friend quizzically? Because gossip said Sean Dare was out there? Was that why she had been so out of sorts since she had returned from Canton, knowing she was losing her heart to a man she insisted 'did not care a fig' for her? If so, Abby could see only danger and desolation ahead for Holly as with others who loved a sailor before her on these love-treacherous coasts. Certainly not the future she, herself, was likely to have if the feelings that were already drawing her to Dr. Tom were returned by him, as she already sensed they were.

Holly set sail for Lintin Island on the Eugenia on a light and bright morning. The distant shore was broken intermittently by low yellow-brown cliff faces or tiny beaches. Native boats dotted the deep green plain of the sea, their great yellow mat sails like butterfly wings skimming low across the fretful water. There was wind enough to set the uneasy water dancing and the Eugenia sliding gently past the semi-barren shores, where waves lazily fretted their steep sides or meagre sands. It was a bleak and uninviting coastline to any weary traveller seeking respite from the ocean.

Lintin Island, its sharp peak crowned with a handsome white lighthouse, both commanded the entrance of the Pearl River estuary ten miles offshore, and provided shelter to warehouse ships unwilling to submit to the strictures of Chinese officialdom. Sometimes in the shallow bay beyond the point ahead where it lay at anchor now, but sometimes at other anchorages round the island according to the season and therefore the quarter from which the wind blew.

As they rounded the point, they found themselves bearing down on three Chinese warjunks manned by a bustling crew although they still lay at anchor. As Holly puzzled why, she had her answer - a loud explosion, a puff of smoke, a high splash of water not far ahead. Jim seized the helm from the mate, shouted a burst of orders which sent the crew leaping for the rigging, and spun the ship on another tack as the sails did their bidding. Just in time to avert another volley, she heeled away from the war junks with their flamboyance of pennants, weapons and warshields painted with hideous distorted faces to terrify the enemy.

As they swept out of the danger zone thanks to a freshening breeze, Holly voiced her perplexity. 'What are these war junks here for?'

'To watch and report to the authorities, to smuggle themselves, to reinforce demands for protection money from smugboats during the season, and to chase all the demon ships away at the end - red-haired, flowery, ocean and white-headed. Which translated means British, American, Portuguese and Parsees. It's rare to find an honest officer displayng his zeal like this one. More often than not, they simply practice their gunnery. Fixed guns mind you so not much of a threat. The problem is there is no way of tellig which is which. A man would be a fool to stick around and find out.'

They crept towards anchorage among the armada arrayed along the wide crescent of sandy beach. No less than 23 large ships of various styles dominated by portly old-style Company ships with unstepped masts, the main warehouse ships at the heart of a fleet of smaller ships with a diligent host of launches, cutters and jolly boats plying between them. These small fry less intent on the big pickings of the smuggling trade than to shift their cargo to dodge the measurement tax of the port dues that operated so unfairly against them. They formed a busy, floating township, chiefly of men not too busy to acknowledge Holly as she passed by, heavy bombazine skirt flapping in the rising wind and poke bonnet tied firmly under her chin.

'How long have all these ships worked out of Lintin?' she asked.

'At least ten years. Ever since Howqua warned the traders they should get their floating warehouse ships out of the river before he had to guarantee the government there was no opium on them at Whampoa,'

Jim eased the Eugenia alongside Joshua Law's depot ship, the Lintin. Holly went aboard the Jarman Malleson depot ship, the Apollo, nearby next day. Captain Macdonald's hearty greeting, capped by a fierce handshake, was 'are you buying opium?'

'Goodness me, no!' Holly protested as her gaze swept the deck. Of all the markets she had ever seen, none was so bizarre as this one: no clothes to buy, food to eat, objets d'art to gratify the soul, flowers to indulge the sense. One article only at the centre of the sharp trading on the busy deck - round opium balls scarcely bigger than her hand, and for all their drab, lustreless appearance as expensive as any jewel.

Captain MacDonald steered her to the starboard side of the ship where East India Company chests of Patna and Benares opium were stacked, stamped with the Company seal of guarantee of quality - pure, with good aroma, and thoroughly dried as proof against mildew. He handed her a sample, no bigger than a small cannonball and just as explosive in its own way in that it exploded in the mind to destroy it more slowly yet persuasive it was the weapon of peace and happiness. Just like a cannonball, it solved nothing under the pretence it did.

'No trash, no adulteration in the Company product,' Captain MacDonald boasted proudly, 'the British importers wouldn't stand for it.'

'British importers?' Holly asked confused.

'Why as much opium goes west to Britain from the Calcutta auctions as comes east here to the Coast. The trade to Europe is growing just as fast as the trade to China, if not faster. And no doubt to America too. Opium is all the rage since some writer boasted it opened his mind to new experiences. What's more some medical authorities backed him up.'

Holly stared at the brisk traffic before her with new eyes. No wonder there was no move to ban the production of the drug in India. No wonder Jarman Malleson were complacent about their own trade in the face of the few voices raised against it.

All further thought of the opium trade vanished from her mind as Sean came on board, overwhelming her with his striking good looks and confident bearing. As yet oblivious to her presence on deck, he disappeared through the door of the Captain's cabin on the quarterdeck. Captain MacDonald left her to follow. She moved to the rail for any distraction that would help her control her racing pulse, her frantic thoughts betraying her even now to a foolish hope that he might be as emotionally vulnerable to her as she to him.

A fleet of long and narrow boats were foaming towards the Apollo under the thrust of huge tan triangular mat sails while their seventy-man crews, wearing conical bamboo hats, squatted on their haunches in chattering circles smoking or playing cards. The boats were armed with large guns on the bows and long rows of bamboo spears and shields at rest along the sides, as well as British flintlock muskets lying about. Suddenly at the sound of a drum they leapt into action. Some struck the sails. The rest unshipped the oars, and stroked in unison to a steady drumbeat. The fleet divided to home in on the depot ships through the great press and scurry of smaller boats. One made for the Apollo, and backed up to the clash of a gong and ship oars.

And there as if at the same signal was Sean beside her, unnerving her more than the 'smugboats' by touching her shoulder as he exclaimed 'Crab boats!'

She turned to find him staring down at her, held the disconcerting brilliance of his green eyes to the stroke of two drumbeats, then turned away flustered, saying to break the spell, 'Magnificent oarsmen.'

'Yes, superb sailors but badly paid, poor devils, like the crews in the revenue boats. Yet they'll fight to the death if cornered, because defeat means certain death. Come! You might find this more amusing.'

Holly felt any other word but 'amusing' might be more apt for such a deadly trade. What did amuse her more was the sight of one of the mandarins on the customs boats coming to dine with Captain MacDonald, whose odious illegal trade he was supposed to suppress. Admittedly the mandarin averted his eyes from stacked opium chests and piles of illegal silver sycee shoes, as he stepped over the bulkhead of the quarterdeck, but his effort to do so and still survey the scene, was comical.

Sean said scornfully. 'That blind eye costs us at least a dollar for every chest, sometimes more, on top of the dollar to the Admiral and five to the crew of the smug boats.'

Evidently the day's serious trading had begun. Chinese shroffs, or money-changers, began to empty their banking bags which held more money than Holly had ever seen. There were dollars of various currencies - American, Mexican, Peruvian, and Spanish - English sovereigns and shillings, Indian rupees, and adulterated coins of all kinds which still possessed some value so long as there was any silver left in them. Of all these currencies, the Spanish was the one most preferred, and the only one left unmutilated. Then there were Chinese copper cash in strings, sycee shoes of silver like small pigs of lead in form and size only brighter, and unidentifiable coins stamped with individual Chinese traders' marks.

The shroffs sorted the profusion of mutilated and dirty coins with amazing speed, stacking them in piles on the trays before them; then began to assess the various orders written out in the back streets of Canton or the byways of the Pearl River delta, their fingers flying incessantly over their abacuses in calculations of the greatest complexity - calculations that seemed to be accurate as no one seemed to question them.

Sean's part in the day's trading was to check the volume of orders, the going price - fickle as Calcutta weather in June - and the tally. Clearly he was a born trader with a good head for figures. She was intrigued with this new insight into his character and reflected that, if this opium trade was indeed a new form of piracy as was darkly hinted among its European opponents and loudly accused by Chinese officials whenever they vented their rage at the traitorous ocean barbarians, then surely it was nothing like the piracy of the Spanish Main - the Drakes and Hawkins descending on the Spanish treasure fleets with poorly paid crews lusting for treasure.

The lust of the Jarman Mallesons of her world was not armed with the cutlass swung across quarterdecks but with the quasi-innocent opium chest in hand. Yet the menace of cannon and musket was there, even if more discreetly in the background. The need to arm could even be justified since they had to run the gauntlet of the fierce Malacca Straits, the Spice Islands or the South China Seas where ruthless pirates eternally roamed the offshore waters.

In her reverie, Holly was unaware of Sean Dare beside her, acutely conscious that he was irresistibly attracted to this striking elf of a girl. How beautiful she was, standing there with the afternoon sun glinting on her hair striking a rich auburn tinge in the dark tumble of curls that refused to be subdued into a fashionable bun! She intrigued him, because she perplexed him. What caused her uncommon gravity at times, her preoccupation clearly running deeper than that of Abby's or Mary Anne's? Was it secret sorrow for the death of her father? Had she come to Macao in marrying mood like so many before her, and been disappointed by the clutch of admirers who danced attendance on her? Or did she have some undeclared involvement with a man already?

He spoke up at last. 'You're very serious!'

She turned sharply in mock fright, searching his high-bone handsome face with challenge in her eyes. 'why not? Piracy is serious.'

Shocked he frowned, 'piracy?'

'It could be argued smuggling and piracy are much the same. Where do you draw the line between them?'

He looked as if she'd struck him a blow on the face. 'Do I understand you're suggesting we practice piracy?'

'I merely wondered if one had to raise a skull and crossbones and swing from the ratlines of one ship to another, cutlass in teeth, to be a pirate?'

He shouted with laughter. 'I daresay I'd cut a dash on a ratline so long as I had a beautiful girl like you to watch.'

Relieved he had a sense of humour, she retorted, 'Alas, girls are always captive in those stories.'

He bowed with an inner glow in his eyes, 'I'd be delighted to make you a captive.' Hers had an unspoken response that needed no words.

'If so, they're always horrified by their plight.'

'Sometimes they succumb. If so the pirate Captain would be very fortunate.'

She could not mistake his meaning and blushed so transparently she was forced to look away. His blood raced as he knew for the first time she truly responded to him. He continued to talk sensibly only with difficulty.

'But this isn't the Spanish Main, my dear Holly, after all.' The 'my dear' hung in the air between them. 'But, if it were, we would have been called privateers, not pirates'.

'The difference?' She asked, her voice steadier now.

'Men who financed their own enterprise. Men who took great financial risks. Men who were traders first and fighters only second. Men like we are. The British Navy is our fighting arm now. In the end, it will fight for us.'

She let the argument go, too astute to wear her intelligence on her sleeve too long. She had seen that frighten men off before. She could only survive in China if she tuned into the comic jest of the world. So she hid the solemnity of her thoughts and teased Sean as they walked the deck with the smiling flirtation of her eyes and flattery of laughter at his sallies; the primeval response of a woman when the still voice of her commonsense was being overwhelmed by her attraction to a man.

A shouted order from Captain Macdonald to lower a boat, and summons to Sean to board it, forced them to wrench their eyes from each other. The fuss, as it swung out from its davit and pulled away to prevent an armed mandarin revenue boat from arresting one of the crew of a small laundry boat, enough to bring the large motherly figure of Maisie MacDonald up on deck in time to explain to Holly why this should involve them in a battle with the revenue boat as it tried to escape. Jingals firing. Shots across the bows. The helmsman shot.

'You can't have these disputes about not paying squeeze in the middle of the fleet.'

'Doesn't it worry you?'

'Lord no, I don't take the conscience of the world on my shoulders nor should you. I stick to my knitting and leave the world to its folly.'

So that was how Maisie could live calmly at the heart of the smuggling fleet, unperturbed by its devilish trade. She hugged the generous Maisie gratefully. 'You're right. We can't play judge for God.'

Well pleased with himself that he had cut a dash before Holly, Sean returned to the Apollo to the more withering fire of Dr. Jarman. 'By the beard of St. Andrew, what was your hell-raising for?'

'We thought a European had been taken.'

'Since when did we acquire the rights of policemen in these waters?'

Sean stood there abashed, his brief vainglory wilted. 'A spontaneous reaction, uncle. We were all in it.'

'All bored with yourselves no doubt, fancying yourselves as rescuing heroes.'

Sean protested. 'It's hard to stand by when a man is seized against his will.'

Dr. Jarman's tone was icy. 'This is a grim trade, young man with some grim reaping. Keep your mind on trade as long as you're here, and nothing else.'

Sean was taken aback at the older man's belligerence. He could see the bumboat had moved away from the fleet under sail now, frail and lonely on the fidgeting water.

'I suppose they could arrest him on shore no matter what we did.'

'Exactly, so why embroil ourselves in trouble? Eight men wounded and one dead. We'll have to answer for it, make up a likely story, appease the magistrate, pay a fine.' He wagged a finger sharply at Sean. 'We could offer you in exchange according to the Chinese law of a life for a life.'

Dr. Jarman took him below and announced over a rum toddy. 'I'm sending you north on the Fairy next week. I want storeships like this one in at least three more locations with smaller brigs like the Fairy as courier ships between them. The profit will be better. No overland freight charges. And no competition from Raine.'

Sean forgot Holly in his excitement as Dr. Jarman had hoped, an excitement briefly dampened when he remembered a troublesome rumour.

'Sir, someone told me the Fairy is manned by a scratch crew. Is that true?'

'We've been unlucky. Her British crew deserted. Whampoa seamen filled them with vile samshu and horrific yarns of deadly typhoons, ferocious pirates and deaths by a thousand cuts. They deserted in a body. Replaced with Filipinos and Lascars.'

'You're asking me to trust myself to a raw scratch bunch of Filipinos and Lascars, sir, one half unable to talk to the other and neither able to talk to officers or mates.'

Dr. Jarman shrugged. 'The Captain's the best on the coast. The ship has all the latest improvements from the galley to the bridge.'

Sean saw all too little of Holly in the following week. When free of the fuss of providoring the Fairy and struggling to help the Captain knock the novice crew into some order, he found Holly had no time for him. She was on shore playing badminton, now all the rage, on an improvised court near the beach. When he could join in, he found himself sidelined by flirtatious officers to fume with jealousy at their flirtatious hilarity over the wayward shuttlecock and brood with bitter uncharacteristic introspection over his stormy emotions for a girl who clearly did not care a tinker's curse for him. Give him a tumbling wild reach of the North Sea and he would show her. He did not guess how she agonised in his absence unable to find one among her eager suitors to match him.

Through that long week of frustration, Sean consoled himself he had a better chance to cut a dash at the ball Captain Clifton was holding on his Red Rover, first of the new fast clippers likely to change the face of trade on the China Coast forever.

As darkness fell swiftly over the fleet on the night of the ball, all the omens gave promise of a magical evening fit to celebrate a magical ship, the pinnacle as yet of man's conquest of the ocean. A faint cool breeze had dispelled the clammy humidity that had bedevilled them all for weeks and the faint haze that had obscured the vast canopy of stars. The ocean winds were dormant and the waves scarcely perceptible. The myriad lights on board flared safely in their sconces.

As Holly stepped on the pontoon, and swung up the companion way, she was amazed to see the deck of the old tea boat cleared of its usual commotion of shroffs, dealers, traders and coolies, and the masts and rigging bedecked with streamers and coloured lanterns. All enhanced by the blazing red uniforms, gleaming instruments of a brass and wind band from Whampoa augmented by Portuguese fiddlers, and the flamboyant dresses of mestizo ladies invited in the absence of the social dictators of Macao.

Sean was waiting to hand her to the deck with his most gracious greeting and most fulsome compliments, comparing her shimmer of white muslin over gold satin to a tropical frangipanni. He led her firmly to one of the few chairs scattered about the deck, buttonholing her for himself despite his Uncle James' hostile stare, knowing the importance of adopting a proprietary stance at once to discourage other swains and to provoke her interest. If only he knew, he had provoked it already with his dark, romantic looks so elegantly offset by the light blue and white uniform of the Jarman Malleson fleet.

The welcoming blare of the band stopped. A skirl of bagpipes rose from the bowels of the ship. A kilt-clad Dr. Jarman, in full war-kit of sporran and band, emerged from the bulkhead to march round the deck as if at the head of an unseen army tramping down the glen. In another time, and another place, he would have summoned up the blood of his clan to lead them once more to war with the English.

The band struck up. Sean swung her through the wild pivots of an endless waltz. She felt exhilarated, bewitched, at one with him - their unison a shield against all grief, all despair, all isolation. If this was love, what magic it was beyond all understanding. They hardly spoke, reading the language of glance and touch unconsciously rehearsed in past encounters.

This was hardly the case when he urged her to join in the furious Scotch dancing. Holly bumbled her way through trying to manage the hopping motion on one foot and pointing the other fore and aft, looking, she thought, like a stork in a fit. She cried off at the end of another set.

'You did splendidly,' Sean lied.

She grimaced. 'I shall get my revenge when I teach you to square dance.'

Sean prompted her to the rail, where she leaned silently for a time to gaze across the swirl of gloomy water at the dark shapes of the warehouse fleet tossing at anchor. What had Captain Macdonald said to her? 'Don't get tangled with the Jarmans. Batchelordom is an entrenched tradition on the Coast, Holly.

Not out of cruelty to the fair sex but kindness. Death walks beside everyone in this country.'

His caution was given too late. She was tangled already like driftwood caught in the wake of Sean's ship, as she knew to the full when he leaned over, eyes locked with her own. Her sense of exhaustion was not caused by the dance. 'I shall miss you as I've never missed anyone before,' Sean was saying.

Over his shoulder she caught sight of Dr Jarman scowling at the obvious intimacy of them both, and knew him for enemy. She came to her senses. 'Miss me?' she gasped barely able to speak.

'I'm ordered north on the 'Fairy' tomorrow.'

'I've never met a woman who intrigued me so much.'

Intrigued? How half-hearted! She was silent in her dismay. 'I believe I'm falling in love with you Holly.'

At last he had made the declaration she had longed for, but now he had given it she bridled. He spoke as if he loved her against his will, where in truth he was merely clumsy in the dance of love stumbling as she had done in the steps of the quadrille.

'You're silent. Have I offended you?'

'No, goodness no. But you sounded as if you resented..' 'My delicate condition? Is it possible that you...' He broke off anguished by his own naive gallantry.

'It is,' she said simply. He gripped both her hands in his own. She drew back. 'Your uncle is watching.'

'I'm my own master,' he responded fiercely.

'Captain Macdonald warned me Jarman Malleson men may not have any entanglements in China.'

'Oh Holly you think you're an entanglement?'

'Captain Macdonald thinks so. Any attraction for a woman like me would ruin your career on the Coast.'

'Holly! Holly!' He shook his head. 'The entanglement my uncle has in mind is of a more unacceptable kind.' He waved towards the women passing by in a whirl, the half-caste progeny of men, highborn as well as low, who lived in a twilight world between west and east because their fathers had loved and left their mothers, and were accepted by neither. 'The rule destroyed the senior de Santios partner, it is true, but only because he married his mestizo lover.'

'A very cruel rule then.'

'Not when she would be outcast in Europe, and let's make no mistake in Macao as well. The Company made the rule out of common sense nearly two hundred years ago. Wives mean demands for permanent residence in Macao or Canton. The Company did not want to plant that seed of colonisation, be obliged into occupation as they had been in India.'

No, Jarman Malleson would never make her welcome, a Yankee miss rating not much higher than a mestizo. But she could not mistake the welcome in Sean's vivid green eyes beseeching her heart.

'You understand?'

Her eyes melted into his own for answer. Yes she did understand the demands of a seaport town, the enforced separations, the long sea journeys to trade, the endless waits.

'When I get back from Chusan Island, we can come to know if we are right.' Right in what? Right in being in love? Right in pursuing that love? Right together in marriage? She did not care being drunk on the balm of the night, the catch of the music, the exaltation of his presence.

Two days later Captain Jim announced they had to up anchor and make for shelter at the Cumsingmoon without delay. The barometer was falling, the wind rising. A typhoon was on the way. 'What about the Fairy, she's heading north?' she asked anxiously.

Jim was curt. 'Jarman should be shot. She won't stand a chance, not with a scratch crew from the dregs of Whampoa.'

Her alarm for Sean grew as the wind freshened fast, black clouds piled high, and tumultous seas thrashed the ship with increasing fury until they reached the spacious harbour formed partly by the Kowloon peninsula on the western side of the river mouth and partly by islands. Well before the storm blew with vehement fury, Captain Jim had all the sails furled with double gaskets.

All night the ship heaved and plunged as if it would founder in the torment of waves at any moment until, at last, a dead calm fell. Holly struggled from her bunk and up the ship's ladder to find Captain Jim, clad in oilskins, checking the rigging. 'Get back to your bunk at once, Holly,' he ordered peremptorily.

'Isn't the storm all over?' she asked naively.

'Worse is to come. You see the storm moves in a circle. The centre is always calm, the eye they call it, but not for long. Soon it will blow even worse from the opposite quarter and the turbulence will be like nothing you've known before. The sea will thrash us like all the avenging furies in one. No one will be able to keep the deck even with a running line. So down below with you, Holly, and hang on for dear life, tie yourself into your bunk if you can or you'll be smashed clear across the cabin.'

He dashed to the wheelhouse to check the barometer. Down to 29 and still falling. He made sure the helm was still lashed firm to hold the ship's head into the wind. In a short time the wind roared in again, this time from the south west, chasing new waves against the headers of the old sea from the opposite direction. The ship lurched and heaved as heavy seas roared across her deck from every point of the compass plunging her rails below the sea time and again. Holly cowered in her bunk as violent flashes of lightning speared through the roaring dark to terrify her with a glimpse of the savage frenzy of the tempest hurling against her porthole.

She prayed for deliverance for herself, her captain and crew, her ship and most of all for Sean. Jim's prayers were not for himself nor even for Holly, for he knew their ship would survive, but for any ship caught at sea this night without the shelter of a port to save it from the rampant storm's vengeance on all humans that dared trespass in its kingdom of the open seas.

The three hours of the height of the storm seemed like twenty four, and the next two days, as the seas gradually abated, like an aeon. Holly wept with relief to see the Fairy limp in under a foretop sail, her top gallant main and maintop sail yards and mizen topmast swept away.

This was hardly Dr. Jarman's reaction when Sean boarded the Apollo to report. He carpeted him, exhausted though he was for the fact the Fairy was crippled. Sean was defiant before his older mentor. He hadn't had to take in the topsails in the icy fury of that wind with nothing but air above and raging water below. He hadn't had to cling there while the ship rolled and tumbled wondering if each monster wave they broached would prove his grave.

'The scum of the sea you gave us ended up standing the ship on her beam ends till I thought the last trump was sounding for us all. Not one of us spoke any language any one of those seacunnies knew except the Captain, and he only had a few words of Bengali or Spanish.'

'You had Dr. Grusson,' Dr. Jarman pointed out icily.

'Bloody useless. Our Chinese spoke Hoklo. He doesn't.'

Dr. Jarman was unyielding. One good lesson China had taught him was that to admit a mistake was to lose face. 'Fortunes of the sea, young man. Storm early for this time of the year. No time to knock them into shape.'

'Where have the standards of the old Company gone? Now we crew our ships like the old-time buccanneers with the riff-raff of every port.'

'Those buccaneers defeated Spain. Enough of that. I'll have to leave you to the salvage of the Samarang. She'd just been beached when the storm struck. Only good for salvage now. You'll have some competition from those Kowloon bandits.' The walled city, notorious for being a law to itself, was near the wreck. 'Don't neglect to carry arms. Avoid using them at all costs. We can't risk an international incident just now.'

The days that followed, while Captain Jim was doing running repairs before venturing to sail out, were days of misery and frustration for Holly. She could see the crippled Fairy lying in shore, yet Sean would not, or could not, visit her. She imagined all his avowals of that seductive midnight were no more than the weakness of a romantic evening. For his part Sean raged that he dare not leave for a moment out of dread that the very clash Dr. Jarman warned him about might occur with his motley crew of Lascars and Manila men spoiling for a fight with the Kowloon predators. They had been growing bolder and more numerous every day nobbling precious iron, nails, sheathing and planking, nimble and resourceful in escape as sewer rats. Firing grapeshot over their heads was useless, killing forbidden. He decided to set a trap to catch a victim to teach the rest a lesson.

It proved easier to catch a man than to keep him. He fought back as two Manila men tried to pinion him, kicking one with his feet, crashing another with a piece of timber. Villagers closed in to the rescue. Oaths and blood flew. Then all at once they fled. Out of chagrin and fury, Sean lost his head. He let fly with his musket winging one of the rearguard with a shot to his arm or chest, he could not tell, as the man staggered out of sight.

'Now you've torn it,' said the bosun, a weathered old veteran of the Coast, 'a dead 'un for sure.'

'Teach them a lesson,' Sean retorted curtly.

'The Viceroy will teach us a lesson more like,' he predicted.

Dr. Jarman was far more scathing when he heard. 'Do you realise just what serious trouble you may be facing. And if you are, so am I. The Governor of the province will demand satisfaction. Expect me to hand you over for their justice. Are you ready for that?'

At first Sean believed his words were mere bluff. 'Rules as old hat as our duelling. Shooting it out like the barbarians they think we are.'

Scorn in Dr. Jarman's voice. 'And what was yours but a shoot-out. You fired the first shot. You behaved as if this were the wild west not a sensitive frontier between two great powers.'

Sean was contrite. He was also resentful as he stood seething at the rail of the ship gazing across the forbidden territory that stretched between himself and the unattainable Holly. Dr. Jarman surely could not be so stupid to think he could salvage the Samarang with the thieving rascals of the people of the walled city of Kowloon nearby. Then if not, what possible explanation could there be? An agreement with them that been breached? If so, then with whom? That slit-nosed fellow he had seen on board that morning with his sinister arrogance and quiet stealth? Riddles within riddles. One thing certain Dr. Jarman's anger was really directed at someone else. He had merely got in the way.

As Dr. Jarman predicted, the governor did declare the murderer must be surrendered for justice when the man died within the prescribed month. But his uncle, surety for him, knew how to play the game of justice by Chinese rules. He hauled up a Lascar, and offered him a considerable bribe to confess to being the murderer overruling Sean's objection that 'that simple fellow can't stand proxy for me.'

'Oh yes he can and has. You can't reverse it now.'

Sean was horrified. 'He'll be executed in my place.'

James Malleson laughed. 'You're still a greenhorn, lad. Money talks here. He'll pay compensation to the family on some face-saving pretext.' He was right. The Governor settled. The relatives made no further fuss. Dr Jarman abandoned the shell of the wreck on the beach for the villagers to pillage to their heart's content as he should have done in the first place. And that was that, except for one magistrate who was scandalised and tried to have the father of the dead man punished for conspiracy.

Sean had a new insight into his uncle, seeing him with more astute judgement as a shrewd politician with the ruthless streak of a good general. If born three hundred years earlier, he would have been calculating the strategy of his troops in the Marchland. Now his mind roved the windings of the China coast and complexities of the Chinese character. In truth, Dr. Jarman was not the tougher of the two as was his reputation but merely the more obvious.

* * * * * *

Kaida Hung Takes John Norris into his Confidence

Kaida Hung arrived at the Jesuit Cathedral of St. Paul in a drenching April fog that shrouded central Macao with its steady cold drizzle and kept most sensible citizens indoors. He shivered from nerves as much as the cold. For today at last he had succumbed to his mother's urging not to delay a moment longer in confiding in John Norris.

Palatial steps rose beyond the neglected residence and nunnery to the facade of this most stately and beautiful of all cathedrals in the Orient, built long ago by Jesuit fathers and Christian refugees from the Shogun of Japan's persecution to commemorate the safe arrival of a black treasure ship thought to be irrevocably lost. As Kaida climbed towards the soaring stone facade, he reflected on the curious irony of fate that led him, a humble commoner, to the very place from which Jesuit fathers had once sought out his exalted ancestors in Beijing to bring them western knowledge with an open-hearted compromise of their religion that their Catholic Church had since renounced as had successive Manchu emperors in Beijing to their mutual cost.

He stood thinking sadly how even those who tried hardest to understand each other, and were given every chance, could so completely fail. How was it that those good fathers had failed to learn that the dragon was a beneficent animal in China, whose image figured on the Emperor's robes and had therefore seen fit to feature a dragon's tail on their seven-headed symbol of evil on whom the Mother of God trampled in victory? How was it that they believed the Chinese would understand Christ's message of redemption through His sacrifice or comprehend a compassionate God, who could also allow His son to suffer those instruments of His Passion so graphically detailed for their witness - the scourge, the pincers, the rope and the Cross?

His mood of melancholy remained as he entered the vast gloom of the cathedral. Those men of God had been good men, missionaries with high hopes doomed as the new evangelists would also be. Their hands no longer tended the exquisitely carved high altar or the ornate side chapels where relics of saints and martyrs rested, including the great Francis Xavier himself. Their glorious testament of devotion to God abandoned to birds and curious wayfarers. No one now to respond to the chant of the High Mass and the Jesuit exhortation 'remember death and thou shalt never sin.'

Kaida found John Norris on his knees in the front pew of the empty cathedral. 'I thought you didn't believe in idols.'

'Strictly speaking we non-conformists do not. But we have a saying 'When in Rome do as the Romans do.' A tolerance the British observe in India when they honour the feast days of Hindu, Muslim and Christian alike. It's the good in the heart of men that matters.'

Kaida urged him into the invisible retreat of a deserted confessional box. 'No one can see us here.'

John submitted protesting, 'why all the mystery?'

Kaida closed the wooden door of the box and thrust aside the rotting red curtain before he answered. 'You have heard many strange things on the Coast, John,' he began, 'but nothing as strange as I am about to tell you.'

He told the story of his father as his mother had - how, as a rebel in his youth, he had migrated south and gone into hiding with the pirate fleet. He explained his mother's determination to give him the choice his father had never had. He hesitated before the final revelation, drumming his deft fingers on the narrow counter between them. Would his old friend believe in the final strange truth, such a preposterous truth?

At first he did not. 'Surely you're joking. You a Ming? After all this time? Why 1664 wasn't it, when they were driven from the Peacock throne?'

'Five or six generations no more,' Kaida reminded him, 'A very short time in our long history.'

'You must have proof, Kaida. Do you have that proof?' The two whispering, heads close together now, although the cathedral was as silent and abandoned as a tomb.

'The first question I asked my mother. Legend is not enough. Yes, there are tablets of the lineage and imperial seals known only to a few. Carefully hidden.'

'Never stolen or destroyed?'

'Sometimes in danger as a short time ago when thieves broke open my grandfather's coffin. But they had been moved as they are from time to time as the Manchu have never given up the hunt for those of us who survive.'

'How do they know you exist at all?'

'Because of the Triads. They were formed to restore the Ming, and are sworn to destroy the Manchu.'

'Does the Manchu Emperor know this?'

'My friend, when a secret brotherhood is as vast as the Heaven and Earth Society it can never keep its secrets entirely secret. It can never totally protect itself from spies least of all in struggles for power.'

'Are you involved in this struggle?' John asked aghast. If so, he would be in great danger so long as he worked in the Viceroy's yamen.

'The Triads know the heir lives, but not that I am he.'

'Surely you will eventually be found out.'

'The time will come when there is another rebellion.'

'And when will that be?'

'When the foreign devils make war.'

'Great Scott!' He reached out to clasp Kaida's elegant hand between his own. His decision could, at best, be only a few years away. 'You are faced with a terrible choice. May God give you strength!'

'Which God?' Kaida asked wryly, 'Jehovah, God of Wrath, or Kwanying, Goddess of Mercy?'

John studied his friend with dismay, by no means happy to be an ally in such a dangerous secret. He could see himself pursued by Triads and Manchu alike, kidnapped and tortured to Kaida's betrayal. He chided himself. Now he was getting melodramatic. But why had he been made an ally?

'Because my mother insisted I could wait no longer,' Kaida told him, 'the Company reign is nearly at an end. The new Trade Superintendent will be here in July. The free traders will drive our chief ally and the only man who understands China, John Davies, away.'

'How do you know all this?'

'Chung Tai Tai has 'long-eyes' everywhere.'

'How much does Viceroy Lu know?'

'Very little. He's surrounded by servile courtiers who only tell him the good news he wants to hear, just like the Emperor himself. He still believes the new Taipan will be like the old President of the Select- in charge of trade but nothing more.' He rose, peeered out of the confessional box, then beckoned to John. 'Time for us to move before the fog lifts.'

John reached out his hand once more. 'I'll never betray you. But I won't join you at the head of a revolutionary army.'

Kaida laughed. 'The only place I'll ask you to join me is on the deck of a retreating ship.'

At last John knew. 'I'm your passport to freedom.'

'One who can vouch for me, convince your authorities I am who I am.'

John put his arm around Kaida's shoulders as he promised. 'I'll be your angel of mercy.'

'Until then my guardian angel,' Kaida responded as he disappeared from the cathedral into the pall of fog outside.

John watched him go with wonder at the terrible dilemma that faced him - whether to honour the hope of his ancestors and all their loyalists or renounce the responsibility that, if he did, he would sanction surrender of any last alterntive to the intolerable Manchu rulers.

CHAPTER 3

1834
The Barbarian 'Eye'

The Heirs to the Company Travel to China

Captain Barron Forge walked arm in arm with his vivacious red-headed wife, Flora, through the bustling East End crowds towards the British East India Company building in Leadenhall Street. It was her first visit to London. She was both excited and overawed by the endless facade of massive structures. Why were they dominated by sculptures of Greek gods and goddesses? How much wealth had gone to create this powerhouse of Empire on Cornhill?

She was relieved to find that the Company headquarters, though also succumbing to the prevalent temptation to present its face to the world as a classical temple, refrained from adding such antique embellishments. Instead it boasted Britannia shielded by her King, liberty in her embrace and Asia pouring treasures at her feet.

'I see Britannia loves gold as much as liberty,' she joked as they passed through the huge public hall to the Council Room where Britannia stood guard yet again receiving offerings from India aided by Africa and the Orient on either side. 'I see the Worshipful John Company worship themselves.'

Captain Forge rushed to the Company's defence. He gloried in the fact he had been appointed Master Attendant of Trade in China in succession to a Company, the grandeur and pride of which was symbolised in the triumphant symbolism of this building.

'They have reason. What other organisation can match it? A world-wide territorial power with its own government, revenue, fleet and army. Author of great names and reputation. Nursery of our empire.'

Flora experienced no such sense of awe and respect until Barron took her down the Thames River to the East India Company Dock in the Lower Pool. There in the biggest dockyard in the world, a whole fleet of black and white Company ships were being readied to sail clear across the world. Every one of them the centre of a frenzied bustle of a dozen trades - some still refitting, some already loading, but all aiming to catch the trade winds that would carry them under the Company flag to India and Canton for the tea season.

'Far more orderly than it appears to be,' Barron reassured Flora, 'the Company is very strict, particularly on the stowing of cargo. Can't have it shifting at sea.'

He held her hand tightly as they stood watching a tug nudging one of the stately ships, her sails already half-unfurled, into the swirling murky Thames past the Isle of Dogs. 'Can you feel her calling you to follow her on our great adventure?'

She returned his grip as she smiled her genuine assent. She was ready for that great adventure. She had nothing to keep her. Her brother alienated from her since he had taken up with the Communards in France, the heroic impulse of the French Revolution corrupted into anarchic nihilism. Her sister usurped from her family by that of the wealthy baron she had married.

'We will be on that tide soon,' Barron promised as he bent to kiss her.

A week later he kept that promise, when they boarded the Artemis shortly before his new superior, the Trade Superintendent, Lord Nash, who acknowledged his salute and Flora's diffident 'bob' with a formal hauteur, echoed by his wife and two exceptionally pretty daughters, which boded ill for their future on the voyage out, or together in China. He turned away abruptly leaving Captain Forge to wonder whether this merely reflected doubts Lord Nash may hold about him as Master Attendant, or an inherent arrogant rigidity in the man.

Captain Forge would not have blamed Lord Nash for questioning his credentials. He had indeed himself found it inexplicable that the President of the new Trade Commission replacing the Select Committee of the East India Company, John Davies, had recommended him as the right man for the job. Davies had only known him briefly when on duty with the Far East Squadron based in Calcutta, and knew perfectly well his stint as Protector of Slaves in Guiana would have little relevance. There could be no other reason than that his family had a long tradition in the King's Service - his father as an Ambassador, his uncle as Governor-General of India, and his cousin in line for First Lord of the Admiralty at any moment.

But equally he questioned Lord Nash's credentials for his new job. For he seemed to have no qualifications whatsoever in the one thing Barron supposed would be the essential requirement for his new job, namely trade; his skills only being in sheepfarming, mathematics, astronomy and the Bible, and his reputation chiefly resting on the fact he was a Trafalgar veteran of the Napoleonic wars.

Captain Forge's forebodings proved more than justified all through the long weeks of their journey together from London to Calcutta. Lord Nash kept him at arm's length whether in the splendour of the Hotel Cairo, on the great lumbering coach to Suez, or during the interminable familiarity of three meals a day at the Captain's table. He had proved eiher unwilling for any joviality out of long habit to discourage more junior officers from becoming too informal, or was incapable of it. He was inflexible and narrow like too many of the older officers in the British Navy, officers certain the British Bull dog who downed Napoleon and all his Admirals, had no need of change.

Captain Forge had decided this was bad enough before he discovered that Lord Nash had been given inflexible instructions by the new, ill-advised Foreign Secretary, Lord Palmerston, which must bring him into headlong conflict with officials of the Chinese Government on either one of two counts - going to Canton without waiting for permission from the Viceroy and refusing to do any business unless directly through the Viceroy.

This brief reflected an ill-timed, ill-thought out reaction to diverse pressures: James Malleson, the manufacturing lobbyists of four different cities, badly-informed Ministers, and a furore in the Times created by Colin Kingsman's unexpected pamphlet under the pseudonym 'American merchant' suggesting the relations of Great Britain with China were harsh, absurd and intolerable.

Some weeks later he found himself standing uneasily at Lord Nash's side dressed 'like a stuffed dummy' in full-dress uniform waiting for the famous Deptford-built side-paddle wheeler steam tug, the Enterprise, to emerge from the Hooghly River; its task to disgorge the Governor-General's aide-de-camp in welcome and to tow them up its estuary to Calcutta.

At last after an interminable and sweltering wait in the distressing humidity of May, he saw it come churning towards them on the flat reach of the river with the excitement of a younger officer who could foresee great changes looming in the Navy, heralded by this remarkable little steamship. Not long before, she had won the prize for the first successful journey under steam from England to India when steamships were no more than tugs on river estuaries. It had been a historic journey by any standard with only thirteen out of one hundred and sixteen days under sail.

Although her lines seemed squat and graceless compared to the aerial elegance of a sailing ship under full canvas, she could generate considerable power with the fuss of her paddle wheels and had far greater refinement of movement with her ability to manoeuvre by reversing towards them, great mill wheels on either side beating the water, able to judge speed and direction with an enviable accuracy as she took take them in tow. She made their clumsier sailing ship seem like a dinosaur of another age.

As she took up the slack of the two, then the weight of the vessel, Forge exclaimed, 'a miracle isn't it, Sir? I hear the Navy's building a dozen at Cammell Laird's on the Mersey.'

'Useful gadgets for jobs like this,' Lord Nash conceded grudgingly.

Captain Forge persisted eagerly. 'Unrivalled on a coastline, sir, and perhaps in wartime..'

Lord Nash cut him short. 'Useful I said with their shallow draft, but nothing more. No guts in them. No safeguards. All sorts of trouble with a single expansion engine, so I am reliably told. Broken spindles and bolts, not to mention leaking boiler joints. No satisfactory system for exhausting steam. Ships could blow up.'

Captain Forge gaped in amazement at this commendable display of knowledge. Lord Nash not such a 'toffee-nose' after all. Genuine scientist enough to have investigated the fine, as well as the crude, possibilities of steam.

Lord Nash concluded triumphantly. 'Not forgetting the iron hulls. Confounded contraptions can play merry hell with compasses.'

For all that, given time to amend those faults, Captain Forge could see how valuable such a ship would be in the conflict certain to ensue when the Company withdrew, leaving them in a vacuum of authority with the Viceroy.

'Surely there would be a role for them in time of war in regions like the Pearl River delta, Sir,' he urged.

Lord Nash gave him a withering look. 'Those tugboats in a seabattle? One shot in those paddlewheels and then what? The sail ship tows the steam ship.'

Captain Forge excused himself. Some day not too far away, someone would perfect a screw propeller and such veteran diehards as Nash would have to change their tune. He found Flora leaning against the rail amusing herself watching Lady Nash's haughty condescension to the Governor General's aide-de-camp who had come aboard. She greeted him with suppressed laughter.

'Will anyone ever be good enough for her daughters?'

They had witnessed her desperate chaperonage of her two flirtatious auburn-headed daughters, besieged by a clutch of officers and colonial buffs returning from leave, determined not to see them married off as army or Company wives in Calcutta. There were no longer rich pickings to be had as in the days of Clive or Hastings, those days of licentious luxury when men lived as splendidly as any Rajah earning Calcutta the name of 'the wickedest place on earth'.

'What does she expect in Macao, I wonder?' Forge mused, 'she may yet wish they both had got stranded in India after all. And her good spouse as well.'

'That sounds ominous, Barr. Why?'

'Our King should have found some other friend for this job, one misbegotten with a Spaniard.'

'What one earth are you raving about, my love?'

'Black hair and dark eyes, sweetheart, go down better in China than red hair and green eyes. They call us red-haired demons, demons for our green eyes.'

'Exactly our colouring, Barr,' Flora said, horrified at this revelation.

He agreed wryly. 'The only thing the chief and I have in common. The accursed Viking look.'

'Does that mean trouble for us?'

'It could, but at least I won't compound the error by affecting the airs of a Spanish grandee as he will. And certainly will never be as tactless.'

He had in mind Lord Nash's famous remark in the Lords in support of the reform of the navy's civil department when Lord Ellenborough had charged that naval captains made incompetent bookkeepers. 'They are as capable of conducting the country's affairs as any member of His Lordship's house.'

At last after hours of towing up the Hooghly, they were at anchor in Calcutta, no longer the tiny fishing village named Kali Hata after the Goddess of Death, a frontier post where the Company Resident had once dispensed justice under a banyan tree with his Bengali wife beside him. Now the 'City of Palladian Palaces', the chief of them the Governor-General's residence built by the brother of the Duke of Wellington, Lord Wellesley, to rival Buckingham Palace itself.

The Governor General received them in a study of stupefying size and luxury, and waved them into capacious red leather chairs to match. He was a man of an easy air of command and a direct manner, such a man as Captain Forge imagined his own father must have been; a diplomat whose intervention, as Governor of Madras, had helped to bring the Mahratta wars to a close in the Indian Deccan, and who later forced two kings - of Naples and of Denmark - to sheathe their swords.

Lord Bentick managed to rebuke Lord Nash with subtle courtesy when he requested a warship to carry him onwards to Canton and for regular visits of warships to China.

'Lord Nash, they should have briefed you better in London. I refused such a request from the Select Committee in China only last year. My refusal was endorsed by the Company Court itself in London.

'Circumstances have changed, Your Excellency. The old Honourable John

Company could command obedience and discipline from its captains, including the country traders. I cannot. Traders will be free agents. I'll need to have a visible demonstration of the dignity and power of my commission.'

'Do you demand our warships to intimidate British subjects or Chinese?'

'Both, Your Excellency.'

'Can they do that without war? Is war your ambition, Sir?'

Lord Nash blanched at being construed as planning war. He hastened to exonerate himself. 'I am told the Chinese believe what they see rather than what they hear, Sir. They are a race who believe that honour lies in appearance rather than truth. Keeping face it is said.'

'You shall have your appearances then,' Lord Bentick assured him, 'but you would do well to remember China is small beer to us.'

Lord Nash, nettled to think his Commission might rate less than he expected in Calcutta, pronounced, 'Sir, perhaps my information was wrong. I am told the opium trade to China provides half the revenue for the Government of India. What would the Company do for revenue if that trade stopped, or England for half the upkeep of the Royal Navy if China could no longer send its tea?'

Lord Bentick was far too used to officials, who fancied themselves as nabobs the moment they arrived, to provoke.

'You must be aware that the Company was forbidden to trade in opium. It is the country traders under foreign flags that do. Therefore you underline the expediency of our situation here. You forget the rules were not made by us but by the Moghul rulers before us. Opium and salt paid taxes long before we were here. In China you could perpetuate problems we left behind in India long ago now that the Company is coming to an end and there will be open season in the opium trade, a free-for-all which could lead to a headlong collision.'

'Perhaps that will be the only way.'

Was that the reason Lord Palmerston had chosen a naval man rather than a merchant for a merchant's job, Captain Forge wondered even as Lord Bentick warned Lord Nash sternly, 'never force a war or history will not let you forget.'

As Captain Forge walked in the wake of Lord Nash through the lofty corridors to their suites in Lord Bentick's palace, he reflected on the calibre of the men usually chosen for this high and difficult office. Their strength and rectitude was as his uncle's had been, a Governor-General prepared to pursue implacable opposition to Warren Hastings when on trial in the House of Commons for extortion in India to the point of losing the Speaker's Chair. But this Governor-General, Lord Bentick, needed even more strength, now the policy of non-intervention in Indian affairs, followed in his uncle's day, had broken down - the country plundered by well-organised brigands and murderous thuggees.

Captain Forge found it hard to imagine this bizarre world of Hindu India as he sat down to Lord Bentick's formal dinner of honour in a banqueting hall, a baronial splendour of red and gold so utterly expressive in its imitative magnificence of the most luxurious London receptions. The ladies billowing bell-sleeved dresses as excessively grandiose as their surroundings. It was hard to believe they were in the heart of India. Only the Indian waiters behind every chair in long tunics and coloured turbans, and punkahs turning endlessly overhead to stir the tepid air, to remind them of that complicated and exotic world just beyond the walls.

To Captain Forge's surprise, tinged with dismay, he found himself seated next to a newly appointed Councillor of India, the redoubtable heavy-browed Lord Thomas Macaulay, historian and famous orator of the House of Commons in every controversy since the Napoleonic War. On the other side his sister Hannah, wife of the historian Trevelyan, but currently hostess to her brother also a new councillor. Scarcely had they begun their subtley spiced soup than Hannah was engaged in spirited argument with a judge on her other side in defence of her brother's new enthusiasm, regularising the legal code to give equality in law for all.

The judge, veteran of the Deccan urged caution. 'Very difficult to play Hammurabi in this land, Madam.'

But Hannah shared a love for the sweep and example of history with both her brother and her husband. 'Anyone should welcome a uniform law code. Look at Rome. Look at Napoleon.'

'They operated in empires that were already homogeneous,' the stout perspiring judge objected, accustomed to his own semi-autonomous domain in the original home of the East India Company, Madras. 'But not India. A quilt of motley states. Rump of the Moghul Empire on the north. The principalities of the Deccan on the south. The Rajahs in their princedoms scattered throughout. Unite them first and then launch your law codes.'

'We could still set an example with a model law code.'

'An example they might loathe rather than admire. An example that might embarrass us one day if we sought expansion to the north.' With a fatigued expression, he dropped more croutons in his second plate of soup. These newcomers wanted to reform India the moment they landed.

Hannah, a daughter of English liberal thought, reacted with horror. 'Conquest? Snatch the kingdoms of those poor Rajahs?'

'Those poor Rajahs might welcome it, Mrs. Trevelyan. A true federation of states, under an overlord, would give the country the unity it needs and the opportunity to create roads, railways and irrigation systems. Until then, any judge in his right mind should arbitrate with some common sense in their ancient way.'

'We must enlighten them with the great advances...'

He regarded her sadly. 'Madam, do your realise how few we are?' He turned to his other neighbour with relief, a vapid woman who could be relied on for the inconsequential but less troublesome talk of Calcutta society.

Flora had been listening in awe to Lord MacAulay expounding his views on education, booming as if addressing the House of Commons, 'the key to change in India, as in England, must be universal education for all. Otherwise any occupying ruler will suffer eternal shame.' Here was a speaker who could command the House to its glory, a man who could lend glory to the crown in India.

She ventured to challenge him. 'What about opium in India?'

Lord MacAulay's growled answer was unexpected from a dedicated reformer. 'Can we change tradition overnight? Always a source of tax in this country, and a great resource of the priesthood for their trances and meditations. Gives them supernatural powers or so the simple people think including their foolish western admirers.'

'I can understand the Government approving a maintenance of opium production, but how can we justify an explosion in crops?'

Lord MacAulay regarded her with the same withering look as once he turned on his Parliamentary opposition. 'You assume, Madam, wrongly that it all goes to China who don't want it. The Chinese are eager to have our Bengali opium because the quality is better than the Malwa opium the Portuguese produce from the Mahratta States in South India, or their own coarse, adulterated product from Yunnan or Schezwan. We have enforced a standard so pure and regular they don't even crack open the chests at Canton for inspection. And before you judge opium too harshly, madam, remember you have almost certainly taken it yourself under its other name of laudanum. The greatest anodyne yet known to man.'

Captain Forge leapt to his wife's defence. 'The missionaries urge opium is a drug of addiction.'

He had listened day in and out to their shipboard companion, a man of earnest purpose who hoped to 'raise a thousand shining temples to Jehovah in the heathen land of China' now missionaries at long last had been given permission to work there.

Lord MacAulay had no sentiment for such hopefuls. 'Confound the missionaries. They will be a headache here now we've been forced to admit them to this country.' He pointed to the judge from Madras. 'My good friend there understands their innumerable gods better than most and respects them. Despite his efforts to explain the unifying concepts of Vishnu, the myriad faces of their religion still confuse me. Will our evangelists try to decipher that confusion and see the face of one God like their own? Will they understand the heart and mind of China?

Captain Forge extended the question. 'Will they understand the opium issue?'

Lord MacAulay shook his head. 'They will jump on that bandwagon of course. Fulminate against opium. Try to ban it, forgetting it is the only panacea from bodily pain - headaches, rheumatism, arthritis, cancer, surgery. What drugs would the missionaries have us use in their place?'

'What if the good always led to the evil?' Flora interposed.

'Endless debate. No answers. Some say yes, some no. Depends on how you take it - through the stomach or lungs. Different answer for every dinner table.'

He lifted his pyramidal glass filled with good red wine to toast their future in China, weary of the subject as they would be in the end but too much the politician to neglect to ask Captain Forge, 'is our noble Lord going to serve demands on China?'

Captain Forge answered with equal directness, 'his very prescence, and the brief he holds, will be a demand.'

Lord MacAulay toyed with a brandied fruit. 'A man to bend?'

'A son of Trafalgar, Sir, a man very much his own master.'

Lord MacAulay curtly opined, 'The Chinese will make no concessions I am told. They fear the same fate as India - creeping occupation.'

'How did England prevail in India, Sir? Was it by diplomacy and negotiation?'

"By default if I'm not mistaken. It's doubtful if India was ever unified in all its history like China. Indeed if Britain could be the first to unify India, it would confer a great merit on this extraordinary continent.'

The toasts and speeches silenced them all. The banquet soon over in a round of formal farewells.

Alone that night at last with Flora, Barron could hardly wait until the last of the horde of male servants had finished their trivial attentions to waltz Flora round the huge bedroom, and to sink into the baronial bed with her in his arms.

'Do you know what happened to my uncle on his first night in Calcutta?' he asked her.

'Nothing so joyous as will happen to us I imagine.'

'He was followed into his bedroom by fourteen persons in white muslim gowns. He might have had some pleasure, as he wickedly said, if the housemaids had not all had beards.'

'Is that where your father got his Byronic propensities?'

For answer he gave her a lingering kiss to affirm his love, desire rising easily in him.

She sighed in her pleasure not entirely from his kiss. 'What a blessing! The bed doesn't move.'

'And wide enough for two.'

He grimaced at the memory of the frustrations of love in a ship's cabin with their canvas walls and hammocks swung from the ceiling. 'not to mention the glorious silence.' No torment of sound from sea and sail or eternal footsteps of the crew on watch above. They celebrated their love with an affection and fulfilment not so common in the arranged or perfunctory marriages of those who surrounded them.

'You're very beautiful,' he told her.

'A woman is never beautiful without a man to love her,'she whispered as his eager caresses affirmed the homage of his love.

* * * * * *

John Davies goes Shooting on Lappa Island

John Davies gloried in his new double-barrelled shotgun as he balanced it in his palm, then hefted it to his shoulder. Such a splendid weapon, easier to handle and less prone to misfire than his old trusty single-barrelled gun, though still weighty like all shot guns.

'Where do you propose to try that monster out?' His managing wife Bettina demanded.

'Lappa Island.' He squinted through the sight avoiding her eye.

'Robber's Island! Not if I have a say.' People were killed or robbed every year over there.

'Well you don't my dear. I can't let Hugh Hodgson down.' He resumed cleaning his gun and checking his gear - shot pouch, priming flask for his bandolier, and container with pre-measured charge and wadding.

She stood over him never ready to yield ground without a skirmish. 'The Portuguese had to abandon their villas on that island.'

He growled back 'because of the Ladrone war.'

'The villages as poor and rundown as any on the coast.'

This was not a day when he was prepared to surrender on the familiar, often genial, battle-field of their marriage. He longed too much for escape onto those beckoning slopes beyond the Macao broads. Out there on Lappa Island he could imagine he was not a target for malice or intimidation in the declining days of the Company, or even assassination as some would have.

Still mindful of Bettina's fears, he was relieved to see no sign of life on the lower scrubby slopes. Nor alas of recalcitrant birds. The snipe refused to break cover.

With the sun already sinking towards the western hills, the burly Hugh grumbled after they had scouted the semi-barren slopes for some hours, trailed by their bearers carrying their ammunition food and game bags, 'we could do with some good hunting dogs.'

'And see them finish up in village cooking pots?'

'Much harder to flush them without,' he complained. A moment later he had a strike.

'There you are. God heard your grievance.'

They turned downhill for home only to find their shots had done more than flush the snipe. Three scruffy men in dirty cotton pants, tied with rope at their waists, were gliding to intercept them from some distance away.

Hodgson urged, 'we'll have to make a run for it.'

But Davies, confident of his fluency in their language, lingered to shoot a bird that had risen almost at their feet, saying 'I can't face that old blatherskite, the Laird, empty handed.' Bringing it down with the second shot.

His panicking bearers refused to fetch the fallen carcass. He hurried towards it alone, oblivious to the fact three more ruffians had sprung from hiding behind him. He was in a desperate situation now, six to one, his only gun useless. He began to parley in Cantonese. For answer, they drew out short heavy axes from their sleeves. The nearest rushed him with axe swinging up to deal a crippling blow. Hodgson charged in to his rescue just in time to crash his own empty gun down on the bandit's arm, smashing both it and the gun. Totally disarmed now except for the mangled butt of his gun, he could do no more than divert a smashing blow away from his head to his shoulder which left him reeling. He slumped to the ground, blood pouring from graze on his cheek and a hideous gash to his arm.

Davies stood over him, screaming in lurid Cantonese at them wanting to know who had bribed them to have him killed. Was it the magistrate of Macao, the Prefect of Heangshan or the Governor himself? How stupid they were! The money they would get for the guns was far more than any bribe those Manchu bandits would ever pay them. They hesitated. The foreign devil was right. Loot in the hand better than a promise from any treacherous Manchu. They seized up the bags and Davies' spare gun and faded away.

Davies tore up his shirt to staunch the heavy bleeding of his friend's wrecked arm. They stumbled together down to the shore in the fading light, Hodgson barely able to stand by the time they reached the beach. No boat to be seen. Stolen as well. Davies swore knowing no other boats were likely to come their way before dawn. 'I hope they all burn in hell.'

However luck soon came their way in the shape of a cutter creeping along the shore, which Davies recognised in astonishment was the Company's own 'Louisa' which had no business to be anywhere near Lappa Island. He soon found out why when he flagged it down to take them off.

When it finally did, after much obvious wrangling, its crew would do no more than back up oars within hailing distance, a 'hideous Charon' of a Welshman at the helm who rejected all Davies' pleas that Hodgson would bleed to death before dawn if he could not reach a doctor.

Still the wreck of a Welshman shook his head. 'If we go back to port, we's in trouble. We stole the cutter. We'd swing for it.'

'Where do you think you can run? Manila? You'd never get past the pirates of the China seas.' Even as he spoke, he knew these sailors were men so inured to hardship they were indifferent to the threat of future rather than present hardship.

The bay was growing darker by the minute, and Davies more frantic as Hodgson lay groaning, pale and shaking from shock and loss of blood.

Davies demanded, 'what's your grievance, men?'

'Bloody captain of the Tara discharged us in Macao, the blackhearted son of Satan. Broke his promise to send us home. Left us high and dry.'

Davies seethed with rage. Jarman Malleson breaking the Company's golden rule since time immemorial again. Captains must never set men like these loose in alien ports to fend for themselves to become the scum and riff-raff of foreign waterfronts.

He promised, 'we'll pay for your keep on landing in Macao and get you a berth in Company ships.'

Protests from the rougher souls on board that they would be thrown in the jug the moment they landed.

'What about us stealing their cutter?'

'I'll go surety for you.'

Argument raged on the cutter. The wilder heads still chasing the dream of making for Manila or Batavia. Or even holding him to ransom. The helsman, for all his savage looks, keeping his head the most.

'You know the Company men?'

'We are the Company,' Davies burst out at last, throwing caution to the winds. 'I am President of its Committee. As such I swear before God I'll not charge you.'

Another burst of palaver on board. The shaken fist of the helmsman prevailed. They seized the oars and rowed the cutter in to ground on the beach shingle. 'Swear,' they demanded before taking them on board.

Davies raised his right hand on high. 'As President of the Select Committee of the East India Company, I solemnly swear before Almighty God to see you safe and bound for Home.'

When the cutter's crew landed them at the tiny stone jetty in the Praya Grande, Davies was as good as his word, vouching for them at Customs and the Hotel Manson. The Welshman, in turn, helped him load Hodgson into a sedan chair which bore him none too gently to the Law house where Dr. Tom, by good luck, was at dinner.

He exclaimed in amazement over the wound. 'Just as well it wasn't six inches higher. No time to waste.'

Davies tried to shield the gruesome spectacle of Hodgson's bloody arm from Holly and Abby. But Abby stoutly followed them all into the ground floor kitchen where they were lifting Hodgson's limp body onto the table. While Dr. Tom stripped his coat, rolled up his sleeves and called for his doctor's bag and boiling water, Abby turned her back without hesitation, untied her lawn petticoat, slipped it off and began to rip it into bandages.

Holly watched from the door intrigued to think Abby's instinctive response might bring her closer to this cheerful young batchelor. Then hopefully she would stop mooning over Adam's lyrical letters and romantic sonnets, dripping with classical allusion, from Canton with their intimations of a world that could never be. Adam had no prospect of inheriting or making any money, apart from the not so minor cosideration he had fights with practically everybody on the Coast through his tongue or pen.

Unfortunately Hodgson, revived by the warm air, was now groaning on his bed of pain. Dr. Tom produced a ball of opium and an opium pipe. He broke off a small piece, stuffed it in the bowl of the pipe, and put a flame to it, saying 'poor devil can't swallow the tincture of opium. Only way to get it into him.' Hodgson's whisper was barely intelligible. Dr. Tom bent close to his lips. 'No mud? Surgery without opium? Can't have you jumping like a grasshopper while I stitch you. Can't have trenches in your face.'

In fact the throbbing agony of Hodgson's face was his most potent argument. He did not resist the narrow stem of the opium pipe, Dr. Tom thrust between his stiff swollen lips, saying 'it won't knock you out but it will reduce the pain so hold still! What we surgeons needs is a drug that can give true sleep. We don't like to be called butchers.' He turned to Abby standing ready to help on the other side with a tender smile of gratitude. 'Grim work but not for ladies.'

Abby challenged his invitation to departure. 'Then time it was.'

Indeed how right Abby was, Holly thought. How foolish it was to put women on such pedestals they could not face reality, at least in outposts where many had to face it daily like the nuns, or missionaries like Mary Grusson.

As Dr. Tom bent to his task, Joshua Law demanded of John Davies, 'do you want me to report this to the Chinese Prefect of Macao?'

Davies regarded him as if he had had a touch of sunstroke. 'And have him round up innocent victims?'

'Let them get away with this it will happen again.'

'We were at fault. We knew Lappa's reputation.'

'If we do nothing, they'll get bolder, especially now the new naval officer is arresting 'smug' boats. I'm told this augurs trouble as you found today.'

Day wondered morosely if 'trouble' was the proper word to use for their fight on Lappa. Surely something more or the bandits would have wounded him like Hodgson. Intimidation? That could mean only one thing. Someone wanted to drive him away from the Coast for ever. Bettina must not know or she'd be urging him onto the first boat to sail for Home.

He answered glumly. 'We're dogs that have had their day. The new seadogs will reign. I pray God I'll live to see their pride have a fall, but I fear it will triumph.'

* * * * * * *

The End of an Era in the New English Factory

John Davies hated the task that brought him to Canton with Ross Newman - to make an inventory of the East India Company's possessions for sale before Lord Nash's imminent arrival. His last act as President of the Select was to sell all the appurtenances of the New English Factory that had for so long signified the elegance of style and orderly power of the Company, that most extraordinary club which had offered him its unique society for twenty years and open bed and board for all comers.

But, in one respect, John Davies was not sorry to see the chandeliers, the great mirrors, the superb silverware, the specially crafted dinner service and other familiar items dispersed. He could not have tolerated their use by Lord Nash who might occupy the New English factory as its legal successor but could never pretend to any of the conventions that made the Company such a remarkable institution. The Latin motto 'for King and Senate', emblazoned over the door of the New English, would now take on a new meaning under the discordant hand of Lord Nash for he would undoubtedly represent a much more aggressive King and country.

As the two men entered the grand reception room they expected to be deserted, they could barely make way for a commotion of servants moving furniture about the room. 'What's going on here?' John Davies demanded of Ross Newman.

Ross Newman threw up his hands in bewilderment. 'Search me! Perhaps Howqua is storing our goods and chattels. It's his right as legal owner of the Factory.'

'Storing them! Moving them round more like.' He accosted the foreman, 'who gave you chop?'

The foreman bowed respectfully ,'Governor chop. Viceroy Lu come.'

'Viceroy Lu? I can't believe him.' No Viceroy had ever visited the New English Factory for one very good reason. The lowest mandarin in rank was considered above any merchant, especially a foreign devil barbarian merchant.

'You'd better believe him in case he's right,' the placid Ross Newman said sensibly. 'He might be curious to see how the foreign devils live. Today's his one chance with the Company officially dead, a case of now or never. But why shove the chairs around?'

John Davies wagged a finger in disapproval. Ross Newman was always too fond of the good life to bother improving his insights into the mysteries of China. 'To conform to the strictest etiquette. You see the Viceroy, as delegate of the Emperor, must sit facing south.'

'Why south for crying out loud?'

'Because the Emperor is the Son of Heaven and therefore of the Sun shining from the south at high noon.'

Ross Newman shrugged his disinterest. 'Mumbo-jumbo to me!'

The hovering foreman jigged in obsequious bows to each man. 'Many high officials come. The Governor, the Prefect, the Magistrate, the Tartar-General and the Hoppo. They want to see the foreign devil King.' He gestured at King George's portrait commanding the wall, now restored by Chinnery. 'You must leave please. Now.'

Davies fumed, 'You cannot order me to leave.

'Yes sir. Company all finish.' More bows.

'I work for new Taipan.' Davies brandished his cane. But the foreman kept on bowing knowing the tenancy of the new Taipan did not begin until mid-summer at the earliest 'Old Taipan go now.'

Davies bluffed. The Viceroy's visit was one he longed to witness. 'I go Petition Gate!' The same form of protest that had earned Dr. Jarman his honour of Iron-headed Rat; one that never moved that gate to open but made sure the whole of Canton would know the Viceroy had made a secret visit to the ocean barbarian factory.

The foreman, terrified by the thought of such a scandal, chose to 'save face'. He pointed to the door in the recess of the dining room which led into the service hall beyond. 'No fanqui eyes on Viceroy.'

John Davies moved briskly away flourishing his stick, Ross Newman sluggishly behind him, saying 'we might hear something to our advantage' for he was fluent in both Mandarin and Cantonese. The foreman ignored him, a Cantonese not so wedded to rigid etiquette as a Han Chinese might be. Let Viceroy Lu's lictors discipline the unruly foreign devils if they would. He could hear them already, their hideous howl announcing the Viceroy's name and titles ahead of his eight-bearer green sedan chair.

Viceroy Lu's face was twisting in distaste as his bearers neared the New English Factory, fingers tangled nervously in his long coral and turquoise beads, at the sight of the naked ugliness of the imposing row of square-fronted Factories. They had none of the graceful curving lines of Chinese public buildings, flowing and blending the one with the other. No, these edifices were uncompromising and uncivilised as one would expect from ocean barbarians.

What misbegotten luck to be sent to Kwantung to keep this truculent region in order, bad luck he had brought on his own head when he had bought the leaders of the Miao rebellion in Hunan Province at the cost of a million taels. How could he repeat that trick of winning a war without fighting a battle when this enemy was so utterly different? Pirates, who had never been subdued in China's long history, free to move on the oceanic fringes of Empire unlike the dogmen of Miao surrounded and outnumbered in their hills and forests. Pirates who would be unlikely to make any treaty with him as they had already formed an alliance with the dangerous red-haired demons. In this monstrous impasse, all he could hope to do was absolutely nothing and pray the vengeance of either Court or Censorate would not reach so far. He did not want to end up in exile like Viceroy Li before him.

Viceroy Lu's bearers carried him through a kneeling Tartar guard of honour and up the marble Grand Staircase. He stepped out of the chair with grave dignity. As the Tartar Hoppo, nephew of the Emperor, and the Tartar-General greeted him hands clasped three times to their foreheads, he returned their greeting in kind, according them equality of rank as High Manchu. Both men were dressed informally like himself in plain blue, red-bordered tunics as they could not appear in full ceremonial dress before barbarians - the Hoppo's emblazoned with a bird, the Tartar-General's with a beast.

The Hoppo led the way into the Grand Salon wearing his perpetual gold-bedecked smile. Viceroy Lu halted impassively before the dominating centrepiece of the room, the unveiled portrait of the barbarian monarch over the marble fireplace. He hid his outraged astonishment with difficulty. How improper! The monarch exposed for all to see! Not concealed by yellow gauze as proper for such an august personage! Dressed without any symbols of majesty like dragons and clouds! Just what he would expect from an uncivilised people!

He turned to the deferential welcome of the lesser dignitaries - the Governor, the Prefect and the Chief Magistrate - before he settled himself in a massive leather chair. He sipped steaming tea from a paper-thin enscrolled cup. He speared dainty sweetmeats and dried fruits from a circular japanned tray. He traded informal gossip of the port with them in a jovial mood as long as was polite. Then at last he turned to the Hoppo and Prefect with the question that preoccupied him most.

'Can we control these new barbarians?'

The Hoppo could not afford optimism. 'They will revolt against the eight regulations again.'

The more ingratiating Prefect could not believe these men willing to disrupt their own trade.

In the silence that ensued while Viceroy Lu knocked the ash from his pipe into a fragile dish, the Chief Magistrate spoke up. 'It's a general rule, Excellency, that the worst of men are fondest of change and commotion hoping they may benefit themselves.'

The three high officials nodded their respect for his opinion as a just and incorruptible official who could be a most preponderating influence against tumults and rebellions.

The Viceroy felt impelled to assert his love of order before such an honourable man. 'We must remember what the first Emperor of the Ming said to his heir "the boat in which we sit is supported by the water which, if roused, will overwhelm it." Remember the water represents the people and the Emperor only the boat.'

The Chief Magistrate's benign countenance concealed his real thoughts. He knew perfectly well both the Viceroy and the Hoppo were only anxious about the foreign devils for one reason. Their income was plunging downwards as the smuggling trade of the Red Circle of the new Triads drove out the old system integrated with the mandarin's cumshaw. But, hoping soon for an honourable retirement to a Buddhist monastery, he did not share the misgivings of the Hoppo and Tartar-General as they watched Viceroy Lu take a pinch of snuff from his snuff bottle. The more deliberate he became, the more dangerous his cross-examination would be.

Viceroy Lu turned to the Tartar-General first. 'I asked you General Ha Feng if we can control these barbarians and you have not yet replied.'

The General smiled, plucking at the ends of his straggling mustache, but his words belied his smile. 'All our thousand war junks could not withstand one of their frigates. It is Koxinga all over again.'

Koxinga, the most famous pirate in China's history, had dominated the entire coast of China from his base in Taiwan in defiance of the Ming Emperor of his day.

The Governor winced at this bluntness, a habit of the Tartar race he could never approve, preferring the subtlety of parable himself. But the Viceroy knew his history. 'Koxinga's heirs gave their allegiance in the end as the Ladrones did.

And so may these ocean-barbarian foreign devils, even if they do smash our thousand warjunks now, even if they land their armies as in India.' Necessary bravado but his hand trembled as he spoke.

General Ha Feng flicked an imaginary piece of dust from his knee. 'If they pass by the forts we will smash their ships. If they dare to land, we will crush them. They carry no shields nor spears. They fight battles in trousers so tight they can't get up if they fall over. '

The Viceroy was satisfied, not by the General's facile assurances which everyone knew to be smoke not fire, but because he had taken the bait of declaring a policy which he, not the Viceroy, must answer for should he fail.

But the Chief Magistrate was in despair. The Viceroy should have grilled the General, insisted on better defences, knowing perfectly well the fixed cannon in those forts demanded experienced gunners trained to judge when to fire at the precise moment they had ships within their sights, not untrained levies from a distracted and sullenly rebellious province who would never withstand a heavy bombardment. Levies were the only force they had as the General was siphoning the necessary funds into his private treasure chest. Yet this was not an enemy to be frightened by terrifying emblems painted on the soldiers' chests or acrobatic menaces.

Viceroy Lu rose regally, admonishing as he led the way from the room, 'keep them in cages like fighting crickets! Even if they demand and win several cages. Let them roam free in China? Never!'

John Davies had been able to follow enough snatches of the conversation for him to assess Viceroy Lu as a man likely to greet any overtures from Lord Nash with absolute rigidity, which boded no good at all for the good lord. 'We can expect no division among them.'

'No, then what chance will he have,' Newman added.

'Against these masters of survival? None!' Davies predicted.

* * * * * *

Rumours of Love and War in Macao

By the time John Davies returned to Macao, Abby was engaged to Dr. Tom and so absorbed in him she had neither time nor thought for Holly. When Holly protested, she brushed her aside saying she had to marry 'all of a rush' and 'a body only gets married once.' The 'rush' seemed to be her determination to get married to Dr. Tom before Lord Nash arrived from Calcutta, so he could invoke his right to be married by the Company clergyman.

Holly was contrite then. Why should Abby be interested in Holly's moody introspections on the theme 'to love or not to love' when her own undivided infectious joy pervaded the whole household like the golden sunshine of a Macao spring on a still day. It was a joy of wondrous enchantment that she had found the love of her life as reward for the gamble of coming to China, that she had found an involvement for her life that would occupy her with more than serving tiffin for idle visitors. Holly envied Abby in her own fear that she, with her more critical character, would never find the same consumnation in her life.

She vowed that she would put such thoughts, bred of the inherent sadness of change, utterly from her mind whenever she saw Dr. Tom's perpetual grin of delight.

On the knotty question of a wedding dress, Abby mourned 'pity I haven't got Adam here to design it for me.'

Mary Ann objected it was hardly 'the done thing' to consult a rejected suitor. It has been such a relief to herself and Joshua when Adam had suddenly departed from Macao and settled in Manila where he was now playing both merchant and plantation owner, thanks to an inheritance, and, among other things, shipping rice to Holly.

'He'd have you in fancy dress.' Holly backed Mary Ann.

Together they haunted the nimble seamstresses feverishly sewing a mountainous yardage of satin and lace for the ultra-bouffant design she had chosen for her wedding dress. Holly jested she would never fit into the tiny Company chapel where the Reverend Vaux was to marry them, let alone the South American singers who had offered to sing at her wedding.

They had arrived on a ship inexplicably blown off course for Calcutta but made the best of it by staging their operas for Macao instead. Everyone who was anyone had turned out for their first performance to pack the little red plush opera house of faded glory, satin programs in hand. Nobody troubled that the Company had neither tenor nor soprano, least of all Holly who had never been to any opera and was vastly amused by the posturings of the singers - 'caterwaulings' Abby said.

Sean surprised her by weaving his way through the crowded foyer towards her. How distinguished and easy he looked in evening dress, unlike so many others who really earned the mockery of 'stuffed shirts', as he bowed over her hand with elaborate formality saying 'I'm overjoyed to see you!'. Nothing formal about the warmth of his grasp or the intensity of his gaze, but no betrayal of the anxiety he felt either.

'And I you,' she replied softly. 'I didn't see you in the theatre. Were you perhaps in one of the boxes?'

'Those attuned to the favours of the Governor of Macao would tell you we Jarmans are relegated to the circle.'

'How very insulting!' She exclaimed, angry for him.

'Doesn't worry uncle, Holly. Opera bores him. As for me, I like to hear the arias I know. Do you sing Holly?'

She grimaced.'Me sing? Screech rather. I know all young ladies are expected to bore everyone to sobs with dreadful renditions of tedious songs. Back home, girls have to learn how lest they be left on the shelf.'

'There'd be a tussle to be first to take you off the shelf particularly as you have other talents that would win any man - business you don't disclose. You are one of us.'

Her pleasure in the intimacy of the moment turned to dismay. She fussed with her fan to buy time to think. Had Jim Peel dropped any hints or had she been too careless with her buying in Canton?

'Who told you?' She asked annoyed, yet pleased, he knew. 'It was Jim Peel wasn't it?'

'No. The little green eye of the God of jealousy did. Seeing you closeted with him as if you were lovers but not so wall-eyed as to see you were not, seeing he was deferring to you as a Captain would to an employer. Then I remembered your knowledge of ships, your interest in prices. You gave yourself away.'

'Does that make me less of a lady?'

'It makes you a more desirable lady.'

'Now you know my secret, does that give you influence over me?'

'I would dearly love to have influence over you but I don't want to earn it by blackmail.'

They were aware only of each other, overwhelmed by their feelings as the crowd swirled around them. The touch of his hand light on her arm, all he dared in this place. 'How beautiful you are, Holly!'

The intensity of both was tinged with despair for each knew without words there was no satisfactory way they could see each other in this tight community, Holly supposing the only barriers between them were the customs of the port and the hostility of his senior parters. She still did not know he was engaged which meant he could not, should not, see her.

In the weeks that followed, Sean found no comfort as Holly did in the fuss and bustle of the wedding preparations, and the devotional comings and goings of all the chief male actors in the drama revelling in their various roles - Dr. Tom as bridegroom, John Norris as best man, Joshua Law as proxy father of the bride and Billy Howe as Master of Ceremonies. Abby, volatile under the strain, would threaten to elope and be married by some captain three miles out to sea, or grow sad to think neither her mother nor father would be there.

Holly was the only bridesmaid to follow Abby down the brief aisle of the simple Company chapel - neither altar nor images to glorify their communion with God. Only the resonant distinction of the Reverend Vaux's Oxford accent and the vibrating splendour of the opera company's voices lofting in the cadences of Keble's new marriage hymn, 'The Voice that Breathed O'er Eden'. Tears in Holly's eyes when they reached the words 'for dower of blesed children, for love and faith's sweet sake, for high mysterious union which naught on earth may break.' Tears of pity for herself that she might never know such dower, love or union; unworthy tears on Abby's high day she chided herself as Abby accepted the golden ring from Dr. Tom, radiating the joy of the dower of each to each with a glow that touched them all with its affirmation of good in God's universe.

* * * * * *

Lord Nash arrives in Macao

Neither Davies nor his wife Bettina normally wasted siesta time. While all Macao slept, he sat in his private sitting room upstairs in the Company headquarters, his quill pen moving fluently as he translated a Chinese classic on the history of the Sung dynasty's conquest by Genghis Khan in the twelfth century. Bettina's needle moved rhythmically in and out of the large tapestry before her creating a scene of idealised European peasants disporting themselves in a leafy landscape.

John Davies paused, saddened by the thought of the last Sung Emperor, a mere boy of twelve, driven by the relentless pursuit of Kublai Khan's troops to leap to his death from a boat off Kowloon. The thought of the dying days of the Honourable John Company provoked the same melancholy. Its structure had once seemed as solid as the spacious stone building in which he now sat or the ships it built. Its fleet would be dispersed. The old teak warriors would be sold or broken up. The like of the stately bluff-ended tea vessels would never be seen again. Their superb reputation for stable reliability, the honour of having served before their masts, would be forgotten.

A sound dragged him from his reveries. Drums in high noon siesta time loud enough to wake all Macao from the dead? Drums to summon devotees to secret rites in the jungle here in Macao? Drums from the Portuguese Governor's residence next door? Obviously not to summon the Governor to some secret rites. He must be elsewhere or he would never allow it. John Davies slammed the window down at first. No business of his if the Governor's caffre slaves felt homesick for Africa and amused themselves. He tried to work on, savouring the taut simplicity of the story before him. Bettina bided her time, knowing an explosion of temper would surely follow if the caffres failed to stop.

A despairing wail began to rise and fall over the ever louder, more frenzied drumbeat. Davies began to pace the room, working himself into a frenzy fulminating against the Portuguese Governor. Clearly the drummers were alone, no one likely to stop them. Seizing his walking stick from the coat rack, he cried, 'I'll drum some sense into those caffres.' He started through the door, Bettina in full cry after him, snatching at his sleeve and begging him not to start trouble.

'Those caffres start the trouble not me.'

He threw her hand off, outraged, and started down the broad stairs. By the time she had reached the street, her husband had vanished within the delicately beautiful facade of the Governor's residence next door. None of the Portuguese guards, usually lolling there in their dingy uniforms, to be seen. Only Maxwell Raine in sight demanding to know most urgently where the President was.

'Oh, Mr. Raine please, my husband's in there picking a fight with the caffres.'

'Raine to the rescue, Ma'am, never fear,' he cried as the door swallowed him.

He found John Davies shouting in pidgin at the swaying, chanting circle of cross-legged drummers, dark defiant eyes glowing in the dark of the candle-lit basement; John Davies seizing the drum from the nearest at hand and giving a furious drumroll on it with his own cane. The drummer frozen, staring at him as he must once have stared at the slave gang that betrayed him in the jungle. No mistaking the look in their eyes. One of them began to drum again in defiance of Davies, knowing he had no right to touch them. Davies lifted his stick and began to beat the crouching figure on the shoulder.

Raine caught his arm. 'You'll get killed some dark night.'

John Davies resisted half-heartedly 'they wouldn't dare.'

'Not if the Governor ordered revenge for trespass? Have you forgotten he barely tolerates us here that you go flogging his slaves?'

John Davies allowed himself to be led away. Raine was right. The Governor was the law in Macao in matters where the Chinese mandarin would not interfere.

'By the way, what brought you here to charge to my rescue like a perfect gallant knight may I ask?' Normally Raine would be dozing after an ample lunch, which never seemed to add one iota to his long lean waistline.

'Disaster, Mr. President,' Maxwell Raine announced as they climbed the stairs to his private quarters. 'the House of Fairlie has closed its doors.'

'This calls for a very stiff rum,' John Davies sympathised as he poured Maxwell Raine one, and one for himself, shocked by the news. The old and stable House of Fairlie's, said to be as safe as the Bank of England, bankrupt! Raine's delivered to the speculative market of short-term finance now and handicapped in playing the price market compared to their fierce rival, Jarman Malleson's, financed by the Parsees of Bombay. This bad news was the precursor of a new unfamiliar era.

John Davies felt bleak, weary and uncertain whether he could play the part of First Secretary to Lord Nash's Trade Superintendent. All of a sudden he felt the time had come at last to return home to England. He hid his troubled thoughts from his old and dear friend, Raine, who had enough of his own now.

'The Company's new Finance Agency will save your bacon.'

'Unless they drive it out with their howls it is the Old Company back under another name.'

Davies added caustically, 'strange how none of them complained of the Company until it was irrevocably at an end, least of all Dr. Jarman who owes the Company everything he is today.'

If John Davies had not already secretly decided to return to England as soon as he could arrange it, his first experience of Lord Nash would certainly have precipitated that decision.

He had gone out on the Company cutter Louisa himself to welcome Lord Nash the moment H.M.S. Andromache had dropped anchor in Taipa Roads to bring him ashore, only to find that Lord Nash had left already on one of Dr. Jarman's fast boats ready for days to intercept him farther out. Worse, Lord Nash had accepted accommodation in the mansion Dr. Jarman maintained for visiting captains instead of the rooms Davies had prepared in the Company residence, excusing himself that he could not be entangled with John Company's past reputation. What of Jarman Malleson's reputation, Davies raged to Bettina?

His summons into Lord Nash's prescence, Captain Forge standing behind him, did nothing to assuage that rage. Summoned not to be consulted but to be told what Lord Nash proposed with all the hauteur of a coral button mandarin towards a crystal. Yes he, not only the ex-President of the Select Committee of the East India Company in China but also a renowned expert on Chinese affairs, told that Lord Nash was instructed to announce his arrival at Macao by letter to the Viceroy.

Davies was horrified. What simpleton had let Lord Nash believe he could write direct to the Viceroy? If he did, neither the Viceroy nor his minions would take delivery of it. He could, and must, write only to the leader of the Co-Hong, Howqua.

'Wouldn't it be best to wait, milord?' he ventured.

'Wait for what?' Angry impatience in every line of the man as beads of sweat rolled into his ruddy beard.

'Excellency, Howqua will wish to greet you first here in Macao to arrange a passport.

'Which means, Mr. Davies, nothing more nor less than I must announce myself first to the leader of the Co-Hong, your Howqua, who I'm given to understand by Dr. Jarman is no more than a mere merchant. That is utterly contrary to my instructions.' He thumped his Royal Sign Manual. 'I'll leave for Canton at the end of the week, passport or not.'

'No chop from the Customs House at the Bogue, no passing the Bogue forts, sir,' his deputy protested, scandalised that he should propose to flout the most basic of China's Imperial laws.

Lord Nash brushed this aside, 'I'm not a merchant to require a licence to trade.'

'But you do require a passport. If you try to pass the Bogue fort at the mouth of the Pearl River their guns will make you think twice.'

'The Andromache will be more than a match.'

Hell's bells, this madman was going to crash through like John Bull personified. Only Captain Forge's warning glance stopped him from reading Lord Nash a lecture on the delicate balance of peace in the port.

John Davies perservered. He must dissuade Lord Nash from this folly. 'If the Andromache proceeds even as far as the Bogue it will give the Viceroy great alarm and offence. You see warships are forbidden.'

Advice which Lord Nash tersely rejected. 'A show of strength will do no harm. They'll pay more respect if we rattle the sabre.'

John Davies resorted to Chinese aphorism. 'A river dammed in one place will find a path by another.'

'What does that riddle mean?' Lord Nash asked crossly.

'Your linguist, who guarantees the ship that brings you up river, will be heavily fined and very likely tortured. And your comprador, Howqua, an old frail man also.'

Lord Nash, primed by Dr. Jarman to distrust John Davies as too soft, too much a Chinaphile, was dismissive. 'Such a civilised country can't be capable of such barbarism.'

Davies desisted. Reason futile. How could he possibly explain the responsibility system of Chinese justice to a man like Nash - that it was the means of maintaining an equilibrium of behaviour in a vast sprawling system of federal government down to the smallest community of households? The system acted as a deterrent, cruel as it seemed in Christian eyes.

Lord Nash pronounced, 'change must start somewhere.'

'And what if it leads to battle, sir.'

'They would not stand up to the fire of a few steady British troops with a hundred sepoys.'

'The Tartar troops may have deteriorated from the glory of their conquest of China but not to that degree, sir.'

Lord Nash rose abruptly to signal the interview at an end. 'Dr. Jarman has kindly arranged a reception this week so my wife and daughters can meet new friends consonant with their station before we leave for Canton next week.'

John Davies left in a rage, wondering if Lord Nash had read the second leg of his instructions in the Royal Sign Manual that he must conform to the laws and usages of China. If he had, he would know that he intended to breach not one, but two, laws of China - the first, if he marched into Canton without the

Viceroy's passport, and the second, if he addressed him over the head of the Co-Hong. Lord Palmerston had either been incredibly badly advised to allow such incompatible instructions to exist in one brief, or he was a devious and naive fool who understood the paradox but wanted a bet each way without the slightest comprehension of the tragedy inherent in the gamble.

He left Lord Nash staring out of the widow's paradisical view, utterly indifferent to it. Why had the Colonial Office given him three such spineless ex-Company men as Sir George Robart, John Davies and Hugh Hodgson as aides? Men said to have the necessary experience. Experience of what? Disarming him so he would have to go into battle like a man with unwilling conscripts. It did not occur to him those conscripts had the wisdom to spare the battle and win the peace, that their determination to fight with moral power might be the better path to defend the honour of Britain than the use of the mailed fist which his aggressive tutors urged.

Over lunch, Barron Forge confessed his dismay at Lord Nash's treatment of John Davies to his wife, Flora. 'Says he won't be beholden to Company men. So what does he do, instead, but become beholden to the masters of the opium trade. Why is he dancing to their tune, for God's sake?'

'Someone in London has given him orders.'

'That would be all very well if Jarman Malleson were paying the purse for the piper not the Company, Flora, who will still bear most of the cost of the Trade Commission, a cost let me tell you far more than that of the old Select Committee.'

'Then make Jarman Malleson pay.'

'And have us all dance to their tune, not just Lord Nash? Never. The fact we don't will be our only salvation, my love.'

'I don't see how you can wage a secret war against your own superior.'

He kissed away her frown. 'You forget that any sailor worth his salt learns how to circumvent his captain behind his back if he's a mind to it.'

* * * * * *

Lord Nash lords it in Macao

As a festive procession of all the acceptable ladies of Macao streamed towards the reception for Lord Nash and his family at the Scott mansion, they passed the annual procession for St. Agnes feast day proceeding down from the convent of St. Clare to St. Joseph's Church. Convent children and nuns with angelic faces bearing the image of St. Agnes aloft on a beflowered platform. Holly was acutely aware of the symbolic contrast between the vision of man's high spiritual life and the reality of the money changers of the temple.

Lord and Lady Nash greeted them at the door as if receiving in their own principality - the ladies ahead of Holly bobbing, even curtseying with a swish of their generous skirts, in their excitement at meeting a real live peer of the realm.

'Heaven help us. Drawing rooms will have to double in size,' Holly exclaimed as the reception room became awash with flounced satin and taffeta.

People were flying at each other in such effusive greeting their guests of honour could never have guessed that many usually ignored each other as of the wrong caste or rank, or conducted gossipy trivial feuds out of boredom.

For the first time since Holly had arrived in Macao she felt overwhelmingly alone. The original foursome of her early days now broken up. Abby married. The jilted Adam in Manila. Her faithful escort, Billy, flirting with a young house guest of Marjorie Raine, having his usual success as a China raconteur to judge by her constant ripple of laughter. Holly suppressed a tinge of envy. After all she had firmly discouraged his interest in her.

She forced herself to move about the room looking, she scarcely dared admit, for Sean. She discussed Walter Scott's latest novel with Rebecca Norris. She cornered Ross Newman to compare the latest music from home. And then there was Sean, Sean squiring Lord Nash's eager daughters in tandem with David Malleson and so attentive to them she was seized by searing jealousy, yet by fury to think she was so much at the mercy of her attraction to him. She tried to assure herself he had been conscripted for duties as a host, then morosely remembered how long she would have to suffer the presence of the Nash girls in Macao - for the term of his appointment.

She tried to see them dispassionately. They had a certain style, good looks that fell short of beauty, a delicacy of tawny and cream colouring and well-balanced features. But they were also undeniably shallow in speech and obvious in tactics like their mother.

For distraction she responded to a summons to see a magic show out on the verandah, magic beyond comprehension. How could a man spin plates, then giant bowls and last water-filled bowls of flowers on sticks? Or make a seed grow into a tree from a marble floor, a tree waist-high and bearing fruit?

She turned away at last to see Sean still in intimate conversation with Rose Nash who seemed to be directing a stream of questions at him, threaded with demure glances, requiring him to bend ever closer to her provocative exposure of curving shoulder and bosom.

If such flirtation in women was what really appealed to Sean, Holly thought petulantly, she would have no more to do with him. She would take Captain MacDonald's advice that any liaison with a Malleson clansman meant danger and disappointment. She would not enable her love to grow like the magician's plant, stage by stage. If she allowed any small leaf to grow she would find it had sprung from a marble floor with a sterile fruit like the conjurer's tree.

She lingered alone on the verandah looking down on the riding lights of the ships swinging at anchor on the light swell of the loitering sea. Tim Bird materialised at her side, his expressive round face full of concern.

'What are you mooning for, lass? Home?'

'Sometimes. But not for home as you mean it. I have none.'

'Women are made for going forward, lass. They have to when they marry. Hence make better colonists than men.'

She retorted with a flitting smile. 'You're still here.'

'Too old to make a new start, my dear.' He whispered conspiratorially, 'Don't get too secure here, lass.'

'Are you warning me against marriage, now?'

'Dear me, no. But be ready to abandon Macao one day.'

She was shocked now. 'Will it come to that?'

'My very word! If the good Lord makes the British lion roar in Canton, the echo will be heard in Macao. They'll flood Macao with soldiers, terrorise the women and create havoc. They'll threaten everyone to teach the Scotch bandits a lesson. You must warn the Mad Davies,' he urged using his nickname. 'He must find an excuse, any excuse to leave Canton. He must be here when it happens. If not his life could be in danger as well as that of Lord Nash.'

Holly was aghast. 'Why can't you tell him all this yourself?'

'Simple, my dear. Too dangerous to be seen with him.'

'Why should I believe you?' Holly asked in sudden doubt. Such whispers of warning were all too redolent of romantic rebels like Paul Revere or Bonnie Prince Charlie. Secret dashes on horseback or messages across the heather.

'I alone in all Macao have no axe to grind. Nothing to lose but my birds.' He slipped away, silent and unobtrusive as they.

What birds did he mean, Holly brooded, his tropic birds or his pigeons? Carrier pigeons! Ah there lay the clue to his riddles, his money. Therefore perhaps she should believe him.

She lured Davies to the verandah to deliver Tim's message. 'You must not go to Canton, or if you do, you must not stay there.'

Davies betrayed no doubt nor surprise, but merely queried, 'how am I supposed to do that when I am commanded by the esteemed Lord Nash to be at his side? Besides I don't believe the Viceroy is sending troops to Macao.'

'Do you mean Tim is lying?'

'I mean the plot is more subtle than he presumes. Men may pretend to be vice-regal troops when they are not for purposes of their own.'

'Who would be strong enough to play such games with the Governor of Macao?'

'The Red Circle who are seizing power from the Elder Brothers of the Heaven and Earth society!' Holly wondered briefly if John Davies deserved his nickname the Mad Davies after all.

Billy Howe studied them curiously. 'What's going on?'

She confessed rather than avoided, 'I was making sure I have a daily news bulletin from Canton.'

'I could have given you that if you'd asked me.'

'Davies will be closer to the heart of battle.'

Billy's head on one side like Joshua's Newfoundland dog. 'You're up to no good, Holly. Do you know whose side you're on this time?'

Because he had struck home she tossed her head and stalked off, leaving him desolate. He went to Mary Ann for consolation. She was the only one who understood that under his jocularity and insouciance he really loved Holly. She urged him to patience. Then, in a mood of mischief, he teased the Nash girls with stories in praise of the Jarman Malleson clan. After all what could serve his cause better than for his infuriating competitor, Sean Jarman, to find a better catch in Rose Nash than Holly?

* * * * * *

Lord Nash is as Good as his Word

Lord Nash left Macao in the warship H.M.S. Andromache without a passport or waiting for Viceroy Lu's envoys, Howqua and Mowqua, already on their way to welcome him in Macao. But not without taking precautions for his own safety by transferring into the cutter Loiusa, which was capable of running the channel beyond the reach of the guns of the Bogue forts.

From the first the elements of China combined to reject Lord Nash. The humidity persisted at intolerable levels. The rain was unremitting. The Pearl River was still in turbulent flood. The Common between the Factories and the river was kneedeep in water. His baggage was broken into at the Customs House. The ground floors of all the Factories, including the New English, were awash with sloppy slimy water in which deadly snakes, scorpions and debris lurked.

In truculent mood, the new Trade Superintendent summoned all residents of all thirteen Factories of the foreign settlement to the Grand Salon on the first floor of the New English Factory. In high formality of full dress uniform he read the King's Commission while Captain Forge wondered what the King, who stared from his portrait with a lofty impassivity befitting majesty, would have made of the incongruity of the setting if he could have joined them now.

Next he dictated a contentious letter to the Viceroy announcing his arrival to his interpreter, Dr. Norris, who pleaded in vain, 'you can't head your letter with the character for 'letter'. You must announce it as a petition.'

Lord Nash dismissed the difference as utterly trivial, 'surely a letter is a letter.'

'In China, a Viceroy can only accept a letter from an equal.'

Lord Nash rejected the objection. 'I am not Chinese.'

'Even more reason why the Viceroy would not recognise any letter from you until the Emperor changes the law which forbids it. You must send it through Howqua.'

Lord Nash flatly refused. Instead he sent his unfortunate secretary to the barred Petition Gate, exposed to a jeering crowd, where he was obliged to stand for three hours exposed to a jeering crowd, insults by soldiers and the pretence of minor officials they were referring his case to some mysterious superior, until he could stand no more.

Viceroy Lu was perplexed. Surely a reasonable man would have written a memorial to the Emperor for his permission considering the exceptional nature of his case? Then this barbarian 'Eye' would not have obliged him to respond by denouncing his presence in a letter of florid and stereotyped officialise despatched through Howqua.

'Even England has its rules. How much more the Celestial Empire! How flaming bright are its great laws and ordinances, more terrible than the awful thunderbolt! Under the whole bright heaven no one dares to disobey them!'

Lord Nash's anger that Howqua was the emissary for this letter turned to outright fury when Dr. Norris, by now mortally ill, was indiscreet enough to translate the mode of address to him literally as 'Laboriously Vile'. John Davies persuaded him the ideograph could also mean low, or mean in station, but was forced to admit Lord Nash had been grossly insulted and to venture that the

Viceroy did not necessarily endorse the letter himself in face of Lord Nash's stormy pacing.

Lord Nash halted in mid-stride. 'Explain yourself.'

'That letter would have passed through several hands, Sir. Through the Prefect of Canton and the Governor at the very least. They both had a grievance against you for assuming a higher rank than theirs. As did Howqua. he made an exhausting and futile journey to Macao to welcome you. You departed without waiting for him. You then grossly insulted him by going over his head, if you'll forgive me pointing it out, Sir.'

Lord Nash knew he would demean his own rank if he belaboured his subordinates' arguments. He dismissed them.

'Who do you think did it?' Captain Forge queried John Davies as they retreated to their quarters at the rear of the New English Factory.

'Howqua of course. He's the one to be ground between those two millstones, the Viceroy and Lord Nash. Don't forget merchants are so low on the scale in China, so laboriously vile themselves, they learn to sharpen other weapons.'

'God help him!' Captain Forge was not so inimical to Lord Nash as to wish him too much ill.

John Davies, more hostile, found a Chinese proverb apt. 'The gods cannot help a man who loses opportunities.'

Meanwhile the man, whose untimely honesty had precipitated Lord Nash's wrath, Dr. Norris, lay writhing on an unbearable bed of pain beyond any care for any Trade Superintendent's official predicament; tortured hour by endless hour by the agony of his swollen stomach, his son, John Norris, in anguished vigil beside him. John wondered if his father had some premonition of his fate when he had stood wan and exhausted before his tiny congregation the Sunday before, leading them with such heart-rending supplication in the hymn 'Jesus, lover of my soul, let me to thy bosom fly.' Had he hoped for release with his great work of a Chinese dictionary complete at last? One thing was already clear. Release was certain.

Dr. Tom had called in the only other surgeon in the port, Dr. Jarman, who had agreed with his diagnosis. Dr. Norris was dying. If they dared abdominal surgery he would die just the same. All they could do was to give him tincture of opium in alcohol, sponge him and hope for the tranquil death his Saviour had so far denied him, his leaving of life itself as much a martyrdom as his life in China had been.

John sat distraught through the lingering hours tormented not only by the dying of his father, but the wonder how his father had sustained his vision so long in a country where he believed Satan kept his throne and where so few had had any curiosity to seek the Book of Inspired Truth. Yet he had endured believing the temple of Christianity would soon be built on the ruins of Chinese superstition and myriads sing the praises of Him whose name was above every other name, and before whose name every man should bow.

His father's dearest wish had been that his only son, bent on a career on the China coast, would vow to carry on his work. But John knew he could not give that vow to his father even to ease his dying. God had chosen him for other work - to use the skills and insights learnt in his adopted country to prevent misunderstanding between East and West.

His sister, Rebecca, was the one who would fulfil his dream, as his father should have known. And it was Rebecca who stilled his guilt that he had not been able to accept an evangelising mission as they knelt beside their father's grave in the walled sanctuary Dr. Norris himself had won from the Portuguese government for a Protestant graveyard when John's mother died and he had refused to commit her to a Catholic burial ground.

As gentle as the mother she had lost so young she replied, 'I could not bear to watch you suffer the same disappointments as he did, John.'

John held up his two hands. 'His converts less than the fingers on my two hands after thirty years, and those in danger of their lives.'

'As yours would be if you pushed the gospel here.'

'I'd never take the risks Leah a Fah has - giving out pamphlets to candidates outside the provincial examination hall. How could he be so naive?'

'Or honest. Urged to spread the Word of the Lord, a Word he saw as the sword of rebellion.'

He seized Rebecca by the shoulders. 'You understand, don't you Rebecca, I could not ask them to become martyrs and exiles as Leah a Fah has become.'

'I understand you were born in China and half your heart is here.'

'Both of us are children in limbo, Rebecca, with eyes to see too much.'

He gripped both her hands tightly with his own. 'No one will ever understand as you do, Rebecca.'

Or as Kaida Hung did, he thought as they strolled homeward silently together. For he too was in limbo, one of the few who thought, as those Ming Emperors had, that men should tolerate religion. He knew the Manchu dynasty, as alien rulers, would write their death warrant if they did. Already its present Emperor, Tao Kuang, could not forget he had never been free of trouble in any one year of his long reign.

* * * * * *

Counter Checkmate by Lord Nash

Howqua maintained an impeccable calm before the other Co-Hong merchants as they sat waiting for the foreign merchants to answer his summons to conference in the imposing Grand Reception Hall of Consoo House in all their glory of embroidered gowns and reticules waving their painted ivory fans in the listless heat. Howqua waited hour by hour as they drank endless cups of tea. The elegance of his conversation betrayed nothing of his mounting fury. Etiquette demanded control even as he realised the scale of the insult their absence implied. Was it intentional? He sent a messenger to find out.

The truth, when it came, was that the insult was intentional. The 'barbarian Eye' had not merely ignored Howqua's conference with the merchant guild to resolve the impasse of the letter and the Petition Gate, but deliberately called a simultaneous one of his own for the sole purpose of raising them in rebellion against the Co-Hong. As he had done by cajoling them to declare against any negotiation with the Co-Hong after boasting that nothing but the point of a bayonet would drive him from the Factories. It tested all the self-discipline of Howqua's long lifetime.

Howqua's gaunt face was taut with the effort to suppress uncivilised anger. He already had plenty of cause for anger. Three times Lord Nash had ignored his polite request for a meeting to persuade him to send missives headed 'Petition' not 'Letter'. Once he had ignored an offer to receive a document at the Petitition Gate jointly with Viceroy Lu's nominee. Howqua had had to report humiliating failure to Viceroy Lu. And now he had been ignored yet again.

How strongly he could agree now with Viceroy Lu now that the men around Lord Nash deluded him in the interest of their clandestine arrangements with Chinese outside the Factories. He sucked at a cold pipe as he turned to Mowqua. The 'Eye' compels us to force.'

Mowqua shuddered, knowing even he had no guarantee of safety from his friend the Viceroy, and swept an imaginary executioner's sword, swift and deadly, across his own fat neck. 'Or we lose our heads.'

'What do you recommend?' The rest of the merchants watched their colloquy in fearful silence.

Knowing all knew too well the crucial importance of appearances, Mowqua, the great survivor, smiled as broadly as a laughing Buddha and rubbed his hands together above his bulging stomach. 'We'll close them down.' Had a blockade of the Factories not always brought them to heel? These foreign devils were full of wind until they had no food, water or servants.

But Howqua saw danger even in this course. They risked throwing the 'Old Iron-headed Rat' further into the arms of the Red Circle. 'We must be shrewd as the God of Justice.' He glanced at the benign gravity of that guardian God whose image stood on their altar, a posture he had so long cultivated himself. 'We cannot act because we have been insulted. Our Emperor himself must be insulted.'

'You'll make the rat fall into the scale and weigh itself.'

Howqua bowed with a meagre smile. 'You'll persuade Viceroy Lu to give the 'Eye' the meeting he asks for, but with the Prefect and the Tartar-General. The 'Eye' will not be able to scorn their rank as he does ours.'

'My esteemed colleague, you must be in your dotage. The 'Eye' would never accept. Look at us sitting here with huge loss of face.'

'He will if our high officials call on him.'

'And if they did, what would it achieve?' Mowqua stuttered dumbfounded.

Howqua resorted to a riddle. 'To make the river between us even wider,' he said mysteriously, not fool enough to confide that the tree he hoped to plant would be as sterile as a magician's tree, and the fruit it would grow would be blunders of the 'Eye' born of fury. Mowqua was too close to the Viceroy.

Howqua's plan of making the rat fall into the scale and weigh itself proceeded smoothly. The officials were persuaded of the cunning at the heart of the plan and agreed to call on Lord Nash. Lord Nash enticed by the illusion of victory agreed to receive them.

When the appointed day came he sat down to an lavish breakfast of bacon and eggs with Captain Forge, John Davies, his secretary, Ross Newman, and interpreter, John Norris, in high good humour. And why not with no less than three senior mandarins coming to pay their respects to him this morning? So much for those sceptics who said a strong line would not prevail.

Moreover, the King's birthday dinner the night before had been a resounding success. Why the cheers could be heard the length of the thirteen Factories when he said he would stand firm come what may. And were heard again when he said he would glory in having his name handed to posterity as the man who had thrown open the wide field of the Chinese Empire to British spirit and industry. Bumpers held high in approval of his words and drained to the bottom.

He drank his tea as if it were another bumper to himself as he prophesied, 'today we'll almost certainly come to an understanding. They'll see we mean what we say and take us seriously.'

'If they don't?' Captain Forge interposed guilelessly.

'I'll order the warships into the Bogue.'

John Davies crashed his knife and fork down aghast. 'If Captain Blackman were to enter the Bogue, sir, he would have to sail so close to the Bogue Forts the gunners could see flies sitting on their barrels. Five forts, sir and thirty guns of heavy calibre in each.'

Lord Nash was in no mood for disputation with John Davies, already diminished in his mind as a China-lover thanks to hostile merchants. 'I've seen those forts myself, Mr. Davies. Those batteries are contemptible. The guns don't swivel. We have fourteen guns a side.'

John Davies persisted, 'what about the Second Bar, let alone Whampoa Reach?

Lord Nash unhooked the white damask napkin from his collar with a deliberate emphasis as if giving orders to his crew, rolled it into a tube and inserted it in a napkin ring as if any such engagement with the enemy would follow motions as precise.

'A detachment, Captain, would act as decisively as I did when I came upriver first. What resistance are we likely to meet? Bows and arrows and pykes that haven't changed since the Manchu invaded China. And muskets on the pattern of ours a hundred years ago. Absolutely useless if the powder's wet.'

Captain Forge felt his temper rising. Lord Nash should have consulted him, the Master Attendant in charge of shipping, as to what he thought, not those burning for making trouble with the Viceroy. He had taken careful note of the problems of bringing hostile ships up river. Its run was extremely easy to defend with its natural bottlenecks of unpredictable shoals and shallows, where stones, spikes and chains could easily be used to block the river. Its defenders would be men who lived on the sea with the same facility as they did on land. They would manouevre foreign vessels into traps as easily as they did fish into their endless tidal snares.

He remonstrated tactfully, 'Sir, I'm told things are not as they seem.'

Lord Nash was in no mood to listen. 'Their army is a joke. They could only muster a few hundred wretched creatures in the city to send against the rebellion last year. One half of these were utterly incapable of taking the field. They would never withstand a strong fire. Why a handful of British veterans with three or four frigates or brigs would settle the issue in a very short time.'

John Davies avoided Barron Forge's eye. Lord Nash looked such an incongruous sight threatening shot and shell in his full uniform over his bacon and eggs. Surely such men as he must have lost the American colonies. The object of their mirth rose, clapped on his tricorn, drew on his gloves and marched to the Grand Salon as if on parade. As Davies followed him in, he warned Forge beside him 'hold onto your hat! The Co-Hong have been at work.'

The Co-Hong had imported their own ceremonial chairs and arranged them with one presiding row facing south, and two rows of five on the east and west sides of the room facing each other.

Lord Nash's expression of smug good humour changed as swiftly as if he had seen Satan, horns and all, suddenly appear. After swearing a few rounds of ripe naval oaths, he thundered at Day, 'what blundering idiot allowed this to happen?'

John Davies, unwilling to expose himself to future blame, had recourse to an old Chinese custom. He passed on the responsibility by consulting the waiting linguists, then gave his answer as if was theirs.

'The visiting mandarins have the seat of honour on the north as they represent the Emperor and you, sir, will be seated on the west with your own officials.'

'Which is the superior side, Mr. Davies, east or west?'

'I regret to say, my lord, the east side.'

If Lord Nash could have breathed smoke and fire like the fabled dragon he would have. 'I'm placed lower in rank than the Hong merchants? These flunkeys sneak in here like thieves in the night and have the gall to order me about on my own premises?'

'Sir, with due respect the New English Factory is not yours. It belongs to the Co-Hong and is on Imperial land. And your meeting today is an Imperial occasion.'

'They have placed us with our backs to our sovereign king. That is an unforgivable insult.'

'With apologies, sir, they forestall a possible insult from you if you seat them facing towards the north. They save you from our own ignorance. That is all.'

His explanation did nothing to appease Lord Nash. 'All? No one dictates to me in my domain. I'm in command here as if on the bridge of my own ship. They will follow my custom.'

Lord Nash stalked about the room studying the strategy of the alien chairs like the Captain of a battleship about to fire a hostile salvo. Then he assigned the waiting servants to shifting chairs like a crew reefing sail on the double, until they were remarshalled round the long table that had graced the Court boardroom of the old John Company not long ago. He would sit at the head facing south, flanked by John Norris as interpreter and secretary, with Captain Forge and John Davies relegated to the bottom end. The three high mandarins were to be ranged on the west side with the Co-Hong merchants opposite facing east.

Lord Nash had only just assumed his seat with a defiant air of challenge to anyone to dislodge him when Howqua and Mowqua glided into the room followed by their servitors. Even Howqua could not conceal his terror at the sight of the profound insult to the mandarins presented by the seating plan.

He urged politely first through John Norris. 'Excellency perhaps your secretary is not aware the order of precedence of the chairs was laid down by Viceroy Lu himself.'

'I don't care whether the order was laid down by the Son of Heaven himself.

The chairs faced away from my King. An insult to my king, sir!'

'The new order of chairs insults my Emperor. Representatives of the Emperor must face south when they meet outer barbarians.'

'Barbarians!' Lord Nash exploded. 'These dog-eaters dare to call us barbarians? Tell him he quibbles.' The nearest word to 'quibble' in Cantonese that John Norris knew meant 'obstinate about trifles.'

Howqua's eyes were agate in a marble face. 'It is no trifle if I have to pay a heavy fine or go to prison.' He bowed and composed himself to a long wait in silent defeat.

'The Viceroy will never take this lying down.' John Davies commented to Captain Forge, agonised at the thought Lord Nash would have to pay an even heavier price than Howqua.

Lord Nash obviously did not think so. He exuded his own opinion of himself as a resolute and independent-minded administrator, as he sat there sweltering in his high collar while time ticked by. He checked his watch constantly all too aware he looked more of a fool with each passing minute. No one made a move to tell him the truth. The Prefect would be two hours late for a man of such low rank as Lord Nash.

John Davies was unsympathetic. 'I could have told him if he'd deigned to ask,' he whispered to Forge, 'but I won't after the way he's behaved to me. He should have informed himself of Chinese ways of doing things.' Captain Forge was left to wonder if he, himself, would ever learn them.

At last the howling of the mandarins' heralds signalled the end of the self-created ordeal of the impatient 'Eye'. John Norris, who had born the brunt of Nash's ill-temper throughout, waited nervously as the three richly dressed crystal button mandarins, their chests ablaze with colourful birds and flowers, appraised the unacceptable etiquette of the seating before them. As incivility to outer barbarians would have been unpardonable, they accepted Howqua's anxious direction where to sit with impeccable good manners, scarcely an imperturbable flicker in their gaze. The very effusion of their smiles, and lengthy protests the honour was so great, were subtle rebukes quite lost on the barbarian 'Eye' as he stared angrily at the smiling officials ignorant enough to believe their good manners to be submissive respect. He was John Bull incarnate in his opening lecture on unpunctuality and his first brusque question address, not to the Prefect of Canton as was proper but to Howqua. 'Did the mandarins direct you they would call at eleven o'clock?' Howqua bowed his head in assent.

'Then ask the mandarins how they dare insult his Britannic Majesty by keeping his representative waiting for two hours.' He waved at the august portrait in question. 'I am an officer responsible to His Britannic Majesty direct. I am not a servant of a private company of merchants such as you have dealt with in the past.'

John Norris' translation of Lord Nash's tirade met with a grave silence from the three officials which angered Lord Nash even more. It provoked him to demand why the mandarins were there at all.

The Prefect of Canton responded. 'To ask Lord Nash why he comes to Canton and when he intends to leave.'

'I come as a competent head of trade at Viceroy Lu's request.'

'The Viceroy asked for a person of the same rank as the merchants. You say you are not. Your rank is higher. Yet your King has not written to the Viceroy to ask his approval for the change.'

Lord Nash parried. 'The King of my country cannot address a letter to a man of lower rank such as the Viceroy.'

'He could have written to the Son of Heaven himself to seek his approval. He has sent no such letter. He is ignorant of the correct procedure.'

John Davies muttered to Captain Forge. 'The Prefect wins the first round.'

The Prefect pressed his advantage. 'Has your King given you new powers not possessed by the President of the Select Committee of the old Company?'

Lord Nash admitted his powers were different.

'So your King instructs you to change our Imperial system which must, and can, only be changed by edict of our Emperor. Why did your King send a person of your rank to Canton when it is well known you cannot deal with officers of the Celestial Empire who never deal in trivial affairs of trade?'

The thunderous, but still haughty, Lord Nash had no answer for the Prefect. Captain Forge, beside him, squirmed with discomfiture. What blundering ass in the Foreign Office had sent Lord Nash and himself out so half-cocked to China? Whoever wrote Lord Nash's Commission had set him on a sure collision course. Was it ignorance or a trap set to that end?

The Prefect, haughty in his turn, spoke of Lord Nash as if he was not there. 'With ignorance equal to his King, his Trade Superintendent entered Canton without a permit, ignoring regulations in force for centuries. He assumed a new privilege for himself without asking for the proper right of entry.'

The only recourse left to Lord Nash was to offer his official letter to the Prefect. 'My commission is set out in this letter to His Excellency, Viceroy Lu.'

The Prefect made no move to accept. To do so would be to concede all that the 'Eye' had asked for. Instead he offered the only possible concession the Viceroy could make. He could accept a verbal statement of its contents. Lord Nash refused in turn.

'Good God I believe the 'Eye' thinks he's won,' Davies whispered to Forge. 'The Prefect knows better. Neither of them have. Both are headed for shipwreck.'

Captain Forge was left wondering at the way in which men could wrangle over formalities, so trivial on the surface, investing them with dire importance or over principles with as much violence as they did weapons.

As the opposing sides joined in obligatory courtesies - toasting each other for longevity and many sons - there was no hint in their correctly smiling faces of past animosity or war to come.

* * * * * *

The Mandarins Weigh the Rat in the Trap

Viceroy Lu knew he could not sit on his hands and wait. He must see the foreign devils trembled and obeyed. For were they not mere subjects of the Emperor, ruler of the universe? He ordered all staff and servants out of the Factories and soldiers in. All Chinese in sight, including the rabble of the

Common, vanished with the terrified speed of a crew deserting a foundering ship. Only one Factory was spared - the American Factory of Peaceful Fountains.

Lord Nash's staff, outraged to a man by the impasse into which his rash actions had precipitated them, resorted to Joshua Law's sitting room for a council of war. Hugh Hodgson, now in business for himself, was there before them, slumped in a chair nursing a hangover. Fortified by Joshua Law's best Southern whisky and delicacies already non-existent in the other beleaguered Factories, they settled to a crisis debate.

John Davies addressed Hugh Hodgson first, 'as you know the 'Eye' leaves the free traders out of his counsels.'

Hugh Hodgson glowered at the thought of his noble chief. 'What a fool the man is! Creating a Chamber of Commerce to hide behind! He compounds his contempt of the Co-Hong if he thinks they'll believe for one moment such a Chamber is anything more than a political engine to destroy their opposition to Jarman Malleson.'

Joshua Law warned them gravely. 'The 'Eye' has a much more destructive engine in mind than a Chamber of Commerce.' Captain Forge cursed inwardly. What was the 'Eye' up to now, and why had he not been told? 'His new brainwave is to appeal directly to the people of Canton over the head of the Viceroy or his minions.'

Captain Forge leapt out of his chair in consternation. 'Madness beyond belief. How does this square with his brief to comply with the laws, prejudices and caprices of the Chinese nation?'

John Davies, almost choking with rage, warned him, 'you'd better be ready, Captain. Viceroy Lu will never forgive him if he tries to rouse discontent in the city.'

Joshua Law spelled Lord Nash's folly out. 'Worse he has attacked the Emperor himself, preaching rebellion.'

John Davies pronounced 'the penalty for that is quite clear - the lingering death.' He moved gloomily to the French windows to look down on the Common occupied by a formidable force of heavily armed soldiers, followed by Captain Forge. 'What in Heaven's name do we do now, John?'

'I know what I'm going to do, dear chap! Wash my hands of this mad affair.' Hadn't Tim Bird warned him through Holly to do just that? His curious sources had proved all too reliable.

Captain Forge doubted Lord Nash would give him leave.

'Meet me at the Customs House at ten tomorrow,' Davies said mysteriously, 'my reputation for losing my temper on occasion will serve me well. The Laird isn't the only one who can put on a show.'

His 'show' turned out to be dancing about in front of two clerks giving a fair intimation of the Laird in full cry, screaming his baggage had been broken into and searched, his lock cracked and some of his goods stolen. When the clerk gesticulated his denial, John Davies began to wave wave and threaten him with his walking stick like a demented creature, landing a blow on his shoulder. The clerk crouched in a fighting stance darting in and out below Davies' chaotic defence to chop him sharply in a rain of blows as Billy Howe looked on, shaking his head, restraining Captain Forge from rushing to Davies' rescue. 'Davies paid the fellow too much. Now he thinks he has to 'all muchee fight' when an obvious black eye would do.'

Captain Forge could hardly believe his ears. 'Bribe someone to beat you up?'

'No Chinese would dare attack a foreign devil otherwise. Not even drunken sailors who assault them.'

'Because they are cowards.'

'Because they dread the police. And, contrary to what you may hear, the police bend over backwards to protect us fanqui. The fact we have no incidents like this, except in a riot, is due to them.'

John Davies staggered and fell with convincing groans. His assailant bowed. His two friends helped him hobble down the steps to the quay to the waiting boat.'He didn't have to half-kill me. Still I have an excuse to go to Macao even though it will be torture to get there now.'

'Half your rotten luck!' Forge said enviously as he helped him on board.

'Invent a reason to abandon this madhouse too!' Davies counselled.

Which he did. He persuaded Lord Nash the frigates had no pilot so he would be needed if they were ordered to force the Bogue. He was as thankful as Davies to settle into a small passage boat manned by Lascars in colourful turbans, and watch the Factories recede as it twisted and turned through the congested river traffic on the turbulent river. He still hoped Lord Nash would not be driven to command the frigates into the river after all. His hope was not to be realised.

* * * * * *

CHAPTER 4

The Nash Fizzle
1835-6

When Captain Forge was obliged to lead the two 28 gun frigates H.M.S. Imogene and H.M.S. Andromache towards the Bogue forts in the cutter Louisa, he elected to emulate a high mandarin by sitting smoking a pipe under an ornate awning in casual calm as if their journey was no more dangerous than a training naval exercise at Portsmouth; a calm that did not escape the wary notice of the Manchu commanders on shore.

In fact, the hazard of forcing their way past the Bogue forts through a narrow channel only a quarter of a mile wide was extreme. Only a noon floodtide and a favourable wind on the shoulder of their sails was in their favour. They came under fire from a dozen war junks in Anson's Bay first. Explosions. Heavy drifts of smokes. No splash on water, crash in rigging. Blanks. Warning shots no more. They forged onwards. A second barrage from the war junks meant business. But the shots fell far short and astern of the frigates. The frigates returned fire. The junks fled among the shoals of Anson's Bay where the frigates could not follow in inglorious desertion of the gates to the Flowery Kingdom.

Now came the worst leg of the journey. They were obliged to tack across the channel within range of the guns of Chuenpi and Anunghoy. Any gunner worth his salt could blow them out of the water with the wind against them on the change of tack as they passed, the sailors working in the rigging 'sitting ducks', and the rest so short-handed they had to work guns both sides. But if there were any Tiger braves worth their salt, they had no heart for battle. Just one flourish of shot from the shore firing wild and high, and one cannonade from the frigates raking the forts, and the battle was over just as John Davies had predicted in allaying Captain Forge's fears.

'They'll let you pass the Bogue. Make a show of making war not make war in fact. That would cost too much in levies to rebuild the fort. In any case, they won't sacrifice perfectly good guns and forts when the defences upriver will bring the frigates to a halt without any cost at all.'

But the gunners suddenly decided to revenge their loss of face with the frigates on Captain Forge's little cutter. They raked her deck with shot. Captain Forge threw himself face down on the deck as several struck home. He raised his head in time to see the gunners in the fort dancing with glee at the sight of the British mandarin flat on his face on the deck. But his real discomfiture was yet to come when they were becalmed below Tiger Island and forced to anchor for the next two days fuming at the farce their rescue mission had become.

When they weighed anchor once more, they were obliged to steer through a narrow channel so close to Tiger Island they were no more than two hundred yards from its fort manned by several hundred reinforcements of matchlock men backing gunners entrenched behind a formidable battery of guns. These held their fire longer than expected, but when it came it was no token performance like that of the Bogue Forts. This time the Andromache suffered a tremendous, well-directed rake of gunfire and cannonade that killed four men.

Captain Forge, now on the Andromache following behind, watched the menace looming above them nervously as the lie of the wind brought her within close range before he could change tack. Every moment he expected a bombardment to sweep the frigate smashing the rigging, disabling the mast, reducing her to a wreck fit only for salvage. The British lion a mouse, the loss of face incalculable. Still they crept on in deathly silence.

Then, as often in action, the wildly improbable happened. Some spark of genius inspired a seaman high in the top. He called for three rousing cheers for victory. The crew up aloft, whether for joyous release from elation or fear, responded with a roaring 'Hip, hip, hooray!' taken up with tossing arms from deckhands and gunners below not once, but time and time again until the ship had passed the danger zone of the fixed guns above, where matchlock gunners were gaping over the parapets at the cheerful confidence of the mad foreign devils, their guns forgotten. What should they make of men who fought with applause? That they practiced magic? Even as they argued, the Andromache slipped away from them to a half-hearted volley of grape shot from the few marksmen less deceived than the rest by the ruse.

The tiny fleet sailed triumphantly on, only to grind to a halt below the Second Bar once more for want of wind, yet thankful enough that the whole damage done on both days of the battle was two men killed, half a dozen wounded, a hole in the side of the Imogene and a few ropes shot away. It was a very Pyrrhic victory as Captain Forge quickly recognised. They were now hostage to the Viceroy unable either to go on or to return without his permission. A most visible humiliation for Lord Nash.

John Norris was right when he said the eastern view of the art of war was different, war not a duel with one man or nation victorious but a state of trickery and compromise which sometimes allowed discretion was the best part of valour.

Meanwhile, in a back room of the English factory, John Norris translated Lord Nash's latest edict with disbelief. How could the Superintendent be so stupid as to write such a document when he had been isolated by the Viceroy to live on bully beef and whatever food could be smuggled in from Little Jerusalem, cut off from all service and surrounded by armed guards on land and water? How could he ignore the fact he had no defence and the frigates intended to protect him were becalmed near Tiger Fort after their violent entry past the Bogue? How could he, a sick man, have so lost touch with reality that he could have written

'I recommend the Viceroy and Governor take warning in time. They have been guilty of folly, wickedness and cruelty. I will lose no time in sending this true statement to the Emperor in Pekin. He will not allow it to go unpunished.'

How could he make the even more crass mistake of threatening Viceroy Lu? How could he insult the Viceroy's by mimicking his stock admonition in adding 'therefore Viceroy Lu, intensely tremble!' How could he fail to realise his actions forced the Viceroy to account to Pekin for the insubordination of these barbarians and to offer up the sacrifice of some innocent man on the altar of his zeal?

Gazing bleakly out of his window at the miniature garden in the small courtyard below that would persist no matter what frenzy of men came and went, he jumped in alarm when Kaida Hung, dressed in servant's garb, appeared noiselessly at his elbow. 'You shouldn't be here. You're taking an awful risk in coming?'

Kaida nodded, as, taking no chances of being overheard, they drew chairs closer together. 'Less now all the servants who act as spies have gone, and I bribed the guard.'

'Why take the risk, Kaida?'

'Because you're in danger, my friend.'

'You didn't have to come here to tell me that. We've expected a mob to come rampaging all week.'

'But not a silent invader to poison your food.'

'Poison in our food? Impossible. We cook and serve our food ourselves now.' John said, unwilling to believe this more than another rumour in the storm of rumours that beset them. 'You can't be serious Kaida. Warning us of murder?'

'Do you boil the water or cook the food yourself, John?'

John's face clouded in panic. He did not know how they came by their water, whether they all drank from the same casks or Lord Nash, fussy about such things, from bottled water. Only that the food came from Little Jerusalem.

Kaida urged, willing John to believe, 'I know the 'Eye' is to die. All I dare say. Because he's forced the Viceroy to lose huge face with everyone. That cannot be forgiven.'

'Doesn't he understand the 'Eye' is no more than an ignorant blundering fool?'

'No, because he's not a fool by nature. He has become one because he is the tool of Jarman Malleson whose one aim is war.'

'Then why not murder Jarman or Malleson instead?'

'The Red Circle would defend them, needing them for the guns they must have for their hour of revolution. But not the 'Eye'. His death will lead to war. War would mean the triumph of the Red Circle in Canton. You must persuade him to leave Canton in time.' His agitation obvious in the nervous interplay of his fingers.

John considered his options. Maxwell Raine might listen to such a warning. He badly wanted the blockade lifted, the port re-opened to shift the tea. But could he trust him? Was there anyone he could trust.

'I have it! The 'Eye' respects one man, Dr. Tom. I could tell him a half-truth. Death threats. Swear him to silence.'

Dr. Tom persuaded Lord Nash the rapid decline in his health made it imperative for him to return to the more benign climate of Macao at once. Viceroy Lu approved the necessary passport with such alacrity John was puzzled that he should so willingly allow 'the dog barbarian, the lawless foreign slave who should be decapitated' to remove from his clutches. He was not puzzled for long.

Viceroy Lu obliged them to travel with a military escort of three war vessels bristling with arms to advertise Lord Nash's departure as one of humiliating defeat. He allowed him to proceed to the town of Heangshan half-way to Macao by the alternative more speedy route through the delta of the Broadway Passage. Then he refused to allow Lord Nash's party to proceed until Lord Nash had ordered his frigates to leave the Second Bar and retreat beyond the Bogue.

So there they remained persecuted by a terrible serenade of incessant gongs and firecrackers, and plagued by chattering curious crowds day and night long enduring an unrelieved purgatory of still humid heat.

Useless to cry wanton cruelty or black outrage. The reality was that the 'Eye' was a prisoner of the Viceroy; a prisoner with no recourse but to obey the Viceroy if he wanted to reach Macao. The 'Eye', who had boasted so loudly that he would not leave Canton except at the point of a bayonet and had in fact called his bayonets into the Pearl River, was humiliated beyond repair because he was now leaving Canton at the point of the Viceroy's metaphorical bayonet for all to see the latter had won a physical as well as a moral victory.

When at last, with his vessels withdrawn beyond the Bogue, he reached Macao, Macao did not save him. He was doomed despite Lady Nash's arduous vigil by his bedside as he tossed and turned in a torment of pain, refusing the one drug that could deliver him, opium; doomed to breathe his last in an alien port where the sweet sonority of the perpetual bells of the many convents and churches of an alien religion had been stilled to ease his agony of body and mind. He was borne finally to rest in the only scrap of ground that could be said to be inalienably English in all of China, the Protestant cemetery.

The six captains of ships in port shouldered his coffin, draped with the naval ensign, into the tiny Company Chapel, too small to hold the miscellany of officer and civilians in the procession behind them. Not one of those gathered there could honestly say amen to the text of the Reverend Vaux's funeral sermon. 'Let me die the death of the righteous and let my last end be like his.' Who would want such a futile death?

The service over, the phalanx of captains hoisted the coffin to their shoulders once more and led by two able seamen, each with the Union Jack limply aslant in holsters, moved out and down the gentle slope to the lower precincts of the cemetery in a slow dead march to the muffled beat of sailor drummers and the salute of minute guns from the Andromache.

The fair skinned officers of the British navy and marine followed in all the pomp and circumstance of their full dress uniforms, next the swarthy officers of the Portuguese army. Last a sombre group of merchants flanking the decorous fortitude of Lady Nash and her two daughters.

Though all in the sad procession were one in their grave half pace, they were not one in their thoughts. Dr. Tom cursed himself for allowing the mandarins to divert their barge through the Broadway Passage, haunted by the thought the Viceroy had staged the retreat to make certain of the execution he thought Lord Nash deserved.

Captain Forge brooded that he and Captain Blackwood might have saved Lord Nash if they had battled up the river in small boats, taking reinforcements with them instead of waiting for an order from Lord Nash which never came.

Captain Blackwood was resentful of the cost of Lord Nash's reckless order to take the two frigates upriver with neither pilots nor proper charts. They could have lost both ships.

Sir George Roberts, now Superintendent in Lord Nash's place rejoiced he, denied the Presidency of the Select despite his long service, because of his reputation for dilatory incompetence, was now supreme.

John Davies reflected sadly the bitter party spirit on the coast which Lord Nash had naively hoped to reconcile was only invisible in his death.

Dr. William Jarman, uncrowned king of the Coast, walking with grave majesty behind him was already rehearsing in his mind the florid rhetoric with which he intended to besiege Whitehall. How compelling his words would sound in the House of Commons!

'We hope never again to see a British representative at Canton starved and insulted at the paltry mandate of the Hong merchants and thus forced to the humiliation of negotiating through them. We should arouse the attention of the Celestial Court by such a remonstrance as never before tingled in Celestial Ears. We should enforce our reception in China at all hazards. We should evidence our naval power in the strongest manner along the whole coast and in every port of China.'

How he longed to end his days there in that true seat of peers!

James Malleson saw victory in Lord Nash's disgrace. Lord Nash had handed him the opportunity he had always wanted, indeed had contrived for so long, to go to London himself, a petition from the entire port in his hand demanding the British Government revenge the insult and death of their Trade Superintendent by sending a fleet not merely to Canton but to Beijing with a plenipotentiary of the highest rank.

But James Malleson was doomed to be mistaken. By the time the petitions reached London, Lord Palmerston, author of Lord Nash's disastrously confusing instructions, had given way to the Duke of Wellington who declared unequivocally His Majesty did not intend to establish commercial intercourse between his subjects and China by force, or violence, but by conciliatory measures. He had accepted the advice of his First Lord of Admiralty that conquest of China would be as dangerous as defeat, and of John Stuart Mill of his Secretariat, that it was 'stupid to punch a large feather pillow like China.'

On the Chinese side of what Billy Howe dubbed the 'Nash fizzle', Viceroy Lu lost his peacock feather for allowing the frigates to pass the Bogue but regained it because the Imperial revenue had not been reduced by 'the value of a hair of a feather duster'. And the Admiral of the Fleet, Admiral Kuan, lost nothing since as he rather euphemistically said 'only the rafters and tiles of the Bogue forts had been shaken!'

Viceroy Lu, a harsh man at the best of times, was now even harsher. What if the people, excited by the 'Eye's' broadsheets, turned on him? He looked for opium traffickers. He sent soldiers to raid the small furnaces in the streets behind the Factories where he arrested dealers or, if they had fled, their families. He burned seven chests of confiscated opium on the military parade ground outside the city. He looked for rebels. He set spies to work everywhere. He arrested Ah Hae.

* * * * * *

The Salvation of Ah See

Billy was perched on a stool absorbed in a ledger on the stand before him when Holly put her arm around him. His heart jumped and a sensation ran through his body inconsistent with his protest, 'you gave me a fright.' No, his intense physical reaction had nothing to do with fright nor her words with the fondness implied by her embrace.

'Ah See's brother has been arrested.'

'Where?' He leapt from his stool all ears, oblivious now to the enchanting sight of her in a drift of blue with an electrifying auburn halo of hair. 'At Reverend Sanders' house. Caught redhanded making metal type for printing the Bible.'

'Hell and damnation! Which prison did they say?'

'None. He escaped. But Ah Hae wasn't so lucky. He was arrested.'

'Hell's Bells. I'd better warn Ah See at once.' Ah See was popular among them all with his engaging ways and the Yankee twang of his fluent English for he had spent several years in the States.

'Can you do anything? Smuggle him out like Leah a Fa?'

'No, Holly. We can't persuade the missionaries to stop seeking converts. We can't convince the Viceroy they're not a danger because they are.'

'It's all so horrible.'

'Holly, if you're going to weep tears for the tragedies of China you'd best catch the boat home with Jim right now. If not them, it will be other converts. Martyrs Dr. Sanders would say.'

'Poor Dr. Sanders. You're so unsympathetic.'

'Then so is our good friend, John Norris. He refused to hang his father's albatross around his neck. God's will his father called it. In the end it is each man's will, Holly. As it is with these converts who throw in their lot with the foreign devils knowing it's forbidden to do so.'

Dr. Sanders' illegal printery was considered a hotbed of sedition by the Chinese with its preparations for another edition of the forbidden Bible not to mention a torrent of religious pamphlets.

She looked up at him mischievously as he stood protectively over her. 'That's not the only problem, Billy. The worst is how to dispose of the body in Dr. Sanders' office.'

'Dispose of a body?' He reeled back in mock consternation. 'Whose body?'

'A magistrate's ferret, so Geli Hung says.'

'So it wasn't the regular police who found him out?'

'No, and Rebecca Norris - she was there at the time - tells me if a man is trying to rob your house and you kill him it's a simple accident.'

'True enough. You're only liable for a fine to the relatives. So they should call the police.'

'Except Dr. Sanders hardly wants to invite police inspection of his premises at the present time. The body's still there.'

'Oh no, Holly. That's why you're here. To talk me into sneaking the body in here.'

'Only till nightfall,' she conceded demurely.

'And if we're caught, how do we explain the body?'

'He was disturbed breaking in and died in a fight. Or we found him dead in the garden.'

'Good enough for your novels, Holly, but not for the magistrate. You would have to know the exact manner of his death as the Magistrate's minions can determine the precise cause of death by heating the body over a fire until the marks show up.'

'Then let's appeal to Chung Tai Tai to bury it at sea for us,' she proposed smugly. 'She has scores to settle.'

And so it was that a mysterious group hustled through the back door of Joshua Law's house, dressed in white shrouds to look like grave ghosts said to roam the night-dark streets in the dead hour before dawn. They staggered down the hill carrying a burden which they loaded into a Tanka boat at the stone quay of the Praya Grande which pulled out into the harbour where one of Chung Tai Tai's fishing junks was already loitering.

And an exhausted Billy sat opposite an effusive Holly at breakfast next morning, knowing he had only taken the risk involved because he was putty in her hands. Putty for nothing, he despaired. All she saw in him was someone to plug the holes in her life.

A week later as Kaida approached the Viceroy's yamen gate he groaned inwardly that Howqua had warned him he could not, and must not, do anything to help Ah Hae. How true the old saying was 'if you have right on your side and no money then don't go to the yamen gate though it stand wide open.' No wonder the tablets at the gate, where any man might write his petition, were blank.

As he walked inside between the rows of cells where prisoners were tortured, he could not close his ears to the long-drawn out screams or thick moans of the victims along that gauntlet of pain. He could not close his mind to the thought the warders must enjoy torturing them, inflicting such vicious wounds with their wire-plaited rattans that death from gangrene was inevitable if the victims had not already been taken to the execution ground. He could not close his eyes to the sight of Ah Hae when he stumbled into the court for sentence, a filthy shrunken wreck with a battered disfigured face, but unbroken spirit. His shining demeanour was of a man at peace with himself, as the lictors forced his broken body to kneel on broken glass before the judge.

What had John Norris said? Ah Hae's vision of his personal salvation in Heaven would sustain him through the martyrdom to which his new found faith had brought him. How fervently he hoped that beyond this suffering Ah Hae would find the Heaven he longed for as the means of his deliverance to that Heaven would be Hell. He would be carried to his execution no better than an animal to the slaughter, crouched trussed in a bamboo cage labelled with his treason. He would be humiliated as he knelt to the executioner's sword. His corpse would be violated, stripped of his new execution garments by robbers, since he had no relatives who would dare to be seen at the execution ground to spare him that last indecency.

Kaida repaired to Consoo House to rail at Howqua 'why is the Viceroy so cruel?'

'He is keeper of the law. These Christians endanger the law with their story of rebellion.'

'So an innocent man like Ah Hae suffers.'

'He preaches treason, my son, as his Son of God did.'

'I do not understand, Old Wu. Am I not a living symbol of treason for the Triads?'

'Ah but a Chinese symbol,' Old Wu declared triumphantly. 'How can a Chinese Emperor of the Middle Kingdom, lord of all the oceans and kingdoms of the earth, recognise another lord of the universe?'

* * * * * *

CHAPTER 5

1836
A battle of wits

Disorders Stir in the Pearl River Delta

Snow fell in the night at Whampoa for the first time in forty years, snow that brought James Malleson on the shout of the watch leaping from his bunk on the 'Lennox' in the grey dawn expecting murder, mutiny, anything but snow. He gazed at the flurry of flakes devoured by the dark swirl of water in disbelief. Snow in Canton, the perpetual sauna? Alas, too late to give them a taste of Merrie Old England for the Xmas season that had just passed them by with all the cheerful ritual of buffalo roasts and plum pudding aflame with brandy, washed down with the best Portuguese wine.

At least this was one night the villagers of Whampoa would not be astir, creatures of the night though these inveterate smugglers were, he thought as he leant over the rail watching the dark swirl of the headlong Pearl River round the hull. He felt secure as few did so near this inhospitable village of ungovernable men. Had he and his partner not successfully harnessed these creatures of rebellion? He would emerge the victor for the running battles certain to ensue on the river would be a civil war amongst themselves, a power struggle to control the smuggling trade.

A grey cloud ceiling hung low over the brooding landscape, Whampoa Island a crouching shape under a white snow blanket dimly perceived through the flurry of snow that frosted their shoulders and the deck. Between them, the barges where the bumboat men warmed their hands at their tiny braziers, cringing from starting the morning's work of loading the late Bohea teas.

Sean Jarman joined his older partner at the rail, homesick at the sight of the silent drift of snow in the growing light of dawn. He had not realised until then how much he missed the northern winter, the clear change of season never to be seen in Canton. He turned to his uncle. 'I envy you the trip home.'

Malleson waved dismissively. 'If I go.'

Sean turned startled. 'I thought that was settled.'

'My partner is due for leave before I am.'

'But he's adamant you're the right man to take the case to Whitehall, not he,' Sean reminded him.

James Malleson studied Sean critically. He could guess well enough why Sean was so anxious to see him away. He wanted to pursue his enchantment with that American miss who looked like a delicate flitting butterfly without a brain in her head, but was as tough as hickory and shrewd as a comprador.

His partner, Dr. Jarman, loomed out of the dark crouched in a row boat, snow dusting his shoulders. 'Couldn't sleep with all the crew turning out to see the snow,' he growled as he came on board. He had slept on the Fairy after doing the rounds of the fleet collecting signatures for a petition to the British government like a Scots clan chieftain collecting rents. His progress had not been without argument with some of his English-born captains. 'Thought I'd take a strong tot of rum to warn my old bones and quench my anger.'

He loomed massively over them, a man too large in every sense for the stage Canton offered. In his brooding hauteur, Sean saw an older generation still cherishing a hostility fostered over centuries of conflict in the bitter frontier marches between England and Scotland.

James Malleson knew he could never match the ingrained anger of his partner against the British government, his desire to stir them into action. He knew his own bias in London would be to adopt the measured argument of the lawyer, his brief commensurate with his training. William Jarman did not prepare for a fight. He overrode it like a captain ignoring a typhoon warning as he sailed out of port.

He urged his partner. 'You should go to London not I.'

'You pack more punch with words than I.'

'Too much!'

'Our demands call for a punch. Nash's death needs revenge.'

'It needs persuasion revenge is necessary. The job of a lawyer not a surgeon. Persuasion that we're not men in the moon in a land as weird and remote as the moon. Persuasion that British honour is worth the price.'

'You're more forceful than I am.'

'A quality I would do well to apply here rather than in the corridors of Whitehall, my friend. Particularly now prices for opium are at an all-time low. A situation that is my forte you can't deny it.'

Malleson had to agree. Jarman far excelled him in sharp horse trading, where bullying, bamboozling and bartering were the order of the day.

William Jarman clapped him on the shoulder. 'Well that's settled. You're the one to go to London. It'll give you a chance to start your run for the Commons. You've always wanted to stand. Sean will make a splendid backstop for me in your place.' For Malleson's own nephew, David, had returned to Edinburgh to take up law, declaring his acute distaste for any aspect of the Flowery Kingdom in general and trade in particular.

The cosy scene was broken by the sound of a shot. They turned as one to stare out into the dark. Two men on the nearby shore of Whampoa Island were making a frenzied dash for the shore, pursued by an irate mob armed with pitchforks, axes and knives. The fugitives leapt into their waiting bumboat in the shallows, almost overturning it. Its four waiting paddlers sheered off as raking pitchforks tore holes in its rim to paddle furiously downstream on the ebbing tide.

Jarman focussed his binoculars on the bumboat, swearing 'what goddammed whoreson is prowling round our preserves, James? Who's blown the lid off the Red Circle's cover? No Chinamen from the look of them. Who are they working for? Not the Viceroy I'll bet my bottom dollar.'

Sean only dimly understood what he might mean. He only knew this was one secret his uncle had no intention of sharing with him, the mystery that plainly had all the dangerous elements of adventure stories of his youth.

No time to linger on the thought. Time to go down river with the onset of the steady blow of the trade winds lifting the ceiling of clouds, floating the flags on the topmast, singing through the sleeping rigging with the senior partners still wrangling. First, as to whether they should push for an Expeditionary Force within the year, then, if it came, whether it should merely subdue Canton or rattle the sabre at the very gates of Beijing. Malleson argued they needed better naval surveys of the coast first.

'And stay at a standstill for how many years?' Jarman demanded.

'You fret because you're older and look to retire.'

Dr. Jarman looked wearily across the river. How often over how many years had he ridden on ships laboriously making their way up this river? 'I can't lead a charmed life for ever. No such thing as magic armour against the four horsemen of the Apocalypse.' He did not need to name the four horsemen of China - plague, cholera, malaria and dysentery.

He pointed scornfully at the Bogue fort on Tiger Island as the tack of their ship brought them under its walls. 'You see how insane the present situation is. We damage the forts because of oppressive taxes on our trade and then pay even more taxes to the Co-Hong to rebuild them. How often must we repeat this ridiculous cycle? We can't allow them to bottle us up here to keep us under control any longer.'

A portentous mandarin boat swept past them, the grave official high on the canopied stern with fawning servants in comical contrast to the indecorous informality of the Taipans sprawling in folding deck chairs among the rope coils and life jackets of the smaller, plainer passage boat with their thoughts eternally on balance sheets. Yet the greed in men of both East and West, was the same for all the formers' pretence to love classical scholarship more. The greed of these men of the West, however, had a more imperial scale than the simple pre-occupation of a local mandarin as to when and where he would retire and with what wealth. It concerned itself with when and where war was possible between great powers, and for how much profit.

As they sailed beyond the Bogue, Sean threw off such unflattering thoughts, all too aware he had no choice but to ride in the same boat as these men. He had no land, no occupation to return to, and therefore no retreat. He must accept his tutelage, his alliance. But he must never forget the harvest they were sowing now would last to untold generations.

* * * * * *

Disorder stirs in Macao

Murder seemed to be the spirit of the times in the uneasy atmosphere that enveloped Macao like an April fog as John Davies kept complaining to Bettina. 'Macao's infested with footpads these days putting decent citizens at the risk of all sorts of mayhem if they venture abroad.'

Therefore he, of all people, should had known it was foolhardy to go abroad in the streets, particularly at night, and even more foolish, albeit with Billy Howe at his side, to involve himself in a Chinese house fire. But he could not stand by in the watching crowd while the flames flaring from the upper story of a corner house took hold. Infuriated by their apathy, he abused them in all the rich metaphors of their own language. Did they want to see the whole street alight? Their own houses burn down? Let them form a bucket chain to douse the fire. Let them wreck those flimsy outbuildings next door, dispose of an explosive clump of pestilential bamboo. Sullen silence. No one willing to tamper with fate.

No need to convince Billy Howe. Together they began to empty the outbuilding, dumping chairs and tables on the footpath. He cursed them again - cruel as lictors, stupid as Caffre slaves. The crowd surged forward at last - some to help but others to snatch furniture away or take revenge for his insults.

A screaming Cantonese bore down on Billy hand out flat, level with his chest, fingers closed ready to strike a deadly blow at his neck. But Billy, equally master of kung fu, swung down and away with a back-kick that threw his assailant onto a fallen table knocking him out. Billy turned to see that a giant Caffre, a madness of hate in his glare, was looming with stump of wood in hand bent on murder over an oblivious John Davies. Billy flung himself forward, throwing Davies to the ground as the Caffre's deadly weapon hissed by to spill the brains from the slack skull of the helpless Cantonese prone behind them.

Billy leapt to his feet, knowing the Caffre would not stand bewildered by the fact the corpse at his feet was not the loathsome foreign devil he meant to kill for long. He was still dangerous. As was the mob even now closing in on them. Only one thing to do. Play David to Goliath. Challenge the giant. He feinted. The giant woke up, lunged towards him. He dodged and weaved, chopping repeated swift blows at the huge man leaving him stumbling aimlessly. Then with agile kicks Billy caught him first in the chest causing him to stagger, and then on the chin with a king hit that toppled him to the ground where he put a headlock on him. Then he turned to bow to the crowd now clapping the foreign devil expert in their art of kung fu.

By this time the tardy police had arrived. Billy Howe with a choice range of expletives demanded to know if they kept order in Macao by letting their foreign guests be murdered by one of the Governor's slaves while doing their job for them.

The police chief was angry. 'You shouldn't interfere'.

'What let Chinatown burn down and our houses with it?'

'You have no authority to damage houses. The Governor will hear,' he threatened darkly, Portuguese resentment always close to the surface.

'I hope he does,' Billy stormed off with John Davies, not very confident the Governor would act with one of his slaves involved. Indeed might have put him up to it.

The Governor had to act however. A Chinese citizen had been killed. An entirely different matter than if John Davies had been killed. He sent the caffre to trial and ensured his own chief judge heard the matter not the Chinese magistrate in Macao. It proved an impotent gesture. The slave had neither counsel nor understanding to offer his defence - that he exacted revenge for the fact John Day had once struck him. Even if he could have pleaded manslaughter the law had no alternative to the death sentence in Macao, not since the Son of Heaven had decreed in 1759 there was to be only one degree of justice for such an offence by any foreign criminal compared to three degrees for any son of China - a decree renewed annually.

The poor dumb giant in the dock was condemned to death, as impotent before the majesty of the law as he had been before Davies' original temper, victim of the Governor's need to keep the peace with the menace of the Red Circle. A contrite John Davies was only able to wheedle a stay of execution saying 'that poor brute shows the Governors ultimate cowardice'.

* * * * * *

John Davies Abdicates at last

After reading a copy of the petition Jarman Malleson had dredged from the Whampoa fleet, John Davies gathered his fellow officials together in the old Company headquarters in Macao - his deputy Sir George Roberts, his Third Hugh Hodgson, and the Company Finance Agency man, Ross Newman.

He announced more in sorrow than anger 'I am resigning this month. I cannot remain in all conscience. This crude, ill-digested petition is calculated to produce and keep alive feelings of animosity in the community; and worse to arouse hostility in the Chinese officials here who must inevitably learn its contents. It is a manifesto for war against China. I must and will use my influence at Home towards some sanity.'

The habitually smug Sir George looked even smugger. He, who had sought promotion in vain under the old Company which judged him as lazy and weak, would automatically become Trade Superintendent now. He made it plain at once he had not changed. 'You can't deny a strong feeling in the community.'

'Is that any virtue when it divides the merchants in two?' Davies demanded scornfully. Really the man was a fool. 'Those who have signed are bitter against those who have refused.'

Sir George boasted 'ninety signatures to that petition.'

John Davies' chortle was an insult. 'All the sweepings of the port! Clerks, midshipmen, passengers! Birds of passage hardly qualified to have a serious opinion about whether we should hold the Emperor of China to ransom or not by demanding he lift his Vermilion Pen to command the entry of our ambassador.'

The burly Ross Newman shared the joke. 'If only Malleson had Jack Tars on his ships instead of Manila men and Lascars, his signatures would have been legion.'

Captain Forge, now Secretary to the Commission as well as Master Attendant of the port, laughed more guardedly. He would have to ride any seesaw Sir George might set in motion between the war and peace parties.

'Our honour has been compromised,' Sir George declared with the voice of Jarman Malleson. 'We can no longer be treated as barbarian rebels against the Flowery Kingdom!'

'From what I know of the alliances of Jarman Malleson that is just what they plan to be,' Davies retorted.

Sir George rose curtly to his feet and marched out, every inch of his rigid back expressing his settled dislike of the man he rejoiced to see departing from the colony.

Captain Forge regarded his reproachful back with alarm. 'Surely he should play a neutral role when you go.'

'He'll be Dr. Jarman's man like Nash. You'd do well to distance yourself from him,' Hodgson growled.

Flora, like everyone else in Macao, treated every gathering as a sounding board for the political weather. So she asked the sewing circle for Mary Grusson's orphans 'you ladies have been here longer than I. Supposing the British Government do send an Expeditionary Force what do you suppose will happen?'

Mary Ann, more interested in motherhood than politics, asserted the view of the optimists. 'The Emperor will negotiate.'

The pragmatic Abby begged to differ. 'Would you negotiate if you were the King of England and the Chinese Emperor sent a navy up the Thames to threaten you if you didn't? Would you, if you read over your breakfast rice that you practiced insufferable arrogance and needed a lesson from the enlightened sons of the Flowery Kingdom to teach you how to behave to foreigners? Do these idiots really think the Son of Heaven is going to bend an inch at their sound and fury off the coast of his Celestial Kingdom? Fiddlesticks!'

'What about the expeditionary force losing face?'

Flora was amused at the earthy cynicism of the American ladies as their debate wore on until they tired of it. It restored some sense of balance in this Lilliputian battleground of Macao. She shared their bent for speaking their mind and their instinct to know when they could take the risk and not be taken amiss. She knew what their answer would be when she enquired, 'do you think all British are insufferably arrogant?'

Abby was damning with faint praise by saying 'you and Barron are the exceptions that prove the rule.'

* * * * * *

Disorder Breaks out in Macao

Holly was playing the 'cheer-up game' with Abby, of what to call her baby due any day, as they sat peacefully sewing nightdresses in the drawing room when the door burst open all of a sudden and Dr. Tom staggered in, face contorted in agony clutching his blood-soaked right shoulder- Sean propping him up on one side and a stranger on the other. Abby struggled out of her chair in shock to hover awkwardly over him after he collapsed into a chair. 'Tom, what on earth..?'

He winced as she seized his hand. 'Just a rock on the shoulder. Nothing to worry about.'

'Just a rock!' she repeated outraged, 'How big a rock?'

'Four pounds at least I'd swear.'

'Who, Sean? Who would do that? Did you see it? Anyone we know? Have you called the police? Who'll deliver the baby if it starts now?' Abby wailed as she fussed over him.

Sean tried to console her. 'It could be worse, Abby.'

What outrageous lack of tact! Holly could not let that pass. 'Not too serious! He can hardly walk. His arm will be useless for days possibly weeks.'

Sean, discomfited, tried to justify himself. 'He would have been beaten up worse if we hadn't come on the scene at the right moment to see him set on by as villainous a bunch of ruffians as you'd meet in a day's march.'

Abby looked up dubiously from her ministrations to the man she believed universally loved. 'Who would set on Tom for God's sake?' A man who ministered to all comers no matter their race.

'That's what it looked like,' the stranger butted in. 'One man egging the other two on, smashing this dirty big rock on his shoulder.'

'Could have been accidental. Mistake for someone else.' Sean hastened to redress his blundering as he folllowed Dr. Tom's orders in pouring a draft of laudunum to deaden the pain.

'Looked like no accident to me. Revenge more like.'

'Who would want revenge against you, Tom?' Abby asked dismayed to imagine her gentle Dr. Tom could be a target for deliberate anger.

'Dissatisfied customers.' He raised a limp grin as he tossed off the potion while Sean eased the coat off his injured shoulder.

'Chinese?' His few patients were only those considered hopeless by their own doctors.

'Or that servant I struck for insolence to you.' He inspected the gash. A few stitches needed there. 'Thank God arms don't bleed like head wounds. Fancy some needlework Abby?'

Abby opened his bag, produced a needle, threaded it with catgut and resolutely advanced on her husband. Holly blanched as Abby pinched the wound together and began to sew, ignoring rivulets of blood.

'Don't force yourself to watch.' Sean urged her away, hand under her elbow.

She resisted. 'I must learn.' She might one day be left alone, no doctor at hand, and be obliged to do just what Abby was doing. Men away too often. Servants too treacherous as Dr. Tom had just supposed. But he was wrong. The Chinese, who had attacked him, were merely mindless forerunners of a riotous crowd- their shouts now clearly heard as they moved closer hunting for undefended houses to overrun and loot. It had happened before.

'Bolt all the doors and windows facing the street!' Dr. Tom cried trying to struggle needlessly from his chair. The stranger was already ramming them home, Sean producing rifles and ammunition from the cupboard under the stair, and Holly keeping watch at the window.

'They're looting Casey's house down the road.'

'That'll put him in a fine temper when he comes back. Funny how they know who's away at Canton or Lintin,' Dr. Tom remarked, his voice slurred.

The sight of Sean at the foot of the stairs, rifle at the ready to defend them single-handed, suddenly struck Holly as faintly ludicrous. 'You look like Horatio on the bridge,' she laughed, referring to Lord MacAuley's currently popular new poem on Horatio's defence of Rome against the Tarquins. Sean looked puzzled. He was no literary devotee. In the upshot he had no bridge to defend.

The Governor had rushed troops, far more promptly than usual, to quell the riot knowing he was the prime target of the mob's anger. He was being blamed, it appeared, for allowing his caffre slave to go to trial over the death of the Chinese. To cap it all, he had given the poor inarticulate caffre no counsel nor supported any appeal. An injustice for which the Chinese mob turned on him when the Caffre was led to execution on the Campo screaming 'strangle the master, not the slave. Drive all foreign devils into the sea', forcing him to pardon the Caffre, give him his freedom and send him out of the country when his own coloured troops refused to disperse the mob.

The affair was not the end for the Portuguese Governor as it was for John Davies. The Governor's enemies said he had injured the British in the eyes of the Chinese in an effort to safeguard his own tenuous existence in Macao. His friends said he should not apologise as the British were their own worst enemies. Those, who were on neither side, had to admit anyone in the Governor's shoes would have to placate the Chinese government to whom Portugal owed their frail toehold in China.

The poor Chief Magistrate of Macao, who had sentenced the caffre, waited for a dreaded rebuke from on high that he, father of these people, had allowed them to riot. His hands shook as he reached for his opium pipe, selected the tiny knife from among the slender tools dangling from a plate at his waist, broke a fragment from the tiny dried opium ball, heated it in the minute spoon over the flame, then dropped it into the bowl of his handsome longstemmed pipe, lay back on the cushions and turned on his side cheek against the bolster. He breathed the excellent European smoke deep into his lungs. It swept him away as ships wafted sailors away from the troubles of the world except for the destruction latent in that sleep. He lay peacefully, his puffy eyes closed, an imbecilic smile on his flabby cheeks.

If he had but known, Viceroy Lu had more on his mind than the pecadilloes of the Chief Magistrate of Macao with the implications of the Queen Mother's death in Beijing. It meant more than the trappings of mourning - head unshaven and white mourning dress. It meant the end of a moderate policy at court on the thorny question of the opium trade. She had insisted for years that if you tried to forbid the evil of the European smoke, you not only made your own society more corrupt but rebellious into the bargain. Indeed, she had said openly that if she had been Emperor, she would have made its import legal so the profits would have gone into the Treasury through customs revenue instead of the pockets of the mandarins and merchants down south. He knew the Queen Mother had been right, and, having just been told by his doctor he only had a short time to live, he had found the courage to send a memorial to the Son of Heaven saying so.

'So long as the commerce in foreign mud is illegal, it plunges officials from high to low into traffic with the most criminal elements of the population and with the uncontrolled and uncontrollable outer barbarians: a situation which grows worse every year and makes law, order or public morality impossible.'

What did it matter now if the Emperor degraded him and sent him to Ili ? He would never arrive. In the meantime he redeemed himself in his own eyes for having told the Court the truth for once.

* * * * * *

John Davies Anoints his Heir

As for John Davies himself, one thought was on his mind as he sat in the wide airy upstairs study of the Casa Garden gazing through the tilted green shutters at the little chapel in the Protestant cemetery next door. It distressed him to leave China for London knowing Sir George Roberts would succeed him as the new Trade Superintendent. He had been a pompous old ass when with the old Company, because he demanded his due as entitled by birth, and still was. How to get rid of him? Then he had it. He jumped up and strode down the spacious stairs shouting for Bettina.

He found her in the lower level of the Casa Gardan secretly feeding the very birds whose persistent shrieks drove him to distraction. Caught in the act she gave a guilty start.

'So you're responsible for my torment,' he accused her more cheerfully than she expected, relieved to find he only had Sir George on his mind. 'The Commission has four officers and two commands. That is simply ridiculous now we have no powers and no Company Court. Leads to a total conflict of responsibilities. Each, if followed, defeats the other. Too many generals without an army. What we do, Bettina, is simplify the Commission'.

Thankful to escape a scolding for taming the birds, she was enthusiastic. 'Because Jarman thought he could divide and rule.'

'Exactly!' He thrashed his arms and the birds rose startled in the path of Captain Forge rounding the corner of the Residence. 'Confounded birds know I'm no birdlover.' He steered Captain Forge upstairs.

'Good news?' Barron enquired as John Davies settled him in an easy chair with a good Manila cheroot in his hand.

'You might say so.' John Davies snipped the end of his own cigar, 'I've untied the Gordian knot.'

'What knot?' Forge waited politely.

'I will see to it that my heir apparent will be you.'

'I?' Forge leant forward in consternation. How could that be when he was only second in line in succession now John Davies was leaving and Sir George had not the slightest intention of rejecting succession as Trade Superintendent on the China coast, a far more important and well paid post than any he could secure at home.

John Davies added to his mystification by catechising him, 'you have learnt what bitter feuds and factions have sprung up in Canton with the new age of free trade?'

'I know that whatever one party proposes the other is certain to condemn most violently.'

'You are aware this petition expresses the political aggression and hostility by which the acts of some of the British merchants have been constantly marked.'

Captain Forge nodded, 'undoubtedly the work of the war party.'

'You know their true purpose is to defend their right to step into the Company's shoes as a virtual monopoly. Old John Company never had more than twenty ships. Jarman Malleson already have forty-five and their capital is considerably larger.'

Forge regarded Davies with dismay. Was he a tired, irascible man too long away from Home, or a more astute judge of a crisis than anyone else because he had been so long away from Home?

'They have learnt much in the Orient, Barron, including the gentle art of saying one thing and doing the opposite. I tell you the trade of the United Kingdom to China will fall into the hands of men who would not be received with honour on the London Stock Exchange. No one who lays claim to the distinction of an honourable British merchant will, in a few years, be able to carry on business in China with credit to himself.'

Captain Forge gave him a wry look. 'You say all this and urge me to the responsibility of heir apparent?'

John Davies had the grace to laugh. 'Rather let me say, if I can urge some reform on Whitehall I hope you will be.'

'Say for the sake of argument, I became heir apparent,' Forge said with an engaging smile, 'What then?'

'You could lose your good name in the battle to come.'

'Even as they will?'

'Even as you will but they will not. These privateers will mislead His Majesty's Government that the Chinese government is weak, ignorant, treacherous, greedy, fraudulent and beneath contempt. You'll have to defend the honour of both their country and ours when they prove to be none of these things. And probably fail to defend either.'

Forge leant back absorbing the full import of Davies' warning. 'What you're saying is I must be my own man.'

'What I'm saying is that you must understand, as Clive of India did so brilliantly, that when you deal with the Oriental you must think like the Oriental and that is never how an Englishman thinks. Let them rant and rail at you, abuse you, call you all the names their fertile brains can devise, but at all costs at all times listen to both your own voice and that of China. That is your lonely path of honour.'

Captain Forge was pensive at the unattractive picture Davies had painted for his future. 'I suppose a Captain, if anyone, is trained for it. But what of Sir George?' After all that was the original point.

John Davies had no doubt. 'He'll hang himself.'

Captain Forge felt as though the prophet Sybil had given him some terrible oracle and, for a moment, thought of the famous heroic Portuguese poet, Camoens, who had spent so many years of bitter exile on this very spot, disowned and neglected by the country that would claim him, long after his impoverished death, as one of their greatest and most honourable sons.

* * * * * *

142

Trade not Always What it Seems

Holly pleaded a headache when Mary Ann went to play whist with the Trade Commission ladies. In truth, she was in no mood either for trivial gossip or for trying to explain the idiosyncracies of China to people clearly not genuinely interested in enlightenment. Like so many visitors, they were blind and deaf to the magic of China, or to its high level of civilisation.

Instead she sat working on plans for the coming season on the verandah outside her bedroom. It was only a matter of days now before Jim Peel's beaming face would confront her with tidings good or bad. Some rumours of a shaky stock market in New York and London had already come on the tide with the first vessels in for the tea season. But others had scotched them. A good phrase she thought for the Jarman Mallesons, who were past master at 'scotching' rumours to suit themselves.

Her thoughts drifted to Sean Jarman provoking the usual conflict within herself to suppress them. What future could there possibly be any future for her with a man of his profession, at least until the Canton system was blown apart and women became eligible to enter China? She admitted grudgingly to herself she ought therefore to support Jarman Malleson's ambition to achieve exactly that concession and set aside her conscience towards them in the matter of opium. So great was her longing for Sean, she could almost be tempted.

A loud argument suddenly intruded on her reflections and brought her back to the present. An argument in itself was nothing unusual. The Cantonese were always erupting into shouting bouts over trivial issues. But this time the altercation rose up the stairs. She moved inside her bedroom in time to face an officer marching towards her backed by a squad of soldiers armed with swords. She stood dumbfounded a moment. Hadn't she been assured Chinese never entered the dwellings of Europeans not even to arrest Chinese, let alone Chinese soldiers? The officer hesitated. So did she. Then his troops began to search her chests and cupboards with bursts of gibberish and hilarity at what they found.

The fighting blood of Holly's forbears rose to the fore. She advanced towards him shaking her fist, 'how dare you burst in here? Where is your search warrant?'

He brandished his sword to bar her escape. The agitated face of their head servant, Afa, appeared at the door.

She shouted, 'go fetchee police.'

Afa replied, 'police no wantee. Afa all gone.'

Holly seized a pillow from the bed, feinted when he lifted his sword tentatively then swiped him about the head from one side, then the other, with a technique long ago perfected in dormitory pillow fights. He evaded and and walked backwards to the guffaws of his own troops and even himself, as she advanced on him screaming 'outside' in Cantonese. With this irreparable loss of 'face', the officer retreated hastily down the stairs and out the front door with Holly in full cry behind until she collided with another young officer on the front step. He announced Chung Tai Tai had sent him aware Holly was alone and would not know an angry Viceroy was on the warpath to make the arrogant fanqui at least tremble if not obey. Holly had never felt so profoundly grateful to Chung Tai Tai as she did now to learn that Chung Tai Tai, unbeknownst to her herself, had been keeping watch on her all the time.

Jim Peel also kept watch on her as best as he could. He arrived next day by the first fast boat from Whampoa to Macao terrified by exaggerated reports of riots that she might be harmed. The relief on his face to find her safely esconsed in the peaceful sunbright morning room was that of a man who has weathered a squall.

She kissed him lightly on the cheek. 'Dear Jim! Such a true friend.' Jim was rueful at the word 'friend', dismayed as ever that she could feel no more for him than the joy of a harmonious friendship, that her response could never match his. She took his hand anxiously as he sat sadly beside her. 'I was worried for you at Whampoa.'

'Only shaking of the fists. Jarman Malleson are spoiling for a fight.'

'What will happen to traders like us then, Jim?'

'Depends on whether we're caught up in the fight or not, Holly. The next time they get the port closed the fight will last longer.'

Her glance was beguiling but her thoughts were not of flirtation. 'Have you any ideas, Jim?'

He clenched his fist to stop himself saying, 'yes, marry me! Trade anywhere but in this God forsaken port.' A port no better than the Buddhist hell of those lurid cartoons in Canton.

Instead he could only gaze at her perched on the flowery chintz couch with such a disconcerting air of fresh innocence. 'The mate of the Eleanor tells me there's a remission of duties on tea in America.' Mundane where he longed to be romantic.

'So you think we should invest?'

'In green tea, yes. Some American vessels are loading up right now. A good season up country they say.'

Holly was incredulous. The news too good to be true. Green tea was in very heavy demand now it was fashionable, and always in short supply. 'Who told you?'

Jim named the linguist of Mowqua, the Viceroy's friend. She forgot Billy had told Mowqua scorned all ocean barbarians and their demon ships, and would happily cheat them blind given half the chance.

'What kind of green tea, Jim, Hyson?' Sharland, the former tea taster for John Company, had told her Hyson meant flourishing spring because its leaves were the tender new leaves on the bush picked before the rain in the early part of the season, then twisted and rolled by hand. Therefore expensive. Jim shrugged his ignorance.

'The real question is will green tea keep?'

'The Company used to ship one sixth of its cargo in green all the way to London - in canisters and double cases of wood high and dry on bamboo platforms.'

Holly ordered Jim back to Whampoa to negotiate quantity and price, no more. She could afford to wait a little longer for trade to get back to normal in Canton. When he had gone, she sampled the tea he had brought, pondering how extraordinary it was that such a light fragile article of commerce should travel so well and so far despite so many hazards for such a profit. It was a miracle, second to none, that those ships had come and gone for over two hundred years as regularly as the monsoon winds whose benevolent rains nourished the tea plants, until it was a vast trade of no less than thiry one and a half million pounds a year to Britain alone.

She chafed once more that she could not be at the hub of Canton's commerce with the men who could parley facts into some sense and exchange ideas over a hot toddy enjoying a life which Billy Howe had cheerfully painted as 'the best club in the world.'

Because of that club, Billy was first to hear a whisper of doubt about the sudden influx of green tea. Not from the usual rumour factory of the Co-Hong merchants but from the unlikely source of Chinnery staying with Joshua Law in Canton while he painted Mowqua's portrait.

'Tea?' Joshua had enquired, unfamiliar with his habits.

'Don't like what they do to the stuff,' Joshua had boomed his bushy eyebrows twitching.

Joshua had thought he meant the treading of tea down in the chest with bare feet. 'Green tea then?'

Chinnery's boom louder. 'Mowqua won't touch it with a forty foot barge pole. Swears it exercises a most powerful and harmful influence on his nervous system.'

Billy dropped his cup of green tea like a hot cake as Joshua coaxed Chinnery to explain why Mowqua was urging everyone to buy it, including himself, if he thought it was so damaging to health.'

Chinnery, abhorring trouble, diverted Joshua. 'Ask Sharland. He says he's detected many attempts to pass off spurious and adulterated teas among the Canton black Bohea in his day.'

'Extraordinary! Adulterated! What could they use?'

Chinnery expanded enjoying the consternation he caused. 'Refuse of Congoo tea! Cheaper Woping! Exhausted leaves! Minced elm or plum.'

Joshua, thoroughly alarmed, begged Chinnery to drag the truth out of Mowqua somehow in one of his sittings. The truth, when it came under sworn oaths of secrecy from Chinnery, was horrifying. Vast quantities of black tea, damaged in the floods, were being dyed green on Honam Island by adding yellow turmeric and Prussian blue and sold as genuine Hyson.

Prussian blue? The words took Billy back to the days of his childhood when his father used to issue dire warnings about touching certain poisons in his pharmacy shop. Prussian blue was made from prussic acid. No wonder Mowqua said it was a powerful and harmful influence. He should have said fatal. He rushed back to Macao on the next fast boat to warn Holly. She must cancel her contract for No. 3 Hyson with Mowqua's son. Threaten to petition the Viceroy if he refused.

Holly threatened to do more. 'I will expose the whole dreadful fraud to the American merchants. I will petition the American Congress.'

'And have the whole American Chamber of Commerce down on your head, Holly, not to mention the Co-Hong. Not all green tea is spurious. Not all merchants are taken for a ride as you nearly were.'

'So you'd leave all those unfortunate people drinking that poison to rot?'

'And all those unfortunate people drinking opium in their laudunum back home! You've been here long enough to learn from the Celestials you can't change the world easily. But there are weapons. Rumour and opinion, Holly, will burn their ugly house down given time. Much more potent weapons than guns.'

She swept away leaving him desolate, deploring the fate that had endowed him with a round boyish face and a flippant manner unlike the swashbuckling romantic heroic looks of Sean Malleson, tailor-made to snatch a woman's heart. What hope did he have?

* * * * * *

Holly Loses her Chaperone

A thick March fog sat on Macao, as a night hood on a bird's cage, reducing all the inmates to silence. The town hibernated under its impenetrable blanket. Only vice walked abroad in its clammy shifting mists.

Mary Ann sat watching Holly tease more warmth out of the fire for Joshua who had sat coughing fitfully all evening as he had often done of late. Mary Ann was not unduly alarmed. He had had the same settled cough before and shaken it off. But not quite like the paroxysm he was having now. Perhaps she should see Dr. Tom about changing the medicine. She shrugged off the thought as the fit eased. He hated it so if she fussed.

Suddenly he pushed his chair away from the struggling flame complaining of its heat. Mary Ann jumped up anxiously. Surely he was not running a fever again? Just as she reached him, shawl in hand to drape around his shoulders, he jerked forward in a fresh spasm of coughing. A thin bright red arc of blood spewed from his choking lips to sizzle on the glowing red coals of the fire as if it were another fuel to coax the flame. Mary Ann was not mistaken this time. That spurt of dear Joshua's life-blood was a declaration of death, an announcement that the close joy of their life together in Macao was now at an end. No need for Dr. Tom to pronounce the fatal word, tuberculosis, as he did when he rushed to their summons.

Joshua Law's household gathered for a grim conference which really had only one decision to make. Whether he should sit out his last days in Macao or sail for home. Useless for Mary Ann to plead the voyage might cut his life short. The tropic heat! The demonic Cape storms! Leave her alone in this madhouse? Never, Joshua said!

Holly lay on her bed plunged into selfish despair while Mary Ann was in a whirl of packing for her departure. She was losing a home, the sister she had never had in Mary Ann, and a father for a second time in Joshua.

Mary Ann chided her for her apathy when she ran her to earth. 'Why the blue blazes aren't you packing?'

Holly sat up abruptly. 'Me packing. What on earth for?'

'Of course you're coming home with us.'

Holly, shaken from her torpor, was vehement in denial. Mary Ann, who had never imagined Holly would insist on staying without Joshua, a fellow American, to protect her, coaxed her as if a recalcitrant child.

'Holly, you can't live here without a chaperone. No respectable woman lives alone in Macao.'

Holly retorted irritably, 'I seem to have heard that ridiculous argument before. Tell me what's the difference between a single woman alone like me and a married woman alone while her husband is in Canton for months on end?'

'Oh don't be so pig-headed, Holly. You know what difference a wedding ring on the finger makes.'

'Not being on the shelf.' Holly said wryly.

'Not being chased by the hunting pack,' Mary Ann topped her. 'Look, if you won't come with us, what about Abby?'

'And be a cuckoo in the nest? If I were just married like Abby, the last thing I'd want is me.'

Mary Ann put a comforting arm around her. 'You can't live alone. The pack would be after you. What would the gossips say?'

'Piranha the lot them. They'd soon find some other reputation to cannibalise when the novelty wore off.'

'But would you get yours back? No, they would hound you. If you must stay, you must find yourself a home.'

Holly flounced off the bed, disgruntled with Sean, with Jarman Malleson, with the batchelor tradition of the East, for the fact she was not married.

'You're quite right Mary Ann. I would declare myself a target for the male pack in and out of port, even though the 'funny club' seems more involved with gambling than girls.'

She studied her neat, if insubstantial figure, in the narrow cheval mirror, amused these new bouffant fashions made women look as if they were fit for little more than gracing the salons of great houses or waltzing at balls. Mary Ann watched her guardedly. What was she up to now?

Holly swung round in a dance step,'I'm going to ask Flora if she'll have me. She might like some company. Her handsome captain's never home. Always dashing round the fleet keeping up a show of trying to keep order. Mary Ann, do be a darling and be my go-between.'

Flora was enchanted with the idea. Holly's forthright style suited her very well. 'We've tons of room. I rattle round in it when Barron's away.' And she was sympathetic to Holly's plight - her parents dead, no ties with home. It was her own.

In fairness to Flora, Mary Ann thought it best to tell her the whole truth, 'besides she has an interest here.'

'An interest? Any man I know?'

'You should ask any ship I know? The answer is the Eugenia. That is her interest. Have you seen her?'

Flora frowned uncertainly. After all there were well over a hundred ships in port at any one time, many of them similar in appearance to the half-initiated like herself.

'Holly owns the Eugenia. In secret mind.'

Flora clapped her hands. 'Bully for her! Why doesn't she tell the world? Let them applaud her for her guts to get in the ring with men? If only more of our fair sex would.'

Mary Ann cautioned her. 'I don't need to tell you the need for secrecy is obvious. If the Chinese Government come to hear of it, they would not allow the .merchants to sell one chest of anything to Holly. Not one iota.'

'I wouldn't want to embarrass Holly.'

'She's worried she might embarrass you and the Captain.'

'That she should dare to be different?'

'That he, as Master Attendant, shelters someone who is flouting the law forbidding women to trade in the port.'

Flora, as yet, was only dimly aware of the ramifications of the responsibility system. It seemed idiotic when women like Chung Tai Tai could own ships and run casinos. Her reaction was forthright.

'Let them dare object. If Holly can defy convention the least we can do is back her up. She is lucky to have Jim Peel.

* * * * * *

Ghosts of the Triad

Holly moved down the path of the little Protestant cemetery, drowsing under its copious trees, parasols in one hand, fans in the other against the rising heat, in a sombre processional to the graveside of Lord Nash. Already she regretted the fact her friends had talked her into a mourning service for Lord Nash at the request of Lady Nash now back home in Scotland with her as yet unmarried daughters. It reminded her all too vividly of that final day when she paid her respects to her parents' graves before she sailed for China knowing she might never return, and oppressed her with the same desolation the three ladies must have felt on that funeral day when they interred his mortal remains in a lonely unadorned grave for ever.

She wept openly when the Reverend Vaux spoke the very same words as on that heart-wrenching day, words to sustain men against grief and disaster.

'In a moment at the last trump, the dead shall be raised incorruptible. Oh death, where is the sting? Oh grave, where is thy victory? Thanks be to God who gives us the victory through Our Lord Jesus Christ.'

Words that expressed the consolation of Christian salvation, the great mystery at its heart. What was the right path of virtue to deserve salvation, Holly wondered? Ask one half of Macao and they would give you a different answer to the other half. Was the path the poor lost soul of Lord Nash had trodden the right path? Lady Nash had seemed to think so as she had stood proudly beside his grave.

When Lady Nash had paused with the Reverend to pay respects besides Dr. Norris' grave because 'he had fallen in her husband's cause', Holly felt rather he had fallen weary of life embracing death with the joy of his own last sermon. 'Blessed are the dead which lie with the Lord from henceforth. Yea, saith the spirit, that they may rest from their labours and their works do follow them.'

Flora's thoughts were otherwise, that some of her friends gathered round this grave might well be unlucky enough to 'lie with the Lord' before their stint in the East was over to judge by the number of men, women and children buried there. Even, she dreaded, her poor dear overworked Barron.

Their quiet contemplation of the hereafter was suddenly broken by a noisy altercation near the chapel. Even more shocking, Holly could see that Billy

Howe and John Davies were in the thick of it.

Lady Roberts, it seemed, had been idling while they were at Dr. Norris' grave, and, hating litter, had picked up a sheet which she declared had a Chinese poem on it, and asked the unwary Billy Howe to translate. He had begun 'Vast was the Central Nation. Flourishing the Central Dynasty' when he halted in horror recognising it as a Triad manifesto, a summons to rebellion. He had jibbed at reading more. But she had insisted until, deciding the more he insisted the more she would persist, he gabbled through the rest.

'A thousand regions sent tribute. Ten thousand nations did homage but the Tartar nations obtained it by fraud and the grudge can never be assuaged. Display aloft the flowery standard.' He baulked at the rest. 'Enlist soldiers, procure horses, raise troops and seize weapons. Let us exterminate the Manchu race.'

Lady Roberts was still suspicious. 'What does it mean?'

Billy lied. 'Street slogans, blown in here.'

'Over a high wall with no wind?'

Memory stirred in Holly - family stories of rebels meeting in graveyards during the American revolution. She murmured absent-mindedly, 'rebels meet in graveyards.'

Lady Roberts pricked up her ears at the word 'rebel.' 'Rebels meeting here? In our graveyard? Planning an uprising? What will happen to us?' Her voice was shrill with fear.

Davies hastened to repair the damage. 'Dreamers, no more. Always endemic in China.'

But Lady Roberts read the Canton press.'Were they dreamers who rioted at the provincial examination halls of Canton?' She dug him in the ribs with her umbrella. They had lived together in the same town for a long time. She knew when he was foxing. 'I smell treason. I must warn the Magistrate.' She thrust him aside, snatching the paper from Billy.

'You're wasting your time,' he warned her trying to keep up with her determined march out of the graveyard. 'He bewails his bad luck that he's no further up the ladder to the clouds than this miserable port daily. Will he jump willingly off that ladder by admitting that treason has reared its ugly head in his domain?'

When Lady Roberts thrust the offensive paper at the Magistrate, sitting like a crosslegged idol on his red divan before a shrine to the God of Law, he blanched as he read. Without a word of acknowledgement he consigned it to the flame of the incense stick smouldering before the God, brushing his hands together in repudiation. 'There is no paper!'

Lady Roberts departed in loud condemnation 'no wonder China's going to the dogs.'

When her 'secret' went the rounds of Macao, no one was more worried about that scrap of paper than Chung Tai Tai. She questioned Kaida anxiously. 'If the Viceroy hears, he'll start a witchhunt in Macao. He's not sure whether new leaders are allied or the old in the cloud of rebellion on his horizon.'

'Then you should make it clear they're not. You will have to pay him more silver.'

She wagged a reproving finger at him. 'Kaida, like all young men you think answers grow in a straight line. When you are as old as I am, you will know they never are. If I pay the Viceroy more to prove my allegiance, he will only ask for more next time. You must begin as you would end.'

'You will do nothing?'

'And be so foolish? No, I will close the back door. But not with silver, no, but with a paper. One for the Viceroy to see. One that implicates Whampoa not Macao where the Red Circle hides, and their leader when he's not in the walled city of Kowloon. One that you will give Holly's comprador, Pu Ping Pang, to deliver to the Prefect of that district. He is an honest man. He knows the price officials like himself will pay if the Red Circle cause trouble here in Macao and the Magistrate does nothing.'

Holly was bewildered when Kaida waylaid her to ask her to do a favour for Chung Tai Tai. 'Why I thought it was she who owed me a favour, not the other way round.'

'She is doing you a favour. If the present conspiracies for war succeed in destroying the trade in this port, how will you survive? Only the giants of free trade will emerge, and you'll be no better than bumboats in their wake.'

Holly demurred. 'You ask me to plot against my own.'

'I thought no love was lost between America and England. Do you believe they should act as pirates?'

'I believe I'm only a very small cog in a very big wheel.'

The allusion was lost on Kaida. He held out a small packet of Hyson tea. This is my real argument. I appeal to your spirit of revenge.

She was startled. 'So you know I nearly got caught. What does she want of me?'

He handed her a doctored duplicate of the paper the Magistrate burned with a few more lines than the original. 'Give this to Pu Ping Pang. He will know what to do with it.'

* * * * * *

Holly loses her pilot

Holly's luck ran out within the week when she lost Jim Peel. Captain Forge brought the evil news to Abby in Macao first, for only Abby was close enough to break the news to Holly.

Jim Peel had made a last minute sortie to Canton from Whampoa to take up an under-the-counter offer of gems from Little Jerusalem. He had travelled in a three man gig with only two sea cunnies at the oars pushing along the overcrowded river to catch a ship about to leave on the flood. He had actually been in sight of the flock of American clippers anchored at the upper end of Whampoa reach where the river narrowed and the current became more turbulent, when the accident happened.

A boat, not over large, had run him down with apparent deliberation ignoring his shouts of protest and brandished fists. The light gig had tipped in the heavy wash hurling him into the water. None of the bumboats or barges went to his aid. Jim, weighed down by the jewels in his webbing belt pouches, had struck out clumsily towards a boat anchored nearby. When he clutched the rail, its grim crew had battered his hands with a heavy stick until he released his desperate grip.

He had swam to another, and yet another, driven away each time with hostile abuse until his last hope was the lifeboat of the Joy frantically rowing towards him in the gloom. It had almost reached him when inexplicably he rolled with one last terrible cry for help as if being drawn down into the depths of hell itself and vanished like a stone.

'The curse of the Pearl River,' Sean explained 'Men sink if they fall overboard in these waters, even strong swimmers. No one knows why.'

It was Abby who volunteered to tell Holly, Abby who found her watching a glorious golden butterfly flitting among the blossom-rich bushes thinking how beautiful all the creatures of this amazing country were. She stared at Abby in growing shock as Abby unfolded the tale, holding her hand to ease the pain betrayed by her stricken face.

'But surely, if anyone could have survived long enough to swim to the Joy it was Jim Peel. He was an excellent swimmer!'

She did know why Jim Peel was handicapped by his burden of jewels however. He was trying to pick up the profit lost by his mistaken advice to invest in that odious green tea. His loyalty to her his sentence of death.

Abby offered the smelling salts from her reticule. Holly refused, looking away to follow the butterfly on the inconsequential flight of its brief destiny.

'Find Sean Dare for me. I have a question to ask'

Puzzled Abby left her. Who could she send to run Sean Malleson down? Not Billy Howe. Not John Norris. She could scarcely go hammering on one batchelor's door after another. News of such goings on would run through Macao faster than a forest fire. Only Tim Bird, the elder of Macao could find Sean. He was above reproach. And he was a man who respected other people's mysteries as part of the necessity of preserving his own.

Holly waited in the garden watching the eggboats flitting across the ochre bay like the butterflies beside her - less colourful, less aimless but with a destiny that made little mark in the world except to add energy and vivacity to the human landscape. Holly knew that she would, in a sense, drown like Jim if she could not reach out with a sense of purpose. She would lose her desire to achieve, her conviction that anything was worth achievement. She would be defeated by her anger at a God who could allow Jim to die, and to die in such indignity. She would become obsessed by a hatred for China's callous indifference.

At first she had summoned Sean out of a primitive need to have consolation from someone who could give it from affection and love rather than friendship, consolation Billy would have given her or John Norris, if she had but known. But she had to be honest with herself that her innate instinct as a trader had dictated the choice of the shoulder she would cry on. She needed another captain for her ship at once if she were not to go bankrupt. And Jarman Malleson had the one man she could trust - Tough Wagoner.

Sean Dare felt as a man who had reached landfall after a long voyage when he saw Holly's desolate face staring out to sea. This was the moment towards which his life had moved, for which his life was meant. Wordless he stood before her, became the landscape her eyes must embrace. He only knew he had been summoned at last. She had asked for him. Her eyes asked for him now, asked him to cross all frontiers of doubt, custom, propriety that so far had stood irrevocably between them. He put out his hands to grasp hers, the force in them such that she rose to meet him and was in his arms, head on his shoulder. Their embrace wordless, speech enough. They stood unmoving in the whispering landscape of evening breeze and birds, experiencing the revelation they had needed each other to become whole. How had they ever been happy before without this profound sense of happiness? How could they be happy again without each other?

Holly remembered Jim with an onrush of guilt to think she could have forgotten his terrible death for a moment. She pulled away and drew Sean to the seat beside her. 'I must be honest. I needed your help. You are the only man in this port who knows my secret. Jim was my captain, my partner. He was due to start the voyage home with our cargo. He lost his life in the cause of our profit. The cause would be in vain if no one can take his place.'

Disappointment dampened his elation. Was she nothing more than a shrewd, calculating minx who sought to captivate him merely to solve her problems? As if she had read his thought she answered his doubt.

'I know you must judge me badly, that I only brought you here to use your kindness of heart to help me out of trouble. But I would not abuse you so. I called for your help because you're the one and only man in all the world to answer my need.'

He swept her into his arms again. She wept against his shoulder inconsolably for the first time. He held her tenderly at first as she lay there racked with sobs. Then as passion rose in him he kissed the tears on her cheeks. She looked up once more with undisguised longing and their lips met to seal a silent bargain of love and trust.

They lingered there into the twilight. When he left reluctantly at last to keep an engagement, he had promised to find her captain for her, but she had not promised to marry him. Not while his fiance still waited for him back home. They must be sure their feelings were true and strong enough to justify such an overturning of all plans for his future.

He left her torn between the wisdom of such caution and his ardent desire to declare his love to the world. Yet she was right. The world, in the shape of his uncle and James Malleson would be less than appproving to see him march down the aisle with Holly at this very moment - with James Malleson away in London calling for revenge, even war, in China and his uncle urging him to trade offshore up the Coast where the dangers were considerable. Hardly a future to offer a new bride even one as stalwart as Holly.

By the time Holly stood in the tiny crowded Company chapel for the memorial service to Jim Peel to hear the Reverend admonish her to cherish no anger against the will of the Lord, her anger was no longer merely directed against the blind whim of fate or the callous indifference of the Chinese boatmen who failed to rescue him. It was now focussed against the boat that had run him down at Whampoa believing its revenge deliberate because Jim Peel had been the go-between for Chung Tai Tai through Pu Ping Pay, causing the Viceroy to arrest a dozen men from Whampoa village.

The Reverend's resonant voice rose loud in the tiny crowded Company chapel with its reproof that anger against the will of the Lord was a rebellion against God himself. She was rebellious. She could no longer kneel and give proper reverence to a God, who allowed such a cruel and uncharitable fate to one so young.

When she met Tough Wagoner again she had to agree God was at least infinite in His wisdom if not His mercy. Tough was more than she could have hoped for with the same sensitive understanding, steady eyes and faintly mischievous smile as Jim Peel. Hopefully he would prove as loyal and skilled a captain. However, he would not be a partner. Jim Peel had left all his worldly goods to her. A windfall that gave her no joy because of the way it came to her.

CHAPTER 6

The Misfortunes of Holly
over her new Captain

Sunday parade of the ladies under the banyan trees of the promenade of the Praya Grande was a chance for inconsequential chatter with those ladies on whom you would leave your calling cards, and for gossip about those on whom you would not. Among them Portuguese ladies of uncertain origin and mestizos whose origins were almost indecipherable - a mingling of Japan, Manila, India or China itself. It offered the chance for mental notes on this new dress or bonnet, and speculation as to whether they were faithful copies or caricatures of London fashion. It was also an occasion for sly observation - Mrs M's immaculate appearance as usual, Mrs. W. with 'the whole workbasket on her back', Mrs. X. with 'the whole lace factory on her rig.'

Holly was too absorbed in this Sunday pastime to see Sean Jarman striding towards her, his admiration for her plain in his eyes. When he loomed up beside her, she felt a jolt at the pit of her stomach, a flush surge through her body into her cheeks - his very presence a physical assault.

Her voice strangely choked in her throat, she murmured. 'You gave me such a start.'

'The last effect I would have on a beautiful lady. Didn't my servant tell you I would meet you here?'

She shook her head not trusting her voice any longer. He smiled down at her, saying 'the half-wit!' Conscious he too had only half his wits about him when with Holly. She wished she were anywhere else than in the formal ritual of the promenade - in his arms, dancing or sitting in the moonlight alone. Beyond that, she did not have the courage of imagination.

Sean serious now. 'Have you heard the latest trouble?'

'Trouble?' she echoed, let down. So he had not come to see her at all, only to use her. The bright pleasure in her face died away. He said nothing to restore it.

'Trouble over the Argosy.'

She frowned puzzled as they strolled along. 'Trouble? How can there be trouble? I saw Captain Tremayne land an hour ago.'

'Not all his officers, Holly. Twelve of his officers and crew are missing. The Captain sent them ashore for a pilot not far south from here. They did not return. Only a boat with a ransom note.'

'Why the undue concern, Sean?' she enquired with lukewarm interest. Such alarums were frequent these days and quickly settled. 'The Argosy is not one of your vessels.'

'I have two friends aboard, one of them Tough Wagoner.'

She stopped in mid-stride. 'Tough on Raine's ship?'

'We have friends aboard each other's ships despite our rivalry.'

'Does Raine know that Tough is a friend?'

'No, he does not,' Sean replied chagrined.

'Would the correct description be a spy?'

'Rather 'tit for tat'. We do it to each other.'

In her dismay she accused him, 'I should have known you would be unscrupulous.'

Disgruntled, she leaned on the stone coping of the promenade wall. He leaned close, his proximity and the intent gaze of his green eyes, so perfectly set below his bold eyebrows and high sweep of his brown hair, unnerved her. She knew only one thing clearly. They were on their own merry-go-round of fate.

With an effort she came back to the business for which he had come. 'You're after the ransom for the unfortunates still on shore.'

'You're after the unfortunates themselves if you want your captain now. Ransom takes time.'

A doubt sprang in her mind. 'Who captured them? It can't be the usual pirates. They avoid foreign vessels.'

He avoided the question. 'Does it matter who they are?'

'Yes it does. Because the mandarins have stuck their nose in.

Holly understood now. Wheels within wheels. The mandarins were concerned to prevent the growth of independence among these villagers whose intransigence, encouraged by Jarman Malleson, could only threaten their own revenue networks and their power. Sean continued, 'the mandarins now hold them hostage in the prison of Canton.'

As if hypnotised she could invoke no will to refuse him. 'What help can I possibly give?'

'See Captain Forge for me. Ask him to go to Canton to apply through the Co-Hong for the release of these twelve men. Nothing less will suffice.'

You're wanting Captain Forge himself to go?' The idea was outrageous. Neither he, nor Sir George, had any official standing with the Viceroy after the fate of Lord Nash.

'He's still Master Attendant in charge of shipping.'

'With no right to communicate with the Viceroy or anyone else. How can he demand that right after what happened to Lord Nash?'

'He can argue a special case. The men have committed no crime under Chinese law.'

He was too close, too obviously intimate. The tongues would be wagging. She forced herself to join the promenade, forced herself to think rationally. There was more in this than met her eye.

'Why doesn't Raine pay the ransom and save everyone the trouble?'

'Pay their ransom once and you put all travellers in danger. Will you ask him Holly?'

She hesitated no longer although knowing her heart spoke against her head. She would do what he asked if only to see him again, but could not resist one last barb. 'You want a spy in their camp as well as Raine's?'

He caught his breath with anger and desire and fear to recognise the two went together, fear of what he might want to do with her if ever they were together alone without a barrier between.

To Holly's relief she did not have to compromise herself with Captain Forge. He had already decided to act without consulting Sir George. He was in charge of shipping, not Sir George. He would join Captain Mahoney of the Argosy at the Petition Gate to plead for the release of the men. He guffawed when Holly asked naively 'will Sir George approve?'

'When he doesn't want any man Jack of us to remain in Canton? Says we should all be withdrawn from the bad influences of the people there?'

'Won't it put you on bad terms with Sir George?'

'I'm afraid so. He'll not take kindly to my independence. It will appear to diminish his authority.'

'But not yours, Captain,' Captain Mahoney interposed.

'No I believe captains like yourself know Sir George is wrong to rule by the letter of the law. You see Holly it was possible to run the Honourable John by ironclad rules but not the quarter deck of free ships. That requires a little 'give' in an officer. Knowing when to stay on the bridge and when to take command on the lower deck.'

Flora put her arm around him. 'Canton is the deck.'

How Holly envied the warmth of Barron's response to Flora. To have such a marriage as their's was every girl's dream. One she would never see transformed to reality, she feared, so long as she was consumed with passion for a man who so obviously did not see his desire for her as the consuming necessity of his being.

Today more than ever Holly felt the Forge household was a God-given refuge for her, light and bright as their devoted relationship and the warm familiar symbolism with which they surrounded themselves. The sweet pea motif of the chintz sofas and curtains, and muted flowers from English gardens on the wallpaper, was romantically reminiscent of the sentimental security of an English home in a world utterly removed from the hostile exoticism of China - from its bizarre population, its extremes of landscape, its enigmatic, most curious customs.

Holly proved right in her warning that Barron's decision would cause a collision with Sir George, who summoned him imperiously to say. 'No I'll not allow you to communicate with that government nor will do so myself until I get my orders from London.'

'That could take many months, Sir George.'

'Until then I command absolute quiescence.'

'Sir, you should protest at the illegal imprisonment.'

'Protest on what grounds? These men had no permission to land.' Sir George puffed away at his pipe unconcerned.

Captain Forge clenched his fist, his voice curt. 'They needed a pilot, Sir George. It's often been done before.'

'They knew the risks,' Sir George opined, his intractable attitude in keeping with his indolent manner.

Captain Forge reminded himself Sir George had been in China so long he treated life as inconsequentially as the Chinese themselves did. He had become case-hardened to suffering. 'What if they are murdered?'

'I will protest to the mandarins. No more.'

Captain Forge rose. 'If you won't act, I will, Sir.'

Sir George rose in alarm. 'You, my junior, defy me?'

'I do not act as second superintendent under your orders in this matter, Sir, but as His Majesty's Master Attendant and therefore outside your jurisdiction. I propose to go to Canton and present an open letter at the Petition Gate marked 'a matter of life and death'.'

Sir George thumped his desk in temper that the Captain had checkmated him. 'You would flout my Commission to conform to the laws of the country?'

Enjoying his advantage in height over the portly knight of the realm as well as in argument, Captain Forge retaliated, 'Sir George, your Commission also tells us to make contact with the authorities by whatever means.'

'You understand I'll have to report your insubordination to the Minister?'

'How can I be guilty of insubordination, Sir George, when there is such a contradiction in your orders?' He sprang to attention, saluted and marched out of the room lest he degrade himself by losing his temper with a man not worth the indignity.

He walked away from the Casa Garden up the rocky hillside to the Grotto of Camoens to let the cool shelter of the shallow cave of stone restore him to calm from the acute exasperation of dealing with a blockhead of an official, much as the poet Camoens himself must once have done so long ago. What an infuriating man Sir George was! Twelve thousand miles from home and he would not lift a finger till London told him when and how. Timid as any time-serving civil servant afraid to step outside written orders unless he should earn a stiff rebuff from his Court of Directors in London. No wonder men like Dr. Jarman and James Malleson were contemptuous saying the timid old supercargoes of the former Company should never have been appointed to the new Trade Commission.

He, at least, had been trained, as a Captain ranging the ocean far from any authority, to resolve problems without orders from the Admiral. He at least had learned it was better to be decisive even if wrongheaded than to be immobilised in face of the enemy. Even Lord Nash had known that.

As he made his way back through the leafy oasis of ferns and banyan trees, he knew he could never mend his fences with Sir George now that gentleman threatened to write to Lodon disowning his actions as rash and unnecessary. Nor could he expect any help whatsoever from Sir George, not since his superior's final jibe at his retreating back that he could not expect to be bailed out if he were taken hostage as no doubt he would be. He recognised a meanness, unusual in his generous character, to hope John Davies, when back in London, would succeed in having Sir George recalled. He had no doubt he would.

For John Davies would see that Viscount Palmerston at last resolved the irreconcilable conflict between them as to whether British policy was merely to facilitate trade, legal or illegal, as well as they could, or to act as emissaries of the Crown charged with establishing better diplomatic relations, formal or informal, with the Chinese authorities. And John Davies would make sure to emphasise the unwisdom of Sir George insisting on living on the Louisa in the middle of the Lintin fleet on the grounds that this allowed him best to control their activities and to avoid trouble with the mandarins. He might have added that it enabled him to avoid danger from the rioters of Macao.

* * * * * *

Holly wins her Captain back

Captain Forge kissed Flora and their baby long and fervently. Her response was tempered with anxiety he was about to march into the heart of the lion's den of Canton. 'You're going with only two escorts my love. I don't like it.'

He kissed her again to reassure her. 'To avoid any impression that I'm being aggressive, my angel.'

'Must you honestly go?'

He caressed her copper hair vivid as a parrot's wing. Given the choice he would never leave her. 'If the sailors in the port are to respect me. Respect is the only weapon I have to control them.'

'Can't you find some other issue?' she asked, proud of the handsome figure he cut in his braided full dress uniform.

He sighed. 'My job is to control the shipping in this port. I must prove I can protect them when in trouble.'

'Even trouble that begins outside the port?'

'Where does 'port' begin and end in this country, my lovely Flora? If a ship is in trouble anywhere on this coast, men must be able to land without fear of imprisonment, degradation or torture.'

'Can you knock on the Petition Gate without that fear?'

He could not, so he prevaricated. 'No one is allowed into Canton beyond the city gate.'

As Captain Forge worked his way up river from Whampoa to Canton, he thought ruefully he hardly presented the stock mandarin image of an ambassador. Assuredly both he and Captain Mahoney wore full dress uniforms, ablaze with gold frogging and epaulettes, and dress swords at their sides. But the fast passage boat that carried them was as plain and unadorned as the meanest Tanka boat. His interpreter, Dr. Grusson, was dressed no better than a scarecrow in his ancient straw hat and badly fitting suit although exhorting them 'face' would be everything.

'Then you should reinforce my rank by showing the greatest marks of respect to me when we get there,' Captain Forge teased him as the towering bulk of the Petition Gate by the Third Pagoda came into view.

'And what might those be? I can't salute. I'm not an officer. Do you want me to kowtow like the Dutchman in Pekin?'

They roared with laughter as the passage boat drew into land. The standing joke on the Coast was the story of the foolish Dutch when the Emperor gave audience to their ambassador forty years before. They had yielded to repeated demands they should kowtow to the Emperor by kneeling, brows on the floor, only to become the butt of the Court mandarins commanding kowtows on any pretext to see the plump buttocks waving in their tight trousers.

'Would a nod suffice?' Captain Mahoney suggested.

Dr. Gustav dismissed the idea. 'A nod means yes. A bow from the waist would do.'

Captain Mahoney got into the spirit of the joke. 'You could make a leg or present arms.'

'With what? A boat oar?'

As it turned out there was no one to impress. Only one wizened shabby old man ambling from behind his tumbledown stall to challenge their entry through the outer gate. Not one official in sight, not one trader.

'This is the gatekeeper?' Forge asked in astonishment.

Dr. Grusson parleyed in the harsh sing song of the Cantonese language. 'He keeps the gate alright and forbids you to enter.'

Captain Forge could hardly turn back on the remonstrance of one little old man of no apparent rank without losing face. He led the trio on through the postern gate, the square courtyard that gave access to the walls, and then through the inner gate before he met anyone of rank. This proved to be a lieutenant of brass ball rank heading a hastily dressed guard of soldiers, who hustled around them spitting on them as they shoved them backwards into the courtyard from which they had emerged. There they threw Captain Forge on the ground where he lay surrounded by the contemptuous laughter of a growing circle of attackers, thankful he had been able to save his sword in the struggle.

Dr. Grusson, a veteran of mob rule in many a Cantonese street affray, had had the presence of mind to jam himself against a pillar spouting ripe abuse and torrential rhetoric to divert the soldiers from the two captains long enough for Captain Forge to struggle to his feet, thankful both he and Captain Mahoney still had their swords to lay about them if it came to the worst. Grateful above all that that dishevelled little man had kept those sneering soldiers at bay with the force of his tongue and a fixed smile on his extraordinary gnome-like face, not a sword. Not only the unruly crowd but also the officer who appeared at last, by demanding the crystal ball lieutenant be punished for attacking a captain of His Britannic Majesty when on business with the Viceroy.

The officer laughed, no proper courtesy. 'Him an officer? Where's his crystal ball or peacock's feather?'

Dr. Gustav rebuked him. 'Gold means rank.'

'Any Co-Hong merchant wears gold embroidery.'

'What do I do now?' Captain Forge demanded of Dr. Gustav, still put out that he now cut a dirty rumpled figure.

'Endure. It's the Oriental way.'

'They try your patience beyond endurance.'

'But if you endure they will conclude your business must be important. A mandarin will come.'

He endured and was ultimately rewarded when several mandarins, preceded by soldiers with whips, finally arrive in state, young Mowqua following behind sporting a crystal ball and peacock's feather which Dr. Gustav muttered must have 'cost him a pretty penny'.

The mandarins enthroned themselves on red pillows and pretended to listen to the letter only to reject it. They could only accept letters, correctly marked as petitions, not marked 'on a matter of life and death.' On this note they withdrew, leaving Captain Forge fuming at the futility of the prolonged farce of his day at the Petition Gate and chewing the bitter cud of defeat. He felt more like a clown than the respected representative of the awesome naval power of His Britannic Majesty, a power that meant nothing to these jesters in uniform unless they were looking down its guns, and perhaps not even then until those guns blew them up.

This gate was plainly a metaphor for the closed door of China, guarded by men of contemptuous hostility or intractable indifference, a door that would not open for diplomacy or rank any more than it would open for the meanest wretch or foam of the sea.

The bedraggled captain allowed his colleagues to draw him beyond the gate where he stood irresolute, letter in hand, still in half a mind to camp outside the gate until someone took the letter. 'I can't abandon those poor wretches,' he argued.

'You won't gain an inch by staying.' Dr. Grusson cautioned him.

'I don't want to have Sir George laughing in my face as well as those confounded mandarins.'

'Better him than they,' Captain Mahoney reminded him.

He had just begun to rage he would send two armed vessels up to Canton, forgetting he had called Lord Nash all kinds of fool for taking that very action, when the mandarins solved his dilemma for him. A lackey dashed from behind him, snatched the letter from his hand, and vanished as fast as the most skilful Cantonese pickpocket. The circus was over. Their face was saved.

Their landing at the Factories was a relief not only to themselves after the absurdities of the day but to the merchants who were about to storm the Petition Gate to rescue him. They had jumped to the conclusion he had been kidnapped into the city, as linguists had found his empty jolly boat with a tricorn in it.

But as they poured into the New English to offer their congratulations on a lucky escape over a hot rum toddy, a thought overshadowed his conviviality. How was it that mandarins had welcomed a deputation of forty commanders and officers in full uniform so courteously within their city gates just over twenty years before, yet now their descendants had unequivocally barred the gate against him without honours or respect?

He received no congratulations from Dr. Jarman in Number 1 Creek Hong. 'What an arrant fool the heroic captain is! Doesn't he realise the more humble and submissive you are with the Chinese, the more cynical and arrogant they become? Just like the bullies of my old school. He'll learn the hard way it gets him nowhere, least of all with me.'

Dr. Jarman was wrong for once. Captain Forge's posture did get him somewhere despite all forebodings including his own. Viceroy Lu heeded his petition and released the men of the Argosy believing no point of high policy was at stake. His intelligence had been good enough to tell him that Captain Forge was not dancing to Dr. Jarman's tune as Lord Nash had done.

* * * * * *

View of Macao.

Jesuit Cathedral of St Paul, Macao.

The London dock, where East India Company ships were built.

An East Indiaman.

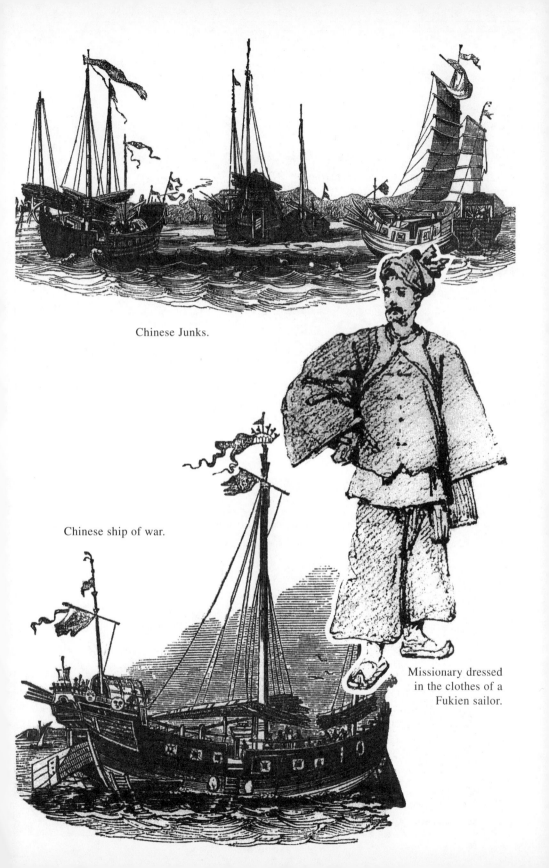

Chinese Junks.

Chinese ship of war.

Missionary dressed in the clothes of a Fukien sailor.

Praya Grande, Macao.

Merchant's residence at Macao.

A Chinese gentleman.

Preparing tea.

View of the Canton River.

Chinese fort.

Chinese soldier.

Military Mandarin.

13 foreign factories, Canton.

Chinese soldiers by a fort.

Chinese artillarymen and gun.

Whampoa, island on Pearl River, near Canton.

City gate.

A prisoner in the cangue.

A beggar 'king' with
three of his organised
gang followers.

Mandarin in his
sedan chair.

Smuggling boats known as 'smugboats' or 'crabboats'.

A mandarin carries the Emperor's official letter.

Paddlewheel steamer destroys Chinese war junks with the new Congreve Rockets.

Port of Ningpo

Grave, as in graveyards,
    where Triads met.

British troops.

Shipwreck at sea.

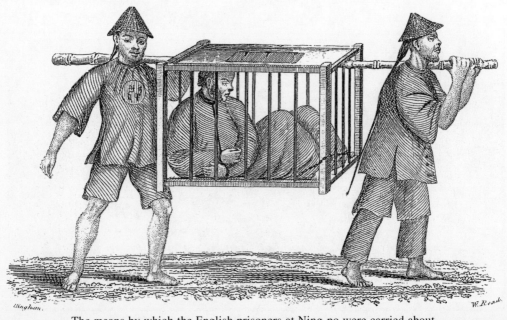

The means by which the English prisoners at Ning-po were carried about.

A Chinese soldier wearing a 'lucky' tiger cap, designed to scare the enemy.

Porcelain Tower, Nankin.

Nankin.

British troops firing on Manchu Tartar Garrison in Chinkiang.

Aboard the Cornwallis to negotiate the Treaty of Nanking

Chinese court room.

Room in a Chinese mandarin's house.

THE FASHIONS OF BRITISH SOCIETY

The *belle* of the evening claims our attention: the lovely dark-eyed girl, so plainly yet so elegantly dressed.

CHAPTER 5

1836
A Battle of Wits

The Winning of Love

If there was a moment when the tide began to turn in Holly's life, it was the night St. Paul's caught fire. Flora and Holly were alone at dinner when they first heard the harsh urgent clamour of the cathedral bells above the blast of an intemperate wind that had roared in from the bay at dusk to an ominous rattle of the shutters. They rushed to the window certain of only one thing, the bells of Macao might be so incessant that one hardly noticed them but they never rang at this time of night in a storm.

'An emergency.' Holly cried alert to the screaming black.

'Yes but where?' Flora was equally baffled as the clamour fluctuated with the gusts of the wind in the clashing palms.

The thought struck them simultaneously. Those bells could only mean one thing. The whole town was being summoned to help as if its citizens were under assault from a deadly enemy.

Holly the first to speak. 'I do believe its St. Paul's.' St. Paul's, the most beautiful of all basilicas in Asia!

They stared aghast at each other. St Pauls was empty. The Portuguese governor quartered his troops in the old Jesuit college next door, ignoring many complaints at their rough and ready ways and warnings about fire.

They threw on their heavy shoes and cloaks, and rushed through the town with their heavy skirts flapping from the rapacious thrust of a hammering wind. As they turned into the road towards the cathedral, they could see writhing spasms of fire and smoke launching a wild pillar of sparks like a brilliant comet across the black carpet of the night from the burning ruins of the old Jesuit college next door, and already laying a gluttonous hold on the roof of the basilica itself. The glare on the straggling streams of people converging to the call of the wild bells made them look like the procession of the damned towards one of the circles of hell.

'Why, oh why, Flora couldn't it have been San Domingo's instead?' Holly mourned in despair. Why must the Jesuit order suffer this last indignity to their proscribed memory - the funeral pyre of the College, once the most famous holy university in the Orient and the church which housed famous devotional relics of their greatest saints such as St. Francis Xavier.

Holly's instant response to the sight of the brothers and nuns darting in and out of the doomed cathedral, clutching sacred icons and gold and silver furnishings from the altar tables, was to dash up the triple steps past the bucket chain of young and old, rich and slaves, shouting to Flora over the uproar 'I must help the nuns.' She plunged through the main door into the vast basilica lit up - as it had never been since its soaring roof first quenched the sunlight - by the glowering fire already crackling in the great vault above her and showering sparks on the long pews below.

Flora watched her rush down the aisle, towards the high altar, one eye on the roof. No way of knowing how rotten those roof timbers were, how old or dry, how long before they would burn through. What chance Holly would have of escape if they burned through now and came crashing down to the floor? A chance she herself was not willing to take.

She felt a violent grip on her arm, swung round to see Sean's fear-stricken gaze in futile search for Holly. 'Behind the altar,' Flora said.

His eyes flew to the roof above Holly already engulfed by terrifying flame. 'She'll be killed,' he roared as he plunged away down the central aisle to find her, a prayer for her safety on his lips, a revelation in his heart. He would be devastated if he were to lose her now. His love for her was his true love, not the pale imitation he had felt for Jean, had accepted because he had known no other until he had met Holly.

No place could be more fitting than this to ask for her hand, this holy place consumed by unholy destruction, this place where transgressing Christians constantly found resurrection.

She was coming towards him from the altar like a miraculous apparition, her skirt lifted high to hold the goblets and icons from the chapels behind. She did not see him, head down to avoid the burning litter of the roof until he was in front of her, arms about her, his grasp holding her burden safe. 'Will you marry me Holly?'

'Sean it's you!' She gaped at him.

'Is that all you can say when a man proposes?'

'Propose here Sean? What a place! What a time! No sunset!' Only the grotesque sunset of the cathedral's dying throes.

'Marry me. Yes or no?' Sean down on one knee in courtly supplication, sparks flying about his shoulders.

'Sean, yes and no. Both. Let's go Sean or I'll be joining you in a funeral not a wedding.'

Sean blocked her way. 'Say yes.'

'Yes of course I'll marry you.'

He swept her away down the aisle on the wings of his exultation and hers. 'When?'

She shouted above the hiss and crackle of the flames. 'I said yes and no. Yes I'll marry you, but no, not straight away. Dismay on his face. 'You in Canton all the time, me in Macao a bride all alone?'

Flora had watched their strange progress towards her with growing amusement at the incongruity of the place and time. But she understood its implications from the shining joy on both their faces, and threw her arms around Holly in congratulation and relief.

Sean persuaded them to the Malleson home as closer than theirs. He took them to the sitting room at the rear of the house, found blankets to drape round their shoulders, and coaxed the dregs of the sullen fire to flare. When it finally burst into flame, he sat down beside Holly on the sofa, his hand over hers.

Flora heeded the strength of the flame that flew between them with misgiving. Could Holly, with her background, ever reconcile her New England scruples with the uscrupulous trade that Jarman Malleson purveyed? She was glad she was there as chaperone because the intensity of the mood of the two lovers could have had only one end.

By some miracle rain fell to quench the fire as the storm blew out, leaving the magnificent facade free-standing in stark silhouette against the still turbulent skies as a permanent memorial to the lost heyday of the Jesuits of Japan and the Court of Pekin.

* * * * * *

Captain Forge defies Sir George again

Captain Forge had an inkling why Sir George Roberts wanted to see him as he swung up the driveway towrds Casa Garden. The goodly Sir Knight was anxious once more that they were about to be invaded by a Chinese army. He was affrighted by every rumour, and magnified one ghost into a thousand. Even his unkindest critics, however, had to concede his delusions were not totally without justification. There were accurate rumours of a power struggle, even a civil war between the Viceroy's braves and Triad smugglers in the delta, but it was unlikely to engulf Macao. And Lady Roberts was claiming he had received a death threat.

However, he was not prepared for Sir George's announcement from behind the solid shield of his splendid desk. 'Captain, we must consider moving the Commission out.' He abruptly mopped his brow with a large cambric handkerchief.

Captain Forge would have treated the news as a joke but for the fact Sir George never joked. He resisted the impulse to laugh. 'Where do you have in mind?

'Where else, of course, but to Lintin Island?'

Captain Forge was stupefied. Sir George, if anyone, should know the Trade Commission would compromise its authority the very moment it moved into the middle of a smuggling fleet.

Sir George continued heedless.'All men, women and children, Captain. I will not be held responsible for any massacre.'

Captain Forge could not let this folly pass. 'Why, sir, has China declared war?'

'China does not declare war, Captain,' Sir George bellowed with exasperation at the instinctive elegance of his subordinate. 'Perhaps you have not been here long enough to appreciate the obscurities of Chinese logic. How can China declare war on people who are her subjects, subjects they are urged to exterminate?'

'Are we about to be exterminated?' Captain Forge asked innocently to stir the coals of Sir George's wrath.

Sir George rose angrily his finger stabbing the air to emphasise his awful warning. 'We are about to be attacked. I have it on good authority. Attacked and plundered by a large party. You know what happens where a Chinese army goes - plunder, rape, kidnap - and in their wake the criminals grow bolder, those very criminals who already infest Macao terrorising citizens. '

So that was it. Sir George had at last become aware of the sinister shift in the wind of politics on the river, the criminal tinge creeping over the Triads in the name of the Red Circle with the accompanying terror of their Red Rods.

Sir George went on, 'the merchants in Canton are hand in glove with the most unruly elements in Canton and Whampoa, and they should be withdrawn from those bad influences or else they will provoke open conflict and reprisal.'

'With due respect, Sir, don't you think they will carry conflict with them wherever they go?'

'Oh yes, all their demands for us to put down the Lion's Paw. If that Paw is to be put down anywhere it should be at Hong Kong. Splendid harbour. A pirate's nest they've never bothered with. It's there for the taking.'

'A taking that would mean war surely, sir?'

Lady Roberts rescued Captain Forge by her summons to tea. She threw up her hands when he hinted over the melted buttered scones that there might be no more such gracious moments for some time if they moved to Lintin. 'What? Miss the social season in Macao? Good Lord no! The regatta? The races? The balls? Especially the play? I was so looking forward to seeing Chinnery in Mr. Sheridan's Rivals. You wouldn't go without me, would you dear?'

'Dear' retired into another scone looking as if he might happily retreat to Lintin without her. 'I can't expose you to an invasion.'

In fact the advancing army turned out to be a gang of six, and her insistence on remaining for the start of the season saved him from appearing an utter buffoon. However, if Captain Forge thought Sir George's phantom army was the end of farce in Macao he was mistaken. This time it was the Laird who flung into the Commission office without notice and threw himself into a chair without invitation to declare 'my buttons have been stolen. Kidnapped on the way to Lintin. You must get them back.'

Captain Forge was startled. Getting sailors back was one thing, buttons quite another. 'Who'd want to kidnap buttons for Pete's sake?'

'You'd better ask the Hoppo's errand boy, the pilot Acha.'

'Then protest to the Hoppo.' Sir George decreed.

The Laird shrugged. 'Your job not mine.'

'I've more important things than a petty consignment.'

'Than 74,000 brass buttons and 43,200 crystal buttons? A pretty penny's worth! That knave of a whore master had the gall to assess them as gold and silver for duty.'

Sir George made no effort to hide his contempt for the Laird or his buttons. No doubt the fellow was trying to dodge duty. 'Are you sure, Mr. Ince, you intended to pay duty on them all and not sell them on the black market? I can't approve you breaking the law of China.'

The Laird thumped the table in fury. 'I was transhipping them, Sir, from a ship bound for Whampoa to a ship bound for Manila. What man in his right mind would pay double duty to that cheating limb of the Son of Heaven?'

Captain Forge had listened to this exchange with amusement. How could the

Laird justify claiming they extend the protection of British law to him for trade he chose to pursue at Lintin where no law applied as Sir George now frostily pointed out?

'If they turn up there'll be hell to pay.'

'What sort of hell do you have in mind this time, Ince? Setting fire to the Customs House again?'

'I could get Wang Chung on the job. Give them a whiff of grapeshot.'

Sir George looked as if he had been given a whiff of the grape himself. He warned the Laird. 'Don't expect me to rescue you from the Viceroy's prison if you do.'

The Laird retreated muttering 'old bag of wind!'

He surprised everyone by confronting the mandarins at the Petition Gate, as Forge had done, after Howqua refused to forward his letter of complaint to the Governor saying the matter was too trivial. Once there he remained obdurate to all Mowqua Junior's wiles to procure his letter until the Prefect himself arrived, then, after more grotesque comedy about whose fingers should touch the letter as it was offered, finally relinquished it to the disdainful three fingers of one more senior than Mowqua Junior. Thus his face was ingloriously saved.

When Captain Forge heard of the Laird's caricature of his own affair of the Petition Gate, in his hilarity he said to Flora, 'he reminds me of a commander I once knew whose idea of strategy in naval warfare was to dash in with all guns blazing without regard to the lie of the wind or the tactics of the enemy.'

The whole affair left Captain Forge with the humiliating feeling he had 'lost face'. He was a tiger without claws. He could not act against the Laird, no matter how unruly he was, unless His Majesty's ships were involved.

* * * * * *

A Matter of Life and Love

The play Lady Roberts was so anxious not to miss was a farce of close encounters, pretences and secrets almost disclosed. Very suitable to China, Holly concluded when she heard. Sean was to play one of the female leads. How she wished she too could have been one of the cast to spend all those intimate hours of rehearsal time with him on a valid pretext. Instead she had to contrive a private comedy of hurried meetings that rivalled the public farce in which Sean also starred.

She sighed with annoyance that she was left to oversee the seamstresses of the lace and satin extravagances the actors would wear with Abby and Flora, complaining that 'it's ludicrous to have men in womens' parts like the old days of opera.'

Flora's response was unsympathetic. 'Would you deny the comics of the port their chance?'

Abby, once star of their school plays, joined her in complaint. 'They might at least have asked me.'

Flora rebuked them. 'If you two had trodden the boards just think how the local gossips' tongues would wag.'

'With woman haters like Chinnery?' Abby pointed out.

Holly agreed petulantly. 'If we acted together in public, the Catholic Portuguese, who think only woman of easy virtue would appear on stage, would be utterly scandalised. And no doubt the Chinese even more so.'

She wondered, even as she spoke, if Chinese women experienced the same sense of frustration at imprisonment within the freedoms, enjoyed by men to regulate the world, as she did.

The play was an enormous success. Dr. Jarman loaned his mansion. Chinnery contrived a theatre from the ballroom, gaudy with Chinese lanterns, with access from the vast sixteen pillar terrace. And one of the stars, Mr. Drummond, insisted on starring to excess by delivering an excessively long prologue beginning 'from Britain's isle the band which plays tonight, unknown to fame presents itself to sight', the band being a sixteen piece orchestra.

'And will continue to be unknown to fame,' Holly prophesied as she shifted uneasily fanning herself in the sticky heat. She forgot the heat instantly when a bonneted Mr. Chinnery minced on as Mrs. Malaprop, advertising himself with every new flounce across the stage as much a clown of genius as an artist. He kept his gravity before the shrieking audience better than the trio of fair 'ladies' when they made their entrance - Mr. Astor as Lydia, the Hon. Drummond as Lucy and Sean Dare as Julia. They came to a halt unable to speak their lines for the suppressed hysterics that overtook them goaded on by the audience.

Sean grimly avoided Holly's eye where she sat crying with laughter. The gales of merriment continued to bring the play to a standstill from time to time and encouraged the actors to even more ludicrous efforts to play for a laugh, most of all in the scene when the Hon. Drummond reappeared as Falkland with a most ardent profession of his impassioned love for Julia, causing 'her' to back off rather than throw 'herself' into his arms. Not exactly, Holly thought, how Sean behaved when with her.

The play over, the chairs whisked away by a gaggle of servants, Billy seized his chance to carry Holly off into the leaps of an energetic quadrille before Sean had time to change and monopolise her. As Billy felt the joy of holding her in his arms, he refused to concede the play was over for him in which he played rival to Sean for her affections. He could still believe he was a knight with her favour on his sleeve, because his heart was pure and his shield bore no sign of the devil on it. He would wait however long it took until she could see for herself he was the right suitor for her hand. If she had to spend her young girl's dream of high romance with the wrong man, then he would have to trust she would ring the golden sovereign in the end and find it spurious.

He prayed a black prayer the gods would see fit to summon Sean back to Scotland on leave sooner rather than later before he put Holly too deeply in thrall. Deep enough already he could see as Sean advanced across the room to ask her to supper, his brooding good looks like august majesty on a Roman coin. Bill took grim satisfaction from the fact Sean could not claim Holly for himself for too long. Women were in such short supply she must change partners every dance, every set of the quadrilles, leaving Sean fuming on the side, praying that all the obstacles that kept him apart from Holly would vanish.

What Sean did not expect in his calculations was the unexpected- Holly in shock when Abby lost her baby. One day robustly smiling as his mother clucked over him, the next seized with deadly dysentery unable to suckle any fluid or finally to cling to life itself. And Abby left to the terrible grief of committing him to a tiny grave beside the many other mournful slabs in the Protestant cemetery.

Holly was forced to face the fact that Abby could hardly be asked to share in any wedding of hers to Sean until her mourning was over, a mourning likely to last months rather than weeks - months during which Sean would once more be obliged to be in Canton with his uncle.

During this time of emotional pause of grief and delay, cholera struck Macao like a thief in the night. No sense in it. Some houses touched. Others not. One side of the street and not the other. No rhyme or reason as to who was struck down. Macao a ghost town. Only the ministering angels like the nuns and doctors abroad to warn, diagnose or ease death as the case may be, among them Dr. Jarman. It was he who came striding up the gravel drive with Sean as Holly lay inert on a cane lounge in the cool shade of the verandah beside Flora busy with her tapestry. Holly, now too drowsy to be aware of sweat trickling down her limbs, to be conscious that Dr. Jarman had broken into a run at the first sight of her, to respond as he felt her pulse and raised her half-closed eyelids.

Sean watched with growing anguish, knowing already what the verdict must be - cholera. The purging, the delirium, the dissolution of life into a blackened corpse in a day.

'Is there hope?' he cried.

'While there's life!' Dr. Jarman exclaimed, dragging Holly to her feet and slapping her face as he ordered Flora 'move, woman, or she'll be dead by dark. Brandy and boiling water! She must not be allowed to fall into morbid insensibility. That's the most dangerous state of all.' Flora rushed indoors.

Next he shouted at Sean immobilised by shock, 'help me to keep her moving.' Together they helped her stagger between them only dimly aware that she must fight to help them help her, and of Dr. Jarman's answer when Sean cried out in despair that cholera was always fatal. 'Not always. We caught her early. We have a chance.'

Flora was back with the brandy. Together they forced a scalding spoon down her spluttering throat again and again. Suddenly she grew limp. Dr. Jarman laid her down, Sean and Flora hovering in frantic desperation. He opened his medical bag, crumbled some dried opium leaf in the boiling water, added brandy then spooned the resulting laudanum down her throat.

Flora watched in astonishment. 'Opium for cholera doctor?

'The universal panacea in India for florid disorders of the bowel,' he answered.

She had neither time nor heart to pause on the paradox that opium could be a blessing as well as a curse to mankind as she bent to put hot compresses on Holly's brow. Meanwhile Sean was urgently moving Holly's limbs at his uncle's terse direction thinking with bitter irony he was permitted an intimacy when she was dying that he had so devouringly desired when she was in the full vigour of life.

Dr. Jarman kept uttering the terrifying words, 'no morbidity yet' although Holly was plainly sliding down the road from torpor into fatal delirium. He was forced at last to declare 'we must try the Caya-puti oil, the last resort of my Hindu friends.'

'Last resort?' Sean watched his uncle fearfully as he reached in his bag again, took out a small phial, and measured a drop or two of the thick liquid with terrifying care as if about to administer cobra poison. 'It can cure. Great danger. A last resort only when death is certain otherwise.' He cradled Holly's lolling head to him, holding her nose to force her to swallow.

They watched as men must once have watched to see if Lazarus would come to life at the bidding of Jesus Christ. The seconds passed like hours. A heavy sweat broke. Slowly, imperceptibly Holly began to stir and mutter as one returning from a profound sleep no more. Suddenly she sat up and looked around her, her return to life as dramatically swift as her decline towards death had been. Flora wept unabashed. Sean stumbled to a seat, head on knees to hide his tears.

A bewildered Holly whispered 'has someone died?'

Dr. Jarman was the only one capable of reply 'Someone has returned from the grave.'

Holly felt as if she had returned from a dream world where the colours and the shapes, through which her liberated fancy had drifted, had such seduction return to the real world seeemed the nightmare. Opium dreams Dr. Jarman explained to her as she lay in a stupor not too deep to recognise her indolent state, indifferent and passionless, was the deliverance from the real world the opium smoker sought time and again.

When Holly, fully restored to the real world, heard it was Dr. Jarman who had snatched her from the jaws of death she knew she could no longer sit in moral judgement of him, nor make her future with Sean stand or fall by moral intransigence towards the opium trade. Although it was a drug of abuse, it was clearly also a drug of use.

Dr. Jarman accepted their profuse thanks distantly, annoyed to have witnessed his nephew so firmly in the clutches of the Yankee lass, all unaware that it was Sean who had Holly in his clutches and not the reverse. Time he packed him off to Manila, he decided, or better still back home.

For the first time Holly thought to ask what these uses were to be amazed by the answer. Opium was the only specific for the aches and pains of malaria, rheumatism, arthritis, toothache, headache, cancer and a dozen more maladies and stomach disorders that flesh was heir too. The Chinese grew it themselves in six provinces, the more distant of these being Yunnan and Schezwan. However their opium was less refined, less pure, less guaranteed in strength than the opium now manufactured to meticulous standards in Bengal province of British India.

Holly, however, was now certain of one thing. When she heard the whisper of angels' wings in her ears, she had irrevocably left childhood behind forever. All sharp confidence the universe offered simple answers was gone. The shelter of parents' law and simplistic dogma was no more. She was not yet certain of the answer to her future, only that it lay ahead as yet invisible across a troubled ocean.

* * * * * *

The hazards of a love match

Holly's gratitude to Dr. Jarman for saving her life had turned to fury by the time he left Macao for the season's trading in Canton. He had played her for a fool, encouraging her in the delusion, that he would not obstruct a match between herself and Sean any longer, by saving her life. How cruelly she had misread his civilities on the many occasions when Macao's incestuous social life had thrown them together. The moment he could no longer keep his eagle eye on Sean, he had deliberately kept them apart by sending him north with the Laird, unlikely to return for months. His assignment to oversee Jarman Malleson's depot ship on the coast near Chusan.

How dare he be so high-handed when he was one of those whom Sir George had berated as 'hand-in-glove with the most unruly elements in Canton or Whampoa', and against whom the fire in Carpenters Square, which nearly destroyed his Number 1 Creek Factory, was a warning. How she hated his supercilious expression and domineering manner, his haughty face, oblivious to the paradox she could so vehemently hate the very looks in Dr. Jarman she so loved in his copper-plate nephew.

Flora could only agree with Holly as she railed against Dr. Jarman over breakfast after a sleepless night. 'the Old Rat banks on the hope absence won't make the heart grow fonder.'

Captain Forge ventured a misjudged joke. 'At least you're safe when Sean can't shop round for rivals.'

Flora rebuked him, 'My dear, it would be more tactful to tell Holly his love for her is so strong nothing can diminish it.'

Then suddenly Sean was there laughing at her fears and forebodings. There to lift her off the ground in a bearhug and tousle her hair with the familiarity of one who claims his own. There because he had defied his uncle by returning with the supply vessel, because he could not bear to be parted from her for the whole season. There to exclaim 'you silly goose' when she said she had been terrified of another Argosy affair. There to douse her agitation about rumours from Pekin of edicts to punish smugglers 'with the full force of the law' because he was trading up coast with smugglers.

'If you only knew the truth!' he said, 'We drop anchor off shore. The local mandarin fires a few shots across our bows. he commands us to be off. We parley we want only food and water. That's legal of course. He reaches into his boot for the decree and reads it out. We can't linger there. We descend into the Great Cabin and get down to the real business of our visit over a cheroot and a glass of sherry.

'He has full information on the latest prices for opium in Canton - all taken from our papers, mark you, as if a regular stock exchange. He gives his order for opium, the bargain sealed with yet another glass. He sails off counting his profits and so do we as we watch him go. $50-$100 more per chest than down here in Canton paid for in sycee silver and this leaves him a good margin of profit. The smug boats heave alongside, load up and away we go with a fair profit.'

She shook him in mock rage. 'Here I was, imagining you in a bamboo cage being hauled off to be starved and mocked.'

'No doubt it will happen to us some day.'

This was an understatement of the truth for there was a darker side to the trade. Gun battles up and down the coast. Men killed and injured. The right of Jarman Malleson and Raine to run a monopoly fought out in a running guerilla war. Not even the mandarins allowed to be neutral but threatened if they dealt with any but the two biggest bullies in the trade.

This time Sean renewed his proposal against a pink and purple sunset as fanciful as a Chinnery theatre set. The fierce intensity of his gaze betrayed his overwhelming longing to pursue possession of her to every reality of his frustrated imagination. A desire that consumed her as much as him, but a desire that could not, should not, be pursued outside marriage in this very proper community where any falling from grace put the sinner forever beyond the pale unless already there.

Alone in the garden one fateful afternoon, Sean kissed Holly with such a desperate passion she had to fight her own most overpowering instinct to surrender all resistance, all common sense, then and there. She felt herself lapsing into a joyous acceptance of his embrace, relishing the sweet taste of his lips, responding with a violence that surprised herself. Alone there under a giant banyan tree, they clung to each other like the roots twining the trunk of the great bole beside them.

'No Sean, no more!' She forced herself away. 'Soon not now.'

His fierce eyes, brilliant with passion, held her own. 'Soon,' he echoed her with fierce promise forgetting for once his uncle was the piper who called the tune of his bread and butter. Cut off by his uncle's displeasure, he would be literally cut off without a shilling.

Twined arm in arm, they agreed on a secret wedding. Abby to give her away as they could not compromise Flora, Billy Howe to stand up with Sean, and Dr. Sanders, no lover of Dr. Jarman, to marry them. All over safely with Dr. Jarman still in Canton before Sean could be called there, and before James Malleson, already on his way back from London, had arrived.

* * * * * *

The Justice of the Yamen

Kaida Hung rose early to go to the yamen for the trial of the pirates of the Argosy. He knew the pirates would plead guilty. They had been caught red-handed with half the stolen treasure hidden in gravel ballast, or in sacks tied to their boat anchors. But he hoped for some new revelation of the identity of the leader of the Red Circle should a harsh judge, rigorous with torture, have be appointed to the case.

He knelt on the icy floor, eyes downcast, as the grim-faced red-robed lictors, in hideous peaked hats of brown wire surmounted with pheasants' feathers, strode through the great door into the cavernous Hall of Justice, crying 'tremble, tremble, tremble' as they rattled the shuddersome instruments of their trade in torture - their chains, pincers and screws. They looked more like criminals themselves than the true criminals in their new black cotton suits kneeling abjectly with a muted rattle of chains on hands and feet to the cry 'accused to your knees' all too aware of soldiers lining the walls, bamboo sticks and rattans in hand.

However it was Hsu Nai-chi who was assigned to the case on his very last day in office, a notoriously kind, just man revered by the people as one who refused to 'shear the sheep' who passed through his hands. He had been merciful to these men. No torture. No lingering death. No stay of execution. Mercy for which Kaida was thankful as he was the clerk assigned to proceed to Potter's Field to verify the executions for the Viceroy and the owner of the Argosy.'

He hurried past the three foot high cages where those to die were being thrust, trussed like fowls, in unresisting resignation, on past the cages where others were still half-alive in fetters and wooden cangues. He averted his eyes. Better the swift death than to be suffering a slow agonising death by festering sores and starvation.

Billy Howe was waiting for him in a narrow lane near Potters Field. A row of executioners was already there before them, their razor-sharp heavy swords and short knives already laid out on a broad plank fixed to the wall behind them.

Billy grimaced at the sight. 'I don't know whether I'll have the stomach for this.'

'It's all over very quickly,' Kaida assured him, forebearing from expatiating on the horror of a lingering death by a thousand cuts.

The coolies lined up in rows before the executioners. They tumbled their burdens cruelly onto the ground, forcing them to kneel, heads bent for the convenience of the executioners. When all was ready, the presiding mandarin dismounted at a table facing the condemned. He swiftly tallied the list of names with the victims before them, then ordered the executioners standing at the west end of each row with their left hands resting on the head of the man to die to raise their swords on high. He paused for a long minute for the assembly to ponder on the dreadful penalty of death, then slammed the heavy square of wood on his hand sternly on the table crying 'behead!' Each sword flashed in a whistling arc too fast to follow. Fifty lives cut short faster than a scythe could sweep away fifty cornstalks.

'There's more in this than meets the eye,' Billy said as they abandoned the execution ground in the wake of the mandarin, the ceremony of death over. 'The Viceroy has been very subtle.'

Kaida was puzzled. 'Because he has protected foreign trade?'

'Because he has issued a warning to Jarman Malleson.'

'Ayah!' Kaida agreed. A warning to the Circle not to plunder the Old Rat's rivals. Those fifty heads were a reminder that piracy had to be licensed to be condoned as much as the legal trade.

When Kaida left Billy at the City Gate, he hurried across the city towards the North Gate where good-humoured crowds were already lolling about, haunted by every imaginable street vendor, entertainer or sharp. They were waiting to acclaim their beloved Magistrate, Hsu Nai-chi, on his way to a new life in Beijing as Vice-President of the Sacrificial Court, a post of honour rather than money and therefore only of interest to a man of the highest probity. At last on a wave of clapping, Hsu Nai-chi emerged through the Gate in a green and gold chair. He stopped before the child who waited to perform a last ritual for him as custom decreed. She presented him with new shoes, undid the old and took them up the stairs onto the wall. Next his most loved servant hung them over the city gate where shoes of popular officials traditionally hung. Last another threw a multi-coloured cloak over his shoulder to wish him good fortune in his new office. A sadness settled on the crowd as they waved him onwards, a grief that more officials could not face the people they governed, nor their ancestors, with the same tranquil mind as Hsu Nai-chi could.

They could not know that Hsu Nai-chi intended on his arrival in the Forbidden City to make a response to a request from the Emperor himself for memorials on the possibility of legalising the opium traffic and admitting it on payment of a duty. He would say the present ban on the import of opium had utterly failed to prevent his citizens buying and consuming it. Worse it had bred crime, banditry, extortion and blackmail which could not be controlled because opium drug addicts would rather suffer death than inform against those who sold it to them. If opium traffic was legalised, the damage would be limited to addicts themselves who would be no loss as the country was over-populated.

Hsu Nai-chi knew he would find strong support for this view in Beijing, but might have been less optimistic as he took to the road towards his destiny there if he had known that he would find a strong enemy in Chu Tsun, Vice President of the Board of Ceremonies.

* * * * * *

The Trade Superintendent steps into the Chief Superintendent's shoes.

Captain Barron Forge never approached the old Company Residence without saluting the wisdom of the long forgotten Portuguese merchant who had chosen this precise spot for his stately house on the saddle between two hills sheltered from the brunt of the inward sweeping monsoon by the low hill and the knoll where Camoens wrote his great epic of Portuguese adventure into the East, the Lusiad, on the other. He had had the good taste to follow the most graceful Oriental mode of western architecture: a harmonious proportion as satisfying in the elegance of long low lines, gentle sloping rooves, and high rooms flowing one into the next within, as the pavilions of Chinese mansions. As he entered the small but beautifully proportioned entrance hall, he already imagined how he woud play host there in its three superb, not overlarge, reception rooms.

Today he felt exhilarated to think he was about to occupy this very house he had envied Sir George. He was about to assume Sir George's post as Trade Superintendent. He was to receive his seal of office and official archives. He had only a twinge of conscience that he, Forge, had some responsibility for Sir George's recall. His savage letter, condemning Sir George for living in the middle of the smuggling fleet, where he had fled from Macao after all, had been partly responsible. It had clinched John Davies' very strong case.

He had been thankful to learn Sir George's anger had not been directed at him when he first learnt the news, flicking Lord Palmerston's letter of recall across the desk.

'The merchants call me a spineless coward when I do nothing. My Minister rebukes me when I do something. That ignoramus in Whitehall has the gall to say I should not have carried on the business of the Commission at Lintin without waiting to learn whether he agreed with me or not. I ask you, Forge, how can he have an informed view about anything when it takes so many months for my letter to come and and go? All the thanks I get for total sacrifice of my personal comfort and separation from my family is to lose my post.' A post that would now belong to his underling, Forge, the fact that galled him most. 'I suppose you'll do the opposite when I am gone.'

Captain Forge inclined his head a trifle in answer. 'You know my mind as well as I do.'

He would certainly try to do what neither Lord Nash or Sir George had succeeded in doing - to create a liaison with the Viceroy.'

Sir George stood to hand over his seal of office. He came from behind his desk gesturing to Forge to take his place. Captain Forge declined to insult him by accepting. Sir George, a shorter if stouter man, tried to overtop him in advice.

'One word of warning. There's no half-way house here. Either submission or removal from the port as you will find if anyone gets killed. They will sooner or later. Then you'll be forced to decide whether to give up a man. If you don't you will defend the actions of men who are smugglers, criminals and rebels.'

Trust Sir George to wish him well with a dose of his usual alarmist pessimism, Forge thought as he countered cheerfully. 'Well, Sir, things couldn't be any worse than they have been.'

Sir George contradicted him stoutly. 'They will be if the Viceroy chooses to wage war on the river with those who steal his smuggling trade from him. I wish you luck, Forge, but you'll fail as my successor.'

'But I'm not your successor in fact, Sir George,' Forge reminded him. 'Your post has been abolished. My post, like my salary is inferior. I don't believe my new instructions warrant the assumption I have a high political character.' In fact he believed all he had was a title without power.

'Not even a Taipan!' Sir George declared smugly taking his leave on one last barb, grudgingly shaking his hand.

Captain Forge held his tongue. What could he say? Sir George was right. He had been given neither authority nor jurisdiction. He had been warned not to achieve any in the ominous words, 'be very careful not to assume a greater authority over British subjects in China than that which you really possess.'

God in Heaven how was he to maintain any semblance of order in the port without any authority? He wouldn't even be a dogsbody let alone a dog that could hold up its head, bark and wag its tail. Of one thing he was certain, he would not stay like a dog chained in its kennel any longer in Macao. Where had Sir George got in all those months of loitering in Lintin. Nowhere!

His mind was made up, Sir George's barbs notwithstanding. He would apply through the Co-Hong for a passport to proceed to Canton and the letter would carry the controversial word 'Petition'. Let the merchants say he was servile and submissive. How else could he follow his instructions to 'respect the usages and refrain from shocking the prejudices of the country'? If he did not possess authority what then did he possess? The chance to establish some reputation for honour and integrity in the port with a race that respected a man who stood by his word.

Four months passed before Captain Forge achieved a compromise with the Viceroy. He might enter the Canton Factories raising the Union Jack there over his Residence after its two year banishment, but must observe the same regulations which had hitherto governed Taipans, and return to Macao at the end of every season with the merchants.

However, once there he found no comfort in the sight of the limp, windless flag as a squad of seaman fired a salute of honour. He could not believe this season would be as peaceful as the last. Present omens were more than a cause for alarm. Unrest in the fleet at Whampoa. Defiance among the free traders. Clashes between the factions up and down the coast. The smugboats of the mandarins and the Red Circle at war with each other in the byways of the delta.

Rumours of new harsh decrees of repression from the Vermilion Pen in Pekin where the oppressive Censor Chu had prevailed against the moderates. Strict confinement to the Factories. Canton and its environs so unsafe there could be no more hiring flower boats for banquets, no more excursions to the Flowery Land gardens in festival time as in the old days, no moments of retreat where weary men, imprisoned in their Factories, could forget the city surrounding them simmered with vice and rebellion that might one day, sooner or later, carry their oasis and all it stood for before their whirlwind.

Pondering these edicts from Pekin, Viceroy Lu lay wakeful in his austere bedchamber, marking the pale glimmer of dawn reflected in the still mirror of the tiny, man-made lake beyond the moon window. He was dying and had no regrets. He saw only vexation and violence ahead in the declining days of the Manchu dynasty. He preferred to look back to their remarkable emperors not forward to the dangerous insinuation of the Red Rods of the Red Circle in the Pearl River delta, the hidden threat of invisible challengers, an enemy unlike the Elder Brothers of the Triads of old you could harness or bargain with. No, he would rather die with the flame of Manchu glory still visible upon him. All he asked for now was to die as swiftly as his cherished friend, Old Mowqua, had done.

Let his successor be haunted with the problem as to who were these leaders hidden in the perplexities of the Pearl River region. He had pursued these names through his spies among runners, officials and torturers of his yamen. Perhaps his successor would succeed where he had failed. He lay slumped in his weakness watching the muted sun quenched in the still artifice of the garden outside his austere stone room as if already enthroned in a sarcophagus in a private corner of paradise.

* * * * * *

It was one of Macao's most ideal spring days, a soft innocence in the windless sunshine as if the demon of the iron whirlwind could not leap from the southeast at any moment to rip the blossom and leaf of spring to shreds. The Taipa calm as a millpond, the Praya Grande deserted for Sunday Mass.

The sedan-chair bearers set Holly down at the park where Billy Howe was waiting. They could debate the issues they had traversed with Chung Tai Tai without being overheard. These were whether Holly should continue to carry so much cargo for Chung Tai Tai and get so much of her cash in short term finance from Chung Tai Tai to enable her to stay out of the opium market, or invest in the British cottons as well as the newer, more competitive, American cottons.

They were only agreed on one thing that Holly should continue to buy her exports through Chung Tai Tai now that tea was up fifty per cent in price, and silk almost as much. She would not go bankrupt as Tinghae and other Chinese traders had done to the tune of two million dollars in debt, chiefly to foreign merchants.

When they had consulted Chung Tai Tai herself, immobile as a carved idol in her expensive jade jewellery and finely embroidered gown, she had advised them to drive a hard bargain. 'Always trust the old bankers.'

Billy had hedged. 'Look what happened to Fairlie and Palmers in Calcutta.'

She had waved this aside. 'Young as the world goes. And there are no Parsees in Britain.'

She had no love for those white-headed demons, the Parsees. They had financed the ships of the foreign country traders to bleed the opium trade away from her grandfather and the Portuguese.

Holly, as ever, had found it hard to imagine the elegant lady before her had planned the battle tactics of her fleet in battle with the new Red Circle smug boats a few weeks before. She was impelled to learn the truth. 'Mr. Howe says you went to sea this summer.'

Chung Tai Tai had paused in the gentle fanning of her writs with a painted ivory fan. 'Mr. Howe is right. A matter of discipline. One is not the policeman without the need to police.'

She had turned to pick up a clear green jade bracelet flecked with airy darker green flakes, then fastened it gently round Holly's wrist, as slim as her own, grieving for the daughter she had once lost.

Holly smiled at Billy when they returned to the Casa Garden after striking a bargain with each other about what she should do. 'I shall miss your shoulder to cry on when you go back to Canton.'

He cocked an eyebrow at her. She hadn't done as much crying on his shoulder as he would have liked. 'But I know only too well how lucky I am to have you there.'

'Your luck may run out yet,' he responded wryly.

'Why, are you leaving the Coast?' She was surprised to feel dismay at the thought. His loss would mean a terrible emptiness in her life. No one could make her laugh as he did. No one could steer her better on a commonsensical course in trade, now Joshua was gone, than he did.

'Not so bad as that, Evergreen. I'm only going as far as the Temple of Longevity with John Norris.'

She was cross with him then. 'Giving me a fright like that for nothing in pursuit of the Red Circle.'

'Not quite nothing. It's out of bounds you know.'

'Quite obviously you two are up to more than looking at old curiosities.'

'Playing at weathercocks.'

'Weathercocks in temples?'

'Temples, my dear Evergreen, are where people gather for every kind of mischief in Canton.'

'Then someone could suspect you were up to mischief too.'

'Like trying to find out if that's where leaders of the Red Circle hide out when they're in Canton. If so, who they are.'

She was dismayed to feel as great a dread that her genial ingenuous Billy was putting himself at such risk as she would for Sean. 'Who wants to know? Barron Forge?'

Billy shook his head. Despite her persistent cross-examination he refused to say. He could not betray Kaida.

'You must take this.' She reached for the talisman Chung Tai Tai had given her, taken aback when he rejected it with a shudder.

'The very thing it would be most dangerous to wear. She's their most treacherous opposition.'

Holly understood. There were two sides to this most strange subterranean quarrel which might still precipitate her on one side, Sean on the other. Then she would have to choose between them when she had hoped to continue with one for friend, the other for lover.

* * * * * *

Temple of Longevity - City of Canton

The pavilions of the Temple of Longevity were set high on white marble terraces with richly wrought entablatures. They must have stood there for many centuries, calm and cool in their beckoning gardens. Foreign devils had enjoyed that calm during that period between 1760 and 1812 when they had been allowed to wander freely there. They had lingered long enough to carve their names and initials in the plastered walls of the verandah of the main shrine.

As Billy Howe and John Norris deciphered the history written there, a crowd of priests jostled and joked around them.

'Do you think they are spies?'

'They could have four ears.'

'Or they could be mad.'

'They all are. They like walking.'

'Aiyah! Just like the tigers in the zoo. It must be all that raw meat.'

'Like tigers when your back is turned.'

'Are they savage?'

'Not if they're well-fed.'

Neither Billy nor John betrayed for an instant that they understood every word the priests said, submitting to their urging towards the Guest Hall with naive imbecilic smiles. Their dissembling was rewarded at last when one, who looked more soldier than priest, said to another as he waved them to chairs.

'Are they spies?'

'They don't look like spies.'

'We don't look like rebels.'

So Kaida was right. Men lived in the Temple of Longevity who were not genuine priests, so they could maintain the new badge of rebellion, an unshaven crown without a queue.

176

They accepted capacious lidded cups of lukewarm tea nodding and exclaiming in sign language over the sacred objects the quasi-priests brought them to admire. They sat wooden-faced as the imposters made even more incautious asides criticising the Red Circle leader for skulking in his headquarters in Kowloon's walled city with Whampoa under siege from the Viceroy's police. They began to take alarm as one, more stubborn than the rest, with his eyes on them insisted the Red Circle never hesitated if they believed a man to be a spy. Wasn't his motto 'if you open the door a crack the tiger will force it open. Then the fanqui will be like the Pearl River in flood.'

'Do you think they'll kill us?' John asked, his smiling face a mask.

'Without mercy. We're going to have to make a run for it,' Billy whispered to John as they rose, bowing as they backed towards the door as if ignorant of proper procedure.

Both were watchful for their chance as their guides steered them by a devious route through swooping pavilions, half-hidden by trees crooked with age, until they rounded a corner to face a murderous barrage of missiles from a terrifying mob armed with brickbats, pieces of broken pots, and lumps of mud and screaming 'fanqui, fanqui'.

John and Billy turned as one, wrenching away from their guardians and pelting up the straight avenue ahead as if the devil himself was in pursuit with Billy yelling 'thank God for all that tiger's meat.' The diet of these people gave them no stamina. A man burst out of a door to rush past them pointing to a different route and calling to them to follow. He led them into a building, charging through a knot of priests into its dim interior, priests who then closed ranks to forbid the sanctuary to their turbulent howling pursuers as they disappeared behind the giant Buddha reigning indifferently there. He saw them safely out of the door and through an archway to a rear gate opening out on the intricate crooked streets of the Old City, then held out his hand.

Billy laughed as he dug in his pocket and gave the man two great rounds. 'That absolves him from any obligation to us for saving our lives.'

As they moved with swift familiarity through the congested streets towards the Factories not far away, Billy warned John 'don't look round. We're being followed.'

'What do we do now? Be marked down by where we live?'

'Nothing simpler, old friend. We'll call on the Iron-headed Rat at Number I Creek Factory. Our spy will think we're one of their mob.'

John agreed gleefully. 'That will see them quarrelling with each other. The story of the tailor and the giants all over again.' A very sweet and private revenge.

* * * * * *

Days of Reckoning

Holly's captain, Tough Wagoner, was one of two captains badly beaten up by Portuguese officers at the Customs House on the Praya Grande - his goods confiscated and returned in a mauled and broken state two days later. Holly fumed when she saw his black eye and swollen jaw. She longed to complain, seething with frustration to know she could not. She could not declare herself a shipowner to the Portuguese Governor of Macao. She could not ask Captain Forge to rush down river from Canton. She did not want to raise trouble for anyone with the Macao Senate. She did not know where Kaida was - whether in the new Viceroy Tang's yamen or tracking the Red Circle Leader down in his lair, the walled city of Kowloon. She was left with only one resort, to see Chung Tai Tai.

She found Chung Tai Tai utterly transformed. Dressed like a coolie in black jacket and trousers. Hair scraped back in a bun. No trace of jade or gold. No cool elegance of manner. Character changed with her costume. Terse and abrupt with a curt welcome as Holly entered.

In answer to Holly's complaint she explained enigmatically 'when you're on the high seas and the enemy is over the horizon you must ask yourself why they fight the battle.'

'Then who are the Portuguese fighting for?' She asked in bewilderment.

'Whoever is winning. Right now the sharks thanks to the Red Circle.'

'But the Portuguese would be the first to lose if they drove all the small fish out of their sea and were left only with the sharks.'

'Not if they gain protection from the Red Circle if they do.'

All the dogged obstinacy of Holly's whaling and Puritan ancestors rose to the fore. 'I will not be driven out of Macao.'

Chung Tai Tai rose from her tiny rosewood seat to stand like a witch's doll in her sombre garb before her to prophesy 'you will be safer in our old pirate haunts as we were before long.'

'What at sea?' Holly asked in alarm aware that Chung Tai Tai might not match her in height but far excelled her in obduracy.

'On offshore islands. You must learn. Come with me. We sail to hunt our enemy today,' Chung Tai Tai commanded her as if she were about to play another game of fantan in her gambling den below.

'Your enemy?' Holly echoed wondering how one, among her many enemies, could be a special object of revenge.

'My spies tell me the Red Leader has left his lair in Kowloon and moved into my territory. He must pay. But first you must dress as one of us.'

Holly succumbed, too ashamed of betraying fear to resist, and envious of Chung Tai Tai for the freedom to go to sea as a true captain. No easy equality for American women at home like Tanka women able to set sail, steer ships and read the map of wind or weather with the same superb skill and instinct for the treacherous coat as the men.

If Holly had not been alarmed at her first sight of the junk in the jampacked fleet, she was terrified when once aboard at the sight of its floating arsenal when her crew removed the camouflaging covers from the sides of the ship. Twelve mediaeval style cannon and a store of ammunition amidships, both powder and shot, as well as muskets heaped abaft the foremast. But she did not dare to defy Chung Tai Tai being so dependent on her by now.

Its crew worked the junk laboriously out into open water, then hoisted the great fans of brown bamboo-ribbed sails up the mast as sailors had done for countless centuries before them. Nothing had changed in the course of time as it had in the west. Not in sail, nor the cumbersome progress of the vessel, nor in the cacaphony of drums and firecrackers to frighten away the demons of the deep, nor in Chung Chung Tai's ritual of lighting an incense stick before the tablet of her father and the image of the Goddess Ama of Macao.

From the first moment Chung Tai Tai stepped on board she stood on the raised stern transmitting orders through her two scowling and obsequious female aides. For all her aloof hauteur, Holly still could not envisage her as another Hawkins or Drake, scourge of the Chinese main. The barefoot crew, half-naked and heavy-chested giants, looked more in character. Some with red kerchiefs wound round their head and necks. Others with wide-brimmed hats. Ruffians all who stared with some hostility as she came aboard, the very incarnation of a green-eyed devil they had been taught to loathe and fear.

Now, as they sailed south out of the Taipa Roads against the orange pyrotechnics of a vivid sunset Chung Tai Tai was frowning at the sight of great clouds racing across the southern horizon, as if God has sent a spectacular huge black curtain for an archangelic tragedy complete with the wind's orchestra across their sails. Clouds with their promise of a driving sea that left the junk plunging all night long, and Holly unable to sleep for dread the junk's famous stability would prove a myth.

At length day dawned on the sails of the homeward bound fishing fleet. The three black junks of the new bandits of the sea Chung Tai Tai sought out were on its eastern edge, the three who were brutal usurpers of her role as protector of this fleet in that they made any villager who resisted them pay a vicious price in mayhem.

At once Chung Tai Tai ordered her junk to sail to the leeward of the nearby island which stood between her and the main fleet where she lay in wait for the oncoming unsuspecting scouting junks. She ordered a shot across the bow of the first to round the point, a large black vessel with three yellow sails. It tried to outrun and outfight her attack, and was forced to pay dearly for trying to outwit the best pirate captain on the coast. Two more chases. Two more surrenders. Two more ransoms. Obviously substantial to judge by the gaiety of the hitherto surly crew and the sudden geniality of their captain. Tamping tobacco in her pipe, she sat down on the deck among them with the air of a parent pleased with the achievements of her children as they crouched around heaped platters of chicken and rice, chattering with animation for all the world as if attending a party not a pirate expedition. Nonchalant foam of the sea, better as friend than foe as generations of Viceroys had learned the hard way.

Holly acted out the question most on her mind. What if the junks did not pay? For answer, Chung Tai Tai snuffed out the incense stick beside her. Who needed pidgin English with such telling sign language? Chung Tai Tai meant what she said when she bore down on another three junks, this time war junks said to be the squadron of Wang Chung, the Red Leader, and gave battle without quarter.

She ordered Holly down below, an order enforced by the crew when she hesitated. All Holly could hear from her dim cabin was the running feet of the crew and their shouts as repeated booms of the cannon shook the timbers, and a dense acrid cloud of black smoke settled around her - its nauseating smell combining with the stale stench of fish to make her violently seasick.

Just as she was losing faith in Chung Tai Tai's fabled invincibility, she was beckoned up on deck to see for herself the battle was over and won. Chung Tai Tai sat enthroned on the stern with musket and bandolier, silently puffing her pipe. The captains of the defeated junks were lying bound on the deck below, their officers prisoners, as they would remain till relatives or friends ransomed them. If not the first demand would be repeated with one of their ears, fingers or hands.

Chung Tai Tai's own officers were commanding boarding parties loading up all the spoils they could find on the abandoned junks, two of which were already slowly sinking. The only spoil of war missing was the one she had come to find, the head of Wang Chung who had returned the Kowloon the day before.

Suddenly Holly understood why Chung Tai Tai had made her witness to the harsh facts of war in the delta. Foreign devils like herself were all too prone to think of news about junk battles, ransom of captains, deaths of crew vanished like a dream as if in a theatre witnessing a play about myths which had no reality. But the reality was that all these dangers and disasters were over who should control the trade in the delta, and at the heart was the opium trade and hence Jarman Malleson.

This meant that, if she married Sean Jarman, she would inescapably be in opposition as Chung Tai Tai had known when she invited her to watch the ferocious truth of her battle for supremacy of the foam of the sea against those of her former allies who had gone over to Jarman Malleson. As Sean Jarman's wife she would be in league with these new captains of the Red Circle with agents in every village, and junk fleets marking prospective victims to snatch them from deck or highway in order to intimidate the rest into submission. For the first time she felt torn from the haze of romance that had hung over her like the orange glow over Lappa Island, and from the trance that removed her from reality although still moving in the daytime world.

She might have fallen back into that trance when she returned to Macao but for the fact that Sean's welcome was furious, and his words infuriating, when he stormed into the Casa Garden to find her alone in the grand salon. She had disappeared. No one knew where she had gone. He had searched Macao for her, was out of his mind thinking she had been kidnapped until at last Billy Howe had divulged her secret. She should have told him where she was going.

She took umbrage. How could she have told him when she did not know he was back in Macao? Besides even if she had, she was not married to him yet. 'Why should I have told you?'

He clutched her arm painfully in his temper. 'I've been out of my mind for three days imagining the most dreadful things.'

'You knew she was the best admiral on the coast.'

'I knew her opposition, the toughest rivals on the coast.'

'Do you now? Have you sailed with them?'

'You think I'm a pirate?'

'No more than you do me.'

He changed his ground mindful of her stubborn face. 'What will people in Macao say?'

'They will not know.'

'The Chinese will.'

'Why should I care what the Chinese say?'

'As my wife you will have to.'

She disengaged herself at that to flounce over to the grand sofa. 'Sean, the woman who can sail with Chung Tai Tai is the woman you propose to marry.'

Sean looked down at the heady vision of the weary Holly stretched out on the sofa, scarcely comprehending her drift in his frustration. Anger fuelled his desire. Holly's independence waa the very quality that challenged him, that aroused him.

'Would you prefer a doll in your drawing room?'

Scotch brides were no dolls, but they were no daring adventurers on the Spanish or any other Main as Holly promised to be. He perched beside her, propped above her with his hand either side of her head, all too aware the rooms around were empty. Captain Forge away, Flora out, and the servants on their day off. Her lips below his were all too tempting to his own, her skin all too beckoning to his touch. He could not resist the eternal challenge of his manhood to tame this exquisite creature he wanted to call his own. The impetus of his passion rose through him when he stooped to her lips. She clung to him, glad to stifle the argument of their minds at war with their bodies. His hands for the first time reached for her bodice and lingered on the exquisite curve of her breasts unable to resist an instant longer.

This was another drowning, not the annihilation of death by water but a resurrection from doubt and dilemma. This was each claiming the other as own, the one and only. This was the desperate demand of one for the other, born of the anger that had seemed to divide them when division was the misery that had plagued them for so many months. This was the hour when they clung to each other through long kisses, touching, caressing where so long desired but so long denied. This was the moment when both abdicated from commonsense that consumnation should wait until marriage, the moment when Holly could not thrust him away as he lifted her up and took her up the stairs into her bedroom to lower her gently on the quilt, to gaze at her delicate fragility with utmost longing, then shed her clothes skin by skin as so often in his imagination he had done. This was the moment when the devil sat chuckling in the corner of the room at their downfall.

She knew no other will than his. She could never have called the first instant of pain and pleasure rape, when she belonged to him at last, because her whole being persuaded him on. Yet he had exercised the domination of his piercing eyes, brilliant with emotion, and his beguiling looks, his passionate urgency to press a desire that only a woman of iron will could have kept at bay.

Three days, days of their honeymoon, spun by. Macao, a honeymoon city, a golden cocoon of sunshine where they pledged themselves to each other in an abandonment made more acute knowing that Sean would be away in Manila for a long year of separation. They parted on a neap tide of eternal love and promises - he to break his engagement, she to wait for him.

When Holly discovered the cost of their unbridled passion, like innumerable women before her, she was less sentimental in confessing to Flora in the cool morning room. 'I've been an unutterable fool! I ignored everything I've heard and read about fallen women. Dupes of handsome men. Left carrying the baby as I am now. No husband! Not likely to have one.'

Flora stifled a smile. Holly looked anything but a novelist's concept of a fallen woman. Admittedly she was in a grim situation. An abortion in this Catholic community, this hotbed of gossip, was out of the question. She suggested the only possible solution. 'Follow Sean to Manila. Marry him there.'

Holly fretted at the window watching the commotion of a flock of birds in the giant trees of the Protestant cemetery next door. 'He should have married me before he went. But he didn't. Why? Because he's under the thumb of those buccaneer partners of his. Which reminds me I would be marrying the lot of them, not just Sean. I could chase him as you say, but every village idiot would know it was a shotgun marriage. Worse he could never be sure it was his child by that time. Besides I wouldn't trust certain quarters not to put out rumours to save their own precious skin. Which shows you how cynical I have become.'

Anguish on Flora's expressive face now. 'You can't have the baby and live alone here. You could go home of course. Mary Ann would welcome you now she's a widow.'

Holly shook her head. Mary Ann's grief over Joshua's death at sea off the Cape was the very reason she could not go to her. Moreover she had learnt to love a life of action. She could not endure the retirement implicit in sitting out her time with Mary Ann. There was only one solution. That was to marry somone as soon as possible, but whom?

'Flora this baby is the best thing that could have happened to me. It has made me look at the future with the same hard-headed sanity my forebears brought to marriage, to see it as a practical contract for a future demanding patience and endurance not as a love affair.'

She hesitated then. How could she tell Flora that, in her more detached moments, she felt Sean's conquest of her was the impulse of a man who wanted to win someone who was not easy to win, to dominate in hors de combat. In the violence of his energy, there was an element of the violation one would expect from a man capable of facing the ruthless character of the opium trade and not turning away. Could her conscience live with this?

She had lost some of the romance of her dreams as many a woman before her when released from the tyranny of desire. She could see the racial gulf between herself and Sean more clearly. Could Scotland mate with Yankeeland?

'How long would our love survive the rejection of Sean's partners? They would express their hostility in a thousand ways. Would his family at home be even better?'

'If you're not going to marry Sean or going home, what on earth are you going to do?' Flora asked distressed.

Holly comforted the comforter. 'Don't fret yourself over me, Flora. I'm going to marry Billy Howe.'

The ever-imperturbable Flora for once was speechless. 'Has he asked you?'

'No, but he will.'

'How do you know?' Had Holly taken leave of her senses?

'How does any woman know when a man's besotted over her?'

'And what if you tell him the truth?'

'Would I be such a fool?'

'Then you'll have to marry him in a hurry.'

'Exactly. A shotgun wedding without the shotgun or father.'

'Could any man be such a fool as not to count the months?'

'A man in love is the perfect tomfool.'

'You'd have to marry at once. Will he agree to that?'

'He'll be only too willing to rush me to the altar in case I change my mind. He'll know better than anyone that I'm marrying him on the rebound.'

'If you have, you might be making a terrible mistake as much for yourself as for him.'

'Flora, we're so obviously right for each other, I wonder I haven't thought of it before. We have everything in common. We're both Yankee. The same background. The same business. The same attitude to China. And most important of all Billy makes me laugh. Laughter is as important as love. Perhaps more important.'

Seeing her doubt, Holly assured her, 'don't worry. There will be love.'

* * * * * *

CHAPTER 7

1836-8 The trials of Viceroy Tang

The Salvation of Kaida Hung's Brother

Kaida rose at the first glimmer of light in the yamen to join the dawn procession of supplicants and courtiers marching from hall to hall, folding doors flying open before them, until they reached the last hall before the audience chamber of the new Viceroy Tang where, lulled by soft music, the principal mandarins waited in exact order of their buttons of rank - red, blue, crystal, white, gilt and copper. Suddenly it ceased to a strident annoncement of the Viceroy's presence as armed soldiers shouted 'tremble and obey!'

The last great doors ground slowly open revealing the Viceroy sitting crosslegged among heaped cushions. He was a man of huge prescence on a scale with the hall, as wide as he was tall like the Buddha of the south but, unlike that Buddha, stern and unsmiling. No hint of levity on his flabby cheeks or thick lips, nor in the brow wrinkled not merely with the cares of office but also dissipation of living. No one knew which. The only incongruous note was the steel spectacles dangling on the magnificent gold and silver dragon coils writhing across his chest, courtesy of Dr. Tom.

The crowd of dignitaries filed in to range themselves round the wall. The courtiers and supplicants knelt so their heads would be no higher than his knees, as for the Emperor himself, and kowtowed nine times. The orchestra stopped. A huge gong crashed. All waited in respectful silence.

Viceroy Tang, deputy of the Lord of Ten Thousand Islands in two of the largest provinces of China, gazed scowling over their serried ranks. Faced with two opposing factions on opium in Pekin advancing irreconcilable policies, how could he speak with a forked tongue any longer? How could he denounce the opium trade in the same breath as he gave commands to the smuggling fleet operating in his son's name?

On the one hand his old friend, Hsu Nai Tse, of the party of compromise which wanted to legalise the trade, capture its revenue for the court and place no embargo on smoking opium, other than on imperial officials and soldiers, knowing what a vexed and insurmountable task it would be to stamp the trade out altogether. On the other hand, the ex-Prefect of Heangshan, now Prefect of Beijing, of the lobby which demanded the trade be plucked out, root and branch, urging his local experience.

His dilemma was insoluble. He could no longer assume the Court in Beijing would be satisfied with token arrests in response to its edicts of suppression. He could no longer relapse into his usual lethargy once he had announced, as he proposed to do now, that the leading purveyors of foreign mud in China-Jarman and Malleson and Raine's- were banished from China forever after the second moon of the Chinese New Year, allowing them to stay so long only out of 'compassionate regard for their long years of business in China', then do absolutely nothing to enforce it?

Yet Viceroy Tang had not risen so high on the ladder to the clouds without resourceful cunning. Once again in his long public career he must call upon that astute political instinct that had stood him in such good stead in earlier crises of his official life. He must know which of those respectful faces making obeisance before him were sham postulants, which were the traitors. And he must prepare himself against their treachery. First he must have a list of all officials engaged in the opium traffic. Second, he must own not a mere four smug boats, but the entire fleet. He must run all other boats off the river. Then, if the Emperor decreed he must cut off the opium trade, he could empty the river of smug boats overnight. With such control he must surely be able to save his own precious hide? Why even better sell them off to Jarman Malleson who were burning to get their hands on more of these craft.

Then he could make token arrests, even order executions. Confiscate opium. Claim sweeping efforts to suppress smuggling. Even gain honours. Then resell the opium at great profits. It never occurred to him the Emperor might recall him and commission someone else to put down the noxious trade.

Joining the gossiping crowd streaming away from the Audience Hall, Kaida learned that Viceroy Tang had failed to announce his real intention - to run both smuggling faction, the Red Circle and the Elder Brothers off the river. There would be bloody war.

His brother a smaller less assured version of himself, sidled alongside as he left the yamen to reach Chung Tai Tai urgently with the news, 'Where are you going brother?'

Kaida responded with a question. 'How did you become a copper button mandarin without passing the obligatory examinations?'

'You know it's possible to buy office here in the south.'

'How low the Manchu dynasty has fallen!'

Kaida studied his brother in disgust that he had sunk so low. Who had bought him office? Someone who wanted an 'eye' in the yamen. Not Chung Tai Tai that was certain. Was his brother then working for her enemies? And if so he must have been bought because of his opium addiction.

'You play a dangerous game, little brother. What will you do when forced to decide from which side you get your rice?'

Geli was evasive in word and look. 'I look to the future not the past. I can hunt with both sides.' His somnolent air lifted for a moment, decision jolted by the thought. How much had opium addled his brains, warped his judgement making him a danger even to his own brother?

'Not if they are at war as they soon will be,' Kaida said curtly. 'You'll get the sword on your neck from both sides, then. You must decide now where your loyalty lies, little brother.'

Geli wiped the perspiration from his meagre mustache. 'I can serve them both but in different ways. The circle as their eyes. The Elder Brothers as their ears. And the yamen as their hands.'

What a recipe for ruin, Kaid thought with pity for the political naivete of his brother. ' You'll get yourself killed by one or the other in the end.'

'Not if I am clever.'

Clever? Geli's wan, drawn face belied it. 'Tell me what is clever about smoking opium?' Although many opium addicts continued to function his brother was not one of these. He was one of the less fortunate who suffered an intellectual decline, an apathy and a confusion. 'You must give up opium, Geli, or your judgement will kill you even faster than the opium.'

But his brother, like all opium addicts, suffered more terror at the thought of facing the dreadful pain of withdrawal from the passive lethargy of its compulsion, or the pain of life without any anodyne. He argued through a long wearisome duel in the tea house.

Kaida insisted with the tenacity of an Imperial prosecutor. 'You want to take part in a Ming restoration one day? Would you be fit to rule if you were doped with opium? Was our Emperor Tao Kuang when he was an opium addict? Why did he give up opium smoking? Because he realised he did not have his wits about him. Opium will cause you to betray the movement and myself.'

Geli was stubborn. 'You have no ambition to rule yourself. So you want to stop me.'

Kaida touched his hand gently. 'Geli, these men use you for their own ambition. Even if they won the throne in your name, they would seize it for themselves.'

Geli rocked in his seat with grief at this revelation - grief at his own tortuous destiny and the evil in men. He was persuaded at last to face the ordeal of giving up opium but only if Kaida procured the Yunnan cure for him and stayed with him throughout.

Back in Macao Kaida took turns with his mother, Rebecca and John Norris to stand guard over Geli and comfort him through the screaming agony of withdrawal despite the cure. Hell itself in his head. Boiling water in his veins. Sharp, hissing whispers all around him. Shaking lights and tolling bells. Disgusting creatures that flung themselves on him and gnawed his stomach. Monstrous beings that wavered about in the air or peered from the dark corners of the room. He crouched in a terrifying abyss of depression and terror, or hurled himself at their menacing faces. Wracked with pain he threw himself against the wall, day after day. Watching the horror on his face John Norris remarked he must have visions of all the terrors of all the circles in Dante's Inferno before him.

After several days the storms that swept him diminished, leaving him a gaunt caricature of the healthy, cheerful young man he had once been, but capable of thanking his warders for rescue from slow suicide. A gratitude Kaida, full of hope his reform would last, was only too ready to accept at face value. He was far more sanguine than the others who had seen too many relapses from grace despite the most fervent intentions.

By the time Kaida went back to the yamen, a vicious war was being waged on the river between the new smuggling fleet and the old. Viceroy Tang was carrying out his naive plan to drive all other smugboats but his own lorchas off the river and away from the depot ships at Lintin . This plan would enable him to win whichever way the Emperor chose to jump. He could claim he had driven out those smug boats currently conducting the evil traffic while establishing a monopoly for himself. A plan, however, that required a crafty trick be played on the Beijing Censors lest they suspect his double-dealing. He declared five hundred chests of opium given him by his son, out of a consignment of five thousand chests destined for the black market, as seized goods.

The people, however, were not so easily deceived. A broadsheet went up on the gate of Viceroy Tang's yamen which read

'Where Yue's lands are broad yet fair

the venerable Tang holds sway.

His bailiffs knock at every door

and drag both good and bad away.

Oh Tang, if from the drug you'd set us free

yourself would soon a prisoner be.'

The laughter of their derision rippled through all Canton, as nimble wits repeated it to those who could not read.

Chung Tai Tai was not deceived either. She was famous for her nose for the temper of a political storm whether a small typhoon or a true iron whirlwind, and the time to shift the fleet inshore to escape the onslaught if need be. Now she judged the time had come to withdraw her smuggling fleet from the Coast altogether and burn it. Her crews, handsomely pensioned off, set the junks alight in great pillars of fire that not only launched great clouds of smoke across the delta, but the sensational news all the way to a rejoicing Imperial court in Pekin thinking they had won a great victory.

Kaida protested at her abandonment of a lifetime's work. How could she be so rash? Was she losing her mind?

She fanned her wrists calmly in the heat. 'Kaida, haven't you heard? The Emperor ordered a search of all junks in the port of Tienjin in the north and found opium from Canton on them all. Now he has commanded the Viceroy to drive all smugboats and depot ships away. It would no longer be enough for me to abandon the smuggling trade for fishing until that storm passes over.'

'I can't bear to think you would destroy a fortune.'

She closed her fan sharply and tapped him in rebuke on the shoulder. 'Would you rather see me destroyed instead, Kaida? For that would be my choice. The Viceroy could argue I am a smuggler, whether true or not, so long as those junks existed. He could arrest me and make me his chief victim to save his own skin with Beijing. He could order me to endure the lingering death as a traitor. I don't fancy that nor would anyone who has seen it.'

He regarded her dainty elegance with horror as he imagined her in a wire cage, sliced inch by inch by an armoury of razor-sharp knives. Never! On the other hand he could not bear to think of the waste. 'Couldn't you have docked them until the danger's over?'

'And have the Viceroy's lackeys steal them, crew them, fake smuggling with them and lay it at my door? You know who they are by now. Ah Shan from Whampoa and Wang Chung from Kowloon. Both evil enough to do that. No, Kaida, I have weathered too many iron whirlwinds in politics not to make port for safety until the winds pass by.'

Kaida had scarcely left Chung Tai Tai on the way to meet Billy Howe at the San Antonio Gate leading to the Campo before the full significance of what she was saying was borne in on him. A flurry of people was also scurrying that way, jostling him in their eagerness to reach the field beyond. As he stood aside at the door of the tiny San Antonio Church to wait for Billy, he saw the reason for the onrush of the mob - the formidable procession of an execution party of one hundred fully armed soldiers as if for a prisoner of great importance when a serious attempt to rescue him might be likely.

But this prisoner was being treated no better than a common criminal, crushed as he was in a foreshortened bamboo basket with heavy iron shackles on his arms and legs, and clearly suffering from the dirt, filth, starvation, and gangrene festering wounds of one who had been treated like the worst of poor felons. Even pigs, carried to market in the same brutal way, were better off.

'What on earth is going on?' Billy Howe asked Kaida as the procession moved on past the tiny church, the very antithesis of the mercy of the Christian gospel preached within.

Kaida's agonised answer was, 'it's Kwok Pung, a little shopkeeper from the inner harbour. I often stopped to chat with him on my way home to my village. What will happen to his wife and family? So poor!'

'Poor? Said to be the biggest opium dealer in Macao!'

'Who tells that lie?'

'The Magistrate! If what you say is true, why Kwok Pung?' Billy demanded as they joined the streaming crowd.'

'Sacrifice one of their own before their hand is forced? Never!'

'Hence the guards in case the crowd tries to save him.'

They emerged from the Campo Gate in time to see the executioner shake poor Kwok Pung out of his miserable cage, more dead than alive, to drag him, incapable of walking, like butcher's meat to one of two bamboo sheds. The magistrate sat in the other, forty yards away, isolated from any need to watch the death throes of the man he had so wrongly condemned to be the showpiece of repression. As he pronounced the death sentence, his uneasy eyes shifted round the crowd as if he expected they might lynch him.

* * * * * *

Holly as Lady in Waiting

Holly luxuriated in her pregnancy, cradled as she was by the jubilant affection of Billy quite unable to comprehend his luck that Holly had chosen him after all. It was a period of quiescence such as she had never known, the impetus of her being lulled towards one precise moment, the hour of her child's birth. She refused to sit about as all the good wives would have her do, or eat for two. She had seen too many matrons look like two after their babies were born.

Holly's son gave his first cry on a luminous spring day after a slow, not too painful, labor until the last brief violence of her final contractions launched him into the world. That last fierce spasm of pain obliterated the spin of doubt and occasional despair that haunted Holly for the folly of his conception.

Scarcely had the midwife cleaned and swaddled him than she begged Dr. Tom to put Billy junior in her arms. Tears of relief welled up in her eyes. Praise the Lord, the child was a replica of herself with her own green eyes, curly hair and neat face. She had dreaded he might too obviously have looked like Sean and not at all like Billy. What a sad and disillusioned man her fun-loving and affectionate Billy would have been if the truth had been written on Billy junior's innocent face. She would never have forgiven herself if Bill had been able to read that truth, he who had been so loving, so affectionate, so patient in invoking her love - a love she had found it in herself to give in time. It was a different love from the turbulence she had shared with Sean, as different as the Pearl River from the open sea, and one which would find an even stronger bond in the miracle of this child.

She had been able to share her business comfortably with Billy. They had prospered, when others had suffered with the collapse of the three 'W' banks in New York, thanks to Howqua who maintained his considerable business in America through them. In the wake of the crash, he had encouraged them to bank through Barings in Threadneedle St. She was content to luxuriate in the blessings of her world from day to day, content she had made the right decision.

* * * * * *

Battles of the Pearl River Delta

Captain Forge sat waiting through many a hot, long day for the inevitable explosion of battles on the river between the boats of the Viceroy and the foreign devils to run out of control. He fumed at the prospect of a teeming world where the only idle person seemed to be himself.

The first trouble loomed in the autumn in the shape of young Sean Jarman, now back from Manila, announcing four lascars had been arrested on the Factory side of the river. They had been manning a passage boat of his uncle's, the Alpha, two miles upstream from the Factories where they had no reason to be. They had been jumped by the Viceroy's men. Two had resisted. One had stabbed another several times. They had all been arrested and were being held for trial by the Viceroy. Now he was soliciting action from Captain Forge as Trade Superintendent.

Captain Forge could scarcely contain his anger. He had warned them time and time again about the risk of smuggling on the river and the consequences not only for the criminals involved but all Europeans in Canton. Now they would expect him to go, cap in hand, to Consoo House to ask for the return of those boats, knowing they were Jarman Malleson's answer to the Viceroy's destruction of all smuggling crab boats on the river but his own. He demanded to know who was responsible.

When Sean admitted sullenly. 'They say our men attacked them first,' he stared Sean down wondering what on earth Holly could ever have seen in this malleable son of a dark trade.

'Did they tell the truth that they were defending their smuggled opium? They were, weren't they Sean?' Sean could not deny it. 'Yet you expect me to defend you after you have broken the law on two counts, when the Viceroy has made it clear he will not tolerate any suggestion that 'the laws of outer barbarians can be practiced in the domains of the Celestial Dynasty.'

He dismissed Sean, angered that he had no choice but to defend his firm in its intransigence not for their sake but because he could not abandon the unfortunate Indian Lascars that worked for them, and this in his first formal negotiation with the authorities as Trade Superintendent. Well if he had to fall on his sword he would do so in style. In full dress uniform to rival the gaudy splendour of the Co-Hong merchants, John Norris at his side, he marched up the granite steps of Consoo House to demand that the four Lascars must be given up by 10 p.m. on his pledge they would be fairly tried according to British law.

Howqua, as expected, declared gravely that Captain Forge was welcome to act as observer of their trial in a Chinese court of law. Captain Forge countered with equal gravity he could not permit trial by a Chinese judge. Howqua refrained from pointing out that Captain Forge was in no position to say what trial he would, or would not, permit to be held as the Lascars were in a Chinese prison.

'I ask you if you, as an Englishman, committed a crime in France and were charged with a violation of French laws, would you demand you were tried by English laws? No, you would be amenable to the justice of tht country. You, as a reasonable man with a love of justice, must agree.'

Captain Forge answered with the same lofty but temperate manner, 'my King will admit the force of this reasoning as soon as the Emperor's gracious will gives Englishmen the same freedom and equality in China as in France.'

Howqua was immutable as the indifferent God of Law in any Cantonese temple. 'Do you presume to dictate to the Son of Heaven what the law should be?'

Captain Forge bowed respectfully at mention of the Emperor. 'My King understands it depends on the wisdom and pleasure of the Vermilion Pen but you cannot deny the present state of things causes great inconvenience.'

Howqua jousted impassively once again, 'we are small creatures to the Lord of Ten Thousand Islands. We promise you a fair trial.'

'Your laws are not as fair to us as to your own citizens. They would be given the right to plead manslaughter and the right of appeal to a higher Chinese tribunal. We cannot concede you the right to try British subjects.'

'Then British subjects should not trespass on our lands in order to break our laws.'

'Have they broken your laws? Where is the knife? Where is the body of a dead man? The victim was only wounded.'

'You must wait twenty days. The wounded man might die.'

'I will not wait longer than 10 p.m. tonight. Otherwise I will withdraw from Canton.'

Howqua remained unmoved. Seething over the impasse wished on him by Dr. Jarman, Captain Forge asked John Norris 'what next?'

He answered in idiom foreign to the rival interpreter, Pao Peng. 'Thump the tub.'

Springing to full attention, clipping his heels and clapping his hand on his sword, Captain Forge announced, 'the Lascars are a very excitable race and will urge their commanders to take some violent path. A large force of men will march on your city gate.' This stung Howqua to a vague promise to see the Governor.

A discomfited Captain Forge marched back down the shabby lane feeling as if he had played the court jester in cap and bells. He had cut a caper between those who had the true power on either side, shaking his baubles for their ridicule and speaking words that could bring down thrones yet raising no more than a laugh or a polite yawn of mockery. Despondency sat like an invisible black cloud on his shoulders as he mounted the grand staircase past the lofty disdain of Britannica and slumped into a chair saying to John Norris 'words are for fools'. What a fool he was to think he could ever win this game of diplomacy in China with nothing more than words.

He gave voice to his despair. 'Three years, that's all, since the Governor-General of India was scornful of any thought of sending a warship to China. One day, not so far away, I, who resisted the thought with every fibre of my being, will be forced to demand one. The day I do should be the day when I run the skull and crossbones up the mast instead of the Union Jack.'

John was amazed to see the affable Captain so grim-faced, so melancholy about the future. 'Surely the case is different now?'

'Nothing will change. Sooner or later someone will be killed as they nearly were this week. I can't stop it nor can I sit and do nothing and let it happen, as my minister would have me do, saying we can't interfere. Does he really want me to sit on this powderkeg until it blows up under me? Then I suppose I'll be punished for not putting out the fuse while those, who put the keg there in the first place, will go scot free.'

John Norris gave a wry grin, 'a very apt simile for our Scottish buccaneers.'

'Who will force us one day to conduct our trade with warships and that will be the day history will blame us. One thing is certain. The time for passive non-intervention is coming to an end.'

John Norris was spared the necessity of further comment by the arrival of Sean Jarman full of loquacious gratitude. 'The Lascars have been released. What was your secret, Sir?'

Captain Forge laughed ironically at the young Taipan so proper and polite with him as if to redeem himself after losing Holly. 'If I knew young man, I might be able to do it again which I doubt.'

* * * * * *

The Ocean Barbarians Gain in the Delta War

If Viceroy Tang hoped to deter the fanqui easily by banishing their smugboats off the river he was wrong. Neither the execution of Kwok Pung in Macao, nor the attack on the Alpha that spring, had stopped the explosion of the hated ocean barbarians into the river in competition with his smug boats. Their mosquito fleet of fast boats grew from one or two to thirty or more. There was constant conflict between them and the government boats, which proved incapable of controlling the complexities of the delta from Foshan on the west to the Bogue on the east. Violence and defiance grew up and down the river in what Captain Forge described in despatches home as 'a complete and very hazardous change in the Canton trade'.

Fanqui smugglers had never flaunted themselves so boldly even to using a ship at Whampoa in the guise of a hospital ship until the Prefect in Canton ordered it broken up, accusing them angrily, 'how can a hospital ship with no sick men be so busy? It is nothing but a depot ship for opium traffic.'

The prevailing violence infected the fleet at anchor in Whampoa and turned its crews against itself. A mutiny broke out on the Marquess of Camden and was only quelled with some difficulty by Captain Hamilton from the Anna Robertson, who suffered a mutiny in turn on his own ship. He decided to make an example of the most drunken and insolent of his own sailors, fighting drunk from a more vicious brew of samshu grog than usual smuggled aboard from a 'bumboat'. He ordered the man flogged before the crew as a warning, who stood sullen and surly in the bright afternoon. The flogger, a burly sailor notorious for his strength, got no further than running the cat of nine tails through his fingers before they broke ranks and surged forward as one to thrust their officers aside and cut the man from the grating shouting 'floggin's agin the law now.'

Captain Forge heard the uproar from the deck of the Marquess of Camden where he had taken up his station at the first hint of trouble in the fleet some days before. He leapt to his feet expecting yet another of the disgraceful riots that, as its Captain had said over a satisfying lunch, 'were the least you could expect from the riff raff and desperadoes that crew the ships into port these days. A violent trade attracts violent men.'

They found Captain Hamilton embattled on the poop by a hostile crowd of a hundred rough Tars, men irate enough to have tossed him over the side if the ship had been at sea but not so out of hand as to obstruct them as they forced their way through to stand beside him on the poop. With hand upraised, Captain Forge shouted for silence, thinking wryly he was in precisely the same position with these men as he had been with the Co-Hong. If he gave into them now, it was anybody's guess where it would end. He paused at length, a trick to gain advantage over the 'lower orders' he had seen so successfully worked by the Chinese merchants and mandarins.

He gazed over the heads of the surly crowd at the village of Whampoa on the island sprawling across the river. Surely the cradle of trouble was not on this ship nor any around, but in the turbulent breed of men nurtured in this, and other coastal villages, whose alliance with the most belligerent among their own must soon produce far more potential death and ruin than this meagre mutiny. He wondered frantically what to say and hoped the sweat would not start on his brow to betray his inward alarm. His lack of fear, his ease of manner, had calmed them all by the time he spoke at last.

'We are all in prison here so long as we are bottled up in this river. We are prisoners of China. Like all prisoners, we can only leave if we have a record of good behaviour. The port authorities remind us of this every day, every year. If we do not behave well, not only will we suffer but the sailors who come after us will suffer. As the people of the Fairy have suffered.'

They all knew of the murder of the 'Fairy's captain - some said not by the Chinese but by his own crew for endangering them by taking too many risks running inshore to do opium deals after dark.

'If one among you, or them, makes one mistake, has one fight with one woman or man on the bum boats, or on these islands in the river, there is trouble for us all. The Chinese sit waiting in Canton for us to put one foot wrong.

Therefore we must keep law and order on these ships exactly as we would at sea. I know the voyage is long. All your grudges and your hates boil over as soon as you drop anchor in this port. But can we afford the luxury of anger in this port, a port where we must sail out again under the cannon of China? I say to you forget your anger. Forget that it is a crime for you to disobey your commander. You!' His wave encompassed the crew who had rescued the man about to be flogged. 'You genuinely believed flogging is against the law. But resistance to your captain is also against the law and it is not for you to take the law into your own hands if you believe your captain is in the wrong. You should make your protest in a peaceful way remembering it is only this Captain's skill that can get you home again.'

Two men in the forefront of the crowd were trying to ease themselves out of sight to let others of the leaders be punished but halted when they heard him add, 'if you apologise to your captain for this affray no man will be punished. I will wipe the slate clean. As to the accused I will tranfer him to another ship. That will be the end of the matter except for one thing. Your instincts were just and fair. Therefore I will look to you men to set an example in this port from this day forward.' The crew's respectful response as he stepped down among them made it clear he had won at least one battle.

Downing a stiff toddy in Captain Hamilton's cabin, he shook his head when his colleague said admiringly, 'you're the one who should have the ambition to stand for the House of Commons not James Malleson.'

'No, my talents, such as they are, are for diplomacy like my father, not politics.'

He offered Captain Hamilton the post of commodore of the fleet saying 'you're the senior commander as of right, the strong man we'll need.'

'Will need?' The comment had an ominous ring, taking away some of Captain Hamilton's pleasure at being given the right to fly the commodore's red pennant from a man he could honour and respect.

'When there's war at the Factories, if not this season, then the next.' When Captain Hamilton heard that as he downed his second stiff rum, he doubted he would have taken the responsibility for any other man than Captain Forge.

* * * * * *

The British Lion Shows the Flag

Some weeks later three warships, led by the Rear Admiral of the Eastern Squadron in his handsome third rater 74 gunship the 'Wellington', astonished them all by appearing over the horizon with orders from the British government to offer an 'open letter' to the Viceroy. Fortunately the Admiral was not one of those pompous seadogs whose sense of humour had diminished with his rise up the ranks. He was able to enjoy the folly of his predicament when forced to lie thwarted by the forts of the Bogue at Cumsingmoon, unable to associate with the smuggling fleet at Lintin or to reach the fleet at Whampoa, with his letter returned unread.

His jest to Captain Forge was 'I came all this way to show the flag but I can't find anyone to show it to.'

'Someone should inform Lord Palmerston about the geography of China, Sir,' Captain Forge returned.

'I would be feared and respected in the west as the colossus who bestrides the deck of a warship that is the awe of the civilised world.'

'Not I regret to say as an ocean barbarian no better than the despised dog men in their mountain huts who understand neither order nor culture.'

'I say. As bad as that?' The Captain of the Wellington struck in, outraged.

'Well, Captain, the Chinese haven't much lately to respect about some of the ocean barbarians you come to protect.'

The Admiral and Captain exchanged glances. Could it be true, as they had been told, that Captain Forge's judgement had suffered from the stress of being an officer without power in an unruly port? So much of what he had told them sounded fanciful by their standards.

They found out they were wrong when the Customs Officers at the Bogue insulted the Admiral. They stopped a decked schooner, the Bombay, twice to ask if the Admiral, his officers or their wives were on board. The Admiral was outraged. Captain Forge agreed he could not afford to let the insult pass. He decided to hoist anchor to insist on 'showing the flag' after all.

The terrified Admiral Kuan opposing him was in no mood for battle. Had he not already inspected Dr. Jarman's new-fangled steamship, the Jarman, when forcing it to turn back from the Bogue two years before? He could never win against these monstrous battleships with his archaic little junks and knew equally well the dreadful consequences for himself if he were defeated, as his imperial relatives in the Forbidden City kept him up to date with all the gossip of the Celestial Court.

The adroit little man was eminently a diplomat not a warrior. With infinite charm, he came personally to present an apology to the fearsome 'ocean barbarians' with a genial twinkle of eye, fiery mao-ti wine in hand for many courteous toasts, and the promise of unlimited water and provisions for the length of their stay. None of which made Captain Forge less conscious that the 'show' of British naval power beyond the bounds of the Bogue had been as embarrassing and ineffectual as that of Lord Nash with the Imogen and the Andromache had originally been.

'What is the answer?' The Rear-Admiral asked moodily as conscious of the irony of his situation as Captain Forge.

'I wonder if there is any answer in the end, Sir. We could storm those forts, win a war, dictate our terms of victory, solve the pressing problems that agitate our leading merchants - freedom to enter their country and equality of status when they do. But we will only open up new problems. We are peoples separated by more than oceans, sir.'

Admiral Maitland, a great survivor whose life-long concern had been the conflict of battle-fleets not cultures, shook Captain Forge's hand respectfully booming, 'we naval chaps only follow orders. Present commission is to show the flag, Captain. Nothing more. Pity we couldn't give you the teeth you need. Count on me to recommend it. Flag follows trade and all that. Can't let the merchants down, can we?'

Captain Forge retreated to his toddy, envying the Admiral his ability to see everthing as black and white as his own flagship. Perhaps he was right. Only a fool would bother his head about matters outside his power.

* * * * * *

Holly had not seen Sean at all. He had been in Canton during the months after he returned from Manila. He exploded into her life again briefly during the regatta at the height of the late summer social season of Macao. The moment she saw him, and his gaze hung on her own for a long minute before he pretended once more to watch a close-fought race between three wherries, she knew there was still a palpable bond between them. It was a magnetism so obvious she was thankful Billy was down on the water acting as starter and not there to observe it. He would have known, as surely as she herself did, that she had not shed her love for Sean, a passion far more overpowering than the more homespun emotion she felt for Billy.

She pretended interest as the crowd yelled and cheered at the Witch and Flower to get back on course. The two boats only veered even further off course. Without a coxswain to steer them straight and true, the more they belted at their oars the more they swung wildly while the spectators on the hill seemed to have their own contest projecting all the animosities of Canton into the betting ring.

When Raine's Dolphin and Jarman Malleson's Dragon fought out the last subscription cup, Sean seized the chance to close in on her, hoping their encounter would pass unnoticed. She gasped when she saw him so close.

'I've come to say goodbye. I'm going home on leave.'

'To be married?' She could hardly speak for the whirl of her sensation.

'It is possible.'

No reproach. No anger. His green eyes unnerved her. If she had imagined his attraction for her had decreased with distance and change, she was shocked into reality. His presence was as electrifying as it had ever been, even with this distance between them.

Billy had never had this devastating effect on her, nor would any other man ever again. Of that she was certain. But the caution that had driven them apart still survived in her brain, reinforced by the reminder of what the shouted hostilities in the crowd around them really meant. She would not have been wise to marry a soldier of fortune on this violent frontier, a merchant adventurer who constantly ventured a course even more dangerous than Chung Tai Tai's had ever been with the same bitter duel of blood and silver. Even if they had lain with their arms around each other, dazed in the wonder of their love, it was a love that existed in limbo. They were in truth starcrossed lovers from opposing houses as Romeo and Juliet had once been. Surely Flora was right when she had said 'a marriage must start on the right foot, my girl.'

Holly made an effort to say, 'if you marry her it will start on the right foot.'

He was relieved to have her blessing. 'We would not have done?'

'Not as things are now. Perhaps if they had changed.'

'Perhaps.' There was grief with the love in his eyes. Grief for the loss of love, the might have been, which she was sure he could read in her gaze as clearly as she in his.

'You go home alone?' Her words gave no hint of the language in her heart.

'With my uncle.' Ah, victory for Dr. Jarman in the end. He would see Sean married the girl.

'You'll both remain there?' She hoped he would never return with his wife, but she knew it was no longer forbidden as it had been in old John Company days.

'Only Dr. Jarman. He'll stand for the House of Commons. But I'll come back here.'

Her heart was wild with pleasure and dismay. Good God, how could she be glad for the havoc that the existence of his new wife in Macao would cause her? He gripped both her hands tightly in his own, saying 'God bless and keep you through all your days.' He vanished into the crowd. She could not feel at that instant, as if God had blessed her, so much as cursed her and Billy too.

Had she but known, Sean was leaving for Scotland because he, in his own way, also felt he had been born under a crooked star. Holly had forced him to take a far more critical look at the price of the opium trade in blood, as he had seen to his horror when an unwilling witness to one of the more spectacularly vicious battles between the Viceroy's revenue cruisers and his own firm's fast boats in the undeclared war of the river. When Sean heard that Emperor Tao Kuang had vowed he could not face his ancestors, unless he put down the traffic in 'foreign mud' once and for all, he knew that he must go home and face his own ancestors to decide whether he would come to terms with the conscience that Holly had managed to kindle in him.

* * * * * *

The Omen of the Comets

Kaida Hung noted a twitch on Viceroy Tang's flabby face when the Prefect of Canton said he had given permission for a great procession in the spring.

'Great? How great?' The Viceroy snapped nervously.

'A viewing pavilion would be desirable for Your Excellency.'

He responded derisively, 'you propose to waste money by building a stand just for an hour or two?'

The Prefect, never calm before this testy Excellency, explained nervously, 'It could take all day to pass, Excellency. Such floats! Such dancers! It will be splendid.'

'Splendid? Who can afford such a splendid procession? Who has money enough in Canton?' He asked sharply, his thoughts on a possible 'cut' for himself.

'The people do it all themselves. They build them with their own hands. Costumes. Everything.'

Viceroy Tang still looked churlish. 'What people, Prefect?'

'A few streets in the Old City, Excellency.'

'A few people? Common people spending so much money? Why? You can't persuade me they would spend so much money for the pleasure of the citizens of the city.'

The Prefect's head bowed low in shame not because he had an answer but hardly dared give it. He gave the superficial answer, 'in honour of the ancient gods of Canton!'

'Not the five rams?'

'No sir, there is no shortage of grain this season.'

'The God of Rain?'

'No, no lack of rain, Excellency.'

Viceroy Tang sat brooding. He had his failings but one was not stupidity. The people sought the protection of their ancient gods in time of trouble, now and to come, out of fear of doom to them and all they possessed. Therefore since there was neither drought nor rain at that precise moment, they had read the political weather more surely than he and sought the protection of their deities.

The Prefect announced nervously at last. 'There have been shooting stars.'

Understanding dawned on the Viceroy. As comets were a sign of impending calamity, the procession was a massive intercession to avert it. Plainly he could not deny it or he would invite some visitation of calamity on himself. He bowed his assent and retired to relish a small smoke of opium in the seclusion of his inner chamber.

As he watched the procession with his family from his viewing pavilion, not altogether reconciled, he demanded of the Prefect 'why couldn't they have donated the money for troops instead?'

The Prefect lasped into silence. Who could be sure the money would finish where it was intended, that the trooops would be flesh and blood and not phantoms on a fake register?

The procession was so beautiful that Viceroy Tang - who was both poet and patron of the theatre - was genuine in his applause for its ingenious artistry as it moved endlessly past with thousands on thousands of people bearing temples, houses, flowerboats, banners, umbrellas of state, female amazons, tables with precious possessions including jewelled European clocks, troops of children, child soldiers, ancient warriors on horseback and much more.

Once the procession was over, the Viceroy sat in the spring pavilion of the Vice-Regal garden sunk in nervous gloom as he chewed arcana nuts. He was oblivious to the artful disposition of the landscape as a setting for the miniature artificial lakes with their lotus bloom and drifting goldfish cunningly calculated to soothe the spirit. He brooded inwardly over his predicament. He had given all the appearance of a vigilant, nay rigorous, administrator.

He had scattered, or driven, the smugglers off the river. He had made arrests in all districts and announced confiscations and burnings of opium in strategic centres. He had arrested dealers, divan and small furnace owners in all districts. He had withdrawn all his own smuggling boats off the river. He had stopped the Europeans, whose fast boats had taken over the river, by refusing chops to go up and down so often and flushing out the chief lair of their crews at Whampoa Island. So why did he have this uneasy fear of the superstitions of the common people? Was he as foolish as they to take notice of a few shooting stars and lampoons?

He reminded himself that he had friends in the Celestial Court, friends he might need although so far away from that awesome focus of power in Beijing. He knew the Council had resolved to suppress the traffic in 'foreign mud'. They could no longer afford the drain in silver from the country now that opium was as valuable as silver. Nor, for that matter, could he in his own province. If the people's copper cash lost any more in value, there would assuredly be riots.

Very well. He would start a few shooting stars, a few prophecies of his own. Let the people beware! And the smugglers!

Viceroy Tang straightened himself with resolution as he stood to answer a summons to the Hoppo, irked that he must suffer that ancient official's solemn hypocrisy on a day made for poetry. Very well! He had changed course often enough with each decree from the South Gate of Beijing and he could do so now. If his pockets would be leaner, his cheeks would never be. He would be prepared for anything.

He was not prepared however for the Hoppo's answer when he complained 'why do you bother me on a feast day? Can I have no peace from the cares of office? You will be the death of me!'

The Hoppo, unmistakeably Manchu, shocked him by retaliating, 'the new Imperial representative will be the death of you.'

'They are sending another Censor I suppose. Hardly a reason to interrupt a feast day,' was Viceroy Tang's surly retort.

No pity in the Hoppo's stare. 'Worse than that.' As a relative of the Emperor he had no need to conciliate the Viceroy. He leaned forward, hesitated over the dried fruits on the japanned tray to keep the Viceroy in angry suspense, then lifted one delicately with his chopsticks and consumed it slowly before he put Viceroy Tang out of his miserable surmise as to what could be worse.

'A special Commissioner!' The Hoppo gave the Viceroy no quarter despite the manifest outrage and fear competing on his crumpled features. 'With the summary powers of the Emperor himself!'

Viceroy Tang, an acknowledged expert on historical precedent knew better than anyone that only one, perhaps two, such Commissioners had been appointed by the Manchu dynasty in all their years of rule, and only in times of utmost crisis like the White Lotus rebellion. 'Who is this Commissioner?'

'The former Viceroy of Hunan and Hupeh, a man called Lin.'

At the very mention of the one man who had agreed with Chu Tsun's memorial recommending the Emperor massacre all foreigners, the most fearsome exponent of suppression of the opium trade in the provinces he ruled, Viceroy Tan slumped forward in a dead faint. The Hoppo was quick enough to catch him before he fell face forward on the stony floor and to thrust him back onto his blackwood throne. It would never do for the servants to gossip that His Exalted Excellency had fainted away at the thought he might be sent the golden cord, and be obliged to summon up the courage he had never possessed to strangle himself.

The Hoppo worked desperately to revive him, forcing rice brandy into his flaccid mouth and slapping his cheeks until at last he stirred into a consciousness of the grim inquisition about to descend on him. Then he warned the distracted Viceroy that the new High Commissioner Lin would pursue the instructions of the Emperor for a 'root and branch' policy against opium to a bitter end.

'Why?' He moaned as soon as he was fit to talk. 'Why has the Son of Heaven decided to send such a high judge among us?' He had known no good would come of those shooting stars.

'Because a junk, loaded with opium, was arrested off Tientsin and its crew disgorged names under torture as cormorants do fish.'

'Names? He has a list?'

The Hoppo spun out his torment with some relish. 'Yes, he has a list of men who say the cost of bribes has risen since you were Viceroy; bribes, his Imperial Treasurer was quick to point out, that do not find their way to the Co-Hong but our noble selves.'

'Do you pay more than your predecessor?'

'Is my name on his list?

'My cousin assures me those on high are not spared.'

The Viceroy clutched his throat as if he could already feel the golden cord about his neck, then chided himself for succumbing to the superstition of the common people. Was he not a man who had always sought to control his fate?

'I will find out who has betrayed me. And when I have his name I will order the lingering death. I will drive the passage boats of the foreign devils off the river.'

'How will you do that?' The Hoppo enquired with sceptical interest. He did not believe it possible. 'You told the spawn of the Old Rat and his allies to go last New Year and they are still there.'

Still dwelling on the evening's regular display of shooting stars Viceroy Tang replied 'light a few fireworks.'

'You speak in riddles,' the Hoppo objected testily.

'Make an example. Punish all opium smokers with death.'

But for all his grim intentions to make the population of Canton tremble, if not obey, Viceroy Tang's campaign of terror did not prevent some anonymous hand from boldly hoisting a scurrious lampoon on his yamen gate, one of many scattered the length and breadth of the two provinces he governed. When he read it, he knew all the terror of a victim waiting for execution. If his name were not already on that Imperial list of the guilty in Beijking, it would be there the moment this lampoon found its way into Commissioner Lin's hands with its obvious accusation that he allowed, even indulged, his son in the opium trade for their joint profit.

Billy Howe's hand trembled as Viceroy Tang's had done when he read it, but with laughter not terror. 'The old fox's got his foot in the trap alright,' he agreed with Kaida who had brought it to him to warn him Viceroy Tang was on the warpath.

Kaida knew this was no laughing matter. 'If you have one last chest of opium in your possession, get rid of it and get your ships out to Lintin.'

Billy hastened to render the lampoon for Holly into what he decried as a cumbersome translation when he handed it to her.

'Over the broad impoverished eastern land
our venerable Tang holds chief command.
His favour falls on those who seizures make
yet in the daring game he holds a stake;
for cruising boats his sons and comrades keep
to scour the waters of the inner deep.
Still the fond father censures not the boy
and, in his halls, he heaps an untold store
of gold; then, still unsatiated, craves for more

while dice and women all his hours employ.
He's blind to reason, no distinction seen.
The good must bow to tyrants and the mean.
But wrong oppression will resistance cause
and mens' indignant hearts assert the laws.

She exclaimed when she had finished, 'Viceroy Tang must have had a heart attack when he read it.'

'When he heard High Commissioner Lin was already more than halfway to Canton more likely,' Billy added wryly.

'Well,' Holly said tartly as she fed her baby son, 'I haven't got one twinge of pity for him or any of those gangsters in the trade who parade as respectable officials or merchants.'

'I'm sure you have a lot of support.'

'Have I? Then why did nobody turn up to the crisis meeting Mr. Kingsman called on the opium question in Canton? Not one solitary soul. Which proves he's the only man who doesn't smuggle opium.'

'It proves nothing of the kind,' Billy said with unusual asperity. "It wasn't a guilty conscience that kept everyone away but the fact that Mr. Kingsman was utterly dishonest calling the meeting in the first place.'

Holly was outraged at the cynicism of her mild-mannered Billy. 'He preaches in Little Jerusalem.'

'Which doesn't stop him smuggling everything else but opium and borrowing money from those who do smuggle it. What's more, he's dishonest in yet another way. He asserts the missionaries can't win souls for the Word of Life because of opium. We all know it's because the gospel itself has no appeal. This land has gods of its own.'

Holly rushed to the defence of her fellow Yankee. 'Someone has to speak out against the trade.'

'Holly what right has he, as a Yankee, to tell the British what to do? To raise his voice in the halls of Westminster? A vote for him would be a vote for bankruptcy - of the British government in Bengal, the whole China trade, the Co-Hong merchants, the British Treasury and not least ourselves.'

'It wouldn't hurt to condemn it formally.'

'Frankly, I prefer the political honesty that doesn't. Perhaps Mr. Kingsman should stop trying to find another champion in the House of Commons who will do for the opium trade what Wilberforce did for slavery. First he should tell the House where to find the revenues to govern India, then tell the Rajputs to stop growing it in Rajasthan or the Ottoman Caliphs in Turkey. When all is said and done the Chinese think Turkey is a state of America because so much of the Yankee opium comes from there.'

By this time, Holly was so distracted by her baby's wailing, and the realisation she was having her first outright argument with Billy, she desisted. She felt the whole issue was one of those Chinese puzzles you could never disentangle. Yet one thought still lingered in the tangle of her doubts. Wilberforce's crusade had led to the abolition of slavery.

* * * * * *

CHAPTER 8

1838-39 The rise and fall of High Commissioner Lin

Clashes on the Common

The rumour that Viceroy Tang was on the warpath brought Kaida Hung to the Audience Hall at dawn where he was shocked to find all eight Hong merchants kneeling before the Viceroy. Their heads were bowed. Wooden cangues rested in front of seven of them. The dread weight was already around the neck of the eighth, the pitiable Punjoiqua. Why had Punjoiqua been especially singled out for punishment? He was not left in doubt long. It was the Laird again. Shades of Confucius, Kaida thought, that man brings trouble on everyone he touches. This time on poor inoffensive Punjoiqua unwise enough to act as his security merchant.

Viceroy Tang did not spare the lash of his tongue. 'This scoundrel has declared dollar boxes at the Customs House as trade goods. But gentlemen, they contained three catties of opium in flagrant breach of the law that goods cannot be smuggled into the Factories. Why does he think he can defy us? Because he has succeeded in his defiance many times before. Who has allowed him to succeed? You have, gentlemen. You will see that Mr. Ince leaves Canton in three days. If not, you will pull his house down over his ears.'

When the merchants heard of this latest 'thundering' from Viceroy Tang they were not unduly alarmed. They had heard it all before. As for his edict demanding they sign a bond not to smuggle on the river any more or to use decked boats, they shrugged their shoulders. Who was in control of the river? The Viceroy or Jarman Malleson and their underworld allies. They shrugged too soon. The Viceroy had other ploys than they imagined.

Billy Howe was the first to see a mandarin procession march around the corner of No. I Creek Factory and head towards the centre of the Common with coolies carrying a prisoner's bamboo cage, followed by executioners and all the impedimenta for a crucifixion - wooden cross, ropes and arrows.

'They wouldn't dare,' he muttered at the sight of the unfortunate being dumped so unceremoniously on the ground with the implements for his death. 'We can't allow it. Not such desecration of our land.'

He reacted with the speed of an old sea salt struck by a squall and charged through the offices of the companies resident in 'Little Jerusalem' yelling 'On your horses, boys! Up and at them!'

Every man within earshot was out of his chair without a second thought, emerging like a clutch of Red Indians on the rampage, as others also alerted came from the rest of the Factories The situation was as self-explanatory to them at first glance as it was to Billy Howe. The very fact the Viceroy had ordered an execution was an outrageous deliberate insult against them all.

Billy Howe led the rush of some to haul the American flag down to spare it such an insult. Others crowded round the magistrate's execution tent, pushed the tent over, trampled on it and broke its poles. Jack Tars from the Orwell, spoiling for a good fight, rushed in more boldly to seize the timbers for the crucifixion cross, smash them to pieces then belay the heads and shoulders of the two executioners and any Chinaman within reach with their makeshift weapons. Not content with this, they overturned the table of the cowering magistrate and would have attacked his august personage but for the merchants who at last made an effort to restrain them and to accost the magistrate.

Billy stepped forward to speak for them all in Cantonese in the loud tones most likely to be effective 'who is this man you propose to execute here?'

'He is Ho Pok Lun, leader of the disorderly and lawless smugglers of Whampoa who are slaves of the foreign devils.'

So, the Viceroy, in his raid on Whampoa the month before, had seized some secondary leader to serve as hostage for Wang Chung who had been warned in time.

'You cannot execute him here.'

'I have my orders. He must die.'

'We will resist any execution on this land.'

Faced with the menace of these bulky foreign devils looming all around him, the magistrate sounded the retreat. His orders did not include an open fight with them. After all he could have the smuggler strangled in Thirteen Factories Street behind the Factories which was close enough to pass muster. But the ruffianly crowd loitered disconcertingly behind as if another act in the drama was about to follow.

John Norris watched them anxiously. 'I don't like the look of them. Not when the Viceroy's determined to strike before the new Commissioner declares war on him.'

'What new Commissioner?' Billy cried in alarm.

'A man so powerful all Canton is in a ferment. One who has had nineteen audiences with the Emperor. Who has the right to ride a horse in the Forbidden City. Who has received honours so exceptional I wonder if there has ever been a precedent. One who has the Emperor's personal mandate to punish every opium dealer and to drive every opium ship into the sea. Only then, the Emperor says, can he face his ancestors.'

'We've heard that froth of words so often before.'

'Then it's been a case of cry wolf so often no one is going to notice the wolf is now at the door.'

'This is really the time of the wolf then,?'

'This time it's war.'

John's prophecy proved all too correct. Within the hour the crowd was growing larger by the minute lingering like ducks waiting to be fed, chiefly in front of Number 1 Creek Factory.

Paddy MacKeane was in no doubt the surly crowd was there to punish the Laird. 'They warned you they would pull his house down round his ears if he does not obey their explicit order to leave Canton.'

The Laird's grimace was like a gargoyle on his scarred weatherbeaten face. 'I've never paid the slightest heed to that bunch of monkeys. Why should I start now?'

'You'd put us all in danger.'

'They always back down,' the feckless Laird said from his vigil over the mob seething below, too many years an Old China Hand for panic. 'Warnings! Warnings! What do they ever amount to? Puffs of smoke without fire!'

Paddy, bred on centuries of fluctuations in the turmoils of Ireland, was more sensitive to the political weather. 'That time is over.' He sent runners for the police.

The sailors from the fast boats, now well primed with drafts of samshu in the recesses of the Factory, crowded the doorway behind him jovially offering 'want a hand with this lot, mister?' They thrust him aside to pour out onto the Common. A wit among them made rushes at the crowd playing the bull in their bullring while his mates barracked, mindless and witless about the consequences of their sport, picking a fight as generations of drunken sailors in Old China Street before them had done.

The Laird stepped forward flourishing his dogshead cane, swearing florid oaths at the besotted fool whose antics might well bring the roof down on his head after all. The capering sailor, mesmerised as any bull by the flourish of a hostile object, charged forward in a stupid rage to dash up the Laird's arm. He hurled the Laird backwards onto the crowd where his cane laid an onlooker's cheek open to spurt blood all over the Laird as he recovered his balance. At first the crowd merely fell back. But not for long. As if in response to a signal they came from everywhere with a sally of brickbats, stones or blocks of wood, not as unarmed or innocent as the sailors had supposed. Some of the sailors, and tougher 'foreign devils', tried to remonstrate. The mob began to hoot and threaten again. The sailors charged once more, driving the sullen force back some distance before it rallied and replied with a second surge of blows and stones. The situation grew uglier by the minute.

'Why haven't the police turned out?' Billy asked fearfully.

In fact the Prefect had deliberately ignored the warning of Paddy's runners and repeated messages from the Co-Hong merchants, who were forced in the end to take the unusual step of coming themselves with their own police to restore order. First they ordered all the Europeans back into their houses as their presence was inflaming the dense throng. Then they prevailed on the restive mob to disperse.

At first they refused. The forward row hurled a barrage of stones and surged forward, knocking the chief of Co-Hong police down and trampling on him as they overwhelmed his force. Gaining in noise and confidence every moment, leaders among them were tearing out the iron garden rails to use as battering rams against the main front doors, already barricaded with iron bars and stacked bales against them. Others were tearing at the Venetian shutters barring the windows shrieking and chanting revenge for two Chinese they believed had been seized and were being kept hostage within.

Just when it seemed nothing could save the cowering foreign devils within, the howling mob miraculously vanished as if they had been a human typhoon that had raged against the Factories then moved on, leaving an empty calm at the eye of the storm. And leaving the foreign devils to emerge from their perilous strongholds asking why the Prefect, who had refused to come so long to quell the furious mob, had suddenly arrived in his sedan chair with a force of his own lictors and police to restore order? Why he could clear the whole Common in fifteen minutes? Why he knew who the leaders were to point them out for arrest? Why he allowed the chief of them to depart with a mere kowtow and thanks for paternal correction? Why he should remain for some time until he was sure the mob had gone?

Even more curious, after neglecting so long to do anything at all, he now set up painted lanterns, tables and other requisites of comfort so the city magistrate and a military officer could spend the night on guard over the Factories to see they came to no harm. Whereupon the pair proceeded to eat a lavish meal to the amusement of Billy. 'The Chinaman, like the Englishman, likes to fight on a full stomach.'

An angry deputation of merchants confronted Captain Forge when he arrived from Whampoa with a force of sailors from the Reliance. Why had the government deliberately left them at the mercy of a raging mob for three hours with the lame excuse the police were engaged elsewhere?

Captain Forge stared the nettled merchants down with angry impatience. Most of these men had openly defied not only himself but Viceroy Tang when he ordered them to remove their fast boats from the river and to stop all smuggling in the delta. They had mocked his impotent lack of authority in the most insulting terms of which 'Viceroy's lackey' was the mildest. Now they expected him to salvage them from trouble they would have avoided if they had obeyed him in the first place. He could only repeat his orders once more. Remove all fast boats in the river. Stop smuggling. See the Laird leaves China forthwith. If possible persuade Dr. Jarman to follow. Or he personally would come and help Howqua carry out his threat to demolish Number 1 Creek Factory about their ears.

* * * * * *

Retirement of Dr. Jarman

In the unkindest cut of all to the memory of the Honourable John Company, Dr. Jarman's farewell dinner was held as of old through many a long year in the great dining hall of the New English Factory. All the appurtenances were there. The towering candelabras on the long dining table of the great dining hall and the massive sideboards, their tiers of candles winking in the mirror wall like a scatter of flickering stars. The handsome crested china and coupes of the East India Company dinner service. The heavy silver service.

The ghosts of the old East India Company men, however, would have risen affronted, Captain Forge reflected as he took his seat at the head of the board. For Dr. Jarman and most of his employees, ranged down both sides of the banquet table, scorned everything those old timers had valued in their respect for the laws and customs of China - obedience to edicts, courteous petitions, repudiation of smuggling. Their rising power on the Coast was a defiant power as the old Company never was.

He turned to Sean Jarman, back from Scotland a more mature and thoughtful man. 'What are the old man's plans when he gets home?'

Sean was courteous. He had come to despise the patronising, rude attitude of some of the new breed of younger men to Captain Forge. 'He's standing for the House of Commons, Sir.'

'So I heard. Lucky man! I'd trade him his chance to reach Palmerston's ear any day.' Anything would be better, even Dr. Jarman's belligerence, than the present drift of Viscount Palmerston, now restored as Prime Minister - no letters, no instructions, no policy.

Sean added. 'There's also talk of him getting married.'

'The Chinese have a saying that a man who is not married is like a coach without a wheel.' Captain Forge commented non-committally although it seemed rather late in the day for Dr. Jarman to be acquiring that wheel. 'Does he confirm or deny?'

'Neither. Simply saying she's fair, fat, and forty.'

Captain Forge's gaze traversed the banquet table with its sparkling crystal, excellent wines, discreet service and first rate food. Every detail was as perfect as any you would find in the most exclusive club of London. It represented the kind of wildly improbably transplantation of home culture in which the British excelled. Haut ton carried off with hauteur. Style that was more than bravado. Survival of belief in the superiority of British civilisation. How much longer, Captain Forge wondered, could this little oasis of elegance last in Canton. After all it had been almost engulfed only that very week in plunder and destruction. He raised the glass of excellent claret he preferred with a baron of beef, admiring its ruby sparkle. It had travelled a long way, through storm and stress, to enliven their evening.

Sean Jarman, contrite for neglecting Captain Forge in favour of Captain Macdonald on his other hand, turned to him again. 'Pity the Parsees couldn't join us sir. They have been the backbone of our success right from the start, and still are.'

'Why ever not?' Captain Forge had not remarked the omission.

Can't eat with us. Will join us later. Zoroastrians sir.'

'I see,' Captain Forge responded although he did not. No one had ever explained to him that the Parsees were more properly Farsis, known as the Jews of the East. They pursued the old fire-worshipping religion of ancient Persia from whence they had come many centuries before.

He added, 'does this apply to Maxwell Raine as well?'

'His taboo is not against our banquet but our company. Or rather our competition. Dr. Jarman bears him no ill-will.'

Captain Forge notched a mental plus for Sean Jarman for accepting the jibe graciously. 'And the taboo of the government on you both? Their intention to say a pox on both your houses?'

'My uncle holds the present edicts are so much waste paper. They can't succeed against us. Hence his decision not to send an express ship to Calcutta to stop all purchases of opium at the sales.'

Sean's glance embraced the confident jollity of the assembly which no doubt imbibed its aura of convinced invincibility from the great Taipan it was about to lose, as did Sean himself along with several rounds of the excellent whisky punch.

'Won't he find it difficult to be a captain without ship?'

Sean, his tongue loosened by liquor as many a man before him, carelessly betrayed a confidence, 'but he won't be, Sir. Captain of a different ship in a manner of speaking, Sir- the Expeditionary Force,' as if the thought were a commonplace which everyone should support.

So that was what Dr. Jarman, so blandly presiding at the head of the table, had been up to these many months, Captain Forge fumed barely able to restrain himself from walking out of the banquet before the speeches to come. That was why his vessels had been so busy in their surveys of coastal waters, why his flags studded a chart of China in logistics claimed to be for his cargo fleet but in fact for a British expedition of war.

He deplored Sean's tacit approval of the plan. No moral concern at the thought of blowing sense into the obtuse Chinese government with guns of men of war. No conscience that it would be impossible to justify war on present grounds in Christian terms. The rest of any of the merchants no better. If any of them were, they would not have stood around Dr. Jarman with such effusive enconiums, nor given such generous subscriptions for an opulent dinner service and a silver plate inscribed with all their signatures. Nor would they have cheered him to his feet, as they did now, their huzzahs so loud they could be heard the length of the Factories. Huzzahs received by Dr. Jarman as Caesar might due homage. Dr. Jarman's rhetorical thanks worthy of Caesar.

'Let me say a few words in praise of this country before I leave it for the last time. I have been here a long time. In all these years I have found our persons more efficiently protected by laws, and a watchful and excellent police, than in many other parts of the East or the world. Business is conducted with unexampled facility and, in general, with singular good faith. The Chinese are courteous in all their transactions with foreigners. As a result, gentlemen, the society of Canton holds a high place among the merchants of the East.'

Suddenly the barb appeared among the flowers, the insult among the compliments.

'I know that this community has often been accused of being a set of smugglers, particularly of late. This I distinctly deny. We are not smugglers, gentlemen! It is the Chinese government and officers, who smuggle, who connive at and encourage smuggling not we.'

As Captain Forge contemplated the gathering standing to cheer this declaration of innocence to the echo, he could only wonder if the verdict of history would agree with Dr. Jarman. Namely, he who supplies a vice is not equally as guilty as he who commits it. He was thankful when he could escape at last into the withdrawing room, created on the verandah by stretching canvas walls between pillars wreathed in flowers, with nothing more than Dr. Jarman's initials, formed by variegated lamps, to remind him a moment longer of that gentleman.

'Why the gloom sir?' His secretary, John Norris, enquired as he sank down on the settee.

'Because the ambition of our man of the hour is war in China.'

'Surely, sir, he'll never persuade Viscount Palmerston.'

'I assure you, Norris, that worthy gentleman won't oppose him.'

'There is nothing like distant gunfire to divert the minds of the common populace from present trouble on the home front.'

'Will there be no opposition, sir?'

'Where, pray, when the chips are down? I'll be under orders whether I like it or not. Everyone else has a vested interest. You've only got to look at the support the old villain's got tonight.'

A support that seemed to extend to the Laird. The studied insolence of his departure next day was more like a victory than a disgraceful retreat with its noisy demonstration of supporters, hurrahs, and long strings or crackers that would do justice to any Chinese celebration. The prancing ocean barbarians in his claque might not have been so jubilant if they had been aware the Emperor had announced that very day, 'I, the Emperor, on account of the daily increase of that flowing filth, opium and the great increase of silver sycee going abroad have ordered that Viceroy Tang must scrub and wash away the filth and must not indulge himself with hopes of shifting the affair from himself. He must not think of sitting still and looking on while High Commissioner Lin Tsi Tse manages the business.'

* * * * * *

Imperial Orders to Scrub and Wash away the Filth

Viceroy Tang examined his conscience nervously as he waited for High Commissioner Lin in a flowery pavilion that had been hastily erected over the quay at the Water Gate. He had quelled the turbulence of the foreign devils. They had not opposed his warning execution on their Common a second time, but skulked in their factories afraid he would rouse another unruly mob against them. He would have been even more nervous if he had known that Commissioner Lin had been lurking secretly in the neighbourhood for some days extending the blacklist of offenders already in his possession.

Viceroy Teng had agonised over the decision as to what would be proper to wear - a highly embroidered robe for a ceremonial occasion or a more sober gown with less lavish ornamentation. But when he heard that the High Commissioner's long journey from Pekin down the Grand Canal, and over the mountains into Kwangtung, had been unostentatious in the extreme - refusing all banquets or bribes and paying for all his retinue bought or used - he knew it would be high folly to meet this powerful man in a grandiose manner. So as the day of his arrival dawned, he and his chief subordinates - the Governor, the Provincial Judge and the Treasurer of the province - stood in sober array as they nervously awaited this dreaded judge of imperial presence and power.

Only the Hoppo and the Prefect could afford to be calm. The Hoppo had abandoned smuggling on his Customs boats some time before. Also by a lucky chance his secretary, Kuo Kui Chuan, happened to be an old friend of High Commissioner Lin from Kiansu days. As for the Prefect, he was the only official who had had a letter reminding him of a law excusing any official for punishment for negligence if he voluntarily turned over those who were guilty of opium dealing from among his subordinates. He had volunteered two such names already.

Behind the august party, a group of interpreters including Kaida Hung waited, for not all the functionaries nor the Co-Hong merchants spoke mandarin, while the eminent Commissioner certainly would not be fluent in Cantonese. Behind them again the President of the Yeh Hua Academy tried to efface himself. Viceroy Tang had angrily questioned his presence until told he had been expressly summoned by the High Commissioner as a personal friend.

If the quay was festive, the Common before the Factories was not, as Billy Howe found when, unable to sleep, he took a turn in the chilly dawn. It lay deserted as if struck by the plague. No sound, no movement anywhere. As he lingered wondering why such a pall of silence lay over a river, normally busy even in the dead of night, he saw the reason why. A red and gold mandarin barge was moving slowly towards him from down river bearing an unknown mandarin gravely enthroned in the stern, who could only be the new High Commissioner, object of so much excited gossip these many days past. He could not believe his luck for normally mandarins of such eminence entered Canton by a different route through a gate upriver.

Maxwell Raine accosted him. 'The early bird catches the worm.'

'I never saw any man look less like a worm.' He could sense the threat of the man even at a distance, no hoary elder but a man in the prime of life projecting an aura of majesty despite his simple dress.

'He'll be like all the rest. He'll huff and puff, spout some rhetoric about opium smugglers and their boats leaving China forever, seize some token opium, execute a few people, line his pockets and then go home.'

Maxwell Raine's lofty nonchalance put Billy in mind of a tugboat pilot who philosophically endures all weathers, certain he can always bring his ship to port, a survivor for so long he forgets one day a storm may blow up that will defeat him. Therefore he would hope for the best in the crisis signified by that stern rigid figure on the gilded boat gliding towards the flowery pavilion and its welcoming deputation. He, himself, knew he must fear the worst.

When High Commissioner Lin landed he peremptorily refused Viceroy Tang's offer of accommodation. He would stay with his friend, the President of the Yueh Hua Academy in Thirteen Factories Street hard by Consoo House. Next he dismissed their invitation to a welcoming lunch with the deputation, summoning them instead to his own.

He wasted no time in destroying any false hopes lesser officials might have cherished. Speaking with stern severity, he announced he had come to Canton to suppress the traffic in 'foreign mud.' He would scourge the horrid filth from the sewers of the ocean barbarians back where it came. He would see they obeyed the laws and statutes of the Celestial Kingdom equally with its subjects. The task would not be easy, as the disposition of the foreigners was as unfathomable as a goat or a dog.

Viceroy Tang picked at his food with delicate appetite, as he fought to conceal his dismay at the enormity of what lay ahead. He would never be able to match wits with this devastating younger man. Had Commissioner Lin not passed the difficult Chinshih examination ten years earlier than himself in age, and achieved rank equal to his own twenty years earlier? Had the Emperor Tao Kuang himself not said Lin's talents were superior to his own? Had Commissioner Lin's immense popularity when Governor of Kiangsu not certainly been superior to any he, himself, had been able to achieve in vice-regal rule. In despair, he clutched at a straw. His only hope of building any bridge of respect with Commissioner Lin would be through their common love of poetry.

High Commissioner Lin next ordered Howqua and the other seven Co-Hong merchants still in business to move into the adjoining house where they remained in dread of his summons for a week. When the summons to his audience chamber came, it was to witness his confrontation of the forty-five public servants he had arrested. Two on the judge's staff, five on the prefect's, twelve on the salt controller's, five on the military commander's in charge of patrol boats, and twenty on that of the two magistrates of Namhoi and Heangshan. All of them, those arrested and the Co-Hong, terrified they might also be arrested at any moment, obliged to kneel before High Commissioner Lin's dreaded procession entered behind the blood-curdling howl and rattle of chains of the Prefect's lictors. Once seated, High Commissioner Lin wasted no time in denouncing them all with chill voice and furious piercing eyes, his face merciless as the God of Justice.

'For twenty years, you have been accepting bonds from foreign vessels to say they did not carry opium when they entered the river, knowing they did. You rented foreign merchants Factories where they, their captains and sailors resorted, where they took our women and boys. In those very Factories, you allowed them to trade in 'foreign mud' openly and brazenly, to write out orders, pass bills for payment, sign chits, and insolently publish their opium prices for all to read in their newpapers. You tolerated them sending their servants to the outside smoking shops and shroffs. You supplied them with the wooden boxes to ship our silver sycee out of the country which has become improverished as a result. I burn with shame for you.'

Worse was to come. They were not only liars. They were traitors. 'You gave bonds to the most notorious opium traders like Jarman, Malleson, Raine and Ince. You acted as spies for them advising them of every decree and policy of the Chinese government. You deserve to die like traitors and so you will.'

He paused to observe fear reducing them to abject fright. The death of traitors was always one of being slowly sliced to death with razor-sharp knives.

'I will give you one chance. If you confiscate all the opium on all the foreign ships within three days and deliver it up to me, none of you will die. If you do not, one or two of the most notorious merchants among you will suffer. Your properties will be confiscated, your women sold, and you yourselves will be taken to the execution grounds for the most extreme penalty of the law.'

The watching crowd sighed and shifted before the gale of High Commissioner Lin's wrath. Howqua fought to maintain his impassive dignity before its bloodlust marking him for its first victim as he marked himself. How could he, or any of his brother merchants force the foreign devils to disgorge all their opium, when, by so doing, they would bankrupt themselves for the season? He dared not argue for his life by pleading he had been ordered to do the impossible. He bent his head in respectful submission as High Commissioner Lin pronounced orders to him as head of the Co-Hong before taking his awesome departure,

'You will advise the fanqui of our edict. Three days! No more! Or I will demand hostages.'

Howqua shook with despair. The very thought of his fate left him drained and nauseous. A fate that must be inevitable as he would never be able to convince the red beards that High Commissioner Lin was different from his predecessors. He meant what he said.

He might have been comforted if he had known that High Commissioner Lin's good friend, Chang Na Shan, one of the most honoured scholars in Canton, had already cautioned Lin against too harsh an oppression of the officials or people of Canton, warning it might well lead to rebellion or war with Great Britain.

At first the merchants treated Howqua's demand as a mere word game, all speaking at once in their first noisy meeting in the New English Factory. Surrender their opium? Commissioner Lin must be mad. Howqua in terror of his life? Just so much hot air. All the fuss just the panic of the 'juveniles' or newcomers to Canton.

'No you're wrong!' Colin Kingsman shouted above the uproar. 'Have you ever seen Howqua show such loss of nerve, such terror before? No, you have not. Have you ever known his son thrown into goal as a hostage? Or known a census of weapons taken. Or the port closed before negotiation has begun? No, you have not.'

Maxwell Raine, a warrior by instinct rather than wily negotiator, lumbered to his feet. 'The Hong is not telling the truth. Where is the order from Commissioner Lin? Let them produce it before I'll believe a word of it. Howqua is merely trying to make himself good with the Commissioner by machinations and lies just like all those mandarins in the past who bought up parcels of our opium to surrender as seizures. They have given us no proof. The juveniles must not give way to panic.'

He looked meaningfully at his much younger brother Alan, as short as he was tall, one of those 'juveniles' new to the Coast's rumour mill.

Colin Kingsman from Little Jerusalem rebuked his recalcitrant audience, 'Howqua's warning should not be swept aside. His terror is not fictitious. He's most certainly under threat of death if our opium is not surrendered. His damnation is not in the hereafter but here and now. Who will damn him but ourselves if we do not believe he's in immediate fear for his life and property? We cannot see this man, our friend and neighbour despite any hard names we have called him in the past, condemned to death out of concern for the profit of our clients.'

His earnest face was suffused with passion. His voice took on the fervour of an evangelist calling on sinners to repent before the Day of Judgement. His rhetoric was as effective as any hellfire preacher coaxing donations from an unwilling congregation. The meeting voted to surrender all chests they personally owned 'under protest' but not those belonging to foreign investors or Parsee traders in Bombay.

Maxwell Raine, forced to conform, muttering angrily to his brother, Alan, 'they should have called Lin's bluff and would have but for that chattering bible-basher.'

The newchum Alan was shocked. 'And see the merchants die?'

'Bleeding hearts. That's what they betted on.'

'A thousand chests should keep him happy,' Alan said hopefully.

'You don't know China. Lin will become more intolerable.'

'We must escape,' Alan rose as if to leave on the next tide.

Maxwell Maxwell restrained him. 'They'll be after my rivals not us.'

'Malleson has taken ship for Lintin. So should we.'

Captain Forge would have agreed with the merchants if he had not already rushed to Macao on news of fireships and warjunks gathering at the Bogue, and soldiers at the barrier of Macao. He would have surprised the merchants by giving them total support for once if they had refused to surrender one ball of opium as the Yankees had. He would have withdrawn all support for the Prefect of Canton, once readily given in the matter of banning British fast boats from the river. He would no longer have earned the abusive accusation of the more intransigent of the British merchants that he was the 'lickspittle of the Chinese government.'

Unfortunately his deputy was in charge, too young and inexperienced to realise that he had made it impossible to refuse to give up all the opium by giving a fraction to appease the High Commissioner.

* * * * * *

Holly stared at the elaborate red New Year card to wish her good fortune in disbelief. Why had Chung Tai Tai come to deliver it in person instead of sending a servant as was more common? She went downstairs at once to find Chung Tai Tai bolt upright on the chaise longue with a retinue of servants, an embarrassing array of largesse, and an interpreter new to her. Holly hid her dismay. Etiquette would demand she return an equivalent display of expensive merchandise from the land of the Flowery Flag. She doubted if she could cull a comparable gift from all her American friends put together, not now at the end of the season.

Her discomfort continued as Chung Tai Tai sipped tea and ate minute bites of old-fashioned English walnut cake for form's sake, appraising the room with its massive Victorian sofas as heavy and excessive as the skirts fashion now obliged western women to wear. Both seemed ponderous and vulgar in contrast to the clutch of dainty women attending her visitor.

Once formalities were over, Chung Tai Tai's manner changed. 'I have come to offer help if you need to escape.'

Holly was thunderstruck. 'I escape? Why should I need to escape? We have no quarrel with Commissioner Lin - no opium trading, no fast boats on the river.'

'He has said he will drive all foreign devils away. His means? Persecution! Death!' Chung Tai Tai was disturbed to see Holly, she now regarded as one of her own, so pale and drawn. 'As soon as danger strikes, come to me. I will carry you to Lintin.'

'We will be safe there?'

'Not if Commissioner Lin orders the villagers of Kowloon to stop selling you food and water as he must now the trading fleet has left the river and put themselves beyond his reach.'

'Will they obey him?' Holly asked in alarm.

'They have never obeyed any high officer of the Middle Kingdom unless they want to obey. Then only at their price not his. We must ask ourselves which way Wang Chung will jump, for or against. And if for, will the fear the villagers have of him outweigh their greed for your money? But you have nothing to fear. We will protect you.'

Holly had never lost her sense of surprise that this frail little figure was her unfailing shield. She went impulsively towards her and took both her hands in her own. 'How can I ever thank you little mother?'

Chung Tai Tai responded to her grip with surprising strength. 'Don't forget to wear your jade. With its magic, you can walk through the forest.' She rose to take her leave.

'Am I in danger from your visit to me today?'

She shook her head. 'If there are spies around they will merely think I owe you benevolence, no more.'

After Chung Tai Tai had gone, she exclaimed over the extravagance of that 'benevolence'- boxes of finest tea, embroidered Nankin crepe, black japanned gift boxes inlaid with pearl, the finest grass cloth, shawls and the choicest dried fruits. She sighed to think so many of her fellow countrymen still laboured under the delusion that these people, who could produce goods of such finesse and exquisite elegance, were an uncivilised race.

She had thought Chung Tai Tai unduly gloomy. But John Norris was even more so, his note of urgency uncharacteristic.

'I don't want to alarm you unnecessarily, but has the Eugenia finished unloading at Whampoa yet? If not get her out of the river as fast as you can. They're going to blockade it.'

'What if they haven't finished loading?' She could not afford to sail without a full hold.

'Sail I tell you Holly.'

'Who was ever harmed in a blockade?' She jogged her son on her knee only half-attentive.

He felt like shaking her. Surely motherhood had dulled her judgement. 'Holly you saw one riot on the Common when Viceroy Tang wanted a scapegoat. This time he will need a much bigger whipping horse to divert the whips of the mob from himself not to mention the whip of the Emperor. He will not stop at calling out the mob. He will call out the whole sea and land force.'

Holly laughed at the vision he conjured up, remembering all the clowning about acrobatic Manchu swordsmen or marksmen firing muskets backwards over their shoulders. 'Holly, China may be a sleeping giant but it's a giant none the less. Slow to move but capable of smashing Lilliput.'

Holly was contrite. 'John, I'm terribly sorry. I've been in a trance since I had Billy Junior, as if it was forever. I'll get a message to Whampoa at once.'

'The fast boats have stopped running, Holly.'

'Then how?' She asked acutely aware the uncommon depth of his anxiety and devotion to her.

'I'll take it myself. I'm going back.'

Wordlessly she took Chung Tai Tai's talisman from her neck. As she handed it to him, she flushed to remember the nuance of his declaration. He bore as futile a love for her as any mediaeval knight glad for the mere chance to do her a service and wear her favour on his sleeve. She felt guilty her very existence caused him such evident misery, and alienated him from any other possible relationship for the time being. Still she reminded herself she was not responsible that the good Lord was not even-handed with the capacity of human beings to love. Their fate was in His hands not her own. Yet she could not exempt herself from anxiety for him

'If there's war on the river, may the Lord protect and keep you.' She touched him gently on the arm as he took his leave. 'Take care. We all love you too much to want to lose you.'

She felt acutely guilty to see him blush and rush abruptly from her too confused for words.

* * * * * *

Holly stood well back from the dense crowd of the faithful who lined the Praya Grande while a column of church dignitaries, nuns and priests moved slowly in a chanting processional of Our Lady of Passion to the humble church of Santa Agostino. It was the day of thanksgiving for the miraculous return of her image from one church to another long ago.

She nudged Flora, an austere Calvinist like herself. 'If only I had the faith of these people. They really believe in miracles, don't they Flora?'

Flora, her bright aureole of red hair aflame in the sun, was a born sceptic. 'Have you noticed, the age of miracles is always some other than your own?'

'Perhaps it's not,' Holly answered with unusual gravity.

'Just in case let's pray for one.'

'An insurance policy?'

'For Billy and Barron.' Flora asked in more serious mood.

'Why not for ourselves? We're in more danger right now,' Holly reminded her, adding 'they say I'm clairvoyant.' She could scarcely put Chung Tai Tai in danger by telling Flora where the prophesy had really come from.

'I'd best warn Barron not to go then. He will if Commissioner Lin doesn't arrive in Macao soon as everyone seems to expect.'

'Maybe he's foxing.'

'Why would he do that?' Flora demanded, more perspicacious than Holly was aware about her sources of reliable forecasts.

'Because they know he's not an Admiral Kuan.'

With that conundrum, Holly dragged Flora into the tail of the procession which had now vanished into the unpretentious church of simple elegance. Inside no empty pew anywhere, many eager worshippers jostling each other to touch the robe of Our Lady, or to kneel for blessing of the priest.

Flora whispered to Holly, 'must I kiss the robe too for our miracle?'

Before Holly could answer, an unknown lady in a black mantilla beside her addressed her in stilted English. 'Excuse me, Mrs. Howe, a message for you.'

'Yes?' Holly enquired calmly enough, too long used to the melodramas of Macao for panic.

'Commissioner Lin will have the opium. All of it. He will stop at nothing till he has destroyed it all, root and branch. He will massacre all the foreigners. He will start a war if he must.'

Holly was too startled by her apparition to ask her where she came from before she vanished into the throng still pressing into the church saying 'we'll call you to the Temple of A Ma.'

As she stumbled out of the church with Flora into a windless eerie fog that had closed in from the sea, so dense they could not see from one side of any street to the other, she was full of dread for them all, but most for her unborn child as she asked Flora, 'what do you make of that?'

Flora, stripped of illusions now, answered sadly, 'that Barron will be forced to fight to save people not worth the trouble'.

Commissioner Lin, since the nightmare of his arrival, would be just as halting as their own advance over the fog-slippery cobblestones. He would test them all in a pilgrimage of terror along his own version of the Stations of the Cross.

'Don't you think they can ride out this storm?' Holly asked hopefully.

'Better than my dear Barron will,' Flora forecast gloomily. 'They will tip the bucket on him for everything that goes wrong, you'll see, and claim the credit for everthing that goes right.'

'Who will your government listen to? Him or me?'

'They have more friends than he.'

'Doesn't that make you furious?' She kicked a stone in her frustration. The fog that enshrouded them was a fitting symbol for the dank, depressing web of politics.

'Not if I know he has done right by his lights.'

'Of all the people I know, you're the truest Christian,' Holly declared, one arm hugging her close as a soft drizzle of rain began to fall.

Captain Forge did not dismiss the message as Holly expected, nor its successor from Tim Bird that they were all to meet at the entrance to the Temple of A Ma, goddess of all fishermen said to have landed there after surviving a terrible storm centuries before. Quite the reverse. Have them all trooping down to the Temple pretending to be a sketching party without him in the plot? Good heavens, no. He wouldn't miss out for the world. Besides he was almost as good a landscape painter as Chinnery and Bird, and much better than either Flora or Holly.

The moment they took up their station before the multi-coloured bas relief stone carvings in the rockface, an instant crowd of cheerful pilgrims gathered round in a solid semi-circle, leaning on each other in their anxiety to see every stroke until Holly expected them to topple over on their easels at any instant.

Chinnery talked as he sketched with the incisive strokes of a master, transforming the scene before him into a metaphor. 'A story similar to our Virgin Mary and child. The Lady A Ma was once a real person like so many gods in this country. Just imagine! She walked to the very crest of this hill above us and ascended from there into Heaven. All that mumbo jumbo with red paper and incense you see on every junk is for her.'

After a decent interval they entered the moongate of the red temple wall into a large greeting hall with a wooden model of the junk which had brought the lady A Ma through the storm safely into port. Once through, they followed one of the sinuous temple paths through the banyan trees, and boulders spattered with verses to the goddess as well as outcrops of joss sticks, to slip unobtrusively into one of the many small neglected pavilions on the hillside.

Tim Bird, shocked to see a fatigue, sorrowful Kaida in wait for them, admonished him 'you've taken a dreadul risk coming.'

Kaida acquiesced. 'No quarter given to spies now.'

'Is Lin hunting down spies then?'

'As no one ever did before.'

When they had draped themselves artistically over the rocks as if in a tableau for Chinnery to sketch, he told them of the to and fro turmoil between the Factories, Consoo House, the City and the Academy. He omitted no detail of how the merchants had at first refused to yield any opium, Maxwell Raine leading the opposition with James Malleson taking a back seat. Then in response to the entreaties of Howqua and Mowqua Junior, they had offered up the opium they said they honestly owned.

High Commissioner Lin had fastened on Maxwell Raine as leader, no doubt regarding the High Devil as less cunning, more malleable than the wily Malleson, and demanded his attendance in the city. The merchants had crowded into the Paoshan Factory to persuade Maxwell Raine from going. Maxwell Raine himself willing to go. His partner, English, volunteering to go instead as less indispensable to the business, and bravely confronting the Chief Magistrate at the Temple of Heaven to say that Maxwell Raine would have come, but the whole of the merchant body prevented him from doing so, believing he would be arrested.

'As he surely would have been - the stupid son of a Thames whore,' Captain Forge swore as he did rarely, 'Couldn't he, with all his years in Canton, deduce they had one aim, namely to keep him hostage?'

'He seemed to think the fact that Pao Pang had returned with High Commissioner Lin from Beijing as his Cantonese interpreter meant he could trust him.' Pao Pang had once worked for Maxwell Raine.

Tim Bird swore in turn to give vent to his alarm, adding 'Pao Pang was always a better confidence man than a comprador. The High Devil was always too trusting.'

Chinnery, a self-declared coward, chimed in 'I'd give a king's ransom to paint the fellow.'

Holly, who had found Raine much more of a thoughtful gentleman than Malleson, was irked enough to enquire, 'Aren't you all being a bit severe on Maxwell Raine?'

Captain Forge, too annoyed for courtesy even with Holly, answered her peremptorily. 'I saw a sailor once, mad with the grog, jump overboard into a raging sea crying it was such a lovely day he was going for a swim. You should have seen the swell. He involved the whole crew in a most dangerous rescue. Just what this idiot Maxwell Raine is doing now, putting the whole foreign community at risk. And who will have to order an emergency force in without any back-up if the party gets rough? I will. Much thanks I'll get from any of them.'

Holly still challenged him, 'surely the very reason he wants to go is so they won't?'

'What can he achieve by offering himself as a lightning conductor? Does he honestly think Commissioner Lin will serve him tea, give him silk and wine as he did his partner English, sit down and have a polite chat about the opium trade? With his hands as steeped in it as MacBeth's in the blood of Duncan?'

The veteran, Chinnery, backed Forge up, 'has he forgotten that unfortunate East India Company official who went into the city, when coaxed, only to spend the next few years languishing in a Cantonese prison?'

Holly, still the doubting Thomas, said, 'he might hope to gain a guarantee of safe conduct out of Canton.'

Kaida denied this softly. 'A guarantee would mean nothing, Miss Holly. Viceroy Tang cannot revoke an order he has already made for Raine's arrest.' The effect of this revelation on those around him was a sensation, Captain Forge the first to speak.

'Do the Factories know of this order?'

'Oh no, Captain. That is why I am here.'

'If Raine does go into the city will they hold him hostage until all the opium is surrendered.'

'No, Captain!' Kaida shook his head sadly, hating the wrack that must overtake his beloved city of Canton. 'The Viceroy must treat him exactly the same as those three opium dealers who suffered a brutal death.'

'Are you absolutely sure?' asked Holly distraught to think she had proved herself so gullible.

Captain Forge sought the reality. 'You mean he intends to have the High Devil strangled in public in Canton.'

'If not Raine, then James Malleson.'

Only Tim Bird was still the optimist now. 'Rumours are ever rife.'

'Not this time, Sir. High Commissioner Lin plans a general massacre of all foreigners who, he says, get the depraved common people of greedy vice in the country to dispose of their opium for them. He will raise a militia from the villages, believing the people there entertain a violent animosity towards foreign devils and burn with impatience to give vent to it.'

Captain Forge rose purposefully to his feet. The moment had come for him to live up to the command of Viscount Palmerston to resist the seizure and punishment of British subjects. 'I must go to Canton at once. These merchants must be persuaded to leave at once. It is impossible for them to remain any longer with safety, honour or advantage. If they do some calamity will ensue.'

He turned to Holly and Chinnery. 'You must leave for Lintin at once.' Chinnery groaned. Even the mildest swell made him seasick.

Tim Bird warned him. 'Have you forgotten Lord Nash?'

Captain Forge renounced him sharply. 'Have you forgotten I'm a man of the navy bred to face the sea and war?'

Kaida assured him softly, 'Chung Tai Tai will protect you. She will divert Wang Chung who can do the most harm, Captain, send a dummy boat to divert his men, set rumours afloat.'

Back at the Casa Garden Captain Forge found a Hakka boatman had brought a message from his deputy in Canton in a bamboo cylinder at enormous risk. Captain Forge must come at once. High Commissioner Lin had blockaded the Factories.

Captain Forge was a small whirlwind. He sent a message to the Captain of the Louisa to pick him up, an assurance to the Chinese Prefect of Macao that he was ready to meet the Imperial will in regard to all illicit traffic, and a proclamation to all British ships at Lintin to put themselves in a state of defence under the command of Captain Blake of the Larne unless he was forced into direct action, whereon they should accept the command of Captain Macdonald of the Apollo and 'proceed to Hong Kong Bay to prepare to resist any acts of aggression'.

He ordered Captain Blake to wait six days, and then, if no message had come from him, to act on the presumption that 'Her Majesty's subjects were detained against their wills and all confidence in the moderation of the Chinese government had ceased.'

He wrote his personal apologia to Viscount Palmerston for assuming an authority he did not in fact possess. The words flew across the page in his precise, flowing hand. The felicitous phrases came easily to him as always.

'There is a natural unfitness of a commercial community, such as this, to take any consentaneous course respecting the delicate and momentous question in hand in this hour of extreme peril to all interests, and indeed generally to human life.'

Last he penned a letter to Viceroy Tang himself.

'Is it the intention of the Chinese government to make war on the British? If execution, and vessels of war, do not amount to a declaration of war, they constitute at best its immediate and inevitable preliminaries.'

As he handed the missive to John Norris for translation, he appealed to him, 'where does a war begin, Norris? Tell me that! With one Black Hole of Calcutta, or a long history of ruthlessness on one side, and indifference and contempt on the other? One thing seems clear. Any government that attempts to untie this sort of knot gets armies when they attack.'

Pray God he would not be chosen to command in this war, which must intrinsically be a semi-naval war, nor some general covered in glory from the fronts in Afghanistan or the Sind.

John Norris kept his thoughts to himself as he sat down to a side table, brush in hand, for the exacting task of conveying the precise meaning of Captain Forge's stiff strokes into the sweep and swoop of ideographs. Whoever came and went on the China coast, there would always be this extremely sensitive work to do.

Flora struggled to 'keep a stiff upper lip' as she handed Barron his kitbag, and her arm went strongly round him as if her love could be worn as a shield in the days to come. 'Must you go to their rescue my love?'

He kissed her gently. 'I'm sorry dearest. It's my duty.'

'Although this quarrel's about opium? Not port dues, nor recognition of you as the King's man? Just opium.'

'This quarrel in the end, my darling, is about more than opium. It is about equality, our right to be treated as equals and not subjects to be bullied into submission by arrogant rulers.'

'All so abstract, my darling,' she objected, obtuse for once out of her love for him.

'Flora, there's nothing abstract about a cordon of soldiers around all the Factories and Raine's Factory in particular. Neither man nor message permitted to leave. All passports cancelled. Universal panic that the threat might grow worse at any moment. Serious division among the merchants as to what action they should take if any. Surrender more opium? Refuse and defend with their lives? They have precious else to defend themselves with.'

She studied him with an unfamiliar melancholy as he shouldered his kitbag, trying to hide her grief that others should force him into danger by their rash and foolhardy intransigence. What on earth could her Barron do to bring the warring houses of Canton together long enough to extricate them all from their present danger in face of that 'fatal division and discord' about which Sir George had fulminated so often and so long when he was in charge on this insubordinate Coast?

She asked as they walked slowly down the spacious staircase, 'what will you do, dearest, when you get to Canton?'

'Do what his Excellency demands. Give him all the opium.'

'The merchants will call you all the names under the sun.'

'The least of them coward and traitor, my dear, but they have called me that so often already I would be lost without it. Besides I can't extricate those warmongers by force, nor leave them to certain massacre.'

Nor could he forget the Black Hole of Calcutta when the Resident failed to evacuate all the British citizens in time. He would never be forgiven if such a disaster happened again. He would never honourably be able to answer to the British government or people if he did not get the British merchants out safely, no matter whether they had invited their fate or not. The only way that could be done was by giving High Commissioner Lin the opium he demanded.

'I would leave them to rot on their own dunghill.'

'Strong words for a fair lady.' He leaned down for a final lingering kiss. 'Remember the commandment "do unto others as you would be done by.' Which in my book means, if forced towards war I will work towards peace. If forced to the clash of extermination, I will persist in negotiation. Despite all the warmongers of Christendom, I may yet be a better follower of Christ than Kingsman.' He held both her hands in his own briefly. 'Go to Lintin at the first breath of trouble.'

He walked swiftly away from the tears on her face lest she see the anguish on his own. He was thankful he had betrayed none of his true conflict of mind at being caught in a terrible paradox. On the one hand, the Chinese government had just ground for harsh measures towards the lawful trade while such a vile traffic existed at the heart of the regular commerce. On the other, as a representative of a great power, he could not accept the violence inherent in High Commissioner Lin's ultimatums nor the active preparations for war in the river forts.

But he was under no illusion. He doubted if he would get past Whampoa or even the Bogue. He prayed Flora would not have to open the sealed letter he left behind with John Norris to be opened only in event of his death. In the event, Captain Forge passed all the hazards on the river safely without any disguise or subterfuge, Captain Wang Chung with his fleet of junks at Cumsingmun, the forts of the Boccca Tigris, the authorities at Whampoa who tried to dissuade him, the pursuit boats from Whampoa to Canton only a mere boat's length behind when he reached Jackass Point at last to jump ashore with sword drawn in his right hand, the Union Jack of the Louisa in his left, and his little retinue of sailors scrambling to safety just in time at his rear.

The mate seized the flag from him, tied it to an oar, then, hoisted on his comrades' shoulders, bound the oar to the stump of the empty flagpole. As it lifted in the strong breeze, Captain Forge shouted the commands to fall in, stand to attention and salute as the besieged came tumbling from the Factories to raise a roar of 'Good Old Blood and Guts' at the sight of this improvised defiance. The crisp response and brave little ceremony brought tears to his own eyes as he thought of the many times he had seen such courageous little gestures of heroism from British servicemen thinly scattered around the world. It was this ability to confront threat with calm discipline and cool bravura that had extended British enterprise to remote frontiers of the world.

Ross Newman's splendid baritone lofted in the stirring words of 'the flag that braved a thousand years, the battle and the breeze.' And Captain Forge dedicated himself to their cause in suitable heroic terms. 'I am with you until my last gasp.' Only a few sceptics stood on the side-lines muttering that that ill-starred piece of bunting had been up and down that pole so many times in Canton, it was the only one of the foreign flags that had grown insensible to shame.

Captain Forge had no time for reflection as to what scenes the flag had witnessed in those thousand years or how many had died in its allegiance. He was too intent to see that this particular flag would not be witness to any death. Calling to Newman and Norris to follow he thrust past the Namhoi Magistrate on guard outside the Pao Shan Factory and the doorkeeper, marching up the stairs into Maxwell Raine's office to confront the High Devil who froze in his chair at the sight of a Captain Forge, he thought to be in Macao, saluting him in full dress uniform, medals and all. He took his feet off his desk and heaved his lanky frame to attention to return the salute in a makeshift manner.

Captain Forge accosted him. 'Mr. Raine, thank God they have't arrested you yet. I am determined to remain until you and everyone in this port is safe. You must leave forthwith.'

His wits in disarray, Maxwell Raine mumbled 'I have promised to go into the city at ten o'clock tomorrow.'

Captain Forge regarded him as an imbecile. 'Mr. Raine, I will not allow you to put yourself and the whole port at such risk. I order you, in the Queen's name, to come with me.'

Maxwell Raine appealed to English and his brother Alan, both as bewildered as he. 'Would that be to my advantage?' The former said no, the latter yes since the Prefect had refused to guarantee him safe conduct out again if he went.

Captain Forge stared him down. 'This is an order, Mr. Raine.'

'An order? What right do you have to order me?' Raine's glance fell on the Captain's epaulettes.

All his gaudy insignia of office was actually meaningless at the Factories. The good captain had no right to order him to do anything, a fact the editor of his newspaper had often rudely pointed out. There was no doubt however that he was on the High Commissioner's hook, and Captain Forge, in all his glory of pretended authority, was his only means of getting off it again. He felt overwhelmingly tempted to take this chance to rid himself of the nervous and quarrelsome merchants who had crowded his premises for days.

Captain Forge made up his mind for him. 'The time has come, Mr. Raine, when people like you must understand the British government has to answer for you and will take responsibility for you, although unwilling.'

Maxwell Raine held out his hand to Captain Forge with the guilty realisation that his acceptance meant that Captain Forge would have to put himself on the hook in his place. 'How will you get round the guard?'

'My answer to that depends on how well you are guarded.'

Raine took him to the roof to show him the disposition of no less than a dozen soldiers around the house.

'Then I must make it obvious that you leave under equal duress from me.'

He frogmarched him, hand gripping his collar, out the door past the incredulous Magistrate and the soldiers on guard through the idling crowd attracted by his arrival and into the New English Factory, where Raine warned him 'you know you've whistled up the wind, Captain, don't you?'

'It would help if you thought of slinging your hammock.'

'My what?'

'Left the coast for good like Jarman.'

Maxwell Raine admitted, 'Howqua threatened if I didn't go immediately, he would send soldiers to force me without any promise of return in twenty four hours. I refused to go. Then he blackmailed me by saying if I did not go, he would be marked to die. Again I refused, banking on the hope Commissioner Lin had realised by now he could not afford to put a rope round Howqua's neck. For who would get him the rich revenue of this port if he did?'

'Why were you singled out and not Malleson?'

'Malleson was smart enough to send two ships away with some seven thousand chests, and order a second two ships to sail up the coast with another two thousand chests until everything died down. I am the next biggest trader as you know. They say I'm a man who's far too inquisitive because I read the Beijing Gazette, inquire about Chinese affairs and teach English to Chinese. All abhorrent.'

While Captain Forge waited for the residents to answer his summons to meet within the hour, he made it quite clear Maxwell Raine must remain in sight at all times. He would not tolerate him going into the city.

The High Devil protested.'I don't like to be mollycoddled. Don't you think I ought to be responsible for myself not you?'

'Mr. Raine, it's not just you, Mr. Malleson or the leading opium merchants who are now under threat. All three hundred occupants of these thirteen Factories, representing the leading powers of the world, are in mortal danger of massacre today.'

'Aren't you being melodramatic? There's no precedent.'

Captain Forge's voice was steely with impatience. 'There is no precedent for a High Commissioner in Canton either, Mr. Raine. The question is not whether you'll be put under arrest tomorrow. You already are. Commissioner Lin has turned our Factories into a most effective prison.' A sentiment obviously shared by the excited crowd of traders that had gathered.

Captain Forge's glance ranged over them wondering how he was to get a common point of view among a group that had not shown one point of agreement to date except that Raine would have been kept by force if he had gone into the city and taken by force if he had not. But they did have one common emotion at that moment, fear.

He regarded them sorrowfully. Here they were in a city once the safest in the world to trade, and now the most dangerous because the legitimate trade had become more and more entangled with the smuggling trade and had fallen by degrees into the hands of greedy, ambitious or desperate men- Chinese as well as European or American- until it stained the foreign character with constantly aggravated disgrace in the sight of the whole people.

What a rogue's gallery they were, these tense and reckless individuals who spent their lives in pursuit of uncertain and often insignificant gains, men who had unquestionably founded their conduct on the belief they were exempt from the operations of all law, British or Chinese. He could see no trace of regret on their faces for the fact they had at last driven him, as representative of their government, into urgent and hazardous measures that well may be paid for in the terrible cost of many human lives. Nor did they have the slightest concern for the fact they unscrupulously turned to the very man they had abused these last three months, namely himself, when they needed gunships at their backs. In extremis, they found it easy to forget the harsh words they had said about his 'toadying' to the Chinese Viceroy. They suddenly remembered how he had twice rushed up river to their rescue at risk of his life from several post stations on the way.

Who was toadying now, he asked himself, as he observed them outvying each other in approving applause when he said, 'I will resist the seizure and punishment of a British subject by Chinese law to the last, be their crimes what they may. I have come here on my own responsibility without advice from any man. If I denied this responsibility for the safety of all men here, the High Commissioner would revert to intimidation against one or more merchants in order to force you all into submission. From his proclamations and his general conduct, I judge the danger to such men, as he is determined to seize, to be not simply one of protracted imprisonment but the sacrifice of their lives. I perceive the moment has come for placing the whole weight of the immense difficulties to be encountered on the only foundation stone where it can safely rest, namely on the wisdom, justice and power of Her Majesty's Government.'

Billy Howe silently applauded him while the rest cheered him to the rafters. Surely he was as undaunted as Clive of India had been before the Battle of Plassey, although his defenceless situation was a travesty by comparison with the defiance of Clive. No army or navy. Only the Blake and a handful of seamen at Whampoa, supposing they could fight their way through. And some three hundred unarmed, and conspicuously unwarlike, fellow contrymen embattled on the edge of a city of a million inhabitants with no weapons to speak of beside half a dozen fowling pieces, a few pistols, a sword or two, and almost no powder. What a joke for old Nash to have said he woud cut his way through with twelve good English tars! Well, many a battle had been won by the rhetoric of a commander. Captain Forge's impassioned delivery and gestures would have done the Macao Repertory Group proud except this was no comedy of which he warned, but high tragedy. Tragedy if they did not unite in one policy, if some made terms and others did not.

Captain Forge got down to practical matters. 'The execution in front of the Factories, the appearance of soldiers at the barrier and fireboats at the Bogue, the refusal to allow anyone to leave Macao, and the threatening attitude of the local authorities, make it impossible for us to stay here any longer. You must move yourselves and your ships out of the river. I will apply for the necessary passports. If High Commissioner Lin refuses, I will take this as sure proof the authorities mean to wring unsuitable concessions from you at the very least, to hold not only myself, but all of you, hostage at the worst.'

James Malleson's sneer declared him the only sceptic present. No need to hear what he whispered to his junior partner, David. 'Our sainted superintendent betrays the vanity of a crayfish brandishing his claws thinking they're battle-axes. He will declare for surrender for all his barking like a mad dog.'

He lumbered to his feet to denounce Captain Forge's optimism. 'As a veteran of this port, I say His Excellency will never let us leave until he has all our opium.'

Captain Forge kept his temper in check. 'If he does, will you surrender all yours as the price of your freedom?'

Malleson's gaze swept the room to see who shared in his scornful laughter at that presumption. 'Only a fool would imagine I would.'

'Will you surrender your opium if High Commissioner Lin pays for it?'

'You know my answer as well as I do. Yes, if he pays the six million dollars it is worth on a good market.'

Captain Forge hit home. 'Even though your cargoes are worthless while this persecution lasts?' Trade was stagnant, prices at an all-time low.

The Laird reminded them that the Commissioner had offered to petition the Emperor to reward any obedient merchant with payment in tea or silk. The crowd took up the cry 'Yes!' 'The Hong merchants said so!' 'They would be as good as their promise!'

Captain Forge listened to the uproar cynically. If anyone had to promise to pay it would be himself, who would then have to force his Minister to keep the promise by extracting the ransom money from the British government. The Minister concerned would be that very Minister who had ignored every submission of his from China for years, returning only the briefest and most dilatory replies, the vaguest of confusing orders, and offering no policy whatsoever except as tacit a support of smuggling through official British inertia as the provincial mandarins of China themselves gave their own. Perhaps if he, Captain Forge, pledged them to redeem that season's tally of opium, he might at last force Parliament to an honest debate on the question, and oblige them to drift no longer turning the blind eye to their most outrageous citizens.

Only when the meeting had dissolved was Captain Forge aware of a wild confusion downstairs as their Chinese servants, one and all, scrambled to abandon the premises faster than rats from a sinking ship with their bedding, bundles and cooking pots hoisted on poles. Those, not already on their way, were busy rushing about 'like chooks with their heads off' as his deputy remarked. An even heavier guard than before had surrounded the Factories to cut them off both from the city and the river. High Commissioner Lin was making sure Captain Forge could not help the hostages escape.

Billy Howe, for his part, returned to the Fountain of Tranquillity to find it anything but tranquil. A shouting melee rushed out, thrusting against another rush of servants coming in with baskets of greens, bread and fruit as well as jars of water and fowls in cages. All the basic needs of life.

He remarked joyfully to John Norris at the sight. 'Howqua's measure of the siege we are in for. Praise be to Joshua Law, wherever he may be in heaven for winning Howqua as a trading partner. May whatever gods he believes in look after Howqua if His Excellency should find out!'

John Norris pointed out as they watched the servants departing as though the black plague had broken out. 'That ancient doesn't seem quite as terrified of His High and Mighty Imperial Commissioner as your servants. They run before the whips of Lin fast enough.'

'As we will run. Make no mistake. We're in for a long siege!'

Billy set himself to draw up a roster for all duties- sweeping, cooking, cleaning, slops- with total pessimism as to the capacity of any of the partners or clerks to do any of these chores after collecting the wildest of replies to all his questions about boiling rice or even eggs.

He castigated them, 'you useless mothers' sons. What a fine collection of men you are to be stranded with on a desert island!'

Then, with his unfailing buoyancy he remembered that Tough Wagoner was also trapped with some of his crew. He rushed along Respondentia Walk to find a disgruntled Tough entrenched with a bottle of Jamaica rum in Standford's Hotel, already half-seas over. 'How am I supposed to get back to the Eugenia? I have a good mind to make a run for it.'

'I don't think you'd fancy the inside of a Cantonese goal as a hostage, Tough. It's not exactly the lap of luxury. Any cooks in your lot?'

'Every seaman has to be able to cook, blockhead. What if he's shipwrecked?'

'Well pretend you're shipwrecked now mate. I need your help.'

'They're a bit hard on the crockery,' Tough temporised, bedded down with the ample grog supply at Standfords.

'You'll starve like stray dogs here,' Billy urged, 'We're the only Factory with fresh meat and vegetables to last a siege.'

Tough needed no further persuasion. He tucked a bottle of rum under his arm and marched his sailors over to Billy's Factory singing a sea shanty at such full bore he silenced the incessant drums and gongs for once, and brought the flitting lanterns of the watchful guard and soldiers on the rooves to peer over the parapets.

'When are those bastards going to leave?' Tough demanded striding past the ghostly apparitions. 'I planned to up anchor by the end of March.'

'You'll be lucky to leave before the end of May more likely.'

Tough exploded. 'Bad for my men cooped up in Whampoa. Bad for the cargo. Bad for trade back home.'

'You tell that to our brave merchants. We don't get out till they surrender their opium.'

'If they agree, how long?' Tough demanded as they wound their way through the labrynthine building to their quarters.

'The opium fleet is scattered along the coast. They'll have to call them I before Lin lets us go.'

'What about me? Kingsman? All of us with clean hands?'

'The innocent will be made to suffer with the guilty. Your crime is the same as theirs - that you are an ocean barbarian.'

CHAPTER 9

1839 War in the Pearl River Delta

Captain Forge Breaks the Deadlock

Captain Forge ate his unpalatable lunch of soggy rice and tinned beef with distaste. Each meal seemed to be worse than the last. His aversion was not, however, only for the meal but also for the news that the merchants, led by Maxwell Raine, wanted to put all the opium they possessed in his care in the hope he would resist demands for its address.

'Just like their hide,' he declaimed to his worn-out secretary toying with his own unpalatable repast, 'to think I would entertain the idea of defending their confounded opium for a single minute. I suppose when the new season's complement arrives, I am to protect that too? The very men who called me a coward in such ringing terms wanting to ride on my coat tails.'

John Norris's looked up in dismay. 'I'd quite forgotten the new season's delivery,' he confessed, admiration for Captain Forge plain on his kindly earnest face.

How fortunate he was to work for this man. No incompetent bluff martinet like so many, but blessed with grace of looks, manner and humour as well as decision, diplomacy and determination. He, if anyone, could extricate this ill-assorted group of individuals out of Canton, this tally of some three hundred people- three consuls, six missionaries, merchants of at least six countries, eighty officers and other ranks, sailors, two agents of the East India Company Finance Agency and supercargoes and clerks from various ships.

The young man abandoned his meal as Captain Forge beckoned him onto the verandah. 'Norris, what chance do we have of resisting demands to surrender? Look at that!'

Some four hundred coolies- transformed into militia with spikes, spears and long heavy staves- patrolled all the Factories under the eagle eye of the linguists from their hastily erected battle headquarters, a bamboo shed by the stone quay at Jackass Point. Many of them had previously served in the Factories, and were identified as such by labels on their conical rattan hats. Two rows of chop boats were anchored in a formidable crescent along the shore to stop any escapee who might elude the amateur army. Beyond these lay yet another row of heavier tea boats chained end to end. Both banks of ships were manned by soldiers armed with bows, arrows and matchlock guns. The Tanka boats, usually crowded there, had been driven God knows where.

Co-Hong merchants were installed at his very door to summon these formidable forces if he should dare to leave the New English. Old and New China Streets were similarly blocked at the rear of the factory. Even if he could have run the gauntlet of the official force, he would have had to face a potential lynch mob in the spectators crowding numerous vantage points overlooking the Common as well as those wandering within it.

Just as he was wondering how long the deceptive calm of the Common would last, a guard marched round the corner from Old China Street towards the door of the New English, bearing a large white placard. He leaned over the verandah rail to see they were merely tacking yet another of His Excellency's edicts to their railing. He sent John Norris down to interpret. He returned, his famous imperturbability shaken as it had never been before.

'Sir, it's nothing more nor less than a death threat!'

'Death to whom? Malleson or Raine?'

'Sir, to yourself! Warning you that you'll suffer the retributive justice of Heaven as the English President of the Select in earlier times and Lord Nash did. They scorned the laws of China- one by trying to get possession of Macao by force, the other by forcing his way through the Bogue into Canton as you have done. This warning cannot be ignored sir.'

Captain Forge sought refuge in light relief. 'There's only one reaction to that. A good brandy. After all a man is not threatened with Heaven's vengeance every day.'

No laughter from John Norris as he hesitated over the precise translation of the rest of the decree. Captain Forge regretted he could read no optimism in John's face. Poor young fellow, humbly shod and dressed, a man without a country. His life had always been spent in suspension between two worlds soon headed for an irreconcilable collision. How could he adopt the only country he knew well, China, which in this placard showed itself so vicious not simply to foreign devils but to John's own missionary origins as well?

John Norris announced the saving clauses. 'If you will now repent and deliver up your opium, you may yet avert judgement and calamities by a well-timed repentance. If not, your wickedness being greater, the consequences of that wickedness will fall more fearfully upon you.'

Captain Forge sought to reassure him. 'Cheer up. We're going to deliver up the opium so no risk at all.'

How John Norris wished for such undaunted audacity. 'Aren't you afraid?'

'After years of action against pirates and slavers? One thing you learn in the navy, my boy, is the folly of fear. Besides why should I be afraid since I don't intend to defy their laws as Lord Nash did?'

John lapsed into silence praying, as his father would have done, that Forge would not misunderstand the complexities of Chinese customs and culture, and, in failing to do so, invite the justice of Heaven.

Captain Forge put his pen down with pride as he finished his answer to High Commissioner Lin. His Latin master would have been proud of him. Brevity, compact lucidity, Ciceronian rhetoric.

'And I, the said Superintendent, do now in the most full and unreserved manner on behalf of Her Britannic Majesty's Government to all and each of her Majesty's subjects, hold myself responsible for surrendering the British-owned opium in my hands to be delivered to the Chinese government.'

Not quite the same metaphoric flourish so dear to the Chinese but in sufficiently high style none the less. He tossed it to John Norris.

'The fell deed is done. Not very many men can say they've bought ten million dollars worth of goods with a stroke of the pen. A king's ransom that is a nation's ransom. At cost price, mark you, if you can believe these rogues. Twenty one or so thousand chests.

Norris was dubious. 'Our government will never repay that.'

'If they don't, a lot of Bombay merchants will be bankrupted.'

'The consequences of that are too dreadful to contemplate.'

'You're forgetting those who go bankrupt every year with the fluctuations of this gamblers' trade. The only thing that is dreadful, but don't quote me, is that those two or three who have made fortunes won't be the ones to go bankrupt. Only the smaller investors behind them back in India, including far too many Parsees.'

* * * * * *

Viceroy Lin's Ritual Sacrifice

In the meantime, Viceroy Tang had been dismissed as Viceroy of the two great south-eastern provinces stretching from the gateway of China and High Commissioner Lin awarded the coveted Viceroyship in his place. So it was he who raised the siege of Canton on Captain Forge's promise of twenty thousand chests of opium. But his new honour did not console him. For he took it as a hollow victory in view of the warning of Censor Pu that the vile traffic would go on in other places by other means.

He kept on delivering thunderbolts of edicts from his new headquarters on a mandarin boat off the splinter island of Chuenpi, set up to supervise the landing and storage of the opium chests in order to burn it en masse. He constantly accused the ocean barbarians of plotting new tricks to continue their vicious, rebellious traffic in barbarian smoke.

The truth was that Viceroy Lin, though a brilliant administrator, was yet a child of the egocentric Middle Kingdom little versed in the complexities of port trade or sea traffic. To get a tally of opium chests that had arrived, or were on their way, on paper was one thing. To get the chests themselves was another. Merchants had to find ships wherever they might be, up or down the coast, and then adjust the original tally by the total of chests sold.

However these very complexities did offer many opportunities to try to hoodwink Viceroy Lin by those slow to realise he was a master in discerning cheats. And cheating there was. Discrepancies from manifests. Chests robbed or repacked to hide the deficit. Chests with false opium or bags of broken pieces. Ships arriving that were unlisted in place of those that were. Ships bearing highwater marks that rode above waterlevels.

The only work that gave Viceroy Lin open satisfaction was the excavation of deep trenches for the destruction of the vast quantity of opium already delivered. These trenches would allow five hundred labourers to stir and turn the opium balls in limed and salted water after they had been broken into quarters, before washing the stinking mass out to sea through opened sluices. He would personally supervise that destruction from first to last to prevent any possible further fraud, despite the awful stench that would ensue. He had decided against his original plan to send all the surrendered opium to Beijing as tribute to his Emperor. He had learned that the despatch of such a rich cargo would be too costly in its demand for a thousand boat crew and four thousand guards, and too likely to be pillaged long before it reached the capital. But he had not repacked it for resale as his enemies said.

Before the ceremonial burning began, he thought it wise to worship in the Temple of the Queen of Heaven, patron saint of all sailors, for forgiveness that he should intend to pollute her ocean. May she favour him who came from the very province where she was born. He lit the candles and offered fruit and flowers! He turned away from the intricately carved and gilded altar and halted before the belligerent glaring-eyed figure of Kuan Ti, God of War, well aware his own bearing was more comparable to this frowning god than that of the God's amiable descendant, Admiral Kuan, who did not even faintly resemble his famous warrior ancestor.

Admiral Kuan was short, stout, laughing, horrified of war and pain, and never likely to have his helmet preserved for ever as Kuan Ti's was in a Shantung temple. His eyes were certainly red like Kuan Ti's resembling the divine bird Kung, but red from his private indulgence in barbarian smoke, gained as bribes from foreign ships, not from any portent of a rare and extraordinary event.

It was a pity, Lin thought in despair that he had to depend on such a useless coward as Admiral Kuan, that he himself was not Admiral of the Navy. Admiral Kuan excelled his famous ancestor in only one respect. His scholarship was more than equal to appreciate the worth of the poem Lin had engraved in most elegant calligraphy on a pair of exquisite ivory fans for his birthday.

Admiral Kuan received them with courteous gratitude and apt compliments, far too polite to express his true thought that poetry was better suited to drowsy pavilions in crafted gardens than to a barge heaving in the choppy waterway of the Bogue. He did not dare admit his real gratitude was not for the poem but for the Viceroy's victory in the opium crisis, which guaranteed him one more season to enjoy the indolence of his life as an Admiral free of fear of annihilation by those ocean barbarian ships, especially their new fire-wheelships. Instead after he had read the poem which began,

'The mist and rains of foreign seas darken Lintin.

I was given a sky of populous stars on a carven platter.'

he toasted Lin with flowery compliments on a poetic skill that so eminently qualified him for membership of the Academy. He hoped he could, by such artful flattery, prepare the way to ask for a foreign warship for his own fleet. They should be going cheap by now with the stagnation of the opium trade.

Although Admiral Kuan was no warrior, he was nobody's fool. He knew only too well his navy was antiquated and full of faint-hearted cowards like himself, men who had been so corrupted by their own trafficking in opium they would be of dubious loyalty or courage in any serious naval engagement. If war should no longer be mockery of war, mere tactical pretence of driving the enemy away, the change would have to begin with modernising the navy despite the entrenched Imperial spirit against change. Perhaps this Viceroy Lin would facilitate such change. If not, then he himself would clearly have to choose between a brave man's death or degradation. There could only be one choice to die with a proud smile on his lips, a fit descendant of the God of War at last.

Viceroy Lin had decided to break with all precedent and choose two of the most worthy despised ocean barbarians to testify that he was a man who lived up to his vow to destroy every last opium ball in his possession. They were the Reverend Sanders and Colin Kingsman from Little Jerusalem. As they were ushered into a viewing pavilion, fully aware of the inordinate honour bestowed on them, Colin Kingsman was enthralled to have his first glimpse of the notorious envoy, amazed to see his dark eyes brimmed with twinkling intelligence and his ready smile lit up his round face offset by a slender black beard.

Overawed by the enormity of the moment, he turned to his considerably less impressed wife, 'do you realise, my dear, we are making history?'

Preening herself, she responded indifferently, too illiterate of Chinese society to know Viceroy Lin could not possibly approve of her appearance whatever she did.

She ignored her husband as he enthused, 'look how many rounds Captain Forge fought to get a letter accepted directly by an official even a menial one, let alone have an audience with one, particularly a man even more exalted than a Viceroy. The equal of the Emperor himself!'

'Are we going to be presented to His Highness?' she enquired her interest piqued. Now she really had something to boast about to the other ladies who patronised her back in Macao.

'Since neither the Emperor nor his envoys have ever consented to any member of our inferior, tribute-bearing race being presented, the Old China Hands insist we will not be,' he responded.

He was caught by surprise therefore when he found himself standing with sweaty palms before the great man. Caught at a loss as to what the correct etiquette should be. Caught in the impasse of doffing his hat to hold it clenched to his chest as he bowed low, instead of kowtowing. The Reverend Sanders followed suit.

Both men were relieved and astonished when Viceroy Lin ordered them through his interpreter to take their ease, presented them with expensive gifts, plied them gravely with questions about life in England and America, and even laughed when Colin Kingsman dared to refuse to answer the last as to who the most honest Co-Hong merchant was.

As Kingsman stood silent and perplexed, Viceroy Lin answered it himself before dismissing them both. 'They all shut their ears while the jingling bell is stolen.'

Finally he turned to the Reverend Sanders to ask, 'I have written a letter to Queen Victoria. Can you see it reaches her?'

The 'ocean barbarians' returned to their seats singing Viceroy Lin's praises as a civilised man, saying how wrong some reports of the barbarism of officials were. They might have changed their mind if they had known that Viceroy Lin believed he was routing the devil himself in defeating the 'red beards'. Or that the putrid stench of the opium, so nauseous as to overpower lashings of eau de cologne, was due to the fact the British mixed the opium with the flesh of gigantic dead crows which fed on dead bodies.

As the morning wore on the stench became so bad, with no breeze to blow it away, they wished they could join the huge popular throng watching at a distance from the hill. They were obliged instead to sit down to a banquet under the drift of the putrescent odour hanging in the sticky air, barely capable of the ease and affability expected of them or of picking at the lavish meal before them. The last shred of their appetite disappeared when the guards, searching the morning shift of workers, found a minute amount of opium hidden in a man's short trousers, dragged their wretched victim up to Viceroy Lin regardless of the hour and forced him to kneel for judgement, the other departing coolies marshalled behind him.

Viceroy Lin raised his hand. The guard lofted his sword and, with one whistling stroke, slashed the man's head from his body. He then held the head up by its queue with blood pouring out, tongue lolling, shocked eyes still open. Mrs. Kingsman gagged. Her husband revised his views on the barbarism of the savages. The Reverend Sanders composed his next sermon on the text of John the Baptist- the victim's head served on a plate to the dinner table where the banquet was of the virtuous not the vicious.

James Malleson gave vent to his resentment of the Reverend in Number 1 Creek Factory to his compliant partners and clerks after a vehement rendering of a Mozart sonata.

'Old fool to think he has a moral right to join the virtuous in their vandalism of my opium. A right to any morality in fact while he busies himself smuggling an equally prohibited religion, which many officials believe to be even more dangerous than opium, into China. Viceroy Lin more fool too for thinking that Bible basher would have any influence with me.'

Only Sean Jarman dared disagree. 'Perhaps he wanted one of ours to bear witness that the rumour-mongering, that he was lining his own pocket with our opium, was all lies. Who else was without stain here but Colin and the Reverend?'

'Still a fool!' Malleson banged the able stoutly. 'What's he trying to prove? That his government will destroy all the opium that now, or in the future, comes to China? If he doesn't know that's just as impossible as Reverend Sander's dreams of building a thousand Temples to Jehovah in China, then the man's as dishonest as all his predecessors ever were.'

He returned to the comforting precision of Mozart, leaving Sean to ponder how a man like Malleson could live so much more comfortably in the world with the reality of his cynicism than any idealist ever could.

* * * * * *

A Law Unto Themselves

Captain Forge did not rest easy until Viceroy Lin's retinue of barges passed safely through the European fleet at Whampoa on its way back to Canton. No salute of guns. No hails of commands to attention. No presenting arms. No honours. Just the hostile ranks of sailors lining the rails of the fleet at Whampoa to witness a spectacle they thought never to see- the passage of Viceroy Lin, a man venerated as a God because he was de facto the equal of his own mighty Emperor, the Son of Heaven and Lord of Ten Thousand Islands. The sailors remained mute and sullen, warned by their Commodore and Captains against any vengeance angry and blockade-weary though they may be.

Once Viceroy Lin was through, Captain Forge announced he was leaving Canton and would take no further responsibility for any merchant who did not follow, particularly the sixteen banned from China forever. As to the bond that Viceroy Lin demanded of every ship, failing which its captain and all its crew would be liable to the death penalty, he told a nervous meeting 'I would rather sacrifice my own life than see one man sign this bond.'

'Histrionics again,' James Malleson grumbled to Sean.

'You're not going to sign that bond?' Sean asked startled that Malleson was overlooking the obvious. Everyone in the port would pay the price of any intransigent boycott on the part of their form, not just themselves.

'The demand will vanish as Viceroy Lin himself will. Opium is too popular in this country among the educated classes to be effectively banned just like wine in Europe. Sit the hullabaloo out for a season or two, and all will be as before.'

'You think the opium trade will ever recover from this crisis?

Sean wondered if Malleson's amazing confidence, sweeping him to success where so many failed, had not turned into a more extravagant and unrealistic arrogance.

'It has already, my boy. New gamblers are ready to get their fingers burned in Bombay and trade which is already picking up again on this coast.'

'The figures for opium sales have never been worse, sir.'

'If you looked at the figures for cottons, Sean, you would see a remarkable increase in the sale of greys, whites and chintzes. In other words, Benares, Patna and Malwa opium.'

Dear God where would it all end, Sean worried as he sought brief refuge with Billy Howe in the Palace of Fountains. The Chinese government would find it as difficult to suppress men like James Malleson as they ever had any of the endemic pirates on their Coast throughout its long history.

Captain Forge first became uneasy that Viceroy Lin was about to begin a new period of harassment when he found his boat stolen. His uneasiness was not allayed when he found the heavy river traffic more provocative than before, as he weaved his way through in it the borrowed gig of the Larne. Other boats were so deliberately aggressive it seemed the first boat to run him down could expect some reward. How easily a boatman could plead he had not known his victim was a high mandarin of the redbeards! Did he travel like one? With the retinue or the embellishments? With the luggage?

As he made his dangerous way down the river, he wryly regretted his decision to rescue the portrait of his erstwhile monarch, King George 4, for fear the New English Factory might be sacked by the time he could return to Canton. After all, Lord Nash had made such a fuss about that wretched portait in the Battle of Chairs it had become a notorious symbol of their honour in Canton. By the time he hung it in the eastern drawing room of the Casa Garden in Macao, it had become an important symbol of his own survival careering down Pearl River as well.

Flora had recoiled from the overpowering image on its arrival. 'My dear, I hope you're not going to bring that monster to Lintin when we go.'

'To Lintin? Why? I thought Lin's threats had blown over.'

'Only while everyone was running scared.'

He took the point at once. 'Who has caused trouble?'

'Your old friend!' His arms dropped away from her in alarm.

'You mean my enemy, of course. I have so many, my dear, although they have tongues of honey while I'm the hero of the hour. But once the crisis is over I'm expendable.'

'I'll give you a clue. It concerns the smuggling of opium. Only eight chests, but ....'

'Only? In the present situation, even one illegally smuggled chest is dynamite. There's just one man who would do that to me, the Laird. Has he been arrested?'

'No, his opium is impounded.'

'By the Chinese?' If so, the fat was truly in the fire.

'No, by Governor Pinto.'

'Thank heavens, Flora. If ever the phrase 'a law to himself' was coined it was for him. If I only had the power I would deport that devil incarnate tomorrow.'

Still seething with anger, Captain Forge strode to the Governor's residence on the Praya Grande, oblivious to the late spring glory of flowers in every garden. No wonder the tally of Viceroy Lin fell short. Ince and his ilk with their petty pilfering!

Only his immaculate manners sustained him when the Laird, arriving ahead of him, accosted him in the Governor's ornate audience hall, his scarred face a gargoyle's grimace. 'I have been illegally detained. You must demand my release at once.'

Governor Pinto, an astute man with long experience in the tricky exigencies of a thinly tolerant Chinese government, did not mince words with the Laird. 'My police hold eight chests of opium confiscated from British sailors in the streets of Macao which they swear are yours.'

The Laird growled fiercely in fluent Portuguese. 'Lying hounds! I gave it to these infamous scoundrels to tranship it from one ship to another. They stole it to sell on the streets of Macao. I demand you return it to me.'

Governor Pinto addressed Captain Forge through an interpreter. 'I believe Mr. Ince proposed to sell the opium illegally in Macao himself in complete disregard of the law and the fact he would compromise me with the Chinese government.'

The Laird shouted back, 'my eight chests are a mere trifle to the quantities of opium that have flowed with Portuguese knowledge and connivance through this backdoor to China.'

'Times change, and with it the law.'

'Law. What law? Captain Forge has no power over me.'

'A fact you have exploited to your own advantage.'

Captain Forge, obliged to follow the gist of this heated exchange through an interpreter, intervened to halt the absurdity of the Laird taking over his own investigation.

'Clearly it would be an embarassment for any of us to admit that any one of our merchants deliberately imported opium to Macao, Governor Pinto. We will simply surrender it to Viceroy Lin without comment.'

The Laird would not be set aside. 'Not yours to surrender.'

Captain Forge rounded on him at last. 'We promised Viceroy Lin all the opium that was either delivered or on consignment to British merchants at Canton.'

The Laird, defiant to the last, threatened him. 'I'll write to Queen Victoria to say her Chief Superintendent interferes with the sale of opium. He has no warrant to do so considering the government of India itself grows opium for China.'

Captain Forge's temper vanished before this ludicrous threat. As if he cared that he might be hung by the government over eight chests of opium when he was absolutely certain to be hung over the purchase of over twenty thousand chests.

He bowed to the Laird. 'You are at perfect liberty to complain to our sovereign.'

Governor Pinto was in a quandary. If he expelled the Laird, it might lead to troublesome enquiries from Viceroy Lin or troublesome incidents like arson from the Laird. He turned to Captain Forge. 'How would you resolve this troublesome matter?'

'If Viceroy Lin has heard there was a Mr. Ince who struggled with the sailors to repossess these chests in an undignified public scene, as no doubt he already has, then perhaps you might assure our eminent Viceroy he acted in righteous indignation to recover these chests from the robbers for no other reason than to surrender them with the rest. After that I would suggest a temporary sojourn at Lintin.'

A smile flitted across Governor Pinto's face. 'A very Chinese resolution.'

Captain Forge bowed. 'One learns Your Excellency.'

If Goveror Pinto sat back with relief that he might see the back of the fiery Laird, Captain Forge felt none. He knew the Laird would be intriguing for revenge within the day, unwilling to concede the man he most despised could outwit him. The Laird himself knew his bluff had been called, but consoled himself that Captain Forge would have his day of reckoning soon enough when the Expeditionary Force that Dr. Jarman would undoubtedly extort from Viscount Palmerston arrived in China. Then that fence-sitter of a Captain Forge would be toppled off his rail. Soothed by this demonic wish he bowed and left submissively enough. He did not hear the Governor's pious wish, 'I hope he falls foul of Wang Chung's fleet on the way.'

Unfortunately it was the Black Joke that fell foul of Wang Chung instead, when she anchored at the south end of Lantao Island on her way from Whampoa to Hong Kong.

When Billy Howe told Captain Forge, he swore 'the devil looks after his own. He goes scot free and poor Mr. Moss, who wouldn't hurt a fly, is horribly mutilated.'

He rushed down to Dr. Tom's house, where Moss been taken while those within were celebrating the purchase of Holly's new ship. He found the hapless young clerk in a horrifying state, not only his right ear but a sizeable part of his scalp torn. Flora was holding his hand, and a very pregnant Abby was clucking over him, bathing his forehead and insisting on brandy while Dr. Tom kept up what he hoped was a distracting flow of conversation to divert his patient from the agony of stitching his ghastly wounds.

'You put up a good fight, lad. No question. If you hadn't, they might have tried to even you up. Taken the other ear.'

Moss was scarcely audible through his black swollen lips. 'Only room for one ear stuffed in my mouth.'

'That was a black joke, my boy,' Dr. Tom teased him with a play on the name of the ketch.

'What happened?' Captain Forge leaned close to his mouth.

'Lucky to be alive!' he whispered.

Billy and Holly told the story. He was down below when he heard his lascars, up on deck, calling 'Waylo! Waylo!' and an outburst of shouting from boats alongside. He emerged from the hatch to find desperadoes, armed with knives and hatchets, engaged in the brutal murder of all his lascars as they desperately fought for their lives. Only one quick enough to jump overboard and hang half-submerged to the tindal. He, himself, had crouched terrified behind the deckhouse as they plundered the cargo below. They had routed him out, resisting grimly, and forced him to his knees where he began to recite the Lord's Prayer believing his last moment was about to come. One of their number laid a trail of the Black Joke's gunpowder to blow up the boat. Then they hacked off his ear and stuffed it into his mouth. Just then a 'merciful providence' had answered his prayer. The Jason was passing by and came to his rescue.

Dr. Tom joined them at last in the drawing room, exhaustion on his expressive features. 'I've knocked him out with laudanum.'

Billy proposed the toast they had postponed. 'To the 'Jason' and all who sailed in her!'

And Abby another toast. 'To Holly who showed them she could.'

Holly had a surge of pride, a warm glow that had nothing to do with her comfortable affection for Billy or her wilder passion for Sean. She had done it! She had increased her hazardous initial investment in the Eugenia to the point where she could buy a second ship. She now stood to make a fortune overnight, this time not from the American run but from transhipping goods from British ships, which could not enter the Pearl River so long as they refused to sign a bond they were carrying no opium whereas her ship, being an American ship, could do so. The very reason why she had named the ship for her son in the hope he could follow the Golden Fleece one day as she had done if not in this ship, then its successor.

The doorknocker crashed once again to a chorus of groans and voices. 'How do you stand this day and night?' Holly asked Dr. Tom as he rose wearily to answer the noisy summons.

'Rain or shine,' he replied as he greeted Captain Douglas, captain of Jarman Malleson's new armed ship from Singapore whose arm had been badly gashed and roughly bandaged.

Abby, veteran of too many wounds now to flinch at the sight of the gaping cleavage, helped the captain ease off the rough bandage improvised from torn strips of shirt, asked 'what have you been up to?'

'A big of a shindig in one of those Kowloon shambles of housing they call villages. Brawl over His Bleeding Eminence putting the kybosh on food and water from all villages on Kowloon and Hong Kong, and backing it up with three war junks. Another round in Our Imperial Bloodhound's war to make it too hot for us to stay in China.'

He downed the ale he had nominated as his 'poison' before cursing the Bloodhound for succeeding too well. 'Those jerks down in Singapore said I would make money to burn. So I hotfooted it here with a half-promise from

Jarman that I couldn't fail. What do I find? No one wants my ship only my guns. Only the Chinks want both. And they're welcome. They're buying the Cambridge.'

Perplexed when his hosts roared with laughter, he reiterated, 'yes, those warriors on the warjunks bought my boat.' Demanding bewildered as they became even more hilarious, 'what are you laughing like hyenas for, that's not funny?'

When he could speak, Billy Howe explained, 'you're the only man in this port who has won even the smallest advantage from Our Imperial Bloodhound, let alone sold him a ship.'

'You don't say. Well I feel a lot better already.'

'What are you going to do now?'

'Buy me a tidy little brigantine I've got my eye on - one of Raine's. Do the Manila run. A goddamned sight more money in that right now. A tidy profit with no risk!'

Holly envied him his ability to up anchor and change course in his career. She fretted, in her more restless moods, to have been born a woman who must always sail on the same ship as her man.

* * * * * *

The Foreign Devils fly to Hong Kong Harbour

Billy Howe was the first to see the board men parading through the streets of Macao's Chinatown, the first to read Viceroy Lin's insulting proclamation couched in terms calculated to incite all Chinese citizens against Europeans. They were to abandon all services to the foreign devils of Macao, whether as providores, house servants, laundrymen or wet nurses.

He waylaid anyone who might known more, and soon learned two thousand troops were on their way from Heangshan to enforce the proclamation. Worse the soldiers were already near Waterlily Neck with orders to surround British homes by stealth during the night. He rushed home to order Holly to evacuate at once, only to find Chung Tai Tai had already warned her and was holding a junk ready near the Praya Grande quay. Holly was delaying only because Flora was still arguing with Barron, who insisted he must be 'last off the ship', and was refusing to leave without him.

'If I look as if I'm skulking off at the first threat how can I hold their obedience before a real threat?'

'My darling, you no longer have to prove your courage to anyone in this port. You've surely done that several times over.'

The stalemate was unlocked at last by a cryptic message from Kaida Hung. Not only was there a body of troops on their doorstep, but Viceroy Lin himself was already half-way to Macao through the Broadway passage in Heangshan rousing the countryside. He was encouraging all the gentry, shopkeepers, traders and even the peasants not only to cut off all supplies by land and water, but to buy arms, attack, and kill or imprison all foreign devils.

Barron Forge was still arguing 'if I run at Viceroy Lin's advance and flourish of troops, it will only encourage him to more outrages against us all.'

She found the argument to convince him. 'He may be shrewd enough to pin you down here so he can play havoc at Lintin.'

He turned to Billy to adjudicate. 'Where do you think the cat will jump Billy?'

'Lintin, no question of it Captain.'

'All hands to the deck then. We sail in an hour.'

The little party moved swiftly through the streets towards the quay, dressed in their most 'drab' with no more than one small holdall apiece, while other foreign devils were still packing as if for a holiday resort, and not for a Spartan life in a congested opium fleet. The now hostile Customs officers at the quayside waved Holly through with a quick smile and salute of brotherhood when she proferred her amulet, then turned their backs ostentatiously to the rest of the party as they scurried after her down the quay to board the waiting skiff with Billy chanting 'see no evil', and Flora remarking 'Sir George would be pleased if he knew. He always said we would be driven from Macao in the end.'

Holly leant sadly over the rail. She would miss Macao's unique blend of colourful houses, churches, temples and stalls surrounded by the wandering walls of its three hills. She was being forced out just as she had learned to call it home. Where would home be in the end?'

'Why Hong Kong, just as Sir George predicted,' Flora promised brightly.

Holly answered bleakly, 'that wild anchorage?'

'All future and no past. That's the beauty of it.'

Holly was unprepared for the scene in Hong Kong harbour, which resembled the Whampoa fleet rather than the warehouse fleet of Lintin. 'Bumboats' were everywhere, hanging in strings at the stern of every vessel or plying back and forth unloading cargoes from those ships that must stay outside the Pearl River to those who could go inside. There were not only ships like Holly's Jason and the two man o' war frigates but also a new fleet of much larger Portuguese-built lorchas between one and two hundred tons, many under Chinese command to judge by the painted eyes on their bows.

This time Captain Forge was faced, not with mutinous crews that could readily be quelled, but with ladies complaining they were cramped in confined quarters without servants, rationed in all fresh food and water as if in a siege, and forbidden to land on the island backing Hong Kong Harbour. He was forced to go from ship to ship with Holly and Flora to pacify them and explain that Viceroy Lin had cut them off by land and water until the shipmasters signed the bonds.

A rebellious Maisie Macdonald threatened to lead a march of women onshore and get rations for themselves insisting 'they wouldn't fire on us.'

'I wouldn't bet on that,' Captain Forge objected.

'We could take the risk better than you.'

'Then I'd have to risk my own life to get you out of prison. Is that what you want?' He protested with some irritation.

He was also obliged to resist the impatience of Captain Barnes of the Volage and Captain Ward of the Hyacinth pestering him that cautionary fire was called for because the whole fleet was up in arms over the fact the drinking wells had been poisoned.

'We'll sink those confounded junks. We'll blow up the Kowloon battery. Why can't we use these darned frigates, now we've sailed them half way round the world to get here?'

He tried to explain his dilemma to his combative colleagues. 'Let us not forget that once the first shots are exchanged we can never undo them.'

Captain Barnes begged to differ. 'I don't believe anything less will knock sense into the blighters.'

'You're wrong if you think it will be money for old rope,' Captain Forge reminded him. 'Just give me a chance to prove to you first that we only have to wave the Union Jack at them and they'll run. Half those conscripts on board are paid little or nothing. Not enough to die.'

But the say was not finally his for the two captains bent on deterrent action were not under his command.

He did not budge from the fore through the exchange of fire that followed, nor flinch when a jingal ball passed right through his hat merely raising his fist in triumph. 'We're better shots than they.'

Captain Ward measured the less than a finger's breadth by which the marksman had missed. 'Just the same your name was on that bullet.'

'Viceroy Lin put it there no doubt.'

'Which is why you'd better stop playing the hero and get behind the wheelhouse on the bridge next time. We're rather short of good supers out here.'

Captain Forge commented drily. 'Or down below? That's hardly my reputation, captain. Perhaps next time.'

'Will there be a next time?' Captain Barnes asked hopefully.

'As surely as the day follows night, and before long. We have bigger issues to settle than poisoned wells.'

'When will it start, Captain?' Captain Ward demanded.

'In this powderkeg of Kowloon sooner or later.'

An explosive incident happened sooner rather than later. Sailors Holly had hired from the crew of the Cambridge to crew the Jason, after that ship was handed over to Admiral Kuan, had landed without permission and caused havoc in a village and trouble for the entire fleet both with the locals and the higher authorities. An infuriated Barron was obliged to castigate Holly for the first time in their friendship.

'That confounded crew of yours have put everyone here in dire danger. They're the bottom of the barrel. A rorty lot of seadogs with the brains of baboons. You should never have taken Captain Douglas' word about them but asked me or Malleson. We would have set you right.'

Holly faced him on deck nettled. 'You commend Malleson to me after the fights his blackguards get into along the Coast?'

'Not unprovoked attacks on friendly Chinese like your sailors. Very many of both sexes. Nor wanton destruction of temples.'

Holly was appalled at the news. She, and her ship, were registered as American but these sailors were British subjects with all that implied. 'Were all my men involved?'

'There were three ringleaders worse than the rest.'

Flora had come on deck, perplexed by the unprecedent sound of her courteous husband's voice raised against Holly. She found the two glowering at each other in a most uncharacteristic confrontation for either of them.

Holly demanded, 'why my men? Why not Jarman Mallesons'? They were there too.'

'My present report is that your sailors, drunk as skunks, led the way into the village, forced their way into the houses, obliged the inhabitants to sell them drink as well as food, and threw stones at a small temple until they had all but demolished it. When the village folk intervened to stop them they made an unprovoked attack on the village wounding men, women and children without discrimination. They behaved like irresponsible maniacs just at a time when I'm doing my level best to avoid a war.'

Holly's eyes blazed as dark as the plain serge dress she wore. 'Surely it's one man's word against another! How can you be so sure Malleson's men aren't shifting the blame knowing they'll get the rough end of the stick from Malleson?'

Captain Forge ignored Flora's restraining hand on his arm. 'I'm speaking to you man to man, Holly, as you have chosen to enter a man's world. I'm forcing you to the same responsibility as any man who owns a ship. We're not just talking about a riot today but a murder. One Lin Wei Te, badly beaten with sticks on the chest and head. He has now died. Your men must be held responsible.'

Holly was shaken at this news. 'Why didn't you tell me that in the first place?'

'I didn't want to blackmail you into facing a responsibility.'

She stared him down. 'You watered the story down because I'm a woman. You've kept something from me, something that would explain why the fighting got so savage someone was killed. After all, fights with the villagers have happened before without ending in murder. What stirred them up so this time, Barron?'

Captain Forge answered with visible discomfort. All his bent was against discussing sex with a woman. 'They went into the houses awash with samshu demanding women. When their menfolk resisted, there was a general donnybrook. Now they want to wear a green coat.'

As Holly looked bewildered, Flora translated the sailor's slang, 'shuffle off all blame. Feign ignorance.'

'How can you possibly identify one as murderer in those circumstances? They wouldn't know themselves if they were blind drunk, not to mention they probably couldn't tell one from the other.'

'You know as well as I do, Holly, Viceroy Lin won't care which one of the sailors actually struck the blow as long as you hand over someone who was there. Anyone.'

'You talk as if you're going to bow to Lin.'

'I talk as if I'm going to court-martial all of them for riotous behaviour and one or more for murder. Let anyone dare try to tell me I don't have judicial power.'

Flora, exasperated by Holly's failure to comprehend Barron's predicament, said, 'Holly, if Viceroy Lin holds anyone responsible it will be you not Barron. He'll deny any American has had anything to do with it, in order to fix the blame wholly on British citizens, and therefore on Barron's shoulders.'

Holly now repentant and frighened. 'What can Lin do to you?

'Force me into the war these opium barons have plotted for so long, the war they persuade themselves can be won with a few shots.' His bitterness surprised even Flora.

'Much ado about nothing,' Holly foolishly assayed a jest.

He spoke more in sorrow than anger, 'if nothing is the first blow struck for war.'

The scourge of his words made her feel as guilty as if she herself had been at Kowloon with her men. If Barron was right and they were de facto at war, then she must be ready for any disaster.

Captain Forge left the 'Jason' moody and morose. Here he was superintendent of a fleet that could not survive with limited food and water for long in Hong Kong harbour. It would always be a hazardous spot for shelter until proper warehousing could be built there. They would never have any right to occupy it unless it belonged to the British crown, a right that could only be won by open war.

War would only be possible if Dr. Jarman had overcome the crafty inertia of Viscount Palmerston; a man who hitherto had behaved like a captain allowing his vessels to drift steadily on to ruinous cliffs before an offshore wind without the slightest concern for the passengers and crew who would implacably drown, but certain he would survive and pick up the insurance. If he, Forge, was cast for any role it was as captain of a ship drifting irrevocably to shipwreck on the eight forts of the Bogue.

* * * * * *

Viceroy Lin Visits Macao

As His Excellency, Viceroy Lin, approached Macao, the shops were already full of oblivious citizens buying moon cakes for the autumn moon festival to exchange with all their relatives, and brilliant paper lanterns of rabbits, cats and butterflies to hang like fireflies in the trees before he arrived. Governor Pinto waited at the Waterlily Neck gate to meet him with a Portuguese military guard of one hundred soldiers in spruced-up uniforms and a military band, and the local mandarins to greet him at the Lotus Temple. Governor Pinto waited in terror that some of the British foreign devils might have defied his decree they must leave while the Viceroy was there or he could not guarantee their safety. For Viceroy Lin was undoutbtedly on the warpath. An unwise warpath in the opinion of the Governor, for it would damage his chances of persuading the British merchants engaged in the legal trade to defy Capain Forge's ban on their return to Canton.

When Viceroy Lin hove into view at last, his sedan chair was borne by only eight bearers, although he was entitled to sixteen as he was acting in place of the Emperor, but his long procession sufficed to assert that rank with the parade fore and aft of troops from different regiments bearing their individual banners and uniforms and marching to the gongs and drums of their timekeepers, the whole led by an officer on horseback.

As the procession halted before the Gate, guns boomed out from the ancient fortress of Morag Ha in salute and the Portuguese regiment presented arms and the band played the Portuguese national anthem before wheeling into position at the head of the procession.

Now Viceroy Lin for the first time, saw so many fanqui in one place he rehearsed the details he would commit to his diary. Their tight garments that made them look like actors playing the part of foxes and hares on the stage. Their round long hats like yamen runners. Their excessive beards. Their velvet or felt hats. Their heavy coats so hot they kept kerchiefs to wipe the sweat away.

He alighted first at the new temple to the God of War where he placed incense sticks in supplication, and next at the Lotus Temple where he passed through a line of carved temple dogs on pedestals of winged dragons into the first Hall to the Goddess of the Sea and beyond to a pavilion off the much larger second Temple to the Goddess of Mercy where he took refreshments and dispensed gifts to the officers and soldiers.

His circuit of inspection took him through the Chinese quarters where all the people stood outside many a house adorned with laudatory scrolls of gratitude for his coming to rescue them from a deadly vice. Not a foreign devil in sight. Macao swept clean by his equally deadly edicts to cut them off by land and water until they agreed to his four demands. He wound back along the Praya Grande past the green latticed houses and the Casa Garden towards the Common, scorning their ugly structures and rehearsing in his demand the new regulations he would impose on the trade to suppress opium traffic, while 50 miles away that very morning the first real blow of a war, that would consume him, had been struck. As often happens it was a slight affair, which had begun at breakfast time.

'Well what does it say?' Captain Forge asked John Norris as he swallowed the last mouthful of his austerity breakfast of rolled oats in the great cabin of the 'Volage.'

'In a minute, Captain.' John Norris still intent on the script.

'What do you expect Captain?' Captain Bell asked politely.

Captain Forge replied tersely, 'Viceroy Lin firing off another volley of words.'

'How will that affect me?'

Captain Bell, a bluff man of ruddy face from long years of tropic service, had little imagination for anything but the wiles of wind and weather. As to the three war junks opposing him, he saw them and their fire rafts as the eqivalent of slingshot against rifles, or arrows against cannon.

Captain Forge curbed his optimism. 'We may have the advantage here in Hong Kong harbour, Captain, but Viceroy Lin undoubtedly has it on land. Out with it John.'

John Norris duly announced 'Viceroy Lin has ordered the people in Kowloon and nearby islands to make war on us. They must kill, capture and starve us.'

Captain Bell snorted, 'you can't take that from a jolly Celestial.'

Captain Forge merely sighed. 'So it has come at last. Viceroy Lin has declared war. And we, Bell, will be the ones to fire the first shots of that war despite all Jarman's prophecies.'

Captain Bell rose jubilantly as if about to prime the first cannon at once. 'We'll pull the Volage and Hyacinth in range, demand our supplies, then, if they refuse, blow them out of the water. That should teach them.'

As Captain Forge studied Captain Bell's great bulk, overpowering as any ship's figurehead, he thought the very sight of him would be enough to inimidate the minute Cantonese.

'And have Whitehall say we intimidated them with our gunpower? No, I say we should go with the schooner Pearl backed up with my pinnance and your cutter of course.'

It took all his finesse to persuade Captain Bell to approach the warjunks in nothing more than three small boats for provisions. Safe, but humiliating and ruinous to patience in the broiling heat, as they soon found out. On the third refusal, they gave notice they would sink all three junks if they did not get provisions within half an hour. The warjunks gave their answer by sending a message boat with orders to the shore battery to get ready to fire, tricing up their boarding nettings and manning their guns.

By the time they returned to the Volage in the early afternoon, Captain Bell was seething with frustration. The Volage was no longer able to stand within range of the junks with the tide on the ebb. The junks, by contrast, could lie close inshore with the shallow draft of their flat bottoms and moveable rudders.

'We could fight them tonight on the floodtide.' Captain Bell suggested, as he surveyed their frustrating plight.

Captain Forge eyed the rafts tied up inshore. 'they'd snarl us up with those damned firerafts.'

'What about waiting till dawn?'

'By that time another twenty junks would have sneaked in and be lined up against us. No, we attack now.'

'With what in this Lilliputian war?'

'With these.' Captain Forge waved at their puny craft.

Had Captain Forge gone troppo? 'We'd all be killed.

'We'll simply run in closer under their guns. Their guns can't swivel. They're all rotten shots. And they have no stomach for war.' He explained just how they would attack.

The three small vessels, their pigmy artillery concealed under tarpaulins, sailed towards the junks as if on another embassy. Once within range they ran down the line of junks, opening up their barrage of shot and grape ripping the hulls of the junks and the great matting sails on their booms. The return cannon fire whistled harmlessly overhead, taking Captain Forge's hat with it.

He swore as it vanished into the smoke pall that now enveloped the schooner. 'I wanted that for a souvenir.' But jested when the sailors crowded anxiously around him, 'when they fish my hat out of the water, they'll send it to Beijing saying they killed the British admiral in a great victory. And our little Admiral Kuan will get a promotion.'

Captain Forge now ordered the schooner to stand off, while they exchanged the exhausted powder barrels for new ones from below and filled the cartridges, then closed in for another barrage. By the time the second exchange was over, the pall of sunset brought a swift dusk and the chance for the crippled junks to be towed to the shelter of the batteries.

The gunduel between the warship over, the duel of words between the two captains resumed back on the Volage. Captain Forge was opposed to blowing up the batteries and sinking the junks. Captain Bell was insisting he should do so or the junk commanders would think they had won a victory as the two warships had not engaged.

'What is victory, Bell? In my book, it's not reducing the Kowloon battery to rubble. They'll only build another one. It's wringing concessions from Viceroy Lin despite the murder of Lin Wei Tse; even negative concessions such as turning the blind eye if his subjects defy his decress to refuse us food and water.'

'Is there any chance they'll defy him?'

'Every chance. These villagers are professionals at defiance. They have perfected the art for centuries against countless officials of Emperors of various dynasties.' He paused to knock out his pipe.

'And positive concessions?'

'He'll modify the bond he demands of British captains before he'll let them enter the Bogue and do it before the typhoon season. He needs the trade as much as we do. He doesn't want to see half the shipping lost in the typhoon season in this exposed harbour any more than we do.'

When all was quiet again, Holly chose to remain in the bizarre floating colony on the Apollo with Maisie MacDonald, while the Jason with a fresh crew ferried British cargo, chiefly cottons, to Billy on the receiving end at Whampoa. And it was Maisie, who exhorted her not to waste her heart looking over her shoulder when James Malleson told her that Sean Jarman had married his childhood sweetheart back in Scotland.

Holly was surprised to find her anger more against James Malleson for so obviously 'rubbing her face in the news' as Maisie put it than against Sean himself. Although she did feel a fierce pang of jealousy against the unseen rival who had always kept them apart, that unknown Highland beauty Jean, who had always had first claim on Sean. Still she preferred to know it was his old love, Jean, who had won him rather than any new love. It was the only consolation she could find.

* * * * * *

Thirty-nine Regulations to Suppress the Opium Trade

Viceroy Lin's temporary yamen at Humen was busy as any headquarters at the height of battle. Major and minor officials, informers and runners, had come in and out from every part of the province night and day. All because he had proclaimed thirty-nine regulations for the suppression of the opium trade, which had instituted a reign of terror.

It reached out to everyone since nine out of ten citizens of the province were said to be smokers. Therefore police searches spared nothing- gardens, temples, the quarters of women, even coffins and tombs. Neighbour turned against neighbour. People denounced others to save themselves. Officers acted as agent provocateurs planting opium, or opium pipes, on innocent victims to spare themselves the trouble of searching at all.

The witch-hunt produced the most satisfying evidence of the successful persecution of the guilty - forty thousand pipes in a great pile like so much old firewood ready for the match. All condemned out of hand, if they had the oil-darkened bowls of habitual use, without regard to any exquisite craft of their wood or ivory manufacture.

At the eye of the whirlwind, Viceroy Lin was a man enraged beyond all reason because his excellent intelligence now told him the burning of the opium, and the order given Captain Forge to banish the opium fleet for ever from China, had been in vain. A new cargo of opium larger than ever before was about to arrive.

Moreover, for all the barbarian 'Eye's' initial co-operation, he was now as intransigent as any outright rebel. Refusing to chase the opium ships away. Refusing to deliver the murderer of Lin Wei Tse. Blowing up the Kowloon warjunks when they were only doing their duty in preventing the purchase of food and water.

Viceroy Lin raged to Governor Tang about the Eye's undutiful behaviour. 'His conduct no longer renders him deserving of Imperial clemency. It is like that of the unfilial Che bird which attacks and tries to destroy its mother as soon as it is hatched.'

Unable to tolerate this public loss of face, he was obliged to order Admiral Kuan to sink and burn British ships and, if possible, bring in the murderer of Lin Wei Tse. Reviewing his fleet of eighty ships from Shakok Hill at the Bogue and watching the agility of the Admiral's water braves shooting arrows from the tops of masts, he composed a poem for the occasion.

A vast display of Imperial might
has shaken all the foreign tribes
and if they now confess their crimes
we shall not be too hard on them.

However, all too conscious that Imperial might was non-existent beyond the Bogue, he was forced to compromise with his pride and bargain with the Red Rods of the Red Circle. He offered Wang Chung, who had used Lin's blockade of the Bogue richly to feather his own nest, the prize of the British ship in the Macao Inner Harbour.

As soon as Kaida Hung heard of Viceroy Lin's plan, he sought leave in order to reach Macao in time to rouse Chung Tai Tai. Perhaps this time under cover of battle in the dark, they might destroy Wang Chung. He used the network of their brotherhood along the back ways of the delta all through the night to travel to his village, where he picked up a small sampan, piloted by his cousin. In the black hour before dawn, it nosed its way towards the shore of the inner harbour of Macao, the faint slap of its oars the only sound in the shrouded hush until it reached the streets of junks clinging to the land.

Just as the rowers shipped their oars, a crash of gongs, a reverberation of drums, a cacophony of screams and yells exploded in the dark; a dissonance that at first seemed as if a stage Battle of Heaven in a Cantonese opera was in full uproar to the discordant crescendoes of its wailing orchestra. Torches flared simultaneously across the crescent of boats as if a director had given the signal to illuminate a demoniacal scene of tragedy.

Kaida could see a desperate wild battle already being bitterly fought on a foreign vesssel by a ghastly set of ruffians against its outnumbered crew with more still swarming up its boarding nets. It was a doomed battle as the new wave of enemies set fire to the inflammable rigging. Viceroy Lin's third bonfire of vengeance, Kaida reflected more in despair than anger. First the burning of the opium, then the opium pipes, now this defenceless ship. All weird sacrifices to the Emperor. Better the bullock before the Altar of Heaven than this. Men jumping overboard to drown at anchor in the harbour not with honour in a storm. The mate fighting for his life back to the mast, flag in hand. A Spanish flag he noted with horror. The ship could only be the Bilbaino.

He turned to his stolid cousin still puffing at his pipe as if a boat on fire were an everyday occurrence. 'Someone has made a terrible mistake.'

His cousin, a pilot who knew everything on the river, shifted his pipe a fraction and answered, 'what does Wang Chung care? He will sell his soul to any devil'. He spat into the water, red-tinged with the fierce glow of the fire. 'But Lin can't buy me.' He would never answer Viceroy Lin's summons to arm against the foreign devil and kill or catch them. A true denizen of the delta, he had no mind to fight for or against either side.

'Let our violent men, the 14K Triads, do the dirty work.'

As the faint red tinge of dawn spread along the rim of the three Macao hills, Kaida picked his way uphill to Tim Bird's house. He could see the smoking hulk of the Bilbaino aleady surrounded by gossiping sightseers, puzzling no doubt as to what lesson they should read from it.

As he lingered in Tim Bird's look-out he knew that Viceroy Lin would go on making misjudgements about the British, as he had when he pontificated that the sailors and troops of the British Navy were so weary with travel when they arrived they were unfit to fight. He could never escape from the narrow armour of Chinese arrogance. Yet withal he was a man of singular virtue among his own kind. He was utterly fair to his subordinates and the only official ever known to consult them. It was unfortunate that no matter how many firerafts and defences he built, how many forts he strengthened, how many land-braves he mobilised, how much resolution he brought to the fray like a tiger in the jungle, he must lose. This was the only fact he refused to understand.

* * * * * *

High Commissioner and Viceroy Lin degraded to Viceroy

Captain Forge swore when he read Viceroy Lin's latest edict. 'Unless the murderer of Lin Wei Tse is handed over immediately, I will annihilate the British ships.'

So that was the Viceroy's answer to his trial and sentence of the five worst culprits, his offer of compensation to the family and village of the dead man. He crumpled the paper on the floor, 'Lin wants war!'

Flora, engrossed with a novel from the last ship into port, paid scant attention. 'I rather thought we did.'

He was riled by her indifferece. 'How can you go on reading at the thought of war?'

She had heard it all before. 'I promise you I'll put the book down when the war starts in earnest. But I've had these alarums and excursions for breakfast, dinner and tea for months now. The excitement is hard to maintain.'

He kissed her affectionately on the cheek. 'It's starting in earnest now. I'm off to give him a whiff of our gunpowder at the Bogue.'

She dropped the book and flew to her feet. 'How much danger to you, Barron? I pay attention to that.'

He put his arm around and lied. 'Infinitesmal.'

'You told me that the last time and got your hat holed with your foolhardy bravado. Next time it will be your head.'

'I have a hole in the head already, my dear, for not contriving to head for home like Davies, Roberts and Jarman.'

As he buckled on his sword, an ayah brought his son into the room, his Botticelli cherub appearance the antithesis of her dark sloe-eyed features. At the sight of the sword the little boy flew to his father in excitement, his small hands reaching to the danger of the blade, pleading as if it were a toy 'does it work?'

His father swung him to his shoulders for one last ride. 'Better than my diplomacy I hope.'

Yet he still hoped for diplomacy. He would try to dissuade Captain Bell from firing that first fateful shot in the Bogue by making a 'moderate but firm' address to Their Excellencies, Viceroy Lin and Governor Tang, asking them to abandon their plan to annihilate the British at Hong Kong. But he could do no more as he only had power to advise, not command Captain Bell.

Nature conspired against him at first. It took him four tedious days beating up wind to achieve the fifty miles to the Bogue. Once there, he faced Admiral Kuan's fleet of fourteen warjunks and fireboats ranged across the narrow mouth of the river. He leaned moodily over the ship's rail staring at the carnival array of gorgeously painted warjunks looking more fit for a festival than war, decked out as they were from hull to topmast with pennants and streamers. He thought how easy it would be to pick off these targets like a marksman at a coconut shy. But the thought was ashes in his mouth. The technical victory would be his, but the moral victory- at least in respect to 'foreign mud'- must remain with Viceroy Lin.

Captain Bell watched the Chinese fleet weigh anchor and bear down to come to rest in a line southwards from Chuenpi. Now was the perfect time to strike while his warships stood between the Volage hove to at the north end of the line of junks and the Volage at the south end. If they delayed overnight they would give the firerafts a chance to slip past in the dark to join battle with the impotent warships, now without protection except their own makeshift armoury.

Captain Forge could not forbid Captain Bell should he decide to hoist the red signal flag to open fire forthwith, but he was still determined to argue for conciliation to the last drop of possibility.

'I'm suggesting you remember Whitehall sits on the judge's bench out there somewhere as well as the future bench of public opinion. Justice must appear to be offered if not done. We must take any chance to save bloodshed although in such an inglorious cause.'

Captain Bell knew perfectly well it was the Trade Superintendent who would have to answer to Whitehall not himself. He had been in China long enough to know that Captain Forge had been consistently left adrift by Whitehall with no answer to frequent warnings of crisis and imminent collision, no orders whether to fight or retreat. He had been obliged to make decisions for the British government, such as more than once had precipitated Britannia unwillingly into

Empire around the globe. Would they praise him in the end like Drake, or condemn him like Raleigh? Would they back him like Clive or ruin him like Hastings? He was only sure of one thing. Captain Forge had not made the fortune of any of them.

He was astounded when Captain Forge insisted on sending not one, but two, letters to Admiral Kuan. He barely hid his impatient frustration with Captain Forge, when John Norris returned from his second laborious crossing over choppy water with another outright refusal from the recalcitrant Admiral, until Captain Forge cried 'let battle commence.'

Now was the perfect time to strike while the tide was in their favour, the junks and fire-rafts hemmed in. Now was the hour for which a naval captain devoted his lifetime of training - action against an enemy. Their crews and gunners manning their stations on sails and guns. Their ships proceeding in order of battle. In this case, each ship bearing away with the wind on the starboard side to run down the line of junks bringing their starboard guns to bear. Their shot and shell ripped mercilessly into the hulls of the warjunks, opening great jagged holes along the waterline while the incessant barrage of deafening return fire from the junks flew uselessly over their own heads into the rigging and spars.

By the time they swung round to run down the line of junks once more bringing their larboard guns into action, Captain Forge could only see bizarre glimpses of the listing and burning warjunks through the billows and plumes of smoke drifting across the unfairly matched battle lines. Before the two frigates finished their second run, three junks had sunk, several more were sinking, and the rest were holed, dismasted or disabled. The Volage would have sunk Admiral Kuan's flagship- where he stood before its single giant mast brandishing his sword to exhort them to action when they would run- but for Captain Forge's urgent signal to spare him.

Viceroy Lin, irate about Admiral Kuan's lamentable performance in battle, was not prepared to give him the same tolerance. He sat down to demand the Emperor dismiss him at once. Governor Tang hastened to stop him, playing on the superstition lurking even in a man of reason like Viceroy Lin. It would never do to disgrace the living heir of a demi-god. It would offend Kuan Ti, who might plot revenge in heaven to destroy them both.

Governor Tang stooped over the parchment instead, sighing as he perpetuated the same lies as so many officials before him in the precise calligraphy for which he was famous- that Admiral Kuan was a great hero who had repulsed foreign ships, and driven them away, when they had tried to steal through after their prayers to enter were refused. The Admiral had cheered on his men to deliver deadly broadsides which killed several tens of barbarians. The return fire of the foreign devils had been like eggs beating on stones. They would never be allowed to steal about the Bogue again, a promise that neither he, Captain Forge nor any of his mandarins believed for a moment.

CHAPTER 9

The British Lion roars

Ocean Barbarians must submit to Chinese laws

As the winter wore on, Captain Forge woke up each day hoping the lull in hostilities would last until the tea season was over. He prayed Viceroy Lin wanted to pacify the people who reaped the Emperor's revenues for him more than he wanted war with the British.

And Holly woke up each morning more and more successful with her soaring profits. She could get the maximum cargo in and out of Whampoa by piling the decks up to the loading blocks as well as cramming the hold. She took out the upper spare to lessen the chance of capsizing. When Captain Wagoner complained of the hazards of taking the Jason in under almost bare poles, she raised his bonus and gave him a percentage, to comply. Whereupon his zeal in goods in and out such as tea, silk, rattans, pepper and cotton more than exceeded her own.

Every morning Holly said a prayer for Billy's safety with an occasional prayer for Sean Jarman's happiness. She was annoyed with herself that she could never quite forget him, eagerly seeking scraps of news about his campaign with Dr. Jarman to mobilise opinion for war with China in London and the Midlands. She no longer chafed against the truth she was still haunted by his image, realising that shedding love was not like a snakeskin sudden and complete.

Yet as her days grew more frantic, Sean slipped a little more from reality in her mind and his memory grew less disturbing. Even her son did not serve as a daily reminder being far more like her than Sean. The clamour of each day claimed her, the gossip and alarms of the extraordinary floating community of merchant ships debarred from the Bogue by Captain Forge following the fresh prohibition of Viceroy Lin against any ships entering the Bogue unless their captains signed bonds by which they agreed to submit to Chinese law for any offence, in particular smuggling.

'Any captain who signs that does so over my dead body,' Captain Forge raged, 'captains must be made to realise that they, or any of their crew, could face summary trial and execution without mercy if any one of them is declared to be smuggling, whether smuggled goods are planted on them or not.'

He was even more enraged when the captain of the Thomas Coutts did sign the malignant bond and slipped through the Bogue reviled by all the other merchants but acclaimed by Viceroy Lin.

On Billy's intermittent visits to Holly, he was full of amusing interpretations of the gossip he picked up along the river. He gave her a demonstration of a thousand men he had seen drilling to fight with double swords, whirling and clashing them as they made hideous faces and horrible grimaces, convinced that the British troops would take flight at the horrendous sight. He did not try to hide the reality behind such displays. He told her how Viceroy Lin incited people to work on fortifications, manufacture armament and fire rafts, raise troops and make all the necessary preparations for clandestine attacks on foreign devils. More worrying news - Viceroy Lin had put an enormous price on the heads of five men, including Barron Forge and John Norris, because the Emperor had downgraded him from High Commissioner and Viceroy to mere Viceroy for losing the Battle of Chuenpi.

Holly found it preposterous that Chinese mandarins should go in fear of life and honour for difficulties beyond their control. She protested 'but he's been so successful compared to Tang and his ilk.'

'My darling, he promised to suppress the opium traffic altogether but failed to do so. He encouraged the Battle of the Bogue and lost. He refuses to believe Captain Forge has no control over the navy, and little over Jarman Malleson.'

'They wouldn't give a hoot in hell for his fate.'

'I don't say they would go as far as to dance on his grave.'

'They would quite happily dig it.'

Billy jigged Jason fondly on his knees making funny faces at the winning curly-headed child to make him chuckle. As always she felt the guilt that haunted her to see Billy's overwhelming affection for the boy, and was troubled by the question as to whether he ought to be told the truth. A truth that could only murder everything they both held dear. So why destroy the loving bond between them now? Billy's grave news was surely a far more vital concern.

'This price on Barron's head. Does Viceroy Lin give reasons?'

'Quite clearly on a placard that's going up everywhere. He's the barbarian 'eye'. He's the Taipan in charge. He has defied Viceroy Lin over the signing of bonds. He's returned to Macao against orders.'

Holly, too worried for child's play, sent Jason away with his ayah. 'What next my love?'

Even the irrepressible Billy was grave. The portents had never been more serious. A new vindictive Prefect, one Yuh, in Macao. Soldiers massing at Waterlily Neck Barrier ready to enter Macao. War junks assembling in the inner harbour. The Hyacinth ordered out of there.

'It's not just Barron who's in deadly danger. But all of us.'

'Governor Pinto will protect us.'

'Governor Pinto has refused because he can't. He's done all he can do in refusing to help destroy Barron.'

Holly look wearily round at the cosy, cheerful comfort of the chintzy drawing room. When she had first arrived to the ebullient conviviality of Macao, she had never imagined she would have to abandon that fun-loving oasis twice in such a short time as a refugee under threat from soldiers and uncontrolled robbers on the street. She packed rapidly, oppressed by the thought that the excellent captain, she had come to admire so fondly, might not survive Viceroy Lin's plans for his extermination. She remembered Lord Nash's fate only too vividly.

If only she had known she had no need to worry. Captain Forge had just received a despatch from England to say Viscount Palmerston, on his own initiative, had authorised an Expeditionary Force to be assembled in India, destination China. The free traders had won.

* * * * * *

Governor Tang leaves with Impunity

Governor Tang had mixed feelings about his departure from Canton and the desertion it necessitated of his firm friend, Viceroy Lin, as they stared in comfortable silence together at the golden carp gliding in the miniature lake of his garden. Of course, he welcomed the chance to turn his back on the past turbulent four years in a region where he had so often been deliberately deceived and mystified by a multitude of officials who spoke a Cantonese language barbaric and alien to his own. Even at the price of being reinstated by Beijing to the lowest possible vice-regal rank, that most dreaded of assignations, Viceroy of the Rivers. It could have been worse, exile to Sinkiang or Tibet. He would be sorry, however, to leave his friend Lin Tse Hsu degraded four grades and embroiled in the same futile struggle that had caused his own downfall.

He would assuredly mourn for their many sessions together in a companionship rare in their arbitrary and lonely official life, moving as they did from post to post every three years in case they formed attachments strong enough to challenge the dynasty. How he would miss the mutual exchange of poems each had written knowing the worth of the other's judgement.

Moreover he owed Lin Tse Hsu more than uncommon friendship, mercy. When first summoned to his presence, he had expected to join the rest of the criminals being consigned to the prison as notorious opium traffickers. Instead Lin had astounded him by the grace of a tacit pardon in the words, 'better the tree whose poison you know than the one you don't.' He had simply demanded his unstinted cooperation in return for that pardon.

'At least we had a good rice harvest this year,' Viceroy Lin commented as he delicately helped himself to the glistening rice, white as the finest porcelain from nearby Foshan.

Governor Tang nominated another cause for satisfaction. 'At least you didn't have to post a placard to say you are incorruptible as the new Magistrate Yuh had to do in Macao.'

'I might have to do so soon if these scurrilous lampoons continue.' He produced the latest vicious one from his boot.

Governor Tang dismissed it with a wave, long inured to such scandalous effusions from the perennial dissenters of the city. 'All that means, my friend, is that you are unpopular with the criminals because you have abolished their profits.'

'Now I'm punished worse than they are.'

'Quite a harvest to reap,' Viceroy agreed taking a small sip of his favourite plum wine.

'I hope it's not the harvest of rebellion my good friend.' Vagabonds and robbers grew by the week.

Governor Tang offered a solution with the negligence of a man about to turn his back on the province. 'Then give them work. Arm them against the foreign devils. Pay them to fight.'

Viceroy Lin was shocked by the idea. Only the Tartar Manchu were ever allowed to own or carry arms. 'Give them arms?'

Governor Tang shrugged. 'Take them back when the fight's over.'

The first naturally would be simpler than the second. What did it matter? Neither of them would be there to reap the whirlwind.

They strolled along the winding, flagged path engraved with emblems for long life and felicity, then stood gazing down at the golden carp swarming for the grains of rice they threw into the pewter surface of the lotus-laden pool.

'This demand of Tsen Wang Yen that you massacre all foreigners and drive out all the trade,' Governor Tang began knowing well it was uppermost in Viceroy Lin's mind. 'It is ridiculous for a man who once lived here to make any such suggestion. He would know that was to ask the impossible.'

Viceroy Lin agreed dourly, 'can I empty the ocean?'

'First ask if you have strong enough swimmers.' Governor Tang put his hand comfortingly on his friend's arm.

Viceroy Lin voiced despair as he stared at the captive golden swimmers of this miniature lake. 'Of course not. Not in a province where there are said to be seven men of the sea for every three of the land, men who, in the final test, are ruled by nothing but the sea.'

Governor Tang sorrowed to hear this confession. What a pity a man of his capacity was not already in the War Council in Pekin rather than embroiled in a futile struggle which could only ruin any chance he once had of ever achieving that lofty position! Unaware of his friend's profound sympathy, Viceroy Lin heard only the Emperor's impossible warning, 'if measures are not taken out to root out this evil, once and for all, you Lin Tse Hsu will be called to account.'

* * * * * * *

The British Lion Puts Down a Paw

Captain Forge would cheerfully have done the sailor's hornpipe to express his feelings when he saw the size of the fleet deploying in the Macao Roads. 'The old giezer's gone to the other extreme,' he shouted meaning the hitherto obdurate Viscount Palmerston, 'not even the sketchiest instructions let alone powers up to date. And now half the British fleet by the looks of it. And, by god, steamships. Steamships that can make their way where sailing ships can't go. Steamships that will make all the difference between victory and defeat.'

They were four stump-masted wooden-hulled steamships from the Calcutta docks on the Hooghly River that looked plain Janes beside the splendid vision of the thirty sailing ships with their soaring masts and majesty of sails - twenty of them troopships - led by the battleships Conway and Alligator and the magnificent flagship, the 74 gun Wellesley.

No need to ask James Malleson, when he met him at Governor Pinto's welcoming reception for the officers of the fleet by what legedermain the fleet had been conjured up. Malleson accosted him first.

'I warned the government a China war would bring them down if they didn't win, and steamships were crucial to victory. You seem delighted beyond measure, captain, they lent me an ear.' He knew perfectly well that it was Captain Forge who had fought against his opposition to have steamships included in the fleet.

The old lion with all his claws intact, Captain Forge thought, refusing to become Malleson's victim in the war of words as he had been in both battles of power fought in the delta - with Jarman Malleson as well as Viceroy Lin.

'Wouldn't you, sir, with nine million pounds of tea on its way and fifty ships to clear?'

Still James Malleson needled him. 'You may be sorry yet. For my book I can only see what our Chinese mandarins will see. It will be hard, even for their gunners, to miss those paddle wheels.'

The Laird, who had stood beside James Malleson enjoying Captain Forge's obvious annoyance, fired a parting shot as they marched out together. 'I'm glad to see you're going to fight a war to save the opium trade!'

Captain Forge left seething not because the Laird had made his malicious remark but because he was right. As it turned out, these men might have treated him with vastly more respect if they had known that Viscount Palmerston had given him equal authority with the Admiral of the Fleet, his own cousin Sir Tryon Forge, with a rank that far exceeded his old status as post-captain of the navy.

At first the traders could scarcely believe it any more than Captain Forge himself until he was piped aboard the flagship with the full ceremonial due his new rank to receive his orders. Then, to his profound astonishment, he found he had been honoured above his wildest dreams with plenary powers of government backed up by an invincible naval force, he, whose every order had been for years the signal for jeers, abuse and denigration from the merchants of Canton during the years they had seen him as a 'paper tiger.' It was an honour he would have thought unimaginable over those humiliating years.

Any exaltation he felt was diminished the moment he met Commodore Brendan, the doddery old commander of the Expeditionary Force under Admiral Sir Tryon Forge, in the Grand Cabin. He was armed with a brief, clearly written by Dr. Jarman, to go to the city of Tienjin at the mouth of the Peiho River eighty miles from Beijing forthwith, a brief that none of the top brass and braid in the fleet appeared to have questioned. Astonishment on all faces as a result when he spoke, 'under no circumstances familiar to me should we go to the Peiho!'

Sir Tryon Forge was the first to speak. 'Regretfully we can't change our orders, Captain.'

Captain Forge would not resile. 'Orders approved by people, Admiral, who know nothing of the geography of China.'

'From people with the advice of a man who does,' Commodore Brendan assured them, 'From thirty years' service in the Orient.' Captain Forge drew no comfort from hearing his suspicions confirmed.

'That advisor, and we all know who he is, has never been to the Peiho,' Captain Forge insisted knowing he was never going to see eye to eye with Commodore Brendan who clearly resented the fact that he Forge, a man of inferior rank, had been placed in joint command with the Admiral over his head.

'Have you been to the Peiho yourself, Excellency?' the Commodore asked Captain Forge exaggerating his new title.

'I've read accounts by those who have. I can make a better assessment of the problems involved for a fleet such as this than he. I'm a navy man. He's not.'

'He had long years of service at sea.'

'Disregarding the contestible facts, as to whose experience is the greater, let's look, Commodore, at the incontestible facts. The shallow approach to the Peiho. Shoals reaching a long way out to sea. The bulk of the fleet obliged to lie so far offshore they would scarcely be in sight of the land. And if they chose to move inshore they would have to breach shifting, virtually uncharted sandbanks. Then there's the tidefall. Or the northern winter. If negotiations should stretch out over months, as in my experience they always do, where is the shelter from the bitter north winds? Let me remind you, gentlemen, there's no harbour at Peiho, no convenient access to food or water. What if the local officials do not provide these essentials?'

The argument wore on for three hours. Charts on the table. Distances assessed. Fingers jabbing in the air. Captain Forge demanding what did they propose to do after they landed at the Peiho? Cross eighty miles of hostile countryside to Pekin? And what then? Did they really expect to find the Imperial Court waiting to receive them in the Forbidden City? The Emperor would have abandoned it long before they got there.

The impassioned faces round the table in consternation. Those orders, that had seemed so clear when they left Calcutta, were by no means as straighforward as they had supposed. All were prepared to listen to him now.

Captain Forge seized his advantage. 'Gentlemen, compromise is the watchword in this Celestial Kingdom I'm afraid.'

Unfortunately they agreed they could not compromise on one thing, their orders to go to Peiho no matter how ill-conceived. So the argument wore on for more weary hours, Captain Forge at odds with Commodore Brendan about establishing the fleet's headquarters at Tinghae, capital of Chusan.

Commodore Brendan, a man bred on European wars, was adamant. 'Chusan is more strategically placed to command the great Yangtze River than Canton and offers more facility in getting supplies.'

Captain Forge did not disagree outright this time. 'Have you considered the local population may not be tractable? They are less accustomed to foreign devils than the south, and like the Formosans, have a long history of truculence to strangers.'

Sir Tryon felt impelled to back up his Commodore, partly to avoid appearing too partial to his cousin, 'the port is more sheltered and a much needed halfway house for the sailors.'

Captain Forge surveyed them with dismay. How could these experienced naval officers have failed to enquire about all the local factors bearing on satisfactory harbourage as they had done with Hong Kong harbour?

'It also suffers from a tidal race and the most vexatious currents. Not to mention the problematical approach, since not all the islands and reefs, so profusely scattered in that region, are on our maps.'

The officers exchanged glances, persuaded Captain Forge had such a preferential axe to grind for Hong Kong and a campaign in the south he could not be entirely trusted. How could Dr. Jarman, a highly successful merchant with far longer and much more extensive experience on the coast than Captain Forge, be wrong?

The chief strike against Captain Forge was that, as far as they could see, the Hong Kong island Captain Forge recommended as a base was a barren and inhospitable spot while Canton was an over-large city, too far upriver, with a history of rigorous and humiliating control of foreigners which their mission was to overturn.

Chusan, by comparison, was an island in a much more commanding position with all the facilities of Canton and none of its disadvantages. Moreover tea, bought in Chusan, would be cheaper without the excessive cost of carrying it on a difficult and hazardous journey overland, solely for the benefit of imperial tolls. What they did not know was that Chusan's reputation as a charnel house of death was worse than Canton's had ever been.

'Regrettably,' Admiral Sir Tryon Forge said with a gentle affability which was the secret of his popularity in command, 'our orders are clear for better or worse. We must go to Chusan and Peiho. We must prove the Foreign Secretary is wrong, and you are right, Captain.'

Of course his cousin's judgement was fair. With the best grace he could muster, Captain Forge joined their toasts to victory at Chusan and Peiho, to Her Majesty and even to Viscount Palmerston. At lease he had acted as devil's advocate first. He had warned them they would have everything in nature against them- the climate, disease, uncharted coasts and not least the treacherous people. If anyone was to die, it would be on their own heads.

* * * * * *

Viceroy Lin rouses the Countryside

Kaida watched the recruiting sergeants openly enlisting new recruits for Viceroy Lin's hastily expanded army on the Common before the Factories. Their test for fitness was simple. They offered them a hundred pound bar and signed them on as officers if they could lift it above the navel, otherwise as privates. Kaida felt sorry for these humble coolies and peasants, joining up as cannon fodder for a few copper cash a week, in the naive belief they would be invincible against the British on land because the red-beards' stiff legs were kept upright only by their tight trousers. Once they had fallen down they would be unable to get up again.

Kaida felt a touch on his elbow and turned round to find his brother Geli standing there. 'What are you doing here?' he asked in surprise, thinking his brother was still in Heangshan prison, victim of Viceroy Lin's harsh test for suspected opium addicts. Imprison them without opium and see if they can survive. If they did they were discharged as Geli had been. He shrugged off Kaida's surprise that he was not facing the executioner's sword by saying that was the thought that had made him endure.

Geli put his arm round Kaida in an unaccustomed gesture. 'You must come home. Someone sold our village poisoned packets of tea. Many have died.'

Kaida seized him by the shoulder. 'Our mother?' Geli nodded sadly.

Shaken by a terrible grief, he allowed his brother to steer him to a waiting boat, asking at last 'who are our enemies?'

'We have no enemies. The poisoning was accidental.'

'Don't be ridiculous. How can poisoning of tea be accidental?'

'Accidental for us. You see the tea was stolen.'

Kaida wondered if opium had affected his brother's brain. His village clansmen were not thieves. Pilots, couriers, postman, farmers but not thieves.

'They bought it from some poor out-of-work pedlar making a few copper cash. He had stolen it and thought to turn a quick profit.'

'Weren't my kinsman suspicious?'

'Why should they be, Kaida?"

Kaida had to agree. Their village, close to the sea, had always been a market for stolen goods including the cheap and common commodity of tea. 'We believe the fool stole tea intended for sale to foreign devils to kill them and so win the price on their head.'

Kaida urged the oarsman on to greater efforts along the windings of the Broadway passage. Geli revealed his mother, believing she would die before Kaida came, had told Geli the secret of their royal lineage. Kaida looked at his brother with new eyes. So that was why Geli looked as if a miracle had touched him. He had become the man of destiny Kaida had never truly believed himself to be. Geli no longer needed the oblivion of opium when he had the intoxication of revolution. He was a man of purpose as Kaida had never been. He would seek out the Elder Brothers, declare himself and set out to lead them when the day came. He would make whatever alliance would further their cause.

When they reached the village he heard a lament for a calamity as devatating as the passing of an army. He scattered chicken and pigs as he hurried to the end of the street where his mother had been living since the rioting in Macao. Half the households in the village, at first glance, seemed to be affected. The other half, including his uncle's, had been saved when they returned from the fields late enough to miss the first sampling of tea.

His uncle restrained him at the door, 'she's gone.'

Kaida stood before the huge closed coffin which dominated the side room where it lay. He bent his head in sorrow. What dignity and repose she had brought to life, what patience with her fate, what honour to her ancestors! His grief deserted him as she would have wished. In her lifetime, one challenge to the Manchu dynasty had failed. Men still plotted for another to come. As he stood traversing the tragedy of her life and her lineage, he knew for certain the time would never come. His brother would immolate himself because he would never come to terms with the need for resignation.

His uncle spoke with a serious urgency foreign to him. 'Her last words were that you must deny her. Speak of her as your aunt not your mother. Or you will have to observe three years of mourning in seclusion here. Do you want that?'

Kaida was too westernised to welcome that ancient custom. 'We will need you at the yamen if this war is to pass without a war on our clan. The Elder Brothers tell me Viceroy Lin has called the people to arms against the foreign devils. The common people as well as the gentry.'

'Viceroy Lin thinks to ride that tiger?' Surely he would know what a dangerous decision it was to rouse the people to arms in the ever mutinous south, arms more likely to be used against the reviled Manchu than the British.

'He will ride the tiger in his lifetime,' his uncle assured him, 'the Red Circle allow him to stroke them until ready to devour him.'

His uncle took him high on the hill among the tombs and found the one sacred object that had been carried so many miles by so many hands over so many years and generations, the Great Seal of the Ming dynasty. He held it triumphantly in the fading daylight. All the awe of office, the might as well as the majesty, lay there in his palm; all the reality of empire so long as men obeyed the commands of edicts bearing its stamp. Kaida wondered what justice, or injustice, had been committed in its name. Now it represented no more than the fantasies of popular rebellions, the hidden secrets of his family, the symbolism of the willow plate and all the secret trials of the Triads. Would the day ever come when one of his family used this very stamp to authorise some convulsion of his country? Would someone then be found to gainsay it as a forgery?

The present decree of his uncle was to hide it again in some place where no one but themselves could find it. They laid it to rest once more, this time in a different place in a crevice of the limestone hill. But Kaida could not lay his own doubt to rest. He knew he would have been home in his village at the time of the poisoning but for a sudden cancellation of his leave. Some spy in the yamen might have betrayed him to the Red Circle but failed to check he had in fact left for home. He felt a sudden chill to the bone in the dwindling dusk to think he, who was trying to kill the man he really believed was responsible, Wang Chung, had almost been killed first by that sinister hand.

Meanwhile a letter lay as heavy in Holly's hand, as the royal seal had in Kaida Hung's, its message of flight and abdication as clear. Sean Jarman had, admittedly, couched the letter in cautiously affectionate terms. She had read it at first with doubt, then surprise, indignation and bewilderment, finally with caustic fury. He had married his childhood sweetheart in a simple ceremony, so he said. Worse he would be bringing his wife back to Macao.

She knew she was being unreasonable. She should not feel rejected as if he had jilted her when it was she who had renounced him. Nor should she feel annoyed that she would have to observe the conventions of their tight little community in Macao and be polite to the woman. She had no business suffering such a violent, illogical reaction, one so disloyal to Billy. There could be only one explanation. She was still in love with Sean.

She threw herself down on the bed, Sean's letter crunched in her hand, and exhausted herself with shuddering tears. Why, oh why, could he not have stayed to stand for Parliament as Dr. Jarman had done? Perhaps he hoped to drive her away from China. Let him hope! She would stay to haunt his conscience like Banquo at the feast. And who would she turn to now with Abby, languid and pale, after her second birth, planning to retire to England with Dr. Tom to take over his father's practice in the Midlands?

Abby gave her short shrift. 'what right have you got to be sorry for yourself, my girl? You've everything a woman could ask for, a husband who is amusing, affectionate and kind - all qualities which are not Sean's long suit. You have independence which many women would give their right arms for. You lead a fascinating life, which would make you all the rage if you went back home and you have the gall to grumble. Just remember you've got no right to be sorry for yourself. It was you who chose to stand on your pride and not tell Sean you were in the family way.'

'To force him back from Manila for a shotgun wedding?'

'I could have taken the shotgun to him at the time for taking advantage of you.'

'It didn't seem so then, Abby,' she remembered with misty eyes. She could not exempt herself from blame.

As she allowed Abby to lead her back downstairs and banish the hungry ghost of Sean, she could not help wondering how many women went about their world mourning a lost love as she was doomed to do.' As she still was when she returned to Hong Kong harbour.

Once there she was one of the fifty-five shipmasters and merchants who signed a protest against Captain Forge's order to move ship to Tongku Bay as less exposed to danger from fire rafts than Hong Kong harbour. The ship insurers heartily agreed. Holly did not. Would Tongku Bay have the floating town that had sprung up at Hong Kong where most necessaries, even some luxuries, were now offered for sale?

Besides who would take Maisie MacDonald's place at Tongku Bay, the redoubtable old Maisie who did more for her sanity at this time than even Flora could? Flora was too anxious over the reward out for her husband's head, too concerned he might be taken hostage the moment he set foot at Tientsin. Maisie was sublimely indifferent to politics and all the wrangling of those around her. Consequently she saw issues more clearly than those who argued with such convolutions in the local press or across their dining tables.

She brushed aside Holly's fear of capture. 'No danger dear.'

Holly clutched Jason. 'Not from rewards - more if alive?'

'Not for women, dear. We don't exist,' Maisie said easily biting off a cotton, 'rewards for women with unbound feet. We have no value thank goodness.'

'What about ransom then?'

'Who would want a fat, middle-aged foreign devil like me? You as a concubine perhaps.' She continued calmly looping thick yarn with swift fingers, imperturbable about her safety from lascivious Chinese.

When Holly recovered from her hilarity at Maisie, and then at tiny Jason for simply laughing because she did, she chided her, 'seriously Maisie, can we trust all these people?'

She gestured towards the string of 'bumboats', spawn of the merchants' fleet like pilot fish attendant on sharks. Their crews looked harmless enough at their unhurried, timeless labour serving oceanic ships, stacking barrels of water and crates of food into loading nets dangling from the brigs.

Maisie soothed her with easy common sense. 'Where better than here? After all this is where the foxes have their lairs? Over there in the walled city of Kowloon. That's where danger lies.'

'When will it all end?' Holly asked wistfully.

'Your Captain Forge will ensure war takes second place until the tea gets home to England and the government gets its tea tax.'

'Will the Expeditionary Force understand such expediency?'

'No, Holly and no doubt crucify him for it.'

A fresh wind had sprung up as they were talking so that loading into the jouncing boats alongside went on with increasing difficulty. In one a trousered woman waited as the ship's derrick swung the net with one last crate towards her. She reached to grasp the net and lower it into position on the deck of her boat. The sailor, operating the derrick's arm, misjudged the distance and lowered it sharply downwards as a surge of the sea made her boat ride suddenly upwards putting her in danger of being thrown forcibly against the beam. She heard the sailor's warning shout just in time and threw herself on the deck with the speed of a cornered rat.

Holly marvelled at the instinct of this agile woman who had been born and lived all her life on the water, this poor unfortunate forced to perform loading on a choppy sea that should properly be done in the untroubled waters of an inside port like Whampoa. She leant over the rail, angry that neither she, nor anyone in the surrounding ships, could share the dangers to which this woman was exposed by their use of this harbour as an anchorage.

Her meditation was interrupted by the explosive uproar of a bitter struggle of boatmen against an attacking force in progress at the heart of the bumboat fleet. She watched with incredulous horror as the defenders defeated the intruders, trussed them with savage violence, threw them into a boat, thrust oil and straw among them, and put them to the torch in a scene evocative of an ancient Viking funeral rite. Their pyre, however, was of living men who struggled screaming from the red and gold rim of fire only to be thrust backwards with long bamboo poles. She turned, hands on her ears to stifle the sound of their agonised screams, to find Maisie gazing with impassive detachment at the terrible scene her knitting needles still in motion.

Holly learnt later the men burned to death had been informers for Wang Chung among the fleet, who had made a list of one hundred and fifty people he intended to denounce as 'guilty of spying for the foreign devils', people guilty of nothing more than earning the money from the foreign devils they could no longer earn at Whampoa. Wang Chung himself unfortunately not, as they hoped, among the victims.

* * * * * *

War comes to Macao

As Holly slowly ate her breakfast porridge, a copy of the Chinese Repository in hand, she reflected what a disagreeable town Macao had become since her arrival such a few short years before. Robbers and kidnappers infested the streets with the audacity of rats in a famine. Soldiers looted the foreign devils. Merchants formed their own street patrols. Women cowered behind locked doors, mourning the lost gaiety of past social seasons with their balls, plays, regattas and picnics. The foreign community had petitioned the Portuguese Governor to protect them now the two Plenipotentiaries were in the north with almost the entire Expeditionary Force.

According to the paper, Viceroy Lin was sending an army of two thousand soldiers to reinforce the garrison at the Barrier and drive the British out. And Captain Andrews of the Druid then in the outer harbour of the Taipa Roads had been asked to protect them. Holly put her paper down, her mind made up. She must head for Hong Kong once more with little Jason. She had already started packing when Billy arrived home with Captain Andrews in tow, saying he wanted to spy out the Barrier from their tower.

Captain Andrews struggled up the tower's winding stair with his gammy leg, spyglass in hand, to study the eight war junks so clearly visible in Fisherman's Bay below. His scrutiny swept the Barrier's two high stone and brick walls one with ten heavy guns to defend the cove of Cashilha Bay in the outer harbour, and one with twenty lighter guns to protect the Inner Harbour and therefore facing the wrong way to be of any help if an attack should come from the Outer Harbour

He closed his spyglass crisply, declaring 'hmph! that little lot isn't likely to give me much trouble,' emphasising as they moved downstairs again, 'one thing is clear. I can't wait until they move into Macao. I must attack first. I've no doubt in my mind our co-plenipotentiaries would agree if they were here.'

His handshake in farewell was expressive of all the firmness of character his words had conveyed. Watching him go, Billy marvelled at the solitary life and death decisions these men of the navy must make and stand by. Merchants like themselves certainly had major decisions of their own involving cargoes that could cost small fortunes, but never decisions the cost of which was paid knowingly in death.

Captain Andrews brought the stately Druid in from the west towards Macao with her attendant flock- the transport Nazareth Shah and the corvettes Hyacinth and Larne- at first under sail and then more ingloriously towed by the wooden steamship Enterprise.

As the flotilla ran parallel to the beach, several hundred people kept up on foot along the foreshore through the St. Lazarus gate and across the Campo to a small hill west of Casilha Bay. There they had a grandstand view of the steamship nudging the Druid as far as possible towards the muddy slope of the shore while the tide was coming in, so her guns could be brought to bear at a time when the junks on the other side would be beached and could not be swung into position to reply. Even so the batteries on the Barrier were still almost beyond the Druid's range at six hundred yards. The gunners on the Barrier were frantically manhandling their batteries to turn them towards the menace coming from such an unexpected quarter.

As Holly and Billy watched from their tower, Holly was staggered by the festive relish of the spectators crammed on hills and housetops to witness the grim dialogue about to begin between two deadly, opposing forces where men would be wounded, mutilated and killed.

But Billy could only rejoice, 'this crowd for once is barracking for us. They dread the thought of occupation by those soldiers poised on the other side of the Barrier. The presence of a body of soldiers is often the greatest annoyance that can befall any Chinese town or village with their rapine and looting.'

The Druid made last minute preparations for battle. Portholes opened. Guns run out. Decks cleared for action. By afternoon the barrage began - a hail of thirty two pounders till the guns of both batteries were hammered into silence and the Campo was swathed in smoke and dust. As splendid a spectacle as any watching crowd could desire. Not as colourful as fireworks to be sure but with much more satisfying explosions and smoke.

Boats carrying some hundred seamen from the Druid and Bengal volunteers from the Nazareth Shah stole on shore under the pall of the barrage to wrestle a field gun onto the beach, and drag it to a position where it could command the barrier wall and begin a second barrage. The defence lost heart. The Chinese soldiers, who had landed with a gun from the junks, ran from the temple on one side where Viceroy Lin had so recently been entertained, while the rest abandoned the defences of the Barrier on the other. By the time the British flag was planted on the Barrier wall, and the marines began to spike the guns and set fire to the Barracks, the field was abandoned.

Holly was bemused to see the spectators vanish as rapidly as if the first blast of a typhoon wind was about to strike Macao. 'Why rush away when the danger's past?'

'They expect the British troops to slaughter them next.'

'You swear that on the Bible?'

'I swear that on my knowledge of what the Chinese would do in the same circumstances. Go on the rampage. Satisfy their bloodlust. Which is why the Chinese soldiers dragged off their wounded as well as their dead.'

'What are they up to now Billy?' Holly pointed to some Chinese scuttling like crabs across the Campo towards the gate.

He peered for a moment, 'Well if that doesn't beat the band. They're salvaging the cannon balls for resale in Macao. Trust the Celestials to turn a dollar out of someone else's disaster.'

Captain Andrews had certainly made his message clear. He would tolerate no attack on Macao and would enforce his prohibition. The troops and junks disappeared. The magistrate in Heangshan was not so easily rebuffed and kept Faunce Wright in prison on Viceroy Lin's orders. Rumour said the Viceroy was seriously considering offering him as a sacrifice to the God of War, a rumour Holly was tempted to believe. The longer she remained in China, the more she was convinced anything was possible in this extraordinary country.

* * * * * *

Holly's Break for Freedom

'So,' Holly remarked when Flora had finished reading her Barron's letter sent, as she joked, by Her Majesty's North China mail service, 'Barron was right. Everything happened as he said it would.'

'That the Emperor didn't lay out a red carpet for them in Beijing? He did in a way, you know, a phantom red carpet.'

He had sent his ambassador, Chishan, to Tienjin who had entertained them in surroundings that were anything but ceremonial, a tent on a mudflat on the seashore, with the absolute minimum of formality. Chishan, an envoy of remarkable charm and tact, had persuaded both Sir Tryon and Commodore Brendan to turn back on the promise of continued negotiations in the south, thus saving immense face for both Chishan and the Emperor with adequate face for the British commanders who had, as Captain Forge had warned, found themselves in a hopeless strategic quandary.

'I can't see that kind of red carpet doing much good for Barron,' a wrathful Abby interjected, thankful she was about to leave the wranglings of the Coast behind for good. 'Not with the backstabbing press of Macao putting the blame on him, saying he's been conned for a right proper fool by Chihshan.'

'Written by his enemies, don't forget,' Flora reminded her, 'who choose to overlook the fact Commodore Brendan was demanding his troops, without one day's experience of fighting, force their way into Beijing across a hostile terrain against seasoned Tartar soldiers.'

'How I would love to have been a fly on the wall in his Great Cabin!'

'You'll be in the thick of the action when they come back.' Holly sighed in her eternal regret her sex denied her this chance.

'We know it will all end up in both sides blowing each other's brains out.'

Abby wondered, as she poured herself another cup of tea in this her last tete-a-tete with the very dear friends she was about to lose forever, whether China as she had known it could ever be the same for those, like her, who would arrive in later years.

Holly realised at that moment she had become like Maisie Macdonald. She had heard it all for so long now, she listened with no more shock than if their menfolk were talking about a day's shooting with the duck or snipe.

She drummed her fingers on the table as she announced, 'I'm renting the Jason to the navy for survey work on the approaches to the Yangtze River. Billy and I are going along for the ride.'

Flora and Abbey were outraged, chorusing. 'Uncharted waters!' 'Bristling with islands!' 'Pirates!'

'The Jason should be safe as houses with surveyors aboard. They'll be taking soundings every inch of the way. Any more objections?'

'Not so long as you don't go to Tinghae.'

Chusan Island had proved the disaster for the British Expeditionary Force Captain Forge had prophesied. The approach to its capital, Tinghae, down the estuary of a river with a bore on the change of tide worse than that of the Wye at Bristol. Rocks and reefs where the flagship, the 'Blenheim', had already run aground. Tinghae itself a death trap of dysentery, ague and fever. The countryside around a deadly region of kidnap and murder.

'The Jason's small and the draught shallow,' Holly insisted, 'we'll stand well out and go well stocked. I'm free to go right now and so is Billy. The season's over and very successfully too. If it'll console you I'll carry my sprig of holly against the gremlins. It'll be like a holiday.'

'I can see you have a new love, Holly, China. Just like Billy.' Abby asserted, confident she could read Holly like a book.

But she could not read Holly well enough to know that it was the old love for Sean Jarman that troubled Holly, and was driving her now to quit Macao with all its memories of him.   Yet there was truth in what Abby said. China was a love she might find it even more difficult to leave behind in the end than her love of Sean Jarman. If only she could have them both.

At first Billy had had to pretend an enthusiasm for the trip to the Yangtze River he did not altogether feel, doubting if it would be quite the holiday of Holly's imagination. Yet he could sympathise with Holly, cooped up for far too long in Macao and Hong Kong harbour while longing for new worlds to conquer. He himself would have preferred to wait for the outcome of the present confrontation rather than head into tacitly forbidden waters, the surveyors on board working too close to shore for comfort. But Holly argued that she wanted to blow the cobwebs of history out of her hair. It needed more than the Perpetual Feast of Hungry Ghosts to lay them to rest.

He had agreed in the end not entirely due to her arguments, but to his own curiosity about this little village on a mudflat near the mouth of the Yangtze river, Shanghai, that Howqua said was the future key to the northern trade. He had to decide for himself whether he was wrong in thinking that key would be turned in his lifetime on the Coast at such an exposed and vulnerable spot.

So it was that he found himself in a deck chair alongside Holly on the deck of the Jason as the willing vessel skimmed the ocean in the wake of another survey ship commanded by Captain Belcher. The fretted waters of the broad gateway of the Pearl River long left behind. The ships forging gently forward through the sloping combers of the open sea under a light but steady breeze, which promised to continue to judge by the fluffy open clouds drifting above in the sunfilled sky.

Holly lay contentedly beside him, her son reclining in her arms, all the baggage of grief and worry of the past two years shed the moment Macao vanished over the horizon. Moreover, she had no responsibility for the Jason on this voyage, Tough Wagoner's command now subordinate to that of Lieutenant Shrewsbury from the HMS Druid. The ship's role, as temporary member of Her Majesty's Navy, was signified by the two quarter deck guns and six marines aboard. She could savour the full joy of winging her way north on magic sails on a quest for some of the mysteries of which she had heard so long, just as her little son reached out to touch some of the magical secrets of rope and sail enticing him from her grasp.

They headed north to the archipelago of some hundreds of islands of assorted shapes and sizes - some conical, some like prows, some round as pebbles - that lay off the most eastern trend of the coast of China and enveloped the island of Chusan only eighty miles from the mouth of the Yangtze River. As they veered towards the capital Tinghae, the Jason battled to keep on course as she rode the waning tidal bore which had been the Blenheim's undoing in the gauntlet of reefs and shoals and spider webs of staked fishing nets.

At Tinghae, they were about to land to admire its picturesque Venetian style canals and picture book scenery at close hand, when the British commandant warned Lieutenant Shrewsbury to leave on the next tide. Tinghae was a charnel house. Anyone who lingered to savour its deadly charms would die as the soldiers were in their scores.

Holly, distraught to learn the emerald island was a whited sepulchre, grieved for 'those poor men dying so horribly so far from home. If only the Commodore had listened to Barron Forge.'

Billy was cryptic. 'Jarman should have told them back Home. He's a doctor.'

Holly was willing to give him the benefit of the doubt. 'His ships never landed long enough to learn.' She lingered at the rail watching Chusan's siren hills, that had beckoned so many to their doom, dwindle astern.

'The locals would believe it's the retribution of Heaven for the conquest.'

Tough Wagoner loomed up beside them. 'The Lootenant told me the locals didn't leave it to the gods to mete out that retribution.'

'What on earth do you mean, Tough?'

'Several soldiers were seized and carried off when they went sight-seeing. One of them, Captain Anstruther, while he was surveying the land thereabouts. No one can find out if they've been killed or not. The word is the Commandant tried to freeze the town. Suddenly funeral processions leaving the town everywhere. When he twigged, Ma'am, he found those huge coffins, they have hanging around years before they're dead, were filled with anything but corpses. Silk, antiques, valuables. All they feared could be looted by us barbarians.'

Soon the farce of the occupation of Chusan Island lay far behind. They skimmed along, the weather as fine and fair as any they had had on the journey. The Jason ran briskly, all sails set, across a translucent sea. Not a sign of land from horizon to horizon, the great Yangtze River, longest river in the world, coming closer with each hour.

Holly lay somnolent in a deckchair in the warm glow of the afternoon sun while her son slept in the cabin below, anticipating no more danger than a tourist on the Mediterranean. The innocent sunlight was like a benediction on her closed eyes, as she wondered if she would ever make the two hundred mile journey up the Yangtze River to Nankin and one day see that seventh wonder of the world, the white porcelain pagoda with its nine terraces of tinkling bells.

The next moment, all the thrusting power of the Jason came to a shuddering, grinding halt, her solid structure shaking as though an earthquake had risen from the sea. Yet the sea was still. She heeled as if turned on her side by the leverage of a whale or a great rock, her masts and sails transformed from her glory to her disaster as their sinking weight dragged her hull upwards, and their own now lethal structures downwards to the surface of the water.

The last thing Holly saw, as she pitched out of her chair and slid irresistibly towards the ship's rail, was Billy thrusting through the bulkhead doorway to dash below to the rescue of their baby son. She was caught on the rail for a moment, but, as the angle became sharper and the rail dipped under the chilly sea, she fell face forward into the water, where each wave, that broke on the hull and tangle of masts and rigging, created a rough turbulence that slapped the stinging salt spray in her eyes and mouth.

She found enough purchase on unseen timbers below to right herself and grip the end of a spar rearing out of the water. To her despair, she could see the cabin where her baby had slept now plunged deep below the water. She could not, if she would, struggle back on board and up the vertical deck to look for her lost child and husband. She felt like screaming as so many others around her were, then like letting her hold go to drift away until she slipped exhausted down into the oblivious deep. How could she live knowing she had brought Billy to his death for a child he believed his own?

At last in continual torment from the salt spray of the remorseless waves with no sign of life from the submerged hull, she asked what Billy would have wanted and knew the answer. She must save herself. She struggled agonisingly across the tangle of rope and canvas, aware that others were doing the same with useless cries for help. She lost her grip once as a wave sent her under and floundered choking, tangled in the rigging, before she caught hold of one of the iron bars that held a lifeboat to the quarter deck.

As she prayed, 'Almighty God, save my husband and child,' she heard a voice hail her from some distance, 'steady on, Mrs. Howe!' It was the Lieutenant. 'We've freed a boat from the davits. Can you swim?'

'Yes!' she shouted back, 'if I get rid of my skirt.'

Her skirt, praise be, was a simple garment tied at the waist, not one of these elaborate bell-shaped affairs buttoned at the waist affected by so many women these days. The weighty serge gone, she could swim sidestroke, her face turned away from the sharp salt sting of the surging breakers to the boat which rode low, swamped with water. She hooked one foot over the gunwale. The men already there dragged her in and then shoved off, although she begged them to wait a little longer in case of survivors. But the water was already up to the thwarts and the tiny craft shipping more with every wave.

'Ma'am I know how horrible it is for you, but we can't save those who are beyond saving. Stay here any longer and we'll be in the drink as surely as God made little apples.'

He cut the rope as he spoke. The current took hold and swept the boat away. Holly screamed over and over then, straining to identify the faces of the crew still clinging to the upper side of the stricken vessel. Not one among them her Billy.

Although the Lieutenant threw the boat's little kedger out, while he and the mate bailed out, the dinghy soon drifted away until the Jason, which now lay low on the reef where it had been wrecked, soon disappeared from sight. Holly sat numb, shivering even in the sunlight, unable to understand how all one's dearest hopes and love could be overturned in one dreadful second. She had read often enough of the catastrophe of shipwreck. Never had she understood the terrible truth of those stories. The steady stability of a ship lost in an instant. The drift without food and water. In her case, the added misery of knowing it was she, who had insisted Billy come north, she who was responsible for his death.

She rocked in silent grief, watching the tidal race of water rushing by like a wall on either side of the boat with its poignant freight of debris from the wreck. Her agony grew worse when the turn of the tide swept them back towards it until she could see the survivors still clinging in a grim cluster to the Jason's maintop shouting desperately for help. They struggled with hands and pieces of board to paddle their half-empty lifeboat closer to the Jason which must soon disappear into the deep below. But they could only come within hailing distance to urge them to build a lifeboat.

Twice more during the next day and night, the lifeboat washed in closer to the Jason in the implacable rhthym of the sea, only to be washed away again. On each occasion, they came within earshot but no further, a prolonged torment that left Holly suffering each time they came close to the last visible remnant of the wreck that was the coffin of her husband and child. When dark came she sat bolt upright, despite the Lieutenant's pleadings, gazing blankly at a moonlight of such lyrical beauty she could only wonder how the same God could create such glory and such black tragedy.

She had never thought to experience such desolation of mind and tragedy. She might have been able to bear her grief more easily if she had been able to put Billy and little Jason to rest herself with the proper sacrament of the church in a known plot of ground instead of losing them forever in a blank desert of water! How could she ever find the place of their burial again to offer any prayer for their salvation?

The Lieutenant consoled her, arm around her shoulders. 'Depend on it, Mrs. Howe, some of them could have been picked up by a passing boat. One could turn up.' Not that one single sail had been seen this past week.

'I wish I had died with them.'

'You must believe God has preserved you for some special purpose.'

'I could not thank my Maker for that.'

'Then just trust in Him, Mrs. Howe. I will stand by you.'

Holly cried herself to exhaustion against his chest. Then she was contrite. God had at least sent her this kind young man to lend her strength in her extremity. He was unafraid although they had no food, no water, no sail.

On the fourth day, a choppy water broke over the gunwales with such violence they seemed likely to sink. The Lieutenant knelt to pray with Holly to ask for God's protection although the mate muttered he did not think letting the ship sink was much of a mercy.

Holly rebuked him, 'we don't have anything else but God to put their faith in.'

When the sea calmed down by dusk they teased the mate that God had heard them.

If Holly was grateful for anything by now, it was not that she had lived, when so many had drowned or been stranded to face a living death, but that the Lieutenant had spared her the embarrassment of her situation as much as he could. The shreds of her dignity, and sense of fellow suffering for the men in the boat with her, had caused her to recover her balance. In spirit, she wore dustcloth and ashes, longing to rip her clothes, tear her hair, and utter hear-rending wails. She was all unaware the worst of her physical suffering lay ahead, and the rescue for which she prayed to God would elude her for some time.

At first it seemed as if God had heard their prayer when the waters calmed down, and a junk hove in sight. They had no sense of panic or fear when its captain took them aboard, nor when he cast them off in a canal leading from the sea with a handful of boiled rice each. They laid down tranquilly enough on the verge for yet another restless night in soaking garments shivering with cold. Next morning they went begging for food with sign language answered by nods and smiles at first, so they trustingly followed the most persistently beckoning guide to a temple.

They began to grow alarmed only when a crowd gathered around, plucking at their clothes and features with ribald laughter like birds pecking at seed. Not a morsel of food to be seen. Not one kindly face. They became uneasy, pushed their way out through the crowd with difficulty to hurry back to the shore followed by the mocking, shouting mob. Before they reached their only hope of escape, a large armed troop, led by a mandarin, cut them off. The soldiers pinioned them by their arms and locked heavy chains round their necks, jostling them cruelly and whipping them with rattan sticks if they struggled. Even Holly, who clenched her teeth to stop herself crying out. Never let it be said the flowery land demons were cowards.

'God forgive these savages, Holly, to treat a woman so,' the Lieutenant cried in anguish.

She bit back her feelings. He needed courage for himself in their ominous plight, let alone her. She assayed a joke, as Billy would have done, when their captors jerked at their chains to make them start walking. 'I've always wondered how performing bears felt!'

The Lieutenant managed a wry smile. 'They'll have us jumping through flaming hoops next.'

Holly had strength of mind enough left to hold her peace on what she knew of the fate of those unlucky enough to be caught in the north; a fate all too likely to be theirs to judge by the threatening throngs screaming 'dogmen' as they were marched into the town. By the time they reached a temple to be locked up for the night she was even grateful for the guard of soldiers. There had been moments when she felt the mob might tear them to pieces. Overwhelmed with hunger and despair, she did not resist as a soldier thrust her into a necklock upright against the wall. But she screamed and fought when he wrenched the golden wedding band from her left hand. The only thing saved from the wreck, the dear pledge of her husband's affection, was gone. All except one thing she suddenly remembered with relief, Chung Tai Tai's amulet around her neck.

She lay back too exhausted to weep as though she had passed some Rubicon of her own. Somehow she was no longer afraid to die and could therefore fight to live.

Her two bearers let her cage crash to the ground for the last time in a small dirty cell of a Ningpo prison. They lifted her out weak from starvation, dishevelled and dirty from mud flung at her by hostile crowds, and dumped her like a sack on the grimy floor. They left her to wonder miserably how she could possibly survive with a bleak wind whistling through the gaps in the roof and gratings in the walls with no comforts of any kind, and no furniture but for an almost derelict table and stool. Very well then, she would summon what little fortitude she had, remembering the old cliche of her youth while there's life, there's hope.

She knelt at the table and, hands clasped over its cracked, gouged edge, she gave thanks to God her terrible journey seemed to be over. She had been forced to walk with her fellow captives many miles for ten long days, dragged along like a dog by the chain round her neck. Then she had been kept bent double in her cage like a pig going to market. She had had little food and less sleep. She had endured being taunted and reviled, spat upon and spattered with mud, serenaded by howls, shrieks and catcalls every yard of the journey. She would have welcomed death many times.

Yet now the journey was over, she wept for the first time not from despair but from guilt. If only she had not persuaded Billy to go on the journey, over-confident their fleet was in control of these waters, over-willing to adopt Billy's own regard for a people he had understood and loved so well. She should have remembered Barron Forge's warning that any invasion of Chusan Island could turn the people against them.

As she drifted off in a merciful sleep of exhaustion, she experienced a moment of revelation. Billy, if anyone, would have understood the sagacity at the heart of the gospel, that no man can decide his own fate, lay in acceptance of its decree however harsh.

But she found acceptance impossible after all when she saw her comprador, Pu Ping Pang, carried into the prison yard, trussed up and hanging upside down from a pole like a pig as an awful warning to any other Chinese who would have 'traitorous connections' with foreign devils, to be released and thrust in the next cell now the public show was over. Yet even he proved to be a blessing. He told her that Tough Wagoner had also survived being picked up like himself from further up the coast than she. For the first time she felt joy that two of her most loyal servitors had survived the wreck, and hope that they all might emerge from their desperate situation safely in the end.

Tough's reappearance was the one true miracle in her life. He gently put an end to rumours from those rescued with him by a passing junk as she had been as they sat talking through the tiny grating between them day in and out. They were only saying so out of charity for her misery.

'Just like the Chows saying what they think you want to hear.'

She fought to put Billy's ghost where he would have chosen for himself, looking over her shoulder with a chuckle.

'Do you think Captain Forge can do anything to save us?'

'Everything in his power to do, he will.'

'What can he do when we're so far away?' She could not imagine any force being sent to their rescue.

'Use us for a bargain maybe.'

'Are we worth anything Tough?'

'Only so long as an Expeditionary Force is hanging about off the coast. If Captain Forge finds out we're prisoners in Ningpo he would threaten reprisals if a hair of our head is touched.'

In Holly's heart, she doubted if any threat of Barron's would carry much weight. Their life and death counted for little. American citizens not British. On a American ship hired by the British but sailing at their own risk. All they could do was wait, and see if charity would prevail though she doubted it as the aristos must have doubted it in the French Revolution, waiting for the grim verdict in their forbidding cells.

Mostly she and Tough talked about what they would do when they returned home. Tough longed to get married, but found no girls wanted a man running off to sea for months at a time.

'She could run with you,' Holly said hopefully.

'Not everyone is like you, Ma'am,' was his wistful answer.

Neither of them spoke of her future as a widow. Would she ever marry again? In her solitary hours, she wondered if it were possible. She had committed her love twice. She was only certain of three things. She would stay in China. She would remain in business. She would buy a second ship to replace the Jason perhaps even own a fleet one day as Chung Tai Tai once had.

* * * * * *

To make War or not to make War

All six weeks the formidable British fleet had remained at anchor just outside the Bogue- no less than three majestic 84 gun first-raters, overlords of a sizeable assembly of second and third raters as well as transports- their commanders had been critical of Captain Forge's insistence on patience during his protracted negotiations with the Emperor's Special Envoy, Chishan. It was a patience they were obliged to exercise since he was the Plenipotentiary in charge, even though they believed Chishan was playing ducks and drakes with him. His treaty, if any, would be a phantom, and no one would care whether he had followed an honourable course either now or in the eyes of history.

Captain Forge was well aware neither Commodore Brendan, nor any of the officers, understood his reasons for tolerance of Chishan's dodges and prevarications. He knew they inclined more with each passing week to sympathise with the merchants' vociferous view that he Forge was a weak and ineffectual Plenipotentiary who dragged Britain's honour through the mud with his spineless and servile delays. The merchants should have known better. They, of all people, stood to gain everything by prolonging the truce, by the hand in the velvet glove, by keeping the port open to clear the season's merchandise.

Their patience, the commanders said, had run out. They must, and would, attack the Bogue forts and teach the Lord of Ten Thousand Islands that His Majesty's Britannic government was not to be trifled with. Its power was not that of a barbarian slave state paying tribute, but the government of an equal civilised power. And at last Captain Forge had agreed that signal 'prepare for action' be sent round the fleet forthwith. However he could not share in their rejoicing for sad amusement to think the enthusiasm of every man Jack in the fleet was not because of any desire for peace and goodwill as the Bible exhorted, but because of a commandment to war.

The commanders themselves had to sanction one more delay to celebrate Christmas day. As the sun rose on Christmas morning, the uproar in that extensive flotilla had nothing to do with the imminent battle. The Jack Tars, lining the rails with their cheers and yells and whistles, were trying to attract the attention of the tardy providoring boats of Hooker and Lane arriving with supplies for the Christmas dinner - prime buffalo roasts, crates of Hodgson's best brown ale, plum puddings with all the trimmings, nuts and raisins, and the best brandy to set puddings aflame. Everyone fearful that Hooker and Lane's supplies might run out before the boats reached them.

The fleet's officers sat down to a Christmas dinner that would have done any London club proud. 'A feast fit for the little Queen herself!' Old Brendan in jolly mood as he downed it with several glasses of rich brown ale and enthusiastic toasts to victory.

Only Admiral Sir Tryon Forge was regretful. The ship assigned to take him to Calcutta for the first leg of a long pilgrimage home, was to leave the next day. And this Christmas was likely to be his last not merely in the Orient but on earth if the pain that seized his heart so often continued. 'Revenge of the East', his surgeon had said. 'These confounded tropical scourges weaken the heart.'

As he surveyed the other officers of Her Majesty's government singing tunefully at the table in the Grand Cabin, he marvelled that his country had had such good fortune in its hour of crisis as to throw up such a sensitive, adroit man as Barron Forge with the good sense to practice both diplomacy and war with indigenous officials on their own terms as Clive of India had so successfully done. How untimely the misfortune that dictated his departure at the moment when Barron most needed his support.

'Well, what now?' He asked Barron as they paced the deck to the distant sounds of lusty singing far more raucous than their own Captain's well-trained tenor.

Barron Forge pointed to the forts ahead. 'So far. No further.'

Even Sir Tryon was startled by that pronouncement. 'Our esteemed Commander-in-Chief will never agree to a minor skirmish.'

'He must and you will persuade him, Tyron.'

'I don't understand why you're holding back even now.'

'The hostages have not been released from Ningpo yet, Tryon.'

'Surely they're not in any danger?'

Sir Tryon had heard that Barron had been able to arrange for letters and supplies to be sent from Chusan to make them more comfortable and there was every hope of negotiating their release. Unfortunate about that American woman, Mrs. Howe, of course. But to hold up the battle plan of an Expeditionary Force for a woman even if she was a friend of Forge. Why that was quite unheard of.

'Tryon, they are now under sentence of death from Pekin. The moment our guns fire on these forts, we make their death more certain.'

'Barron,' Sir Tryon protested, ignoring the pain that tightened in his chest, 'you, yourself, told me that hostages have generally been returned in good shape, albeit with some trouble.'

Barron pressed his argument despite the stress written on his cousin's drawn features. He had no other ally of value. ' I also told you it could not last. Times have changed. Beijing is in the mood to teach us a lesson. Therefore I fear for these hostages.'

'Is your intelligence reliable?'

'Barron Forge stared across the water at the challenge of those forts, as frustrated as Tryon. Yes his intelligence was reliable. Kaida had brought the news from Viceroy Lin's yamen to John Norris, who had repeated the ominous words with a terrible anguish on his sorrowful countenance.

'The Emperor has sent a new governor to the province to see that Holly and the rest are sent to Beijing as rebel subjects, where their fate is to be the lingering death before the Emperor himself. They say he is very partial to seeing rebels suffer the torment he believes they deserve.'

John was the only one among them all who had witnessed that most hideous of all deaths and the inexpressible suffering of a victim.

'Surely not Holly?' Barron had asked.

'Her most of all. They think she is sister to the Queen of England and will without doubt flay her alive. They are not merciful to enemy monarchs.'

Barron Forge spared no detail for Tryon. 'The condemned is not simply a passive victim in the vicious mockery of his own death. He is forced to take part in a terrible lottery. Confined in a wire mesh straitjacket, he faces a basket of exquisitely sharpened knives, each numbered for an equivalent part of the body. The key to those numbers is unknown to the victim. As he calls the numbers so the knives are drawn and the torture governed. You see the Chinese are in every essential gamblers.'

Sir Tryon was scandalised into silence. How could Barron say these people were as highly civilised as themselves?

Barron continued, 'If I let that happen imagine the furore. The Black Hole of

Calcutta would fade into insignificance. Imagine the demand for armies to land, for revenge to be slaked in Beijing.'

'There'd be no end to it,' Sir Tryon agreed appalled. 'Do I understand you're telling me our Expeditionary Force is in fact held to ransom to save those few prisoners that awful death?'

'I am. We can't do more than threaten Chishan till he sees those prisoners are back in our hands.'

'Meanwhile the threat we have over him is these two forts, no more?'

'Exactly.' Barron looked gloomily out over the restive fleet.

'What chance do you have of prevaiing with Chishan?'

'Every chance. Chishan, once one of the most powerful men in China, has fallen out of favour with the court. I can help him restore his fortunes by making him an offer too tempting for him to refuse; the chance to tell Pekin he has persuaded me to return the island of Chusan to China in exchange for the prisoners.'

'Return Chusan! There'll be a howl to high heaven after the men we've lost to capture it.'

'What about the waste of men to keep it, Tryon? There'll be less of a howl if both of us agree.'

Sir Tryon shifted his ground. 'It was one of the stated objectives of our campaign.'

'It was one of the grosser follies of those who drew up the plan of the campaign.'

'I'm the one who must argue your case when I go home.'

'Then tell them how our soldiers looted and got drunk in Chusan even after Commodore Brendan ordered all the liquour tipped into the drains. Tell them how we lived in a state of siege in Tinghae. Far better that we demand Hong Kong in return for Chusan.'

'Which they mock as a useless island.'

'All the better I say. Few inhabitants. No city. No chance of any man who stirs outside the city walls being killed as happened in Tinghae.'

Sir Tryon eased himself painfully onto a bollock. 'So you have your truce. You get your prisoners back. You get the cargoes loaded and headed for home. Then tell me what will our Expeditionary Force have accomplished for all its effort and expense other than to restore trade to the position it enjoyed before we came?'

'We'll have Hong Kong. A base to store our goods. A harbour to call our own.'

'I have to admire your fortitude as Trade Superintendent. Fighting the merchants every inch of the way.'

'For all their snarls that pack of curs will be the first to shoulder each other aside to buy land and build their warehouses in case I might happen to be right.'

'They'll never agree unless you take the war to Canton and that will be one hell of a war.'

'You've forgotten the Nemesis captained by my old friend, Roger Hall, Tryon. She'll be here by that time. All our instant strategic experts forget one salient fact. Without the Nemesis, we can't fight this war at all. Our Nemesis will be theirs with her five foot draft and her Congreve rockets.'

Sir Tryon nodded his agreement. Every officer on all of the ships had his theory about how the war should be fought. But most were bred like himself to strategies that had won the Napoleonic War, naval strategies evolved in the open sea. None of them had any experience of a sneaking war in the watery maze of a large river delta where sailing ships could be so easily trapped by baffling winds, no winds at all, or grounded by shoals and sandbanks. Helpless before fire rafts and surprise night attacks. Prisoners of a region whose rice paddies were as deadly as the Dutch lowlands to any land campaign.

Sir Tryon regarded his younger cousin regretfully. 'Good luck, Barron. You'll need it. I feel as if I'm abandoning you to play Daniel in the lion's den.' The sweep of his hand encompassed the whole fleet. 'But just one piece of advice. Let our sainted Commander-in-Chief be the one to plant the flag on Hong Kong. I suggest you find urgent business elsewhere that day.'

He put out his hand. Barron took it in both his own. The two golden heads drew closer to each other, the hair of one thinner and flecked with grey, the other with all the golden burnish of a youth not quite lost still upon it.

'I'll miss you more than I can say. May God go with you!'

Commodore Brendan could not believe Admiral Kuan had sent him a flag of truce with an old woman and man in a tiny boat. Was this his measure of 'loss of face' after the spectacular defeat of his fleet with eighteen Chinese war junks sunk or damaged, forts silenced and reduced to near rubble, and a massive Chinese casualty list compared to their own?

'I thought you said the higher the rank the more the show, Captain,' Commodore Brendan grumbled with the emphasis on Captain Forge's lesser rank to his own.

Captain Forge ignored the slight. 'Admiral Kuan doesn't need to prove his rank. Not as direct descendant of the God of War himself.'

Commodore Brendan scratched at his beard, disconcerted, 'I'll never understand these people.'

'Just understand they are highly civilised people.'

Commondore Brendan spent the next three hours arguing with Captain Forge before he would accept the flag of truce. He wanted to continue into the Bogue, now his men and ships were primed, and demolish the other six Bogue forts so irresistibly within his grasp.

Captain Forge thumped the table insisting, 'I am under orders to use maximum restraint in the use of military force.'

'And I am under orders to do the opposite - to use military force to gain all the objectives for which we came. Have we got the indemnity for the opium, the apology to yourself or any one of the concessions in dispute? Or only the right to negotiate with the old fox again?'

The set of Captain Forge's jaw was stubborn. 'I will make peace if I can.'

'Peace will not be permanent if you make it now.'

'I need peace right now, Commodore. For the next four months at least.'

'Peace to their profit. Time for them to strengthen their defences, amass more troops, throw in more junks.' The arguments were stale.

Captain Force conceded their justice. 'They will bring seasoned troops from three provinces, I know,' he said wearily. He too had heard troops were being brought in from Szechwan, Hopeh and Kweichou. 'None the less these four months are months we desperately need. You saw the petition from the merchants complaining they bear an intolerable burden of costs and demurrage so long as they are blocked from the port. They must be able to get in and out of port now, not later in the season. Three million pounds worth of cargo is waiting to be unloaded in the roads and more is on the way.'

But Commodore Brendan was a bluff, blunt tough officer whose sole business was war, 'as sole Plenipotentiary you must contiue to hold the strong bargaining position we have given you to force the treaty we were ordered to obtain. Anything less and how will you account to the Foreign Secretary in the future?'

'Commodore, I have to face the merchants today. I'm their Trade Superintendent. These merchants represent a huge slice of Crown revenue in tea tax, a tax that helps to pay for this very force. Will Palmerston pay that out of his own pocket if Canton remains a closed port for the rest of the season?'

If Commodore Brendan thought he was sorry he was wrong. Seven years in this vineyard was enough. He could not in all conscience use this engine of war against any crowded city of innocent citizens, let alone one the size of Canton. Not on the issue of opium. Equal rights yes but not opium. Let someone else wear that crown of thorns on his head.

Commodore Brendan continued to argue through lunch and beyond, growing more vehement the more rum he quaffed. 'We should follow up our advantage and run through Canton.'

Had the Commodore been deaf all these months? 'And get ourselves bottled up on the river?'

'We've proved our shells and rockets a weapon they can't resist.'

'You've also proved some will resist to the death.' As they had in Chuenpi fort when surrounded on all sides, hurling themselves from the battlements to drown, seeking suicide rather than the death they expected from surrender.

'We should give Canton a taste of our guns.'

Captain Forge groaned inwardly. Lord Nash all over again. 'Commodore, not one vessel could get within 11 miles of Canton.'

'We have our troops.' The Commodore in a mood to be obtuse.

Captain Forge contained his rising impatience with difficulty. 'Where can they land? Slapbang into a maze of rice paddies? The swarming residential areas of the riverfront of Canton?'

They wrangled longest about the return of the Bogue forts, Commodore Brendan shouting outraged, 'thirty eight men wounded to win them and you want to give them back?'

'I must give them back to allow Chishan to recover face.'

Captain Forge rose and paced across the cabin to study the barometer. Good weather ahead! 'With due respect, you have forgotten they hold the survivors of the Jason hostage.'

'The surrender of Chusan should suffice to safeguard them.'

'He won't sign if you don't surrender the Bogue forts.'

'Too high a price to pay,' Commodore Brendan was admanant, his face even redder from restraining his volatile temper.

'The crew of the Jason won't think so.'

'What about our dead when we have to take the forts all over again in the face of fresh troops, fresh fortifications?'

'Chishan is as anxious for peace as I am. He knows we will defeat him in battle.'

'How long will his truce prevail?' Commodore Brendan was sceptical. The mood of Pekin was belligerent.

'Long enough to save the prisoners at Ningpo,' Captain Forge said grimly knowing Commodore Brendan weighed those few too light in the scales of justice and would never understand the subtleties of his diplomacies when he made a treaty with Chishan as he proposed to do.

* * * * * *

The Rescue of Holly

When Holly was summoned to the House of Chun, Prefect of Ningpo, for a banquet so lavish she could hardly eat after weeks with little or no food, it was Pu Ping Pang who translated her answers to Chun's persistent questions about Her Majesty's Government, the British Expeditionary Force and the income and ranks of its officers - questions as foolish as those of ignorant Europeans on their first arrival in China.

Holly found it difficult to restrain her mirth. They had been treated worse than creatures intended for slaughter in the prison. They had been living in filth like beasts for weeks. They had been carried to the banquet in cages like performing animals. They had been cleaned up and dressed in Chinese costumes to make them fit to appear at the banquet. They had been treated with honour and ceremonial as if ambassadors. And now she was summoned once again to appear before a mandarin newly arrived from Beijing.

For weeks, she had hesitated to produce the jade amulet Chung Tai Tai had given her for any time of trouble. For what trouble and where? Trouble in Fukien as well as in Kwangtung? Perhaps it would get her into trouble in Fukien, not out of it. She discussed it with Pu Ping Pang who had no answer. She saw no desperate need to take the risk until Pu Ping Pang was distraught about talk he had overheard that the mandarins proposed to send her to Beijing. He warned her this could mean the lingering death, sparing her no detail of what this would mean. She was horrified. Who would ever imagine becoming a victim of such a cruel and vicious custom oneself? But what could she do? Who could come to her rescue? No one of her own. No one, it dawned on her, but a Chinese official. What had Chung Tai Tai said to her an age ago, this amulet will save your life if it ever comes to that. She had laughed at the time but it had come to that. But where could she show it? To whom?

Perhaps now was the time, she decided as she was paraded before them in 'fancy dress' as she thought of it. Her fingers strayed, as if nervously, from the clasps on the ornamental Chinese jacket to the modest amulet scarcely visible in the dazzle of embroidery - a symbol that could only have meaning to an initiate. Meaning she saw at once to Prefect Chu, whose eyes were drawn to it and kept straying back. When his guests left at last, he commanded her to be brought back to him with Pu Ping Pang, and demanded to see the amulet. When she refused to hand it over to him, he made no move to force her, merely asking her to come closer and turning it over so he could read the writing on the back. He looked up sharply, his tone in sharp contrast to his usual urbanity.

'Where did you get this?'

'In Macao from the Pirate Queen.'

A flash of surprise in his eyes that a white woman had been honoured as a member of the brotherhood. 'Why did she give it to you?'

'She owed me a debt. She said it would protect me in time of trouble.'

As soon as she had left Prefect Chun sank into gloom. who should he believe - his own officers who swore Holly's ship had been an opium ship, or her sailors who swore it was only a survey ship making maps of equal use to China? Was it against the law for them to make soundings as far out as they had been from the coast? He could not put the question to Pekin for fear of being berated as an incompetent fool? He was certain of only one thing - he did not fear a rebuke from Pekin so much as revenge from Chung Tai Tai. He had no doubt her revenge could reach so far. He shivered at the thought. He knew the pirates' reputation.

He sent the fanqui back to their cells, and sat distracted through two opium pipes before he made a decision. Captain Forge was said to be in Chusan Island even now negotiating the early release of the prisoners. Very well! He would protect his rear. He lifted a small drumstick from the black japanned table beside him, and tapped the small suspended gong delicately with his round padded head. His secretary padded swiftly in and bowed low before him. He gave his orders decisively. The prisoners were to be moved into more comfortable quarters. He sent Pu Ping Pang to Tinghae in Chusan in answer to a fire-express request for their release from Envoy Chishan in Canton. But he warned Pu Ping Pang he must return or the prisoners would be killed. He did not warn Pu Ping Pang he intended to keep him as sacrifice to the bloodlust of Beijing for revenge. He must have one victim at least.

The reform in arrangements was not quite as pleasing for Holly as he supposed. They sent her an old crone for company who drove her to distraction by incessant mumbling and scratching. The bed that was supposed to make her more comfortable was as ancient and filthy as the old crone. And she was separated from Tough Wagoner. She fought against despair. She felt as a monk must, when he has renounced the world to live in a tiny cell, his wants reduced to nothing but the charity of bread, the compass of his world, prayer for salvation from any vice, any desire. Bare walls for austere needs. Joy in the smallest things - a bird picking at seeds, an insect crawling over the concrete floor, a leaf in flight past her window.

She scrutinised her past without the distracting bustle of a fleet around her. If she survived, did she want to go on floating on the tide of Imperial expansion and accept the bad with the good? Should she simply regard it all as the irredeemable lunacy of the world as Billy had, living as a jester on the edge of a vast cosmic joke? Should she simply see opium smoking as irrepressible as whisky or gin drinking in the British Isles? She knew only what she could not do, and that was regard herself as an evangelist bringing enlightenment to heathen darkness.

The news that Pu Ping Pang brought back at last seemed grim at first. The British had formally handed Chusan back to China and were busy evacuating Tinghae. She felt Barron had abandoned her, and her amulet had failed in its promised magic. However, it was working better than she knew. Prefect Chun had already signed orders for them all to be escorted back to Tinghae, all but Pu Ping Pang himself. The last British transport would wait until they arrived.

When Pu told her sadly he would be left behind because his work for foreign devils had now been judged a crime, her voice broke with remorse.

'Why did you return then, Pu? Why didn't you stay in Tinghae.'

'Because I was hostage for you.'

Holly was aghast at this devil's bargain. 'I will negotiate for you, Pu. I will demand you join me. Just give me time.'

She did not know she had no time. A vengeful Yihshan arrived in Ningpo from Beijing only two days after they had gone, bent on consigning them all and her in particular to a lingering death. He had vented his frustration and anger on the wretched Pu Ping Pang inflicting that death on him instead.

She felt overborne with guilt by the time she returned to Macao. For Pu Ping Pang's terrible death, for Barron's unpopularity with the merchants because he had strung out negotiations with Chishan until she was safe thereby earning almost universal scorn, even for the news Barron broke gently that Sean Jarman had lost his wife in childbirth because Sean had been the ghost looking over her other shoulder in Ningpo.

* * * * * *

The Nemesis to the Rescue

The iron-hulled steamship, Nemesis, arrived in Macao at length. An untried ship of experimental construction, she had made a heroic pioneering journey round the Cape. She had survived one of those ferocious storms off the east coast of Africa, which struck without warning. Under the fierce battering ram of the sea, she had begun to split amidships, the crack yawning to a terrifying five feet at the rim. Her crew had struggled to bolt plates over the gap in the raging storm and limp onwards until they could effect repairs at Calcutta. They had proved the Admiralty wrong in their belief that this steamship with its cumbersome side paddlewheels and shallow, flat hull could ever survive a hostile sea.

No one in the cheering crowd on the Praya Grande that greeted the ship knew or cared she had just performed one of the great voyages of history. They simply saw her as an exciting novelty which terrified them briefly, as she ran close enough inshore along the embankment for her crew almost to touch the outstretched hands of onlookers. She had fired her bow and stern guns in salute as she churned by and the guns in the three forts above had roared their reply.

Captain Forge had his own private moment of triumph when he stood in the wheelhouse beside her captain, his old friend Roger Hall, while she pounded her way towards the Bogue, and recited the curious dramas that had already taken place there: the bone-headed entry of Lord Nash, the burning of the opium, the smoke and blood-ridden battle that won them the Chuenpi Convention. All had led inexorably to this moment when they had won the right to surge through the narrow passage of the Bogue past the forts manned by unarmed Tiger Braves and unprimed guns and decked by a rash of flags where there had been nothing but deadly cannon, jingal and musket fire only three short weeks before. This was the right to rendezvous in the river with the Emperor's Envoy to ratify the first treaty in history between their great nations.

Captain Hall decided to repeat the practical joke that had thrown Macao into confusion saying 'I'll scare them with a little fire-wheel ship magic.' He swung round to bear down on them until his yardarms almost touched their bastions, knowing as well as Captain Forge did the apparition of the huge eyes painted Chinese fashion on his bows scared them as much as the daring manouvre of the strange fire-wheel demon ship. At last even Captain Forge protested, 'you're scaring me as well.' He did not fancy being wrecked just now, not since Viceroy Lin had put such a high price on his head, more if he were dead than alive.

As the Nemesis churned its way upriver, Captain Forge exulted in the sense of freedom conferred by the power of those giant engines, hissing and thumping below, instead of sails above; in the emancipation from the tedious necessity to tack back and forth in the changing hazards of river shoals. What a blessed miracle this steamship was! Ugly perhaps, as some said, but with no complications of rope or canvas. No eternal need of repair of torn sails. No one aloft in peril of their very lives with every change of sails. Auxiliary sailing masts, it was true, but mere stumps compared to those of the 'Blenheim'. No vulnerability to adverse wind or tide. No masterly tricks of timing for going about. On the positive side, the most perfect control in that most dread disaster of the sea, going aground. He could understand utterly why his friend had committed his career to steam all those years ago.

Captain Forge caught sight of a man on a treadmill, patiently turning its chain of buckets to sluice a rivulet of water to the now-dry fields. Strange to think genius was so elusive in mankind, it had taken many centuries to learn how to transmit that principle of energy without the donkey labour of man; a principle so simple that once any man saw a Watts engine and knew how it was born of a homely kitchen kettle, he would marvel ever after why no one had ever thought of it before, or why it was invented first for the improbable reason of draining a mine and not driving a ship. History was such a story of whys. Why industrial revolution in one country like Britain? Why stupor in another like China? China in the age of the treadmill still, a sleeping giant slow to change under the dead hand of the Manchus and mandarins. England, by comparison, a convulsion of change transformed by the magic hand of its ironmasters.

Captain Hall had no thought for the imponderables of history. His questions were all for the present. Why were there no maps of the Pearl River delta? Why had no commander of the many ships that visited the river annually over the centuries never been prompted to explore the passages of the delta that opened up on either side from time to time? Were they never bored or curious where they led?'

Captain Forge answered without hesitation. 'No ship could enter without a river pilot. Their orders from the Hoppo were very strict. No other passage but this, the main branch.'

'And no commander ever flouted his decree?'

'Roger, any man who strayed off the beaten path went in fear of his life. The whole of this delta is a natural smugglers' lair. The long arm of the law in this province doesn't reach into its tangled ways. Given all that, would you go exploring?'

Captain Hall gazed reflectively at a beckoning arm of the river. He would not have entered in a small boat as sailing ship men would have had to do, but he would in the 'Nemesis'. He would dearly love to have a shot at it.

Captain Forge for once had no preoccupation with such tricky strategic questions. He felt a sense of relaxation he had not been able to indulge these many months, not only because he had either been the pilot himself or sweated on the pilot's every move in case of disaster, but because on this very day Commodore Brendan would have occupied Hong Kong. He would have taken formal possession of the island in the Queen's Name on a small shelf of rocky waste land in a bowl of hills, dubbed it Possession Point, and drunk the Queen's health to a rousing fusillade of musketry. A fait accompli carried out swiftly in case the Chinese changed their minds.

He warned Captain Hall of 'Her Majesty's opposition in China'. 'James Malleson hasn't a good word to say of this glorious page we've written in British history. Says the choice is wrong. The site's poor and there are too many hills, too little water and too little protection from typhoons. We should leave it to the pirates and outlaws as the Chinese themselves have always done.'

'Let them boycott it, Barron, and count your lucky stars!'

'Would it were so, Roger, but I'll lay you a bet that Malleson plants his house flag on the best waterfront available before you leave Canton, or Forge is not my name. And the Laird will follow. God knows why they keep that man at their side like a caricature of themselves.'

'Like fools at court I imagine.'

'His antics will haunt me as long as I'm here,' he prophesied. But he was wrong. The Laird had died with far less trouble than he lived, of a swift heart attack in Macao. His body would remain, where he had lived so rambuctiously, in China.

The Chuenpi Convention between Britain and China was to be signed at the Lion Reach of the Pearl River on Envoy Chishan's barge, after they were received in his audience tent near the Pagoda of Lotus Flower Hill. Captain Forge was well satisfied. Its four main articles were concessions such as no Imperial representative had ever made before, let alone one of Chishan's stature. An ambassador to be allowed in Beijing. Direct official intercourse between the countries. Cession of the island and harbour of Hong Kong. Last, but not least, 6 million dollar's indemnity to the British government for the confiscated opium.

Therefore he came into land with mixed feelings of awe and pity for the great man; awe because he knew the great price Envoy Chishan would have to pay for the treaty, and pity because no one in this huge crowd of spectators in the horde of pleasure boats or the environs of the small and large audience tents where Chishan awaited him, was in the least aware of the high tragedy about to be played out. They chattered, laughed and pointed as if watching some farce of their street theatre- not a contingent from a Great Power dictating the humbling of a great Emperor who believed he ruled all the lands and oceans of the world.

Captain Forge's entourage of British officers from various ships of the Expeditionary Force - the eighteen foreign officers, the sixty Royal Marines and the band of the flagship, the Wellesley were more like children at a carnival than men aware they were making history. They pointed excitedly to the oddities of the vast crowd, the gaudy splendour of the mandarin boats, the Tartar soldiers in their baggy red and white uniforms, Chishan's tent with its silken yellow dragon flags.

As Captain Forge, in all the gilt splendour of full-dress uniform, stepped onto the landing, roofed with bright cloths and plantain leaves, he wished he could stop to draw the bizarre scene much more reminiscent of Chishan's Manchu ancestors, who once entertained ambassadors from remote corners of the earth in the days of Genghis Khan who had so often practised majesty in venerable palaces, than China.

Captain Forge's escort led the way towards the golden tent to the tune of 'The British Grenadiers' from the drum and fife band, the tramp of their feet like the sound of one man. They wheeled, manouevred and came to a halt, presenting arms before His Excellency Chishan, with an exact precision that brought loud murmurs of appreciation from the watching crowd.

All Captain Forge's buoyant good humour vanished the moment he saw Chishan. The Imperial envoy welcomed him without any evidence of imperial rank upon his simple sable gown but with the yellow girdle, without any appropriate retinue of mandarins - sad and diminished in manner as if a fire express had already descended from the Vermilion Pen in Beijing with scorching disgrace as indeed it had. But with the same courteous and unpretentious dignity as he had when confronting the Expeditionary Force's deputation in the Emperor's name on the Peiho River a few months before. The smiling courtesy of his greeting was in marked contrast to the sullen dignity of the local mandarins grouped behind him, most of all of that superseded dignitary, Viceroy Lin. Captain Forge did not have to guess at the cause of their anger. Envoy Chishan had ignored them from first to last. He had made no effort to consult them on any aspect of the negotiations, and had concluded a treaty obviously highly objectionable to them.

When all the formalities of banqueting in the larger tent were over, Chishan was agog to satisfy his curiosity on details that had evidently astonished him. He examined Captain Forge's dress sword as if he had never seen one before. He exclaimed over the percussion rifle of the office of the guard, and even more over the fixing of a bayonet. He declared the diminutive midshipman Grey, all of fourteen years old, should still be at school.

He felt for padding of the chest and arms of the two tallest British marines as if a cannibal chief testing missionaries for the cooking pot. He watched attentively as the Marines gave a marching display to quick and slow drumbeats. He restrained his laughter with difficulty when the Marines opened ranks too quickly for the Tartar braves behind them, and trod en masse on the Tartar toes to howls of unbrave pain. Only the Tartar-General scowled. His efforts to impose European-style drill on the Tiger Braves had dismally failed not long before.

The long-postponed treaty signed at last, Captain Forge saw respect in his adversary's eyes and a ghostly smile on his fate as if from a friend. He knew in that instant that Chishan was the only man, of the many within the port, who knew that he, Forge, had acted with the same statesmanlike perception as Chishan himself. He had gained at last what he had always sought - a moment when at least two men of the opposing races saw each other as similar and equal, a moment for which they would both pay in the end at the hands of their respective governments. How he would have loved to have reached across the barrier of language to wring Chishan's hand in salute of a very great man.

He boarded the Viceroy's gilded barge for the return procession down the river to the Nemesis rejoicing for himself that the culmination of his years in China was a remarkable treaty achieved with a minimum of force. But he could not rejoice for Chishan, whose foresight and diplomacy was likely to be overturned by the narrow, obdurate bureaucracy of the Emperor, unwilling to accept that the opium trade would not have become great enough to disturb the balance of China's trade if his own Viceroys and mandarins had not been equally involved.

As the Nemesis moved steadily downriver, Captain Forge gazed moodily at Lotus Flower Hill, where he had just participated in one of the momentous moments of Chinese history, he prophesied, 'Roger, you have just met a remarkable man, the only man who cared more for his country than himself. And did so knowing he would be doomed to failure. That failure means war.'

'Did you honestly think he might have succeeded?'

'No, but he knows as I do, we must go down in history as having made an honourable attempt. We might even have been foolish enough to think it would succeed for a week or two. But what can you do with a throne shrouded in lies?'

What he did honestly think was that Canton must sooner or later face the sack of war. The Councillors of the remote government in Beijing might condemn its people as fierce, rapacious and intellectually inferior, but any British merchant of any perception, who had been long enough in China, knew the hostility of Beijing derived from the fact that too many Cantonese had become too well-disposed to the red-beards for their liking. He knew that not only Chishan and Howqua - who had lost a million taels worth of foods due to a disastrous fire in the warehouses of Honam Island - but also the people themselves would lose heavily from the Emperor's guerilla war with foreign traders.

As Captain Forge feared, Chishan was recalled to Pekin in disgrace not only for signing the treaty in the Emperor's name, but also for daring to tell him that he had no defences worth the name. His vast fortune of a thousand acres of land, eighty-four shroff shops and some six million taels in gold and dilver was confiscated. He was degraded in rank, exiled to Tibet and replaced by three new Commissioners including the nephew to the Emperor, the famous Tartar-General, Yihshan, who had executed Pu Ping Pang. Yihshan was supremely confident he would live up to his new name of General Pacificator of the Foreign Rebels by succeeding where Viceroy Lin and Governor Tang had failed, namely in suppressing the fearsome red-headed foreign devils.

* * * * * *

CHAPTER 10

1840 The Stop and Go War

The British Expeditionary Force remained at an anchorage in the mouth of the river for the period of truce specified in the treaty. They lay three miles below the first of the forts the Chinese believed impregnable for the defence of the Bogue. The first two were on islands on the west and east sides of the river channel. The next two were three miles upriver beyond Anson's Bay, one on the east side and one on an island in the middle of the river. The fifth lay three miles further up again on Tiger Island.

These forts, strongly built and well furnished with Tiger braves and cannon, could withstand a powerful attack if they were stormed by frontal attack. But the British commanders, aware that all those guns faced the river, decided to attack the lowest fort from the rear with a force landed from the Nemesis two miles south. 1,400 men of the 26th, 49th, and 37th Madras infantry and Bengal volunteers together with a 24 pounder howitzer and two six pounder field pieces drawn by seamen from the 74's. All accomplished unobserved while warships distracted the garrison with a fierce pounding from off-shore.

This sortie over, the Nemesis rounded the point to join in the action at Anson's Bay. She churned through the shifting white drifts of smoke, shot through with black and grey, with the din of battle resounding in their ears. The crashing blast of cannon. The whine and ping of smallshot, grape and canister.

In Anson's Bay the Nemesis fired her first Congreve rocket. It homed in on the magazine of one of the largest war junks there and blew it into matchwood. Then it created equal havoc on eleven more. Captain Forge could hardly believe the battle was over so quickly.

At the end of an hour and a half, the Chinese forts, entrenchments, barracks and magazines were all in ruins, beaten down, set on fire or blown up, the sappers already spiking the five hundred or so guns of the batteries and destroying the ammunition. Many braves had fought fiercely believing the British took no prisoners. On Chuenpi, two Chinese officers fell on the bayonets of the marines rather than be captured. The general's son jumped into the sea when he found his father had died courageously in the forefront of his men. By contrast, four boatloads of officers and their followers had fled panic-stricken from a fort on Wangtong Island at the sight of the British ships under weigh but not before barring the gates to prevent the rest from following. On the British side no one had been killed, and most of the wounded were only slightly hurt, the bulk by an accidental explosion in the lower fort.

As Captain Forge watched the Chinese encampments burn in a spectacular triumphal bonfire that cast a strong glare across the sky and over the waters of the Bogue, he wondered how much more terrible the sack of Canton might be. He could not exult like the crews of the fleet rocking quietly around him, at peace after their deadly day's work, for dread of the destruction that must yet come as the war moved even further upriver to the ultimate fortress of the city of Canton.

At last, a favourable time to move on to the First Bar. The iron-hulled Nemesis once again led the way followed by the wooden steamship Madagascar. All the way Captain Forge remained standing anxiously in her bows beside the leadsman, who twirled the heavy lead with a tireless rhythm, heaving it ahead of the vessel into the wayward stream with its constantly shifting shoals and sandbanks, then hauling it in again as the mate called the depths for the seaman in the stern to hoist flags on long bamboo poles to guide the following ships.

By the time the steamers had reached the First Bar, the other ships had lagged behind as the wind had lapsed to a meagre breeze that scarcely blew across the limp water. Once there they were confronted by a fort to one side of the river and a strong line of mud batteries, extending along the riverfront and an impassable raft of immense tree trunks reaching across the river backed by a number of warjunks and the Cambridge on the other. Captain Hall appraised the Cambridge through binoculars. She was nothing like the warship she had once been with her gaudy red bows and banners on her thirty or more guns. 'British guns by Jove!

'Paid for with opium brought from Jarman's by the Viceroy, then sold on, no doubt,' Captain Forge remarked grimly.

But Captain Hall had no time to fathom the perplexities of smuggling now. His quick strategic eye was at work again. 'They should have sold them spring cables when they sold them guns.' For the Cambridge guns were useless owing to the fact her rigid moorings left her unable to swing around to bring her bring her guns to bear. Only her bow guns were of use in defending the tree raft. 'As for the war junks, what do you think?'

He handed the binoculars to his colleague. The warjunks seemed less formidable close up than at a distance. 'I think they'll make a run for it when the first shots are fired.' He swung the binoculars round to scan the river bank. 'It's the jingals on the left flank of the batteries you'll have to look out for. They are far more accurate and easier to handle.'

Captain Hall bit his lip in his quandary, 'The burning question is do we go into action now or wait for the rest?'

Captain Forge hesitated. They must ask rather could they afford to lose the Nemesis? Neither man was willing to admit they were both chafing for action themselves after all the weeks of what they had nicknamed 'the stop and go' war. Captain Herbert, on board as Commodore Brendan's observer, gave his casting vote. The Nemesis should commence battle, while he went down in his own gig to bring up the rest of the force.

Captain Hall anchored the Nemesis with springs on her cable seven hundred yards from the lower angle of the nearest fort. Her two mates opened up a barrage from her bow and stern guns while others manned the new Congreve rocket launchers. Their appearance so slender, their angles so reminiscent of fireworks, it was hard to regard them as serious a weapon as more massive guns of lower trajectory until they opened fire. Then the awesome spread of their exploding rockets made it clear to any experienced gunner that here was a weapon potentially much more powerful than ever before.

Captain Hall argued heatedly with his friend, as shot flew all around them despite the crew's efforts to jockey the Nemesis out of range by manouevring her on her spring cables, whether he should go below. 'You'll get your head blown off if you stay here.'

'While you stay on the bridge? Never!'

'You're more important than I am. How will we get along without you?'

'Some would say very well. They might be lucky enough to get someone with water in his veins instead.'

'Is that what you're trying to prove, there's blood in yours?'

Some well-aimed fire into the spars and rigging nearby caused them to duck their heads as an engineer rushed up to say one large shot had passed completely through the outer casing of the steam chest.

'A fraction closer, and it would have blown up.'

'And blown us to smithereens with it,' Captain Hall added.

Just then Captain Herbert came aboard to ask Captain Hall and the crew of the Nemesis to join him in storming the fort, which must be captured before they could attack the barricades.

Captain Forge tried to dissuade his friend. 'You and your best engineers thrown to the wolves. What for? To play heroes?'

'Probably the only chance I'll have on this campaign.'

'Then I'll come with you. Act as your bodyguard.'

Captain Hall playfully sparred with him by way of protest. 'Not if I can stop you. If anything happens to you who will act as Plenipotentiary?'

The thought of Commodore Brendan in sole charge prevailed. Captain Forge stayed on board while Captain Hall's courageous little force rowed in to land and disappeared into the smoke-fog. He prayed the drifts of smoke might throw the Chinese gunners off their aim as they rushed up the bank. He was on tenterhooks until Captain Hall reappeared to plant the Union Jack on the crown of the fort, in agony as he watched a Tiger brave raise his bow and fire four arrows in quick succession at the indomitable Captain; in thanksgiving when a marine dropped to one knee, and killed the Tiger brave with one well-directed musket ball; and in terror as he saw his friend now rowing with the Lieutenant of the Calliope in the boat its crew had manhandled across the raft bridge on a course that would bring it within range of the Cambridge's formidable armament.

Only a miracle could save them from such foolhardiness. And to his amazement a miracle did. The crew of the Cambridge fought and jostled each other to escape down the nettings they had thrown over the far side of the ship. They had no desire to stand and be slaughtered by the ferocious redbeards like the wretched garrison in the fort. The marines swarmed up the other side, and, once on deck, danced a crazed fandango to find themselves in possession without a single shot or blow. Then they disappeared below to reappear in a purloined medley of Chinese uniforms and flags in grotesque parody of the erstwhile enemy as if in some fantastic Oriental fair. Hardly the behaviour, Captain Forge thought, he would prefer from men asserting the dignity of the civilised nation of which he was now the sole Plenipotentiary.

When Admiral Downing arrived well after they had blown apart both the Cambridge and the improvised bulwarks it had defended, as they had the Bogue forts the day before, he found them broaching a keg of rum to 'splice the mainbrace'. He warned them 'The Commodore's fit to be tied.'

'Because we stole his thunder?' Captain Hall asked placidly as he poured the Admiral a healthy tot of rum.

'Because you didn't wait for the land troops.'

'They had their day of glory at Chuenpi. Let the navy have their battle honours this time.' He added the news certain to be unpopular with these men of action. 'I have signed a three day truce.'

'With whom?' Admiral Downing asked stupefied.

Well he might ask, Captain Forge knew, since Viceroy Lin had been hauled off to Beijing in chains, Envoy Chishan was about to be, and Yishan, the new Great Pacificator of the Rebellious, was not yet in Canton. Nor his two offsiders, Yangfang and Lingwang.

'With the Prefect. There's no one else.'

'The Commodore says you should follow up your advantage while you still have raw recruits opposing you.'

'He should remember ours are not better. China is not Afghanistan nor the Sind.'

This jibe was aimed at Sir Hugh Gaunt, who had just arrived to take over from the elderly and ailing Brendan with a considerable reputation founded on those turbulent regions. A man of authoritative presence and booming voice, he came easily by the air of superiority of which the British Raj was so often accused. He had already given Captain Forge the impression he thought that lessons learned in the rough and tough campaigns of India were equally relevant in China, forgetting that India was a patchwork of rival quarrelsome states compared to China with the disciplined overlordship of its central government evolved over centuries.

From the first moment of their meeting, Sir Hugh Gaunt had voiced Captain Forge's correct title of 'Excellency' as if it were a bone stuck in his throat outraged to think he, a general, should have to defer to a post-captain. Worse he was expected to act in concert with a man he was told had been excessively cautious and dilatory in using the costly and unbeatable Expeditionary Force sent with the express purpose of defeating the Chinese in war.

Captain Forge had decided at once it would be a waste of breath to persuade Sir Hugh Gaunt that the British soldiers and the Indian regiments might be equal to none under reasonable conditions. But these were not reasonable. They would be faced with a city, eighty miles inland, which had proved difficult to capture since time immemorial and would be more so once fresh Tartar troops, being rushed from all parts of the Celestial Kingdom to defend it, had arrived.

* * * * * *

The Great Pacificator of the Rebellious

Kaida walked through the bustling yamen where preparations for war had drastically changed its unflurried pace. Officers of the regiments, that had arrived from provinces near and far, hurried in and out. Runners rushed back and forth with news of their fights with local militia in the streets or quarrels with the citizenry over their looting and abuse. This very morning the worst incident to date had occurred, a riot in which a number were killed, all over cutting off a man's queue.

The continual chaos and disorder had kept Yihshan in a perpetual bad temper since his arrival, which grew even worse when he heard how readily the glorious Chinese braves had deserted their posts in face of the vile red-beard demons, how quickly the warjunks disappeared up the river byways, how willingly the citizens of Canton were abandoning their city. He raved at them all for cowards.

Kaida no longer felt safe in the yamen. He was forever on the alert, nervous and anxious that luck might abandon him. Someone would denounce him as a spy, a 'treacherous native', in this time of fear and suspicion when every man's hand was turned against one another. Everyone went in fear and tremblling of reprisals. The shock, when it came, had nothing to do with himself.

'Wang Chung on trial?' He could scarcely believe the clerk. 'Viceroy Lin's great ally?' The Red Circle leader finally meeting his just deserts?

The clerk assured him there was no mistake. Viceroy Lin had betrayed him before he had left for Beijing. He had used Wang Chung as Wang Chung had used him, but only as he might a snake to milk off its poison before destroying it as an evil thing. Kaida was confused as he rushed to the courtroom. Surely Yihshan would not need Wang Chung, as Viceroy Lin had, to defeat his enemies? Or could he, unable to weld the insolence of the out-of-town troops, the smouldering sullen countryside, and the cowardice of the militia into any forceful defence, hope to harness this rogue as Viceroy Lin had done? At least he was sure of one thing, he would see the brutal author of the raids on the Black Joke, the Bilbaino and the Hong Kong trading fleet face to face for the first time.

He was consumed by a chilling excitement as he entered the court, crowded with curious yamen officials because the word had got around that the infamous Wang Chung of the slit mouth had been hauled in from his lair in the Walled City of Kowloon. But Wang Chung had not, he saw at once, been hauled to kneel on broken glass before the stern Table of Justice for the torture and instant death Viceroy Lin would have ordered once he had finished with him, but to stand comfortably before his superior who addressed him in a respectful, almost apologetic manner, about enlisting his aid. How Viceroy Lin would have shaken with anger to see Yihshan, the swarthy, saturnine avenger so suave and polite to this rich smuggler.

'You know our ancient Martial City of the South is threatened by treacherous foreigners?'

'I do, Your Excellency.' Wang Chung spoke with eyes wary rather than apprehensive. An arch veteran trader in dangerous enterprise, he could smell a deal from afar.

'You know how many of our citizens have been the guilty hands of the foreign devils' unlawful trade?'

'I do, Your Excellency.' As well he might. His were the most guilty hands of all.

'You are one of their chiefs.' Yihshan suddenly lashed out like a mongoose playing with a cobra. His high-flying eyebrows gave him a naive, mild-mannered expression of genial humility apt for the small shopkeeper he had once been. Wang Chung bowed his head submissively. He had too often used the technique of terror not to sense it from afar. 'The very least you deserve is confiscation of all your property and death.'

Wang Chung was untroubled. His property would be hard to prove or find. His only wish now was to accept whatever Yihshan might offer in order to avoid the otherwise certain death that would be Yihshan's revenge. 'I am yours to command.'

'I do command. Since you and your ilk put Canton into this terrible danger, you will defend it.'

Kaida admired Wang Chung's self-control, barely a flicker of shock on his fact that Yihshan, the Great Pacificator of the Rebellious, wanted to embrace an unregenerate bandit like himself to his bosom. He was obliged to see Yihshan, a Manchu Tartar from a race that had survived as rulers in China so long, in an utterly different light from his reputation as a truculent belligerent fool with his back to the wall- as a shrewd ambassador swift to read the lessons of history by embracing generals and rebels willing to change sides. As Wang Chung did now. No torture and lingering death for him. Yes, he would assemble a fleet of boats in the service of the Emperor. Yes, he would defend the vulnerable western approach to the city. But he must have arms. Yihshan, shrewd enough to know he faced an enemy such as never before, was obliged to agree.

Kaida was left to wonder if the Manchu rulers would not pay too great a price in the future for the bargains of today. Would Wang Chung really put up a fierce fight against the very men with whom he was in an unholy alliance or return the arms to be given him by Yihshan when the fight was over? As Kaida studied Yihshan's sinister new ally, he understood why there were times when wise leaders forgot to hate knowing that for every leader killed there was another standing in his shadow. With the thought his own hate of Wang Chung ebbed from him. It was a useless hate. He might kill Wang Chung but he would not end the Red Circle and its evil ways by cutting off one head. Another Elder Brother would step into his shoes. The assassination of a king did not end a dynasty while it had loyal allies as the Red Circle did with the Red Beards. But even as he lost his own hate, he knew the price of that loss was that he could no longer lead.

The only way he could help his people was to follow the true vision of the old Triads to whom he belonged - to help all those village people yoked to the plough of a foreign Manchu government for their food, taxes, armies, those people who always suffered most in wars. All that mattered for them was a quick end to this war, the British and Tartar troops sent home again. And all that mattered for himself was to help Captain Forge bring the quick and just peace only he could bring, a peace with the least slaughter rather than the most honours in battle. In the Captain he recognised a man like himself, essentially a man of peace.

When Kaida was able to slip away from the yamen and reach Macao in the hope of finding Captain Forge there, he told Chung Tai Tai about Yihshan's new ally. She scoffed, spitting into the spittoon beside her.

'The Pacificator thinks he will use Wang Chung. The rogue will use him.'

'He will not defend the city?'

'They're frogs not sharks.' Her tone was expressive of the contempt all deep sea sailors felt for boatmen of the delta.

'Will the boats gather at all?'

'Ayah. If he asks they must or go in fear of their lives.'

She spat again in contempt for the recent expansion of the Red Circle, a criminal version of her own empire. They had become collectors, mentally blind beggars of the Beggar King who returned as bullies if their victims refused to pay to protect themselves against their illegal activities.

'If the Pacificator Yihshan has nobody to protect him but that gang of criminals he must be desperate.'

A servant glided in with a tray, placing it on the low rectangular table between them. She leaned forward to pour the tea, folding her deep silk sleeves back with a quick movement, as precise as her hands on a gun.

'A threat to the Pacificator as they will be to me.'

'The British commanders are determined to occupy the city.'

'They are as big fools as the leaders they oppose.'

'Surely the city will be easy to take, abandoned as it is already by most of its citizens and defended by troops fighting amongst themselves.'

'The climate will fight the battle for Yihshan without another shot fired. Remember how many red-beards died of sickness on Chusan Island.'

Kaida was not convinced the terrifying prospect of the battle for Canton could end so simply, given the new Governor was declaring he would fight to the death as his ancestors had done against invaders.

Chung Tai Tai brushed this doubt aside saying tartly, 'that old fool! I knew him when he was no bigger than a child's paddle. He says that to please the Emperor now he was wangled his way up to the inner council. But he has forgotten this city lives by trade. Whoever rules should never forget it. Captain Forge never does. Chinese appreciate him better than his own.'

She paused to refill her cup, and drank before she passed judgement as to what must be done. 'You must go to Captain Forge. He's back here in Macao. Warn him to take his fire-wheel ship up the Macao Passage from the Inner Harbour to the western flank of the city where Yihshan will send Wang Chung to defend it. His sailors will have no stomach for battle with a fire-wheel ship.'

'What about the shallows, the bends and the narrows?

Chung Tai Tai had not been an Admiral for nothing. 'The fire-wheel ship draws five feet of water. She has a moveable keel. She can go anywhere any junk can go. I will give him a pilot.'

Kaida was not altogether reassured. 'What about her length?'

'She can back like a barge with a pole.'

He must be sure before he urged Captain Forge to go where he could be trapped with the only ship that could win the campaign for him.

'What about snags?'

'Iron will take more punishment than wood.'

He yielded to Chung Tai Tai. She was as skilled in the ways of the water as he with books. A wise, wise woman, he thought as he put down his own cup more at ease with himself now the urgency of his mission was justified. 'I will go straight away, and tell him if he agrees, he will have the best pilot on the water.'

* * * * * *

The Nemesis goes where a Junk can go

The moon was no more than a glimmer in the dark haven of the inner harbour below the sombre bulk of Lappa Island when Captain Forge stood on the bridge of the Nemesis with John Norris and the Captain of the Samarang to welcome Chung Tai Tai's pilot on board, a small ancient, brown and wrinkled as a Chinese date. Nothing reassuring about him, Captain Forge objected when he saw him. 'Look how fearful he is!'

John reassured him. 'He's only terrified you might punish him if you turn back for any reason. Your incompetence not his. Your panic. Your fear of the forts on the way.'

'Punish him? How?' He had no authority over the man.

'Is that the custom here?'

'No payee, no get better.' John explained succinctly.

Captain Forge thought how old and wise the young man was despite his smooth almost childish face. Had this clever efficient youngster ever had a youth? 'Set his fears at rest.'

John Norris spoke to the pilot in a harsh jabber of Cantonese. With a grimace of a smile he took his place in the fore, hard by the leadsman standing on the channel ready to heave the lead. Three boatloads of men were in tow behind them, two from the Samarang and one from the Atlanta.

Some of the forebodings of the pilot were justified. It took five days to make the journey. As they did so, they wondered whether they were waging a war or staging a show. The people of Heangshan Island within the delta were out in their legion on the surrounding hills, river banks, housetops, boats and barges to watch their noisy skirmishes as they subdued the forts that lined their way one by one.

The mandarins of the town of Heangshan were not so anxious to watch the passing parade. They jostled each other to jump on barges to flee in the opposite direction almost as fast as the two war junks supposed to defend them. They need not have been quite so afraid of being caught. As the Nemesis gave chase she ran aground in the narrowing Broadway Passage, her bow and stern both buried in the muddy rim of flooded paddies, prompting some wit on board to ask if this was a new way of going overland to England. Towed on the tide at last they emerged at the junction of the Broadway Passage with the main river to find Wang Chung's flotilla gathered at the mouth in expectation of an advance farther up the main river, all unwitting the fire-wheel ship had churned her way towards them from the rear. When its fearful apparition appeared behind them, they showed no more courage than the mandarins, bumbling against each other in their desperate confusion to escape, some of them beaching their boats so the crew could flee overland. The crew of the Nemesis paralytic with laughter at this spectacle of terrified cowardice from these notorious bullies of the water.

'Will Yihshan demand his money back from Wang Chung?'

One final moment of comedy was theirs, when they arrived at the Factories at last to repossess the Common and the New English. Captain Morrow waved the standard of the Nemesis from its windows in challenge to Captain Belcher as he ran the Union Jack up the flagpole to a gun salute to claim flag honours for the Survey. As Captain Forge strolled out on the deserted Common to greet him, his gaze turned to the intractable city walls beyond the Factories.

Not all his buoyant good humour could stave off the thought neither he nor the fleet had yet progressed any further with all their present armament, and the running battle of the past five days, than any European had ever done before them. The gates of Canton still remained implacably closed, a difficult challenge to the cordon of smaller warships the captains were now setting along the southern perimeter of the city. They still had no bigger force on shore than the two landing parties of Captains Hall and Belcher.

His meditation was interrupted by a sudden volley of shots from Captain Hall's party, which had just landed a little further away. Chinese braves had rushed in from Hogs Lane with hoarse yells and grotesques grimaces brandishing rattan shields and spears, and were hurling themselves forward on Captain Hall's party as they raced to join Captain Belcher, expecting the foreign devils to be helpless until they reloaded their weapons. Far from it. Armed with new weapons of war in the shape of repeater rifles, they discharged a second volley at close range. Most of the hapless braves pitched screaming in tortured postures at their feet. The rest fled the field, rattan shields on their backs.

'We've put the fear of God in them now,' Captain Hall exulted as he cleaned the percussion gun which had terrified the braves. He was lucky to have one, the personal gift of Admiral Sir Tryon Forge when he left England knowing he must bear the brunt of any Expeditionary Force campaign.

'You're ship's going to be a brute to defend in the front line so you may as well have the best and latest,' he had said looking uncannily similar to his cousin Barron. So far only the marines had been issued with them and were, as a result, the envy of all the soldiers.

Captain Forge demurred. 'Next time they'll have their revenge.'

'Why so gloomy this morning, Barron?' Captain Hall demanded.

Captain Forge stared out at the grim city walls soaring above the huddled Factories and the streets behind. 'The moment order breaks down they'll be back here like rats up a drainpipe.'

'Not the soldiers again after the dose we gave them?'

'Alas, the people. They've been roused too often against us.'

'Aren't you afraid one of them will be after you with such a price on your head?' Captain Hall rammed the wadding down the barrel of his gun again with the same meticulous care he demanded of the crew on the guns and engines of the Nemesis. 'Do they have courage enough for that?'

'No, nor hate enough. But they are greedy and stealthy. Rats that come like thieves in the night. Who can control rats?'

'My dear fellow, you're too obscure for me at times.'

'If the mandarins can't control the people, how can we?'

'In other words, you've no stomach for occupying the city.'

'What man in his right sense would?'

'What's the alternative?' Captain Hall looked down the barrel with satisfaction. Clean as a whistle.

'Ransom.'

'And give them a chance of saying they drove you away like they did each time the fleet withdrew after a truce?'

Captain Forge replied testily. 'I'm not playing at building legends for the firesides of Britain in the future, but for the lives of men thrown into the furnace of Canton in the present.

'Then you'll have two battles on your hands, Commodore Brendan and General Gaunt,' Captain Hall concluded, ignoring his friend's rebuke. This port would try even a saint's patience.

The battle for Canton did not, after all, begin straight away. Yet another uneasy truce ensued, demanded by Captain Forge to buy time. Time to get the trading ships out under the protection of the guns of the war fleet at Whampoa. Time to repair the 'Nemesis' at Macao. Time for Commodore Brendan to go to Calcutta to ask for supplies and reinforcements. But also time for the indestructible Chinese to make a multiplicity of preparations for war - new cannon, firerafts, stakes and stones - and time for Lung Wang to arrive in Canton with a large reinforcement of fresh troops.

Time also for the entrenchment of an embryonic community at Hong Kong in tents and matting lean-tos. Time for Jarman Malleson to conjure up the first of their great new go-downs or warehouses from Hong Kong's barren soil. And time for Holly to decide whether to stay on in China or not.

No, she would not return to New York although violence, even war, was likely to be endemic on the coast for a long time to come. The shipwreck had left her bereft not only of family but of fear of China. What worse could happen? Yes, she would remain in China where she had invested so much love and hope. She would buy her own block of land at the next land sale in Hong Kong and pitch a tent like the rest until she built a home.

When Flora objected to the crude life she would be forced to lead there, she argued 'if the frontier women of America can do it, so can I.' When Flora reminded her she had once been squeamish about the morality of residing among the opium fleet in Hong Kong harbour, she replied, 'Ningpo changed me. It taught me to live and let live. Each man chooses his salvation in his heart and mind in his own way, not in the company he keeps. I can't play God and condemn them. Only God can stand in judgement.'

'Surely you don't support the opium trade,' Flora said still anxious to dissuade her, considering the hardships of Hong Kong rather than the company she would keep.

'I can no longer be sanctimonious about it.' Holly dismissed the subject thinking of the elegance of Chun's opium ritual at the Ningpo banquets, 'so long as I think our dram drinkers are more disgusting in their cups.'

Flora gave up the argument. Holly had changed in the past year. She wondered what effect this would have when she saw Sean Jarman again as she surely would. He was due to arrive back any day now but not with his wife as they had expected. She had died in childbirth just before he sailed, the child that had been her death warrant still-born. She wondered if, at last, they could find consolation with each other for the sufferings they had endured, now that Holly seemed to have lost most of the scruples that once divided them.

* * * * * *

When Sean arrived in China, he bypassed Macao and went straight to Canton. Aloud he said 'I must be where the action is.' To himself he admitted he was afraid to meet Holly. Could they take up again where they left off with the memory of their marriages a barrier between them? How much had she changed? How much had his feeling for her changed? Could he hope to go back to the beginning knowing how seldom life offered opportunity twice? Still his longing to see Holly persisted during the weeks at Canton while he and other partners of Jarman Malleson raced against the clock to conclude the season's trading in half the usual time.

They were almost ready to move down river when Captain Forge called on them with the ultimatum he could not long postpone the crisis they had all expected so long. They must leave by sunset or he could no longer be responsible for their safety. How could they argue? The dense river traffic, normally energetic as beetles on a pond, had altogether vanished. Guards blocked the streets to the Factories. Soldiers moved in the streets behind with slow matches to fire their matchlocks already burning in their hands. The last enduring shopkeepers had frantically shifted their property and households out of the back gates of the city to the villages.

He thought Sean Jarman's reaction the height of folly, when he ignored the plea to leave at once, still anxious to get the last of the Jarman Malleson records down to the boats. 'Don't worry about us. You warned us. It's our funeral.'

'I hope it won't be,' he had replied grimly.

Sean comforted himself with the thought that no matter how Captain Forge played the prophet of doom his two men of war - the Modeste and the Nemesis - lay upstream, guns loaded, double sentries on the watch and cables ready to slip. Their captains and their crews slept fully dressed, ready for instant service, and the Nemesis stoked ready to get up steam at a few minutes' notice.

And he had the new young clerk, Johnnie Adair, with him who politely told Captain Forge, 'we'll be as safe as houses. They haven't declared war yet. And the Modeste will still be in the stream.' More fool he, Captain Forge decided as he pulled away from the deserted shore. Did he really think the Chinese authorities would fire signal guns to announce 'let battle commence'?

Sean was uneasy enough to insist they stayed upstairs where their frail lamp was the one solitary light burning in all the quiet gloom of the deserted Factories. The only life astir in the sultry palpable darkness of the warm late spring evening the countless winged creatures that swooped into the tiny circle of their flame. All the customary flickering flames of the boat alleys had vanished. No sound was to be heard in the eerie silence, none of the customary drums and gongs to mark the hour. This brooding dark not in the least like any eve of battle in his story books, where the winking campfires of embattled armies faced each other across the battleground of tomorrow. This secret furtive eve of battle had no certain frontier. He peered nervously into the Stygian gloom for reassurance from the pilot light that marked the anchorage of the Nemesis.

The burst of fire upstream was a shock when it came. One fire after another, giant torches exposing a whole fleet of firerafts chained together in twos and threes bearing down on the Modeste to fasten like barnacles on her bows and consume her. However, Sean soon saw someone had miscalculated the swirl and set of the river current. Most of the fire-rafts were drifting away from the Modeste towards the shore.

'Glory be if that's how they fight a war,' Johnnie whooped at the sight, 'what's that old woman of a superintendent, Forge, so worried about?'

The panicstricken crews jumped overboard as their rafts rammed the bank. The riverside houses turned into bonfires instead of the ships. Hapless victims, engulfed in flame, screamed from every door.

'Poor illiterate farmers without the wit to develop a second plan when the first doesn't work,' Sean remarked, pouring himself another ale as Yingwan's new batteries opened up on either side of the river against the two ships downstream, the Louisa and the Aurora.

'We have a grandstand seat for the action,' Johnnie exulted, congratulating himself they had stayed behind.

They watched the two smaller ships, exposed in the light of the fires, forced to dance on their cables, veering and shortening, to dodge the blast of the cannon and the popping of the jingals.

Johnnie soon regretted his self-congratulation. As God lifted his blind on the world next morning, he scanned the river with some dismay. All the British ships, engaged with the enemy the night before, were gone. Someone had taken the small boat they were loading during the day. They were now stranded, enforced prisoners of their Factory. Downriver they could hear a new cannonade. Dense columns of black and white smoke billowed and belched upwards from massive explosions to the west and the south of the city.

'To be sure, the Nemesis has flushed out some more fire rafts,' Johnnie, hanging out the window, reported to Sean, 'Lord what's that, now?'

Invaders were beginning to trickle in from Hog Lane, ominous as a first run of water signalling a flood overbrimming the banks of the Pearl River. They were ragged looters of the most desperate and vicious kind headed, staff or axe in hand, for the New English Factory. He hurled himself down the stairs in time to drop the heavy bar in its solid iron catch, then rushed back upstairs to close the doors to the upper verandah as the looters streamed past brandishing useless pieces of its famous mirrors and chandeliers.

'Versailles all over again,' Johnnie joked.

'Sans-culottes against us?' Sean was afraid. This time, unlike all former crises, they were alone.

Anything that could move was moving in a wild and immoderate caravan. Even the famous marble statue from the great staircase was not exempt, hauled out for a blasphemous orgy of hatred towards the foreign devils and all they stood for.

'My God!' Johnnie exclaimed, astounded to see how they gouged, chipped, hammered and battered the marble.

Whereas Sean, more experienced in the quixotic nature of the Chinese mob remarked, 'pity they don't fight with the same fury.'

Just at that moment Johnnie saw the Nemesis round the bend and asked hopefully, 'do you think we could make a run for it?'

'Not if you want to end up like old Adonis there.'

'This is no laughing matter,' he said primly as Sean, hitherto surly, doubled up with laughter. 'How can you treat such a serious matter as our lives in deadly danger as a joke?' Johnnie demanded angrily.

'That fancy dress ball is.' Sean pointed at the masquerade in progress aboard the steamship. Its crew was out on deck, prancing about playing the buffoon. Between them they paraded all kinds of hats and follies of dress. Some had

Chinese pigtails tied to their caps. Some had the shields or uniforms of tiger braves. Some had embroidered mandarin tunics. Captain Forge himself was standing alone on the bridge, scanning the other farce being played out below them on the Common. Johnnie waved frantically yelling 'help!' as if Captain Forge could hear him over the shouts and howls in a pulsing roar around them.

'He doesn't know we're here. He'll never see you. Even if he does, what can he do?'

In fact, Captain Forge had seen them and was weighing up his chance of doing anything to pluck them out. He surveyed the crazed scene of destruction, the excited rabble armed with timber from doors and windows they had already dismantled. He could, of course, shell the Common, and destroy the Factories far more swiftly and completely than the rabble were doing. But the buidings were owned by the Co-Hong merchants, who had so faithfully loaded British ships twice under excessive difficulties and threats during the two periods of truce. He could assault the mob on the Common. But he could not, in all conscience, order the valuable crew of the Nemesis, who were about to play a crucial role in the landings to the west of the city, into a strategically useless and potentially futile rescue, nor be the first to fire deliberately on civilians in this war.

Captain Hall was not on the bridge for a very good reason. He had gravely burned his arm when a Congreve rocket had jammed in its slender launching tube after being fired, threatening to blow the entire ship sky high. He had saved them all by plunging his arm into the redhot stream of the rocket with a tool to force it on its way.

Knowing nothing of the logic behind that decision, Sean watched in disbelief as the paddlewheels of the Nemesis churned steadily by without pause, decked with flags and costumed players prancing about in carnival mode, as they gave three rousing cheers, whether for themselves or the 'sans culottes' of the Common Sean had no way of knowing. What he did know was that he and Johnnie were now at the mercy of the government of Canton and could expect no rescue. He cursed himself for his folly, denying Captain Forge as he had as a surrogate for Holly.

Just as they seemed likely to be forced out into the raging mob by flaming torches brandished at their door, police of the Co-Hong merchants appeared with the Prefect to arrest them. As they marched away, Sean had a confused impression of gaping mouths with broken teeth jeering obscure insults as hands reached out to prod and punch this way and that, too many for the whips of the police. He cursed his own witless audacity he had not left with the rest of the merchants again and again. He, if anyone, should have known what it was like to be a hostage. He had not forgotten the Aurora, nor the suffering inflicted on Holly, as it was now for them with chains on hand and neck like common criminals, spat on and derided in their humiliating march through the streets.

'Now I know how Christ must have felt,' Johnnie groaned as he tripped and was jerked onwards.

'At least we don't have to carry our own Cross,' Sean jested to hide the real dread he felt from the unfortunate Johnnie, a victim only through staying to help himself.

'I'm not the stuff of martyrs.' He groaned again as a rattan fell on his shoulders.

On their way, they passed teams of soldiers and coolies dragging guns towards the Factories. 'They must expect a landing there,' Johnnie guessed.

'They'd better sack the Tartar-General if they concentrate their defences on the river,' Sean returned, 'since our lot will be landing at Tsingpo on the western side of the city.'

'The west?' Johnnie was aghast, 'they've got my sympathy. Rice paddies all the way.'

They entered a great gate in the long inner wall that divided the New City from the Old to find themselves in the headquarters of the Tartar-General himself where there was a great bustle and confusion. Officers of every grade, city guardsmen, couriers on horseback, grooms, and an immense crowd of Tiger braves lounging about. Hurled to the flagstones they crouched there surrounded by a human jabbering wall, three or four deep. Each row leant on the one in front until Sean thought the whole scrum would fall on top of them both. All curious to see the Red Beards they had never seen before and had come so many thousand li to fight.

Sean did not need to understand their words to know they were arrantly hostile. He prayed the guard might keep the crowd at bay, or they would be in mortal danger of being kicked to death like stray dogs. He prayed again as he had never done before that the combined naval and military force had made their way up the creek on the west of the city and would win their battle quickly. Yet he knew well the Tartar soldiers were likely to vent their vengeance on their prisoners either way. They looked menacing enough at rest with those devilish faces painted on the rattan shields of their four banners - yellow, white, red and blue. He shuddered to imagine what they would be like in the flood tide of their fury.

Their tiny, filthy cell looked like a haven of peace after the huge threatening crowd. Sean never thought to have welcomed prison bars with such relief. 'At least we are safe,' he reassured the by now hysterical Johnnie. But he could not persuade himself this was true. They were far worse off than Holly and the wretched sailors of the Jason had ever been.

When he saw Yihshan, the Great Pacificator, had sent 'Captain White' to be his interpreter, he groaned inwardly. The man was a Jackanapes, who could never understand any English words beyond the business of buying and selling opium and tea, a fool who told them now that Yihshan was like the God of War. They must tremble and obey. Obey what? From his pidgin jumble, Sean understood the price of three of the fanqui - Commodore Brendan, Captain Forge and John Norris - was fifty thousand taels. They might earn this reward and their release if they could lure any one of them on shore where the Great Yihshan's men could seize them.

Johnnie was outraged. 'He must think we'd sell our own mothers.'

'Oh no, Johnnie, it's that we are dogmen. We have no morals.'

Sean smiled disarmingly at the pretentious 'Captain White'. 'Bring me paper. I will write a letter to entice them into the hands of the great God of War.'

When 'Captain White' had strutted out with an air of agreeable surprise that this foreign devil should be so compliant, Johnnie burst out, 'you'd really write such a letter?'

'What the eye sees is not what the hand does,' Sean answered, not in the least put out, 'Captain Forge would have to be more fool than I take him for to believe a word of it. At least it will tell him we are alive and where we are.'

'You think Captain Forge's worth appealing to?' Johnnie leant against the cold, harsh wall of the cell wearily. Surely there was no hope now. 'I've heard no good about him since I arrived.'

'When he's gone as he soon will be, you'll hear on all sides how popular and respected he was.'

'That's like everyone praising a man only when he's dead.'

'Johnnie, you've arrived in the middle of a war. You haven't been here long enough to know this is a hothouse of frustrated emotions from an impossible situation. Someone becomes victim.'

'Who will it be after Captain Forge?'

'If you stick around long enough, you'll find out.'

'If I'm still alive,' Johnnie said dismally kicking away the few strands of smelly, bug-ridden straw before he lay down.

Sean lay curled against the wall thinking of his argument with Holly about Chinese justice and how no European should ever be obliged to submit to it. He had never imagined then that he would be faced with that very dilemma while a war was fought beyond the walls that now held him imprisoned, a war that would leave him to the merciless judgement of Chinese courts if his side lost. He clenched his fist as if to urge them on, then knelt and prayed to a God he had forgotten for a long time.

The very thought of Holly gave him such a desperate sense of longing for her that he felt a surge of energy which made him straighten his back and tell an astonished Johnnie, 'I must get back to Hong Kong.'

'Why so desperate all of a sudden?'

'I intend to propose to a lady. This time no words can come between us.' His words sounded strangely angry to Johnnie for a man touched by the tender magic of love.

No stupid issues would divide them as they had done in the past - whether there was an irresistible tendency for opium smokers to self-destruction and death, or whether the conscience of the trade should ride with those who sold it or those who smoked it. Why the very thought the opium trade had been like a rival suitor to their love was monstrous. The only issue was whether they could live without each other any longer. He could not. If his uncle still objected, then he would leave the House of Jarman Malleson. He had paid his dues. Perhaps she too had changed and no longer wanted to beat on closed doors, no longer bore a fierce conscience for China.

Sean woke in the first sour glimmer of dawn to a commotion of argument and clanking of key in the lock. He dragged himself up, rubbing his neck already raw from the iron grip of the collar that held him to the wall barely allowing him fitful sleep. Two men in the garb of guards entered. As one of the two stepped towards him key in hand, he threw up a defensive arm to stop him unlocking his collar, fearing worse to come.

He challenged him. 'What on earth's going on?'

He was astounded when the younger man whispered in fluent English as he helped him to his feet. 'You are going to the Factories where you will be rescued,' then added a warning as he straightened up. 'I no speekee Inglisee.'

A bleary Johnnie struggled up, 'where are they taking us?'

Sean whispered urgently, 'shut up, Johnnie. Leave it to me. Do as you're told.'

Johnnie by now was too cowed to argue.

The mysterious young man waved them to waiting sedan chairs, shouldering one end of the pole which bore Sean leaving him to his thoughts. Why did this man of education pass himself off as a coolie? How could he do so without being caught? Was the young man acting with or without authority? It must be without to judge by his nervous tension. No wonder, therefore, they moved at an undue speed through streets just beginning to stir with those still left the city.

Sean winced with every jolt from the pain of his raw neck and ankles already festering with sores. The journey seemed endless. When at last the sedan chair crashed to the ground, Sean crawled painfully out straight onto the marble chips of the ruined statue from the New English Factory. He threw his arms round Mercury's shoulder and kissed his ruined face.

'Have you gone mad?' A battered Johnnie demanded.

The young Chinese masquerader urged Sean to his feet whispering 'We've got to make a run for it.'

'Run where?' He looked towards the Factories, expecting to see a wall of troops ready to mow them down.

'The river, sir. Look the Cameronians.'

'Good grief!'

There was the Atlanta steamship drawing into the beach like a vision in a mirage. Without pausing a moment longer to wonder why the Common was empty, he picked up Mercury's staff and brandished it on high as he rushed with Johnnie and the young coolie to the bank of the river where willing hands grasped them to drag them on board. When their helping hands reached for the Chinese, however, Major Pratt gave a curt order to reject him.

Sean stood fast. 'But he saved us.'

Major Pratt brushed him aside. 'On someone else's orders. They've taken fright after yesterday's victory.'

'No, Major, he has acted without any orders and risked his own life. He was one of our bearers.'

'I have no orders to rescue any native, Mr. Jarman.'

Sean stared helplessly at Major Pratt, whose knowledge of the Chinese was so far confined to brief skirmishes and the prevalent belief they were an inferior species, particularly coolies.

But the 'coolie' could look after himself. He was not going to be rejected by a mere Major. He whisked a paper from his cloth boot, stepped forward and handed it to the Major with a flourish declaring in his flawless English, 'My pass is signed by your Captain Forge, Sir. I am an officer of your intelligence. My name is Kaida Hung.'

Major Pratt, and all those grouped around him including Sean Jarman, gaped at his sudden transformation from obsequious coolie to the dignity of a British intelligence officer with a pass from the Plenipotentiary himself. Major Pratt could not gainsay him, but had to remain until he had put batteries of the Madras Artillery ashore together with sappers. Then he backed offshore to make their way upstream against the tide to join the attack of the Modeste, the Hyacinth and the Algerine on the battery of eleven heavy calibre guns that lay between the heavily armed forts of the Dutch Folly and the French Folly, protecting the residences of the highest officials of the region.

Within the hour, all three escapees were more at risk on the river than they had been in all their long-drawn out hours in the cells. In the heat of battle, the Atlanta's captain, without a river pilot, managed to run her aground hard abreast of the dreaded Dutch Folly. The Modeste and the Hyacinth sent oarsmen to drag her off the sandbank under an acrid blanket of smoke that enveloped them all. Their jocular curses and self-mockery could be heard across the dangerous reach of water, where they were raked with jingal fire as they sweated at their oars. Sean watched them with wonder. These humble ratings could teach them all how to wring grim laughter from the heart of war's essential tragedy with their insouciant courage. They understood the ironies of battle because no commander, however excellent, could ever anticipate all the ridiculous complications that might arise from the basic imperfections of man's judgement.

Major Pratt now bundled the three escapees into the Atlanta's pinnace with orders to join Captain Forge on the Modeste. By the time they reached it the artillery duel, in which it had engaged, had died down and its captain and mate were appraising the damage to its rigging and spars. Sean hailed them. 'Message from Captain Forge'.

Seeing Kaida beside him they hailed back, 'What sueing for peace already?'

'News from within the gates. We were prisoners.'

The Modeste's captain beckoned him alongside. Kaida was first on board just as Captain Forge came on deck with John Norris hard on his heels. John rushed forward to throw his arms round Kaida while Captain Forge pumped his free hand.

'Will someone please explain what this is all about?' The bewildered captain demanded.

John, his arm around Kaida and tears on his cheek, answered. 'This is Kaida Hung.'

Kaida, bowing, addressed him as formally as if he were being received in a county drawing room and not on the deck of a fighting ship in the heat of battle, 'I am delighted to make your acquaintance, Sir.'

The captain asked the inevitable question, 'where did you learn your English?'

'Mostly in England, Sir,' Kaida answered, amused as always. Englishmen had such fixed ideas about other races, as fixed as the Chinese themselves who thought of Chinese scholars like himself as men who never travelled.

John spared him further embarrassment, 'he went to England with my family. We're like brothers.'

'You treat him as if he'd returned from the dead.'

'In a sense he has. He was about to be thrown into prison.'

'To join my brother who was likely to betray me under torture.'

Captain Forge interjected thankfully, 'then you are safe.'

'And for the moment so is he thanks to the rebels in the hills,' Kaida answered gravely, 'they paid the bribes to get him out.'

'God in Heaven!' John Norris swore.

What a hot-headed idiot Kaida had been to compromise his family by throwing in his lot with the riff-raff that claimed all the highest motives of rebellion only to pursue their own criminal ends. It left him with only one choice, abdication, not only from his destiny but China itself. It was an abdication from a mystery, a legend, a lost dream, from any hope of a normal career even a modest one in the middle ranks of the hierarchy of mandarins.

Captain Forge took a last anxious look at the storm clouds massed over the city with their promise of torrential rain before he took Kaida and John Norris below, isolating them from Sean Jarman and Johnnie. What he had to say was not for the ears of any of the Jarman clan. He sat them down to steaming hot porridge. As they attacked the thick mass crowned with dark treacle and butter, and washed it down with an equally dark hot cup of tea, his first question was of the weather. Would it rain today?

'Buckets to borrow your phrase.' Kaida minced no words, as he ate his porridge politely wondering if he would ever see his preferred steaming rice gruel again. 'Your men on the heights will find it hard to keep their powder dry.'

A critical point, Captain Forge was obliged to concede. How could the force to the west of the city attack the northern hills tomorrow as General Gaunt proposed if they could not keep their powder dry? Particularly since three of the four columns the General intended should occupy the four hills to the north of the city, escalade the city wall or blow up the North Gate would be out of range of the protection of either their nine pounders or their muskets. He raged inwardly.

Had General Gaunt taken leave of his senses, or forgotten that only a handful of marines from the 'Blenheim' had the new reliable percussion muskets? What had been the use of dragging the nine pounders, as well as the twelve pounder howitzers with such grinding labour three miles round the lowlying rice paddies across the spurs, broken with hollows and covered with rocks and monstrous gravestones, up into the Purple Cloud Hills overlooking the city, only to employ tactics that made no use of them? The threat of the guns over the city would be enough without General Gaunt's bulldog attachment to the idea he must enter the city by the formidable North Gate, and seek to dominate it from the hill within. Couldn't he see the city was spiritually in his range already? Didn't he understand how dangerous it would be to prolong the battle by a day or an hour in this death-laden battleground? Hadn't he learned the lesson of Chusan that the real enemy was not the citizens inside the walls of Canton but deadly malaria and dysentery that lay waiting in the open country outside - at its most treacherous in this sticky weather? Could he not foresee the half of the fighting force that had survived to date would follow those who had succumbed like flies in Chusan Island?

He thought sadly of that extraordinary, lively procession of men in red and blue he had led up Browne's Passage to the west of the city in seventy boats, towed by the Nemesis, the longest-ever tow of a single train of boats ever attempted. A weird motley of boats, not only from a dozen navy vessels, but also from Wang Chung's abandoned junks and anything afloat that could be commandeered from the river. They had been a chaffing, jocular cargo of men with an air of going to the fair, rather than their own doom in an implacable countryside.

He voiced his anxiety to Kaida, 'our esteemed commander seems to think once we breach the walls and occupy the hill that dominates the Old City our problems are over.'

'They will just begin, Sir. How can he dominate a city of a million people?'

'I'm told the city is a shell. Many of the civilians have left, Kaida.'

'Their houses remain, sir. Each street is a little walled city. And two armies of troops to defend them, Tartar and Cantonese.'

'Do they have the will to defend?'

'The Tartar yes. They will fight to the death. Surrender is a disgrace no Tartar can bear. He will kill his women and children before he kills himself. He will set them on fire, cut their throats, throw them down wells, kill them by any means rather than bear the shame of defeat. The strength of the Tartar rule in our country is the terrible majesty of their courage to die.'

'Ye Gods and little fishes!'

A chill went through Captain Forge at the apocalyptic vision conjured up by Kaida, as a spatter of heavy raindrops swept across the porthole. Menace from the skies as well as from the Tartar New City within. How could they face forty-five thousand suicidal Tartars inside Canton with less than two thousand men?'

'You would be much better advised to reach a truce, Sir.'

'Would Yihshan accept a truce?' Captain Forge eyed Kaida doubtfully.

'He might prefer that to defeat which can only mean disaster for himself and danger to the monarchy.'

'A truce?' Captain Forge pondered glumly, 'our Expeditionary Force no longer trusts truces.'

'The officials and the people of the city would welcome you with open arms.'

'Would they say afterwards they had tricked us into peace as they have before?'

'No matter what you say, sir, they will distort your truth to suit the image they want to see in their mirror.'

If Captain Forge had learnt one thing in his years on the China Coast it was that the same facts could appear absolutely different between himself and Chinese mandarins.

Kaida finished wearily with a warning, 'Sir, you can't invade the city. If you did both armies would fight as one. You must divide and rule. A truth you once told me that goes back beyond the Romans.'

Captain Forge squared his shoulders. Well, he was still sole Plenipotentiary. He could conclude peace single-handedly. He could ignore General Gaunt with his dream of a general's triumph, a dream nurtured under altogether alien conditions in India. It centred on the domination of an entire city by his guns planted on one strategic hill, no matter what the cost or the sequel.

Yet he thought, staring as Kaida had done at White Cloud Mountains where their victorious troops must be getting drenched in their flimsy tents, he could not merely retreat from that position now so hazardous to health. What could give him the victory, render the city without battle? His thoughts drifted into the past. What had other commanders done in like situations before him? What had Clive of India done? At last the solution struck him.

'They will have to pay ransom.'

John Norris spoke up at last. 'Gaunt will be furious.'

'Why for God's sake?' Captain Forge asked irritably, the weariness of three nights with little sleep overtaking him.

'You intend to use the ransom money as indemnity to the merchants for the loss of their opium?'

'I intend to keep the promise I made when I surrendered it to the Chinese government in the first place. The merchants will be paid at least a percentage without the debt His Britannic Majesty has already so summarily repudiated.'

'Surely if General Gaunt does not get the ransom he considers his due, he will seize it from the city.'

'Do you suggest the British Army would loot the city?'

'Could you guarantee they would not?'

John Norris could justifiably ask the bitter question. Had the troops not got drunk in Tinghae, assaulted some of the population and wandered off at various times to be kidnapped or murdered? How much temptation could they withstand if the local population put it in their way? Particularly the sepoys from Madras of lower caste, or no caste at all, unlike the higher caste Bengal sepoys.

Captain Forge stretched, stood up, reached for his oilskins and led the way back onto the bridge to scan the weather once more. The clouds still hung massed over White Cloud Mountains to the north of the city. The rain seemed to have set in for the day. He could imagine the soil turning to thick mud that clung to boots, adding lead to the weight each soldier already carried with every step.

Kaida's thoughts were elsewhere as he huddled in the lee of the paddlewheel housing. 'I forgot one thing, sir. Just a rumour you understand.'

'And that is?'

'The patriotic gentry called to arms by the Commissioners.'

'What's new about that, Kaida? Lin raised that self-defence force months ago. We've given them no cause for quarrel.'

'Oh, but you have sir.'

Captain regarded him doubtfully. He seemed shaken, suffering from loss of nerve. 'Has someone told you we've attacked any of their villages, violated civilians?'

'Ah sir, what is violation?' Kaida responded with gentle sadness. 'They say you have desecrated their graves.'

'That's absurd. Who would want to loot or open up graves? My men would be far too superstitious for that.'

It was John Norris who remembered how he had seen soldiers manhandling their guns across the tomb-strewn slopes, and had wondered whether to warn the Captain of the consequences.

'The Madras gunners dragged their guns across the hillside yesterday sir. This is desecration of their ancestors' graves in the eyes of the villagers.'

With his friend's support, Kaida ventured more. 'They took buffaloes for their mess, and some sepoys took women.'

'Are those rumours fact?' Captain Forge demanded, his brow thunderous as the pendulous clouds to the north. All goodwill lost by the crimes of a few. Tinghae all over again.

'Who knows. What we do know is that up till now the villagers saw the quarrel as one between the Manchus and yourselves. Now they see it as their own quarrel against you. Therefore you face a new danger from the patriotic troops to the rear of your camps on the northern hills.'

'A development which the General can ill afford in weather like this,' Captain

Forge said angrily. The news gave extra urgency to his decision to bargain for a truce. He could no longer afford to wait for ideal conditions. The time had come to act. 'Everything depends on the speed with which we can get ransom.'

'Howqua is on his way.' Once again Howqua was to be the bottomless bank for the follies and failings of his rulers.

'Where is Howqua now? Where can I find him?' Captain Forge asked anxiously, dreading he might be as far afield as Foshan.

'There he comes now,' Kaida pointed to Howqua's unpretentious barge hugging the ravaged bank on the Honam side of the river near his burnt-out warehouses. 'One favour, first, an urgent favour. A matter of life and death for me. Will you grant me citizenship?'

Captain Forge was contrite. This thin, sensitive man had risked his life time and again for him, giving him intelligence that had made balanced calculations posssible. Yet he had not spared a moment's thought that, as an isolated spy, Kaida was in more danger than any of them. He put both hands on Kaida's shoulders as if to invest him with the safety of the sovereignty of Her Majesty on the spot. 'Of course! You wish to go to Hong Kong?'

'I am safe nowhere else. May I have a passport at once, sir?'

'Won't tomorrow do? You'll be safe on board here.'

'Sir, with apologies. If you were killed today, who could swear to my services.'

'It is I who should apologise. You'll have your passport at once, and, if I had the choice, it would be delivered to you with all the honours of an investiture.'

When Captain Forge handed Kaida that fragile guarantee of his freedom and safety a few minutes later as all officers present stood to attention and saluted, Kaida accepted with tears in his eyes saying, 'at last I will be able to speak free English!'

Only John Norris was aware of the dangers of Kaida living in the open. 'Hong Kong is not far enough for that, my friend. You will still have to live in the shadows if you don't want your life shortened!'

There was no time for Kaida to argue if his friend was right. Howqua's barge had slipped alongside, Howqua himself in the plainest of robes on a plain chair in the cabin below. Howqua was as discreet as he had been in all his negotiations with the city fathers these past two days. The exhaustion Howqua felt showed on his face and prompted Captain Forge to wonder whether he would last long enough to free the city.

Howqua refused all gratitude from Captain Forge. 'Thank Chung Tai Tai. She has paid her debt to Holly.'

'To Holly?' Holly a crucial factor in the war?

'The young Mr. Jarman and Mrs Howe have twin fates.' So Chung Tai Tai had turned matchmaker, as he was, in a larger sense marriage broker for Canton through Howqua.

Howqua maintained the niceties of the meeting. Haste was improper even on a field of war. Captain Forge waited while he savoured a pinch of snuff from the delicately fashioned, stoppered bottle at his belt, offered him tea and listened gravely while Howqua complained that the Hoppo had curtly opposed his desire to retire as he wanted to put his affairs in order before he met his ancestors.

Grave and courteous in return, Captain Forge thought how ludicrous the affairs of the world were, that he should sit here negotiating with the one man he had most sought to set aside in any negotiations when he had first come to Canton, as a man too mean and humble in the hierarchy of power, as a man whose very existence as intermediary humbled the English envoy far too low. Yet here Howqua sat, undeniably the real power, deciding the fate of both the High Commissioners and the Tartar-General, who had reviled him on their arrival as a sheep existing only to be shorn. Well this shearing would save the lives of them all.

At last Howqua broached their most momentous business. Encouraged, Captain Forge catechised him. Could Howqua speak for the Prefect of the city? For the City Commissioners? For Beijing's Great Pacificator? Throughout, Howqua's steady regard was that of an old man without anxiety, fear, anger or passion. A man whose life, unlike his own, had already sailed into calmer waters because he felt close to death.

Howqua's answer was laconic. 'The majority will prevail.'

'Against the Tartar-General?'

'The Tartar-General only wants one enemy at a time.'

'He's afraid of rebellion?'

'He's afraid of anarchy, Your Excellency. We are very close to anarchy. The people of Canton have overflowed beyond the walls of the city like the Pearl River when it floods the plains. They don't want to be there, a burden on the villages. And the villages don't want them. An instability almost as dangerous as a full rebellion. A breakdown in the law which holds the whole countryside to ransom while foam of the land are rampant everywhere.'

Howqua opened the bargaining at three million taels' ransom for the city. Captain Forge dragged the figure slowly upwards, refuting Howqua's arguments with tedious patience. Liabilities of the Co-Hong. Debts of their bankrupt brethren. Impoverishment from opium loss. Chains of copper cash worthless as stones. Taxes now onerous from inflation. Finally injustice of the war.

Captain Forge dismissed his rhetoric on war sternly. 'The justice of the war has nothing to do with the facts of the battlefield.'

When the ransom price reached six million taels, Howqua became obdurate. Kaida advised him the old man, once implacable, would not be likely to change.

'Going, going, gone,' Captain Forge cried, baffling even Kaida. 'I will accept that final bid on one condition, and one only, that all troops and the three Comissioners must leave the city, bag and baggage, in six days and move no less than sixty miles away. Only the troops from the province of Kwangtung can remain to keep order. In return, we will withdraw all troops beyond the Bogue and hand all forts within back to the Imperial government. One last proviso. The money, all the money, must be paid by sunset.'

If any doubt lingered in the Plenipotentiary's mind at having settled for an immediate peace for a moderate ransom, it was set at rest by the end of the day when news arrived from General Gaunt's command on the northern hills. Just as Kaida had forecast, the Association of the soldiers of Righteousness had roused fifteen thousand braves from the villages with the will to fight that had abandoned the townspeople, hanging over the city walls as the citizens of Rome might have once welcomed their heroes returning in a triumph, waving myriad white flags and screaming 'Forge! Joss!'

Worse, the rebellious braves claimed to be on a divine mission. Had they not seen the Genii of the Ram hovering over the city? Imbued with fanatical fervour, they were advancing en masse armed with muskets, spears and pitchforks screaming rapine against the weary, sodden and heat-tormented British troops in their footholds on the Purple Cloud Hills.

As Captain Forge heard the ominous news, he wondered how General Gaunt could possibly fail to accept the necessity to forego the right to sack the treasure of the city, as loot for his men, in face of the reality of the question what use reward could be to men who would be dead and gone by the time it was amassed? More spoils to the victors who were left, one might say. But would it be General Gaunt who would answer to Parliament for the sacrifice of one half of the Expeditionary Force to the greed of the other? He knew only too well he would be the lamb of sacrifice on that altar.

He did not prophesy for himself that General Gaunt would prove his implacable enemy. When he heard that the Plenipotentiary, Captain Forge, had signed an armistice with the city and cheated him of the glory of occupation, he raged the money paid in 'ransom' was the army's right as the fruit of battle. Had they not paid the price in men dead from sunstroke, gashes, amputations and agonising cramps of dysentery? Why should the money go to honour an old promise to the merchants for the cost of their confiscated opium?

General Gaunt took his wrath to the only court of appeal open to him, the Minister. How dare His Excellency, Captain Forge, sign a truce with the enemy without consultation with his Commander-in-Chief in the field! How dare he withdraw when the city of Canton was in his grasp! How could he justify ending a war so timidly that would only have to be fought all over again? Let him stand at the Bar not only of Parliament but the British nation! Let them judge who was the hero of the affair - Captain Forge, who cheated the British Army of its victory, or General Gaunt!

* * * * * *

CHAPTER 11

1841-1842
The Fragrant Harbour

John Norris stood up as Holly came with swift steps into his office at the Casa Garden. The rising heat of an early summer's day could not account for the overwhelming sense of all his being overturned, of a confusion and fear worse than any he had felt in the Battle of Canton. He managed to overcome his shyness sufficiently to say,

'Holly, how glad I am to see you.'

Now or never he must try to court her before any in the multitude of batchelors snatched her up. He must find the words to seduce her heart not her mind. But even as he hoped for the slimmest chance to win her, he knew the controlled reserve of his nature, deeply instilled by his father and imprinted by his Puritan religion, would probably handicap him beyond that chance. He would remain like a commoner, doomed to admire majesty from afar. And what did he have in common with her?

He took both her hands in his own and said merely, 'Oh Holly, it's good to see you so restored to health.'

'More flesh on my bones, it's true,' she laughed returning his grip, 'they didn't keep an imperial table in the Ningpo prison.'

'I was shocked to see you when you first came back.'

'My faith kept me going as you know, John. Now it's my faith in the future of Hong Kong.'

'You're going to buy in there?'

'You've guessed it in one.'

His heart soared with a quick aerial lift, a flash of brilliance in the dark green of its cage like one of Tim Bird's parrots. 'You're going to remain on the coast?'

'Why, John what did you expect?'

'That you would leave.'

'This place is where my best friends are - like you, John.' She caught his hands again just to feel the solid reality of this man of truth everyone loved. His hands shook in her own as if he were coming down with malaria. She regarded him anxiously, oblivious to the urgency of his love. 'Why should I leave?'

He could barely answer. 'Because of revulsion from China over your sufferings.'

'Yes and no, John. More no than yes. That's why I need to see Barron to ask him if I should buy land in this auction.'

'I thought you'd made up your mind.'

'Everyone is adamant they'll stay away, each for a different reason.'

When they found Barron, he chided her. 'The very merchants, who ridicule me today, will turn up to the auctions next week.'

Holly asked anxiously, 'a rush to join, you say?'

'My advice is to wait till that rush dies down.' Barron spread a topographical chart of Hong Kong on his desk and pointed to the lots for sale near Possession Point. 'These are all waterfront sites, good for warehousing you'll agree.'

'Which is why I had one in mind. One of these possibly, Barron,' she suggested, hovering over the chart.

He cut her short. 'First ask the question, will that site be sheltered in a typhoon? Remember the last real typhoon that hit Macao? How will warehouses there withstand the kind of waves and winds that shifted those huge stone blocks in Macao some years back? Blocks that take eight men to lift each one.'

But that was before Holly's time. There had been no typhoon for several years. Their ravages were merely local legend.

'My advice is to wait,' Barron repeated, 'let others take the risk.'

'Why shouldn't she take the risk if she wants to?' Flora protested.

Holly agreed. It was all very well for Barron to be cautious. He had experienced no urgent desire to found a permanent home as she had when standing on the shore of Hong Kong Island. Barron, like so many executors of the burgeoning British empire, seemed to have adapted to a nomad way of life, making home in any country where he pitched his metaphorical tent with an ease undoubtedly facilitated by the congenial radiance of his marriage with Flora. Obviously, home to them both was wherever the other was. Holly, however, was alone and happiness could not be transferred from the place where she had found it. She wanted to remain where she had her happiest memories and her most likely hope of redemption in the future from present grief. The sooner she could build hard by the sea the better.

Only Barron fully understood what a grave mistake this would be and searched for the words to convince Holly. 'Typhoons are not the main risk, Holly. Hong Kong fever is.' He spoke with such gravity, all three stared at him as if he had announced an outbreak of bubonic plague. 'All the soldiers bivouacing there are going down like flies.'

Flora gasped. 'On top of your sicklist from Canton?'

Nearly half the Expeditionary Force were already desperately ill from their eight days exposure, alternately drenched and roasted during the Battle of Canton. Now ill from ague, dysentery, diarrhoea, fever and war wounds.

'Yes, our surgeons, familiar with the dreaded yellow fever of Panama and the African jungle fever, say this scourge is a cross between them. The Chinese burn joss sticks and say it is retribution on the Red Beards for their siege of Canton.' He pointed to the sites of the camps immediately to the east and west of the land to be sold on the waterfront. 'Do you really want the risk of living between those death camps right now?'

'Why have those proposing to buy there not been warned then?'

'Because we don't know who is right. Those who declare it deadly ground because of its aspect, or our surgeons who say the sickness is due to the effect of heavy rain in the heat on newly opened ground.'

Some of the fatigue of the last weeks showed in his weary demeanour. He could have done without this fresh complication.

'How long will that be?' Holly longed to leave all her memories in Macao and begin again.

'Until people have built and lived there in different areas at different levels. Some on the flat. Some on the slopes. We can judge then which is healthy or not.'

Holly had listened in bewildered silence. 'It's my belief the China Coast seems to foster every calamity known to man except earthquake.'

She left it to John to ask, 'how many cases exactly?'

'Too many considering I must lead this insane expedition north in a few weeks' time,' Barron replied.

'Why don't you keep the soldiers on the ships then Barron?' Flora asked sensibly.

'For a very good reason. Possession means occupation, as the thousands of Chinese asking for asylum under our flag already understand. Never fear, Holly, we'll look after you.'

'With all this, Barron, it seems crazy to rush into the land auction, Barron.'

'If I waited I would risk our government renouncing my treaty with China, forcing us to live in some much more accursed spot like Ningpo or Chusan because some Whitehall buff thinks it falls at the most strategic place on the map.

He folded up the chart, his movements of the same precision as his mind in the chess of diplomacy. 'You know there's not much difference between myself and the Chinese mandarins. We both have our war and peace parties at Court and the respective Majesties in pendulum beween them.' Aware of the bemused look on the faces of the three people most near to him in Macao, he continued, because of that pendulum Hong Kong will stay whether I'm here or not. There's an old saying, possession is nine tenths of the law.'

Holly decided to keep an open mind, and to go to Hong Kong in order to see for herself. It was possible Barron was too battle-weary to be reliable in his judgement on its future.

* * * * * *

Reunion

Sean strode in nervous anticipation towards Kingsman's makeshift warehouse on the Hong Kong harbour waterfront, where he knew he would find Holly. He found her sitting in a tiny pigeonhole checking bills of lading with her new comprador overwhelmed, like all merchant shipmasters, with the demands of the Expeditionary Force. Once he would have been dismayed and confused by such a scene so inconsistent with his notions of love and marriage. Now he understood her commitment only as an enhancement of marriage, a dimension that would spare marriage the narrow boredom he often saw in others. Here and now was the utterly right place to propose, here in the heart of the trade she had chosen for herself.

He knew her heart jumped, as his did, when she looked up and saw him at the door eyes alight with the intense flame of his love. She rose with surprise, relief, joy succeeding each other in the exuberance of her welcome, hands reaching out for him. 'Thank God, you're safe. I heard you'd been arrested. I died a thousand deaths.'

Her comprador bowed low and disappeared, magician of discretion as of all trade.

Sean threw himself on one knee, hands clasped round hers. He would propose properly. No random possession this time. 'Holly, I had time to think in prison. I came to China with only one thought once, to make my fortune without regard to means. I imagined like everyone else that was the way of it on the Coast. I did not see it as an individual matter of conscience. Then I asked myself who am I to change it? I won't be rich, but I have enough for a start.'

Holly suppressed a smile. Trust a man to turn a declaration of love into a manifesto of self-justification. Why couldn't he simply say 'I love you and want to marry you' instead of complicating a simple proposal by turning her into a sort of devil's advocate?

'What are you saying, Sean?' she asked softly, her eyes full of affection and amusement, 'that you're retiring from the Coast?'

'That you come first with me, Holly. You always will. I can't live without you. Will you marry me?'

This time her answer was unqualified. 'Yes, Sean no one will divide us ever again.' Her only reservation that she would not marry him until the war was over. She knew he was to follow the British Force shortly when it went north to Nanking at least as far as Shanghai. She wanted no marriage with another death like Billy Howe's.

When he took her hand and pulled her gently to her feet, she allowed him to sweep her into the violent embrace for which she had so often longed, and which now said all they had to say - that they would always stay together come hell or high water 'until death do us part.'

Holly intended to waste no time in telling Flora the news when she returned to Macao. But when she landed, she was astonished to encounter frantic crowds along the waterfront banging gongs and exploding little bamboo petards until at last she caught the chanting of 'typhoon' in all their wailing and shouting. The signs were ominous by the time she arrived at the Casa Garden - huge threatening black masses of clouds shot through with brief flashes of vivid lightning, deafening peals of thunder, and a sultry oppressive atmosphere.

Flora's first words as she welcomed her with a generous hug, 'do try and talk Barron out of sailing to Hong Kong tonight. Says he can't let Commodore Brendan down. Insists he's seen all that commotion before, says such uproar in the universe has often turned out to be nothing more than a huff and puff of the gods to remind men they can't trifle with their elements.'

'What's so desperately urgent at Hong Kong that he couldn't wait the day out?' Holly asked as they proceeded up the grand staircase to her baronial bedroom.

'First and foremost the Admiral has Hong Kong fever and is odds on to die. Second, the entire fleet of the Expeditionary Force is anchored in Hong Kong Harbour - men o' war, steamers, store ships, transports - all close together some with not even enough room enough to veer cable. A storm could not only wreck the bulk of that fleet, but all plans for launching an attack on the north. There's no one there with the necessary authority over the whole caboodle to order them to another anchorage. Barron and old Brendan could not possibly have foreseen this crisis, when they rushed over here to insist the Governor protect us British citizens against the renewed threat of the patriots. Now it has come, they can't get back quickly enough.' Flora helped Holly stow her clothes with an enviable calm.

Holly never ceased to marvel at the cheerful stoicism of these wives on the frontiers of Empire. 'Aren't you worried?'

'In ordinary circumstances I would be Holly. But to tell the truth I'd rather see both men get away from Macao right now. I can't forget the size of the price on their heads - one hundred and fifty thousand dollars between them. It's literally a case of between the devil and the deep blue sea. Better the sea.'

'The devil here in the Casa Garden? It's hard to remember that murderous kidnappers lurk round any corner,' Holly said wistfully as she leaned out of the window. 'How I love the serenity of this view!'

'You prefer it to the bay?' Flora envied others their hilltop views.

'Those old trees! They speak for all eternity and cut our human follies down to size.' Suddenly she was aware they were still as any painting. 'Look, Flora, how lifeless they are. I've never seen them so still before.' From across the wall drifted a rising crescendo of gongs and firecrackers as if the whole of Macao were a battleground. 'Unnaturally still. As it is before a catastrophe.'

Flora leaned out beside her. 'The dogs are not howling. They do before earthquakes so they say.'

'It's as if all the hungry ghosts of Macao haunted this one spot alone.'

Flora, suddenly fearful, was out the door with Holly giving chase, saying, 'I've just remembered. A typhoon in the sixth moon blows with the greatest violence.' She hurtled down the stairs calling out to Barron in the hall below, 'Barron, I'm afraid.'

'Time to go, sweetheart.' She embraced him so fiercely, he protested, 'darling, I'm only going for a week.'

'But never through a typhoon, Barron.'

He tipped up her chin with a smile of reassurance. 'The Louisa's brought me through fire at Kowloon and battles at the Bogue forts. She's my good luck charm.'

'But not through a typhoon yet.' She clung to him still.

'We'll dodge the worst of it, and if we get roughed up a bit, why she's stable as a good, stout whaleboat. We'll be as safe as houses.'

Holly stepped forward and touched his arm. 'Do me a favour, Barron,' she pleaded, 'take my good luck charm with you. My guarantee of safety.' She slipped the amulet she wore on a chain round her neck over her head, and handed it to him.

He hesitated before taking it. 'A strange sort of weapon.'

She ignored the flippancy. 'Blessed in the Temple of Kwanyin.'

'And this guarantees my safety at sea?' He eyed it dubiously.

'Your safety on land, Barron. Remember I never expected to be shipwrecked in Fukien.'

Barron did not gainsay her after that reminder. He took it from her to stare at the neatly engraved symbol. 'It doesn't look very strong medicine to me.'

'Very powerful. I can vouch for that. It sprung me from prison.' Holly noted Flora's stricken face with guilt. How insensitive of her to frighten her dear friend with asserting an overt prophecy of doom, driven as she was by some strange prescience.

'I must weigh anchor.' Barron kissed Flora, then ran down the short flight of steps waving the amulet with a cheerful smile. 'Kwanyin will look after me. or my father's award for diplomacy in Denmark.' He waved the Hanoverian medal he habitually carried.

Flora teased Holly as the hours passed harmlessly, the evening almost tranquil as they went to bed. When the thunder began again, at first it was a mere distant rumble then world-shaking crashes which died away for a time. But when it returned it came in a heaven-rending battle of the elements detonating the very universe. And after each flash of lightning, exploding its weird blue light across the landscape in eerie revelation they were plunged into a pitch-black darkness. Then an excessive deluge of rain began, flung slantwise across the window panes on fierce squalls of wind whose roaring blast could be heard between every round of thunderclaps.

Flora crouched at the window in terror of her husband. 'My God, I hope they're past Lantao Island, and not out in that!'

By the time the heavens had exploded into the full, awesome rage of the storm, the Louisa had been fighting to make way for hours with a rising gale from the north-west, tossing like a toy boat on a roller coaster of mountainous waves. Commodore Brendan's native servant was standing by him in the wheelhouse, teeth chattering with fright, as Captain Forge was fighting a losing fight to keep head on to the sea; a fight more desperate when the fierce wind smashed their mainboom like a twig. The sea drove them backwards when the mate was jibing the mainsail. The crew barely managed to get the gaff topside down, to twist the topsail off and lash it, then could do no more than abandon themselves to the whims of a storm too terrible to battle.

By dusk they were slipping fast to leeward, while the driving squall of rain and haze of spray had reduced visibility to their bow. They could see nothing but the nightmare conflict of the elements with each other. No wonder, Captain Forge thought, the Chinese say a typhoon is a mother gale abroad with her offspring, the gales from all four quarters of the heavens. The only comfort he could find, if there could be any in their hopeless situation, was that a typhoon that turned about from east by north to west, as this one promised, would not be as bad as the other way round.

He could find no comfort in the sound he suddenly heard, as dark closed in, the terrifying sound of waves breaking on rocks. The mate had heard it too. Together with the bosun, he struggled to get the anchor overboard in the desperate hope it might hold them from drifting onto the jagged menace of the rocks, only dimly seen as a thin, high line of breaking spray. That done, they could do no more than try to conserve their strength while they rested and pray the small sheet aft with the mizzen forestay sail could help to keep them head on. They pitched and rolled all night long, sleepless from the deafening tumult, soaked to the skin with the icy spray that penetrated every corner of the vessel, nauseated by the stench of vomit, intimidated by the violent fortissimo of interminable thunderclaps.

Captain Forge never thought to have seen the dignified Commodore crouched all night on the cabin floor, arms clasped round the table legs, shaking from fear as much as cold, moaning 'we'll never survive.' No shred of his famous courage under fire to be seen.

Captain Forge patted his shoulder encouragingly. 'Never fear! We'll ride this one out. She's shipping very little water yet. She's riding well.'

As if to bely his words, the gale seemed to increase every moment against all possibility. Before long, Captain Forge knew very well it would be a case of all hands on deck to survive until the typhoon reversed to blow from the opposite quarter. The first light of day revealed a more daunting scene than Captain Forge's worst imagination. A dense haze, thick as a London fog, stretched across the tormented landscape. Dark, massive clouds scudded wildly overhead from the north with an endless barrage of drenching rain. The gloomy seas were sculptured into huge trenches by the terrible hammer of the wind. It seemed impossible to believe the gods of vengeance, striding their heavens, could summon up more legions from hell. Yet that was what their barometer prophesied, dropping so low it had plummeted below all reading.

If Kwanying could survive such a storm in her junk when she lived on earth, then Captain Forge consoled himself, as he struggled forward to lash himself at the bow to act as lookout for the dangers he expected to lie ahead as they continued to drift inshore, so could he. He saw no reason for hope that he could succeed in averting their annihilation, as he watched the debris of innumerable wrecks driving swiftly by them. He was seized by bitter despair as he realised they were swept on the thrust of a rising fury in the gale. The waves, thrashing him where he stood, reared to such a height it seemed impossible they would crest each one and not be overwhelmed like the flotsam on all sides.

Captain Forge hesitated. The lives of all aboard depended on what little wisdom of the unrecognisable deep he had to withstand the grievous whips of this tempest. What would be the best? To hold the Louisa head to the wind so she would neither stand on her beam ends nor turn turtle? To hoist a token sail or none?

At this moment a lull fell that could only last a short time as the eye of the typhoon passed across them, and the force of the storm began to blow from the opposite quarter. He urged the crew to slip the mizzen forestay sail, cut away the mizzen mast, and hoist a forestay sail. They fought across the slippery, lurching deck to finish in time, swearing at the clumsiness of their cold hands. The forestay sail was scarcely up before the wind came in again with such force as to blow out the sail and whip it off at bullet speed. The Louisa drove for mile after mile with Captain Forge peering grimly into the fog of spray, expecting to be swallowed in the gigantic seas or to be battered on rocks it was impossible to see.

Suddenly he saw doom ahead. The little cutter was driving down on an evil line of foam that advertised the dreaded land ahead. 'Land ahoy!' he shouted. His crew could not hear for the wild flapping of torn canvas. He gesticulated towards the ominous, towering line of spray that suggested the high cliffs of a large island. It was if they were looking into the mouth of hell itself.

He gave the only possible order across the shrieking wind. 'Hoist the peak of the mainsail above the gunwale.' By a miracle it would hold the Louisa steady. As they slipped closer to the murderous surf, moment by moment, they could clearly hear its roar over the piercing whistle of the wind. A huge comber fell ravenously on the deck. The mate struggled to free the peak where it had fallen and jammed in the larboard gangway. The greedy backwash of the waves whipped the tackle like a noose round his waist and flung him into the deadly sea.

The crew, still working in grim unison for their survival, managed to rig a scudding sail while the helmsman fought to hold the wheel steady and save them from a certain death sentence on a deadly precipice to larboard. Their salvation was short-lived. Beyond there loomed yet more breakers and another precipice.

Captain Forge took the wheel himself. The Commodore crouched beside him in the wheelhouse awed by his Plenipotentiary's seamanship, all differences between them forgotten. Here, if ever, was a born sailor tested to the utmost. He watched in terror as yet another precipice slid by almost close enough to touch, the meagre scudding sail just enough to keep the Louisa from turning turtle on the clamorous thrust of the tumbling seas along the cliff-face constantly breaking over her decks. Through it all, Captain Forge fighting the bucking wheel, she ran. Once nearly on her broadside. Once with the wind abeam.

Suddenly Captain Forge saw land dead ahead and felt a new surge of terrible despair. How could they possibly survive being dashed against that formidable cliff-face with its fringe of spray fifty feet high? He peered through the spindrift. Curse this coast with its hostile shores. All cliffs. No beaches. Not even a fringe. He searched that forbidding surf for some keyhole no matter how small, surf towering above the Louisa's mast. The wind howled and shrieked around him. He made a point out just in time to spin the wheel hard to port. The tough little boat turned grudgingly as the scudding sail tore to ribbons with the strain, and carried her with an agonisingly slow response just clear of the point, with the surf tossing them savagely, and straight towards a tiny aperture in the rock wall confronting them giving entrance to a scrap of beach.

'Good old Kwanying,' Captain Forge cried to the wind all nerves keyed to their salvation. One small mistake, one tiny shift in the wind and they would be doomed.

He headed for the gap through the rocky headlands, foam boiling and seething round their fringe, the crew standing ready to let the anchor go the moment they struck, and drove through with grim cliffs lofting above them on either side. A wave reared to dash them onto the rocks. The seas drove her onshore, surf breaking above them in a deluge that swamped the vessel. As the sea drew back for the next assault, the strongest swimmers, led by the Captain and Commodore, jumped overboard to scramble for their lives across the slippery rocks, coiled ropes slung around their necks to fasten life lines for those still left on board.

Once safely ashore, Commodore Brendan left Captain Forge to take stock. All the crew were alive even the Commodore's blackamoor, except for the three swept overboard earlier. Only half had all their clothes. Fewer had shoes. They had thrown them off before jumping into the seething water, or had their trousers ripped by the fanged rocks as they scrambled above the waterline. Their eyes were red and sore. Their hair was stiff with salt. The Commodore and himself were travesties of officers with their clothing wrecked, their faces scratched and bleeding, their knuckles raw from clutching at the barnacled rocks. Almost no one had weapons.

Worse, they had no idea where they had been wrecked. Captain Forge knew they would be safer if they had been lucky enough to be thrown up on one of the small islands that dotted the river estuary. But if on the islands of Heangshan or Lantao, or the mainland, they would be safe only so long as they were clinging to the narrow rock shelf they had reached just above the full flux of the waves. Safe but not comfortable. Only half their number could huddle for any protection in a tiny cave formed by a fissure in the rock face, the rest forced to suffer outside. All were equally damp from the percolating runnels of the endless and remorseless driving rain.

For all their misery, Captain Forge raised a laugh with, 'my, oh my, we do all look a bunch of scarecrows.' He added to the Commodore beside him, 'thank goodness, they won't be able to identify us.'

He and the Commodore laughed uproariously as they took a good look at each other. Who would be likely to take them for officers, dressed as they were with ragged and torn shirts and trousers, no sign of rank, no shoes? Just as well with such a huge price for their heads, dead or alive.

'Who are 'they' sir?' the burly unshaven bosun asked.

'Whoever finds us as they will. I don't need to tell you mum's the word if you want to save your lives because the safety of your necks depend on ours. We're not officers. You're not Queen's Navy you understand.'

The men would never have refused Captain Forge obedience for a moment after his superlative performance at the helm the past day. They had seen with their own eyes. Not one man in all that fleet in Hong Kong could have excelled his seamanship. There was no doubt he had saved their lives. Let any man jibe at their captain from that day forward and he would buy a fight.

Captain Forge sent them foraging on the ebb tide, lashing themselves first to rock stumps even though only the waves were not only shadows of those dashing themselves on the narrow jumble of the water's edge in the full fury of the storm.

He laughed to see their booty of eight bottles of gin. 'Well if that isn't the strangest lottery. Not as good as rum but it will serve to warm your guts.' He passed a bottle around and they took a good long swig apiece. 'Why, blankets and a tarpaulin. What no mattress to match?'

As for the Commodore, he winced at the prospect of a night's torment, bolt upright in a circle on tumbled stones with cascades of water from above, behind and between. But still better than the lot of those crouched under wet blankets and a sail outside.

They sang and dozed all through the long soaking hot night until the first grey light of morning when Captain Forge could send some of them up the cliffs with the bosun, others down to the fast disintegrating wreck of the Louisa only her taffrail and deck planks now showing even at the ebb. As Captain Forge watched them, debating what to do next with twenty two men without food and water on his hands a loud hail came from the bosun above.

'Some Chink wants to talk to you. One of the boys say they know him. A Tanka from Macao. He's waving a paper at me, Cap'n. Your signature on it.'

'My signature?' He was dumbfounded for a moment until he realised it must be his pamphlet about the fact his quarrel was with the government and not the people. What an irony he thought as he scrambled up the rock cliff. The propaganda I condemned first in Lord Nash, and then in myself, might prove my salvation in the end.

The bosun gave him a hand onto the ledge where the Tanka, dressed in the dark blues of a boatman, was waiting.

'Pray he knows the Pirate Queen.'

'How's that, cap'n?' The bosun stared as he tugged at the pocket of his shrunken trousers, hoisted out Holly's amulet and extended it towards the Tanka. The Tanka's eyes flickered with surprise as he pointed across the sea saying 'Ama', then raised two fingers saying 'two tousand taels'. The price of their rescue. Captain Forge raised three fingers in return repeating the Chinese name for Macao, 'Ama'.

The Tanka nodded and beckoned him to follow with all his men. His village, some distance away in a valley beyond two hills, was not so welcoming. The waiting crowd of men flourished billhooks and rakes as their women ran away. Captain Forge called on his men to halt, warning them not to fight or they would sign their own death warrants. Perplexed by their passive stance, the truculent villagers bundled them into a rough house little better han a cowbyre with its whitewashed daub walls and mud floor. An insatiably inquisitive crowd came and went all night long until the air was foetid, and the noise of their chatter a din. They touched, prodded and fingered them all endlessly but most of all Old Joe, the Commodore's servant. One tore off his earrings, another tried to cut off his ear, a third his twisted black knot of hair. Yet more scratched at his black skin to find the white skin underneath, believing the black to be painted on like japanned lacquer to turn him into a slave.

Captain Forge, uneasy at the malice and hate that lurked behind the mocking laughter, forced himself to fight against his weariness as his men slept. His forebodings were justified. They woke to the clamour of villagers, led by men bearing three dead Chinese bound with ropes, crowding into their prison, all of them plainly demanding their prisoners' execution for murdering the Chinese sailors to judge by exaggerated motions of cutting their heads off. This lust for revenge, despite the fact it should have been obvious to all of them as it was to Captain Forge at a glance, that the bonds on the dead Chinese were such as they would have used to lash themselves to the mast of their junks during the typhoon as was their custom.

Captain Forge made an effort to look cheerful despite their desperate plight, cursing the fact he had not taken time to learn a few phrases of Cantonese. He was as helpless now as he had been when trying to cross-examine Gambia natives on the raids of slave-traders. Ah, had he not drawn pictures as for tiny children? He looked vainly for a stick, then remembered Holly's amulet. As he plucked it from his trouser pocket, he saw a flash of recognition in the eyes of the villagers' most aggressive leader. He knelt down and began to sketch crude pictures first of a junk with Chinese sailors bound to the mast, next of the junk being broken up by huge waves. Then, with a vigour that turned the ugly atmosphere into harmless hilarity, he acted out the drama of the maelstrom and the drowning of the poor victims before they were washed up on the beach. The village warriors were so taken with his performance they joined in, acting out their threats of execution to make him repeat it over and over until he was tottering with exhaustion.

Their torment lasted through a second night before the storm wore itself out and guides appeared repeating 'Ama' and signalling to the Captain and Commodore to follow leaving their men behind as hostage. Captain Forge delayed, unwilling to abandon his men in case they suffered the usual treatment for crews stranded as they were - to be thrown into a squalid, unsavoury prison. Or worse, killed for the bounty still standing on the head of any foreign devil - a bounty larger if captives were dead than alive.

After a swift colloquy, the bosun spoke up for the men in urging them to leave. 'You go, cap'n. You can't talk us out of here if you're still here. We'll take our chances.'

They left then, still sceptical these poor, semi-starved villagers who were their saviours had not, in the meantime, found how much higher a price was advertised on their heads than the three thousand taels they had promised to pay. They soon found how lucky they had been. They had been castaway on an isolated island. Their barefoot Tankas were honest. They took them down the cliffs to two rundown sampans on the shore and ordered them to lie down on the bottom, repeating over and over that 'Ladrone pirates' were about, then covered them with straw that had seen better days. They lay half-smothered, drifting between sleeping and waking to the flap of the heavy mat sail and the slap of the sea on the hull above their heads, profoundly thankful for the benign sea and the gentle stability of the little craft after the catastrophic typhoon. Suddenly an altercation broke out overhead. Captain Forge peered through the straw to see their Tanka boatmen shaking with fright.

'Ladrones?' the Commodore whispered.

'Our headhunters methinks. Being headed off in the opposite direction from where we came, it seems.' The Tanka boatmen now filling opium pipes with shaking hands.

Captain Forge woke from an uneasy sleep to a second loud hail across the water. This time one of the Tanka boatmen shook him roughly awake as he thrust the straw away from his face and pointed to a Portuguese lorcha heaving to hard by, its rails lined with Portuguese and Lascars sporting a heavy armoury of swords, muskets and pistols. The Commodore joined him, shouting 'Englesee, Capitaos.'

Captain Forge identified himself, 'Eu sou Capitao Forge.'

'Capitaos?' The dapper Portuguese Captain smiled at the clownish appearance of the two men. Captain Forge doubled up with laughter as the absurdity of their bedraggled state and their craft. It spread to uproarious laughter among everyone on both vessels except the pompous Commodore who had never been blessed with any appreciation for the ridiculous

The Portuguese captain welcomed them on board the lorcha, hitching the Tanka boat in tow so the boatmen could claim their reward in Macao. He rifled the crews' sea-chests for clothes to fit. As they were largely slender or diminutive, and the two refugees were sizeable men, he could only produce striped trousers and jacket for the captain and a blue worsted sailor's frock for the Commodore with low-crowned sailors' hats to top the outfits prompting the captain to break into a sailor's hornpipe.

The Commodore reproved him, 'really, Barron, do you think that consorts with the dignity of your office?'

'No, but it consorts with my mood at escaping the wrath of God and man, and expresses my relief at my rescue.' He waved his hat to cool himself down again.'

The affable captain was ready with a drink. He could, after all, speak passable English. 'Very good, Capitao. God is good. No Ladrones. Lucky no Ladrones. Ladrones everywhere. Storms. Make money.'

Over the first full meal they had had in days he told them of the devastation in Macao. Trees stripped of all leaves. Large masses of granite washed from the seawall in Macao. Houses unrooved. Ships in the Taipa wrecked. Looting everywhere. Heaven knew how many more shipwrecks out in the open sea. Too early to tell. Finally over a large cup of very strong tea, he produced a copy of the 'Canton Press'. And there on the front page, a fresh shock for Captain Forge. A sketch of his face with news of his recall and Sir Hugh Pottinger already on his way to take his place.

Captain Forge was not shocked to be recalled. He had expected to be General Gaunt's victim over Canton. But he was shocked that the news came not, as it should, in a private despatch from a Minister of the Crown but with maximum disparagement in the local gutter press published by his arch enemy. He could never remember being more angry than he was now.

Commodore Brendan, now his greatest ally, was incredulous, 'that's preposterous!'

'Is it, Commodore? You, youself, said the army would not tolerate taking orders from the navy any longer especially from a junior post captain.'

The Commodore read on, 'and to give as a prime reason that you disobeyed your instructions. You should have kept Chusan Island. You should have gone north first. You should not keep Hong Kong. How can those brass hats in Whitehall have the gall to sit in judgement on us out in this hell hole of China? They ought to be sent here themselves as punishment. You have my deepest sympathy. It's a disgrace that you're in disgrace, Barron.'

Captain Forge refused to go onshore until his honest Tanka boatmen had their reward, sending the Commodore instead to tell Flora and the Governor of their rescue. The Commodore returned, fully restored in dignity in a fresh uniform, with the warning the Governor had ordered a guard of honour and band to welcome him with full honours at the quay to show 'his thanksgiving for our resurrection from the dead.'

'Does he know I'm deposed?' Captain Forge protested, annoyed with the thoughtless Commodore for his failure to bring him any uniform. 'You go straight back and tell him I can't expect a guard to present arms with a straight face at the ludicrous sight I offer.'

But the band would not be denied its moment of glory. The Captain was after all obliged to step ashore to their dirge-like playing of 'Rule Britannia' saying under his breath 'Britannia doesn't rule these waves.'

The fleet in Hong Kong had been too late making a run for it to the open sea. The storm had caught its ships tight packed in that enclosed reach of water and hammered them on each other like a madman's marble game. Wrenched this way and that, many were partly, and four totally, dismasted. Six with bowsprits, mainmasts or spars lost. Hulls cut by collisions. Twenty merchant vessels and transports driven onshore to be torn to pieces along with the new Hong Kong Houses and buildings along the shore, including Jarman Malleson's new warehouse. Many others driven out to sea to witness appalling scenes of stricken junks riding to their certain doom.

'Time for us to go. I believe I've pushed my luck far enough,' Captain Forge said without regret as he returned the amulet to Holly. It mightn't have worked on the Yangtze River.' Which was where Sir Hugh Pottinger was now destined.

Holly nodded. Barron was right. Chung Tai Tai's influence would not reach as far north as Shanghai. 'I'll miss you both terribly.' Her desolation was obvious.

'For us it's the end of an era. For you the beginning,' Captain Forge said in a forlorn endeavour to cheer her up. 'There'll be a new surge of energy into China, spreading north from Hong Kong. You'll be a pioneer on a new frontier, doing what you Yankees seem to do best.'

'You've become as dear to me as family.' She threw her arms around Flora.

'No one is irreplaceable, Holly. There'll be new faces, new friends as dear to you in time as we have been.' In truth she thought the dearest face would be an old face, that of Sean Jarman who was her only hope of resurrection of family and children beyond the terrible grave where the 'Jason' lay buried with Billy and baby Jason.

Tears stood in Holly's eyes as she asked. 'No regrets, Flora?'

Flora smiled gently. 'Would you be sorry in our shoes?'

Weariness on Captain Forge's face as he spoke for them both, 'I tried to postpone a day of reckoning as best as I could. I paddled against the flood with a leaky boat and an oar full of holes. That day of reckoning is getting closer. I don't want to be here. Holly, you've seen great changes overtake this country as we have. Commissioner Lin found these great provinces in the south tranquil and flourishing. In less than year he reduced them to the verge of ruin and insurrection to conform to the dictates of the Vermilion Pen. Now pirates and robbers stalk abroad unpunished.'

'Yet you recommend I stay here?'

Holly's wry smile left Barron him apologetic for his rhetoric. 'You can always...' he faltered.

'Find a good husband who'll look after me?' She could hardly tell him she had found Sean Jarman again, not when men like Jarman and Malleson had had him thrown out of China in disgrace, blackening his name.

Flora took up the theme. 'There would be no shortage of candidates with the fleet in port for repairs, Holly.'

'Maybe I can look after myself, pirates and robbers and all.'

Even as Holly spoke, she knew the truth of the remark. China had been a hard taskmaster. She had gained strength, but more important she had lost fear. She had learned to hope for God, and not to walk in terror of the devil. Therefore if she gambled with the devil himself, the gold she might win would not turn to autumn leaves.

* * * * * *

Defeat of the great Conciliator

Holly stood to attention on Penha Hill as the Portuguese Governor's twenty-three gun salute thundered out in farewell to Captain Forge and Commodore Brendan as Her Majesty's steamship 'Atlanta' dwindled rapidly over the horizon, her funnels trailing plumes of smoke. She wept, not because her Barron had gone and with him her closest friend in Flora, but because he had been so shamefully treated.

The merchants had ignored his departure in shabby contrast to the ceremonies for Dr. Jarman two years before. No banquet. No farewell calls. No escort of ships. Only the Portuguese Governor rendered him due honours, understanding only too well the diplomatic finesse of his achievements. As did Howqua, who sent him rich gifts with an apology that age prevented him coming in person and the compliment he was a 'Number One Vellee Man'. Barron had laughed at that when he heard.

Holly wondered whether he would have laughed at the vicious epitaph that had unfortunately been published in the scurrilous new rag, the 'Hong Kong Press', for him to read. 'His public acts in China may become a valuable rule to those who succeed him. They will know what to avoid, acts that were a series of errors due to his total misconception of the character and genius of the Chinese and their government.'

The only man in all Hong Kong astute enough to see, and courageous enough to say what a serious loss Captain Forge's departure would be, was John Davies who had returned to confound all those who had said his career in China was finished. He had sprung from the earth like a second miracle within days of Captain Forge's return 'from the jaws of death', as he put it, jovial as ever.

Captain Forge had welcomed him back with genuine pleasure. 'You kept your promise to return after all!' He had pumped the hand of the little man, more rotund and grey than when he had left China, but with the same irrepressible smile, the same latent edge of irascibility.

'Only because I have the misfortune to speak the language of the Celestial Kingdom. They want no mistakes about any Treaty with the Forbidden City.'

The new Commander-in-Chief, according to John Davies, was a man who would be respected by everyone but be popular with no one. 'Quite a reputation in India in the Sind campaign. Not the man I would have chosen,' he had said, finishing with with a jibe, 'but Dr. Jarman expresses himself well satisfied.'

Captain Forge had been less hostile. 'What matter if he makes the Emperor sue for peace. At least they've left Hong Kong alone. Dr. Jarman must have realised its enormous value at last.' Hong Kong was the one achievement of his that Viscount Palmerston no longer scorned.

Captain Forge's resignation to his fate had been genuine. He had watched the extensive fleet of the powerful Expeditionary Force sail north without regret. The Foreign Secretary had been right to recall him. He was not the man to see busy cities occupied, civilians slaughtered, Tartar generals disgraced, Tartar garrisons of that proud, if now degenerate, race driven to mass suicide, moderate Tartar envoys, who tried to negotiate with the west, humiliated and sent into exile. He would have hated to see more British troops sicken and die in their hundreds in the wrangle to come to terms with an intractable China. Let that great force of ten men of war, four steamers and twenty two transports attack Amoy, Ningpo and Shanghai! Let them recover Chusan island, block the Grand Canal, blockade and sail to Nanjing up the Yangtse River! He would prefer not to have that war on his hands.

John Davies had confided in him, as he was about to leave Macao for ever, that when the Treaty that would ensue was signed, sealed and delivered he, Davies, would be Governor of Hong Kong. 'Then we will see.'

'Why didn't you tell me earlier?'

John Davies' wry look was answer enough. 'You've been in China long enough to learn secrets get wings of their own.'

'Lord Palmerston not so hoodwinked by Jarman after all?'

'Let's say I became a successful antagonist. I convinced our Minister that the merchants and their minions must be curbed or Hong Kong would become the headquarters of the Red Circle to its cost.'

'Did you dare spell that out?'

'Would I be such a fool as to give them warning and put a price on my head? I handed the baton to you. It's fitting I take it up again.'

'And pay the same price?'

'No doubt, or worse.'

Holly's sadness was matched in that of John Davies as he stood beside her in the soft late spring sunshine to watch the Atlanta fade away over the horizon. She pledged whatever help she may.

He shook her hand warmly, his lingering in her own. 'One true friend is worth a hundred fair weather friends.' He prompted her to leave and put the past behind her. 'When do you go to Hong Kong, my dear?'

'Tomorrow. I will live in the High Devil's house until my own is built.'

'That should be a new experience for you, Holly.' Raine's Pagoda House, built by the Chinese in their own fashion, was a standing joke in the colony.

Holly dismissed the implied criticism. 'Beggars can't be choosers. I can't exactly live in a tent with Seth Law. The Pagoda House is said to be at the healthy end of the township. Unless I live there and supervise the building myself, I won't get my Connecticut cottage but another Chinese pavilion. The Chinese would be the last to respect me if I became an imitation Chinese.'

She was silent on the one most compelling argument. She must keep herself busy so she had no time to be afraid for Sean, who proposed to enter Shanghai in the wake of the fleet when it went upriver to Chinkiang and Nanking leaving only a handful of soldiers for garrison in a hostile countryside in Hong Kong. The scale of her fear she knew to be the measure of her love, overwhelming.

CHAPTER 12

1842-Hong Kong rises from Canton's Ashes

The treaty of Nanking

John Norris sat utterly exhausted beside Her Majesty's Plenipotentiary, Sir Hugh Pottinger, on the warship Cornwallis. He forced himself to be attentive to yet more of that indefatigable Excellency's endless demands. He had been too exhausted for any excitement the day before, when Sir Hugh had offered him the post of Colonial Secretary in Hong Kong after the campaign was over. He had merely gaped like a country yokel and stammered his thanks at the great honour. Six months ago he might have shouted the news to the universe that Sir Hugh had given him the right to stand tall as any merchant the day he would ask Holly to marry him.

Now he only felt despondent. Tired enough to admit the truth. He had never shouted. He had never enjoyed himself. Work, nothing but work, and no play since he was a child. How true the saying was that all work and no play makes Jack a dull boy. He was diligent but dull. He had always been in a batchelor community. Never had the chance to mix, to enjoy himself with young people or acquire any social graces.

He knew only one overpowering emotion at this precise moment, namely relief that the gruesome events of the capture of Chinkiang would not be repeated. Nanking had surrendered. The Emperor had sued for peace. He would not be obliged to witness the appalling rites of death committed by the Tartars in Chinkiang all over again. All their houses filled with the dead and dying. Women with their throats cut from ear to ear. Children thrown down wells. Men immolated by fire or self-strangulation. Barely five hundred surviving out of four thousand. The terrible indifference of the looters pouring into the ruin, and destruction of the town, to pillage and out through the broken walls loaded with plunder in endless streams like ants.

He had prayed in thanks to God that the only embellishment of those formidable walls of Nanking that loomed above them was a rash of white flags of truce, and they would not have to turn the massed gunpower of that great, ominous squadron against them.

Now the moment he had never believed possible had arrived. The Emperor had at last sent mandarins of the highest rank - Viceroy Ilipu of the two Kian provinces and Envoy Chiying - to make a genuine treaty of piece yielding all they had asked for during three long years of intermittent violence between their nations.

At first there seemed no room to greet the mandarins on the deck of the Cornwallis as officers of the army, navy and marine assembled, serenaded by the band of the Royal Irish, still perplexed by his warning to wear no more than half full dress as the mandarins would be wearing the plainest of travelling robes. He had answered their objection that no ambassador of any European nation ever turned up to such a historic meeting in anything less than the most splendid dress, by insisting Chinese etiquette demanded they appear as if they had left the Court at the Emperor's most urgent order, dressed as they were.

By the time the three gun salute announced the approach of the Embassy's barges, the congregation had miraculously resolved themselves into a semblance of order. The Admiral, General and Plenipotentiary were on the quarter deck, the principal naval and military officers on the poop and a guard of marines faced the gangway ladder.

The leading barge, bearing the Imperial yellow ensign, drew to a scrupulous stop. As the stout Viceroy Ilipu stepped laboriously onto the deck, the Marines presented arms with the sharp slap of hands on rifle stock and brisk stamp of feet the only sounds in the hushed silence. The ambassadors indeed as plainly dressed as foretold with no more adornment on their plain blue tunics for this high occasion than the red girdle of rank on Viceroy Ilipu, or the yellow girdle of membership of the Imperial family on Chiying - not even a yellow cape like the Tartar-General although himself a famous Generalissimo. Their dress was even less assuming than that of the blue and white button mandarins in their entourage. Even their ubiquitous interpreter 'Captain White' more of a peacock than they.

The introductory courtesies over, Envoy Chiying asked to inspect the ship. 'Certainly', the Admiral obliged with an aside to his aides, 'far more likely to convince the blighters than all the regiments we've put on shore.'

As Envoy Chiying, Viceroy Ilipu and the Tartar-General led their retinue on a tour of the armoury of guns, rifles and swords, it was plain these three Tartars were the only ones among the mandarins capable of appraising these engines of war. All three had won their spurs in battle. The rest were traditional Chinese scholars forbidden the knowledge or use of weapons.

Viceroy Ilipu's eyes lit up with the days of his glory as they rested on the general's sword in the aftermost cabin. 'May I try the sword of the great general of the intelligent nation?' he asked.

So we are 'the intelligent nation' these days are we, and not the 'outer barbarians' any more, John reflected with amusement, as he translated the request.

Sir Hugh drew his unadorned cavalry sword from its scabbard and offered it, grip first, to Viceroy Ilipu. The Viceroy took it with a surge of revived vigour, straightened his stooped back, tested its weight and balance with a swing up and down, a jab and swipe wide enough to cause Sir Hugh to jerk back in the confined cabin. Then he seized the sword blade, point in his free hand, and, much as he would test the spring of a cross bow, forced it upwards with an inward pressure of both hands and a strength surprising in one of his age. As Sir Hugh expostulated at this cavalier treatment of his heirloom sword through a translation too slow to stop the old Tartar warrior, the sword snapped in two to shocked apologies from the Viceroy protesting he would replace it with a better one.

Sir Hugh bowed with constrained civility and terse orders to the junior officers that they were to bring their best swords at once, and let the junior mandarins test them in case the latter ran away with the idea British arms were inferior to their own. John Norris believed the self-same mandarins would be far more interested in the cherry brandy wine, and rum laced with sugar, in the wardroom than any further test of British arms. They were not too stupid to know it was the guns that counted, not the swords. He was relieved to be able to sit down at last before the banquet in the Grand Cabin that proved they had more culinary masters in the Fleet than anyone had imagined. Cakes and sweetmeats that conjured up memories of winter high teas in solid English homes. Creations that caused their guests to pause politely as they themselves did before delicacies of fungus or hundred day eggs - eating as they did when faced with such a dilemma, bolting small samples down quickly then washing them down with wine.

How strange it was to break bread together in a tranquil meal with its promise of a signed treaty which would ensure this ancient city of Nanking would rest untroubled behind its endless city walls of vanished days of Imperial grandeur. All the while, as counterpoint to their frail mortality and perishable treaties, the Yangtze River flowing insistently past their vessels in medium flood, rocking them with a rough hand. A flood which already overflowed the embankments creeping across the countryside as it had done since time immemorial, laying it open to invaders far more ancient than themselves - bandits who smelt anarchy from afar and swarmed in to plunder homes, empty granaries and open prisons.

John Norris sat bemused throughout the banquet to think he was present on such a historic occasion - a Son of Heaven obliged to accept another race as equal. When he had learned mandarin at his father's knee, he never thought to meet the Emperor's councillors on equal terms, never dreamed he would be present when they signed a treaty acknowledging defeat. Still less that they would pay reparations for the Expeditionary Force that imposed a Treaty on them, let alone the value of the opium confiscated by High Commissioner Lin. Nor did he believe Envoy Chiying would suffer with exile to Tibet and confiscation of his fortune as Envoy Chishan had after signing the first Treaty.

John Norris felt this war had made him old before his time, cynical beyond his still youthful twenties, this war, which seemed to solve all the grievances, yet somehow seemed to solve none. He was too sceptical of the victory which caused them such jubilation to share in it. Could the British officers on board not see this war had brought a shame on the Son of Heaven he could not afford? Samson had shaken the pillars of his temple and cracked his foundations. The Emperor could not remain content with such massive loss of face and honour to men scorned yesterday as outer barbarians, no better than the piratical foam of the sea, to men whose undoubted high aims still had opium at the rotten heart of their victory.

John Norris could not shake off this depression through all the rituals that led to the signing of the treaty except at moments so ridiculous he could forget his huge and most subtle responsibility in this most extraordinary moment of history. As when the British officers, ablaze in scarlet and gold, abandoned their onshore solemn procession on the way to meet the Envoys at the Temple where the Treaty was to be signed, and scrambled like children to be first in the sedan chairs; or when the British band of the 18th led them through a double line of Tartar soldiers into the second court of the Temple playing British Grenadiers in loud competition with two Chinese bands esconsed between rows of colossal

Chinese gods. Most of all he laughed to witness Sir Hugh Pottinger riding his horse up the steps, regretting he had ever told the Plenipotentiary how Chishan had once been allowed the very highest honour of all for any man in China - to ride his horse in the Forbidden City - an honour he had decided should be central to this final ceremony.

At last the whole melodrama, with its weird blend of solemnity and grotesque farce, ended with a final flourish when four copies of the Treaty were signed - the ends of the ribbon glued to the paper so no page could be abstracted in one last touch of distrust - and a twenty-one gun salute for the Emperor of China was fired from the flagship.

At last they could up anchor and away, none too soon as so many men on every ship in the squadron were so ill with all the complaints known to Old China Hands they could barely crew them. As they dropped cautiously down the treacherous high flood of the river, John Norris needed no imagination to forecast what must follow. Out of the eight Powers that wrestled for a toehold in China, the British above all would prevail. There was an old saying in the East - 'the first thing the French build is a fort, the Spaniards a church, the English a warehouse.'

* * * * * *

New destinies

By the time the Treaty was signed, Holly's house stood half-way up a hill overlooking the Jarman Malleson warehouse on the foreshore and Hong Kong bay beyond. No matter that neither she, nor anyone else in Hong Kong, had a legal right to build when they did. By the time it was finished, she had made so much money victualling the British Expeditionary Force, she regretted she had not planned for a house twice as large.

Yet as she stared down on the burgeoning settlement from day to day, she still was not certain after all whether she wanted to commit her life to its future. It was raw as a California gold rush town, a slapdash mixture of scattered burghers' mansions, ponderous warehouses and improvised Chinese shanty towns as they flooded in in their thousands. A single street, imperfectly planned. A few sporadic buildings on the hillside. A spluttering progress, depending on whether the prophets of doom, who pointed to Happy Valley as a valley of death, prevailed or not. Already a haunt of pirates, who infested Chinatown and lorded it over the high seas with weapons they had refused to return to the authorities after the truce in Canton.

As she sat in her bay window posing for Chinnery, while he roughed out the portrait he would hang over her mantel, she knew Sean would soon be home. She could not postpone decisions much longer - whether to marry now or later, whether to live in Hong Kong or Shanghai.

'Tilt your head a fraction, Miss Evergreen,' Chinnery ordered as his pencil moved rapidly on the huge canvas. She smiled that she could still be 'Miss' in Chinnery's mind as when he had first known her - vivacious, vulnerable, unsullied yet by grim experience.

'You will hang in the Hong Kong Art Gallery one day, Miss Evergreen, immortal as the gods.'

Sitting in a Queen Anne chair, borrowed from the Casa Garden in Macao for the purpose, Holly felt absurd dressed in a formal gown as if for dinner at Government House; a dress of the new fashion for whale-boned bodices over wasp waists and billowing skirts balanced by imbecilic sleeves. Clearly what was haut ton in London was grotesquerie in an outpost like Hong Kong. Here she would sit, all dressed up and nowhere to go. How she wished Mary Ann or Abby could see her now. They would see it as one more proof of the lunacy that was life in China. Chinnery peering at her over his half moon glasses, dipping his head up and down like a honeyeater pecking at pollen. The servants peeking through the long windows at the missee 'sitting'. How ludicrous to behave as if she were sitting in a New England manor to add yet one more to the dynasty of portraits that advertised the changeless drama of family. Here all was change. Here society was unstable and turbulent.

'You're not going to live here, Mr. Chinnery.'

'Why no, Miss Evergreen. One needs peace at my time of life.'

'Once you came to Lintin to escape the uproar of Macao.'

He eluded her. 'Miss Evergreen. You don't need me to tell you the uproar has moved from Macao to Hong Kong, and is worse than ever. Therefore Macao will be peaceful again.'

Holly nodded gloomily. 'Two fires in Chinatown already and a riot after spies were caught, spies they said were from the walled city of Kowloon.'

'I was down at Jarman Malleson's yesterday. They say that Chinatown is nothing but a nest of pirates.' Holly laughed outright at this. 'Is robber and murder so amusing, Miss Evergreen?'

'When it's a case of Jarman Malleson's smug boats being robbed by those from whom he snatched the trade in the first place. It's known as dog eats dog. You might call this undeclared war one between the foam of the land and the foam of the sea.'

'Since you're so knowledgeable, Miss Evergreen, who will win?'

'The advantage at present lies with the boat people, disorganised though they are since Chung Tai Tai retired.'

'That's not what I heard on the grapevine.'

'Oh yes, she has what her enemies call these disgraceful establishments. Perhaps they are pawnshops for stolen goods, or merely for those who gamble in her casinos. But the Ladrones at the Bogue have new captains, and the Red Circle moves into Hong Kong in the shadow of the merchant princes.'

'You see, Miss Evergreen, why I prefer the peace of Macao. My home and friends are there. Praise God, I will be dead by the time rebellion, provoked by the loss of face we have inflicted on the Son of Heaven, breaks out.'

Holly was about to ask Chinnery why he made such a ghastly prophecy, so out of character with his jocular nature, when Kaida Hung was ushered in. She did not leave him standing as Chinnery expected, ignorant of his real eminence. Nor could she give him his due. With two Triad groups at war who had only one thing in common, their loyalty to a Ming heir, it was a matter of life and death that he remain anonymous.

She spoke first. 'When do we leave for Canton, Hung?'

'Madam, I came with a warning. It would be dangerous.'

'The Treaty allows women. Are they more of a threat than men?'

Chinnery, the famous woman-hater peered humorously over his spectacles at Holly. 'Perhaps they're shrewd enough to see that letting you ladies in the open door would be the ruin of their male domination, as the Manchu see that letting your husbands in will be the ruin of their rule.'

'Speaking as a refugee from petticoat rule yourself, maestro?'

Kaida waited patiently through this exchange, thinking how he wished he had the courage to ask Chinnery to paint his new love, a girl from the Norris School in Hong Kong. She was the girl he hoped to take to America as his bride to work for the American government, if Chiying went to New York as rumoured and an interpreter was needed. Lost in his dream of the future, Kaida did not hear Holly's question.

'Is it Howqua who sends the message?'

Kaida nodded. 'Howqua says you must not come. Food and water could be poisoned.'

'The mandarins are still at war with us?'

'The people are. They say you're the cause of all their misfortunes.'

'I don't understand Kaida. What people?'

She turned her head back on Chinnery's testy orders.

'The villagers. The Patriotic Associations, who believe they could have driven the foreign devils out of Canton, if the Prefect had ot betrayed them for a bribe from the Red Beards.'

'You and I know that's ludicrous.'

'Perhaps but they believe it.'

Holly was sceptical. 'How do you know all this, Kaida?'

'Because they have pasted placards in all the streets behind the factories saying so. Not only that, they have distributed gunpowder and bombs so rebels can set fire to the Factories.' Factories only just rebuilt. Both Holly and Chinnery giving him full attention now.

'Any chance of massacre?'

'Surely not, the Prefect would never let it come to that,' Chinnery ventured.

'What is Howqua doing for God's sake?'

'Howqua's dying. He will not see out the summer,' Kaida said.

'He says he'll be glad to die. And the Co-Hong has lost its power.'

Young Mowqua had survived the war in triumph. He had won a decoration, a promotion in rank and the highly prized salt monopoly for Kwantung - the profit from which financed his new fleet of war junks - for no more effort than buying a British officer's uniform and cap from a looter in the field and sending it in triumph to Pekin.

'The end of an era,' Chinnery sighed, taking up his pencil again. Howqua had seemed to be the indestructible pivot of the Canton trade. And when he died, as seemed imminent, a grace, a dignity and a trust would be gone. Qualities he believed he had caught in Howqua's portrait so all would remember the man who ranked so high, yet was a man without rank. Truly immortality lay only in the brush.

* * * * * *

Celebration

When Holly was handed on board the Cornwallis for a celebration ball in the gown she had worn to sit for her portrait, she could not recognise it's scrubbed spic and span any more. The old warrior ship was more like a Chinese warjunk with all the embellishments it now wore, an eruption of flags of all nations, variegated lamps, flowers and chandeliers of crossed bayonets on masts, rigging or rails.

Sir Hugh Pottinger and the Admiral were receiving on the maindeck, standing side by side, sporting the new GCB decorations, they had awarded each other to a gun salute that very day, beside their long strip of campaign ribbons as they played the gallant and kissed Holly's hand.

'Mighty sure of themselves aren't they? Bringing those awards, or rewards if you like, along in their kit in the supreme confidence they were going to win,' Holly grumbled to her escort, John Norris, as they moved away.

John Norris laughed. 'Scratch a Yankee and you find an irritable critic of our glorious heroes.'

She groaned in disapproval. 'Where are Barron Forge's medals, may I ask? He did the spadework of their war. Where are your medals? Your skill with words was far more important than theirs in blowing holes through a few walls.'

'Hang on Holly. I wouldn't go as far as that,' he murmured in dissent. 'Besides I have been honoured this very day. Appointed Colonial Secretary and Councillor of the new colony of Hong Kong.'

She drew back in exaggerated appraisal. 'You are a dark horse, John. The rank outsider galloping to the front. No wonder you look like the cat who's just had a bowl of cream tonight. Stupid me thought it was the fact you were letting your hair down for once.'

'It was also because I was taking you to this ball.'

'If there weren't such a big crowd here, I'd give you a big hug of congratulations.' She grimaced at the blaze of uniforms and ballgowns around them.'

Racked with nerves, he seized both her hands. 'Oh Holly, if only you could. I know this isn't the time to speak out now, but if I don't a dozen men will snatch you from me before the night's much older.'

'Do you want me to keep the supper dance for you?' She asked disconcerted by his unusual boldness.

'Oh no, I want you to keep your life for me.' She struggled to hide her amazement as he raced on. 'I want you to be my wife. I have prospects, Holly. I am second only to the Governor now.' How he wished his tongue did not feel so hobbled and cobbled, that he had more of the suavity of a Sean Jarman. 'If only you could say yes.'

Anguished for him, she stood dumbfounded to think he had suffered for love of her, as she had for Sean, and she had never guessed. How well she knew what that hopeless love must have cost him in the past, what this hope he might yet win her love cost him now. If only she could say yes and save him from the same despair she had once known herself. How cruel this dance of love forever was. A dance of death for so many. She could not deliver that blow, dismiss him to face lonely regret, not here and now in a celebration ball as much for him as anyone.

She searched for the words as she tightened her grip on his hands. 'Your love is more than I deserve. To accept it would precipitate a very serious decision for me. I would have to fit into an official life. Perhaps even sell my ships. Can I think it over?'

One of the matriarchs accosted him, insensitive to their intimate dalliance, seeing John, as everyone did, only as a man eternally busy with work. She turned away to find Sean Jarman bowing over her hand, kissing it with excessive pressure and a lingering gesture.

'Very different from the first time we met is it not?'

'You've had a war since then, Sean.'

'Won the war and lost the girl.'

'Have you Sean?'

'Have I not?'

As they stood silent, eyes locked, both knew he had not. She had given him her answer once more. They were two halves of one being, utterly whole when together, all differences of mind or heart melted away, recalled to the present when the band struck up. Holly was relieved to see John too far away to have noticed. Poor John! How guilty she felt now. She would have to subject him to all the pain of a rejected suitor, the one man, above all others, she would least like to hurt. Her answer to Sean could mean only one answer to her future. She could not live in any place that held John as her despised love. She must leave the new house she loved, her first real home, to go to Shanghai or Scotland - anywhere but remain here with her love for Sean so plain for John to see.

Her despairing thoughts were cut short as the Chinese national anthem brought them all to attention for the banquet on deck. The Envoy, Chiying, waddled forward with the less portly Tartar-General, Huang Lu - their pendant double peacock feathers bobbing behind their little black acorn hats - to seat themselves and proceed to imbibe too freely much to the amusement of the two attentive officers on either side of Holly. She explained they were Tartars, who, unlike the Chinese, did not believe a banquet was a banquet unless they got roaring drunk.

Chiying was not so 'roaring' however as to be incapable of presenting a gold bracelet from his wrist to Sir Hugh Pottinger with the promise that he would only have to show it wherever he travelled in China to meet many friends. But 'roaring' enough for him to express the extraordinary hope he might see Sir Hugh's legs under his table in Pekin by virtue of the fact he had just overseen a war to prevent any such possibility. And to sing a love song, his robust wailing so weird to the British ear all of Her Majesty's subjects present were hard put to it to keep a straight face, and demand that Sir Hugh Pottinger oblige in kind. Since Sir Hugh had no reciprocal desire to make a spectacle of himself he goaded Captain Quin into singing 'Poll of Wapping' more off-key than on so as 'not to let the side down.'

The banquet over, Sean commandeered Holly for the quadrille and was galloping across the floor with her when Tung Fat decided to get into the spirit of things by seizing the equally inebriated Chief Justice and capering about more in imitation of the sailors' hornpipe than the quadrille, ricocheting from one to the other in his thick sole boots with his partner's long thick legs ridiculously encased in tight shining black, exactly like an elephant dancing with a stork - exempt from censure only because he had the luck to be married to an imperial princess.

Holly danced on, oblivious to all but Sean, thinking of that other time when they had danced on the deck of the Lintin in a dance that was a pledge to each other. Was it only so few years ago? It seemed like a hundred. She had seen and done so much. She saw that naive young woman now as a stranger long gone and with her all the romance, sentiment and idealism of youth. She understood only one thing. There were no answers. Not even the catchcries such as 'east is east and west is west but only the Chinese are grotesque', no matter how mandarins such as Tung Fat might give the lie. Sometimes an answer would stare you in the face and you would be too blind to see it as she had been twice with Sean.

Holly was frantic when she heard just days later that John Norris was mortally ill of Hong Kong fever. He himself sent a message she was not to come. This blend of the yellow fever and the African jungle fever was too contagious. His last act one of thoughtfulness and courage. For weeks, she was tormented with guilt by the small voice that said he won't have to face rejection, he won't have to live with a rival he does not respect, until she found an answer. He had died with the universal love of everyone in the colony, a much rarer love than the so often corrupt emotion between two people. He had been buried in the Protestant cemetery alongside his father with unqualified grief and plaudits from all.

'A prince among men whose pure soul rose above the common clay of lesser men,' the Reverend had said. Lesser men who far too often thought themselves greater.

Tim Bird slipped away in another sense. He simply disappeared. Seth Law's first thought was of his outstanding debts. Surely the six hundred dollars Tim Bird had borrowed from him, just before he vanished, would have met the payment he could no longer render the Chinese agents of his creditors abroad? No one would have thought worse of him if he had defaulted. After all everyone was feeling the pinch in Macao by the final shift of trade to Hong Kong. But Tim had had a sense of honour as became apparent when at last, after months, his body was found buried in the sand of Casilha Bay.

Everyone who crowded the tiny Company chapel then asked the same question. All Macao had been his friend. Why had he not turned to any of them in his trouble? A small unnoticed trouble in the wake of Viceroy Lin who had destroyed his fragile means of keeping afloat and put him in fear of exposure.

The respectful dignified comprador was there to tell an ironic tale of how his body came to be in Casilha Bay if he had committed suicide. Wanting to save face, he had gone to a tiny settlement at Fishermen's Point there and told the men they would find a dead man lying on the beach nearby. As the Chinese nearest to the dead body, they must bury it otherwise the mandarins would hold them responsible for the death. When they had argued they would appear guilty if they did, he had pleaded with them in their own language by the light of their own superstitions. He threatened the dead man's spirit would haunt them. They would grow no rice, catch no fish, until he was buried. And so they buried him. Which left the final question unanswered. Had he wanted to die among the people he understood and loved so well?

When Holly heard of Tim Bird's melancholic but triumphant end, she was left to wonder what could become of that most perfect expression of his love of the Orient - his aviary and his garden. He, at least, had tried to leave his mark in other terms than the begetting of silver.

John Davies' Resurrection

Governor Davies ushered Holly into the withdrawing room of the temporary Government House, seated her on the ottoman and stood before her.

'Your note asks me to give you away, Holly. I'll be more than delighted. I'm only sorry Barron wasn't here to stand in my place.' He leaned forward to kiss her lightly on the brow. 'But I'd better warn you it's just possible all the worthies in the entire colony might stay away from the wedding.'

Holly regarded the sprightly little man with amazement. 'Why ever should they do that?'

'To show what they think of my appointment as Governor of this colony.'

'They didn't do so when you were President of the Company Select. They wouldn't do so now when you're his Excellency, the Governor.'

'Wouldn't they, Holly? They don't depend on me for licences now, don't forget.' He sat down beside her, one arm along the curving back. 'Holly, you understand what you're getting yourelf into, don't you?'

She looked so innocent in her soft golden dress, so much like a bewildered child with her poignant blue eyes, and delicacy of manner. 'I'm marrying into Jarman Malleson's.'

'With all that implies!' Was she strong enough, he wondered?

She asked with assumed naivete. 'What does it imply?' He so clearly wanted to play the father to her.

'Look at the facts. For centuries, the Portuguese dominated the smuggling trade and paid a levy to a whole hierarchy of mandarins to turn the blind eye to the distribution of those smuggled goods by means of a large fleet of smug boats. This ancient balance of power has been overturned in favour of the free traders, the chief of them your family-to-be in alliance with new 'running dogs' in the Triads.'

To Holly, this was now a familiar tale. She protested. 'I'm marrying Sean not the firm.'

'Will there be any difference my dear? Think well.'

'Chung Tai Tai and you speak with the same voice.'

'Did she spell it out, dear Holly? Cruel that it would have been to do so. But she, or I, would be more guilty if we did not. She did well to retire.' Oh, how he dreaded disillusion after marriage would go hard for Holly.

He paused to stare out the window at the diligent Chinese workmen on the half-built mansions hard by before he began slowly, 'if I had known how bad things had become, I doubt I would have succumbed to Lord Palmerston's urgency he needed a man who could speak the native languages on the spot. The horror of my situation is that I do. I learn the truth.'

'And that is?'

'This new power, as Barron told it to me, seized control of the Pearl River delta. You know their battles in his day better than I do.'

Oh yes, how could she forget the running battles, the massacres that were a prelude to the real war; the time Barron said Viceroy Lin opened the floodgates to the new criminal economy by wrecking the old.

'This new power is busy seizing control of the sea, putting the whole coastline in the grasp of their blackmailing confederacy by landing to terrorise the villages away from the Ladrones of old, by rape, murder, burning, destroying all resistance if there is any and sometimes even if there is none. Why these men in their junks and Portuguese-built lorchas are an infinitely more infamous scourge than the pirates ever were.'

'Don't the Ladrones try to stop them?'

'Of course! Wouldn't you if all your trade was poached from you? Oh yes, they set spies among them, board their vessels and take their booty. Some bloody battles follow, I can tell you.'

Holly shuddered at the recollection of atrocities she had heard. Butchery that made poor Mr. Moss's bloody half-scalped head seem mild. Sinews torn out, limbs chopped off, eyes blinded. Ferocity that knew no bounds.'

'Their spies infest our bazaars, European as well as Chinese. European guns for hire are the worst of all, they say.'

'What can you do?' She asked in distress, not so much for these warriors of war to control the smuggling trade but to think Jarman Malleson could have such allies. Was she being too insouciant after all?

'What can I do? Nothing, since our precious Sir Hugh gave Chinese full control of Chinese shipping, except do what they demand. This is to arrest the Red Circle members and pack them off to Canton with a brand on their cheeeks so there can be no mistake if they try to come back as they will.'

'Wouldn't there be a furore about that?' The very idea of branding humans raised all the ghosts of the humanitarian movement on the slave trade.

'Don't you think you should ask Sean Jarman that question?'

'What are you trying to tell me, John?' The room that had so much charm a moment ago now seemed oppressive.

'What a father would tell you if he knew as much as I, retire to Scotland. Urge Sean to take up any career there. Trade, politics, even the Commons in the footsteps of his uncle. They say he's about to retire. But not Hong Kong or Shanghai.'

James Malleson was retiring soon to take Dr. Jarman's seat in the house of Commons when he died after an agonised battle with cancer.

'I tell you Holly, it's easier to govern twenty thousand Chinese than it is to manage a handful of Europeans, at least the kind that find their way out east. I haven't got the faintest hope of carrying out Lord Palmerston's edict against the opium trade in Hong Kong now that Sir Hugh lets the Apollo sit out there.'

He pointed to Captain Macdonald's ship anchored near East Point, busy transhipping opium into brigantines, clippers, lorchas, junks in flagrant defiance of the law.

'I can stop them warehousing on land, that's all. I have no power, whatsoever, to stop this trade on the sea. All I can do is try to prevent this island from being used as the point from which the British smugglers depart on their illegal adventures. My edicts will be as useless as the Viceroy's have been. They will mean nothing. No one has ever controlled this gateway to China. No one ever will.

'You're saying what Barron Forge said when he left. We've not only opened the door to China but also the door to anarchy.'

'To the terror and ruin of another White Lotus rebellion. Will the roots of the smuggling Taipans of all nations grow free from the mire where they seeded?

Can they?' Holly rose as he spoke these gloomy words. 'You still want me to give you away. You aren't angry?'

No, she was not angry. She merely looked pensively down at him. 'I wonder what Billy would have said. He saw the best in people.'

'He refused to play God and make judgements as I'm doing.'

'That's why you'll make an excellent Governor and a good father of the bride. But seriously, your Excellency, how can you control this monster you describe, John, ?'

He rose to join her, a whimsical smile on his face. 'Tread a tightrope as Barron did. Then retire before I'm kicked out as he was. One more question. Which preacher is going to marry you?'

'The Reverend Legge from Malacca College.'

'Ah, a good Scot from Aberdeen and the only honest man in the colony besides myself.'

As Holly stepped into her sedan chair, she wondered what future Billy would have forecast if he were with her now. Why surely he would have said, 'you'll be the new Chung Tai Tai, the future Pirate Queen.'

She laughed at herself then. She would take what the gods gave and be thankful. But she doubted if she would end up running a casino in Hong Kong's Chinatown in retirement increasingly embattled against the growing predominance of the Triads 14K like Chung Tai Tai.

Holly thought the exuberant bustle on her wedding dress looked ridiculous as the tailor pinned it in place. She had sympathised with Envoy Chiying when he lifted a lady's bustle at the ball on the Cornwallis to see what lay underneath believing the affronted lady was stuck to the cushion she had sat on. Alright for ladies built like junks.

'But not a sampan like me,' she told her good neighbour, Betty Harrow, in fact her only neighbour. Betty was a chatty, uncomplicated soul like Mrs. Macdonald, that breed of indomitable Englishwomen who could travel halfway round the world and establish their small replica of England without a tremor in the most outrageous places.

'Good for the cake gluttons,' she said cheerfully now, 'who look like cushions everywhere. But a sylph like you, who looks as if you'd blow away on the first strong gale, it makes you look more formidable.'

'I thought I was supposed to look the helpless female on my wedding day.'

'Just beautiful, lass, which you do.'

Holly turned sideways to admire the line of her pale blue taffeta dress remembering what Sean had said when he had insisted on blue for the blue of her eyes. 'Why not the sea blue?' she had asked. 'Too dark,' he had rejoined, 'too angry.' Yes, he had been right. It was an angry sea, hereabouts. So she had chosen a blue a shade darker than forget-me-not. Hetty Macdonald would wear a slightly darker blue as matron of honour.

As both the tailor and Hetty white fussed over Holly's fitting she suddenly felt very alone. Here she was preparing for the most joyous moment of her life with two virtual strangers. All her friends scattered - Mary Ann, Maisie, Abby, Rebecca, all gone home. Too many of the roving wives of men in the services still remaining drunk, rough, flighty, or faithless. Her only two close friends men. These two, Tough Wagoner and Adam, who was already on his way from

Manila with his new Spanish wife for the wedding.

'Missee likee,' the tailor asked, the last tuck taken.

'Missee likee velly muchee,' she felt like shouting as she saw happiness luminous in the face that stared back at her from the mirror.

She ushered them out exhausted and went to bed early. She slept fitfully as she had done since Major D'Augila had banned the nightwatchmens' hourly gongs so they could all sleep undisturbed, uneasy because robberies had been a daily occurrence on and off the water since the curfew on the harbour.

She lay thinking of Chung Tai Tai who had said that very day, 'it's the Ladrone war all over again. But this time my people do not fight the government. They fight the foreign devil Red Beards, the Portuguese and all the foam of the land who work for them. My poor Tanka people. They would drive us off our old ancient islands, even Hong Kong.' With a weariness in her eyes, Chung Tai Tai no longer looked as indestructible as when Holly had first met her.

Holly had asked her gently, 'will you fight?'

She had answered. 'I remember when the Portuguese navy helped the Manchus we had to surrender. We must do the same if the British Navy help the Red Circle.'

'Is the government in Hong Kong like the Manchu?'

'Be careful, Holly. If they know I'm your friend then...' she had left the sentence in mid-air and turned to pray at her shrine to Kwanying that Holly be safe on the seas of her life.

Warnings. All those around her gave was warnings, she fretted as she drifted off into a light sleep. She woke to the harsh reverberation of her own watchman's gong, the shout of the watch, abrasive thuds on the doors and walls outside and the apparition of a coolie rushing in shouting 'bandits!' as she stepped from her bed.

Was the house surrounded by them? How many were there? Had the coolies locked the doors? She took a quick look out the windows as she thew a voluminous cape round her shoulders and tied the strings under her chin. A flare outside revealed a demonic scene at her front door, bandits, too stupid to break a window, trying to break down the door with some heavy mass. She ran to the back of the house, shouting to the distraught coolies bunched uselessly in the kitchen holding choppers and bamboo staves. 'I go soldiers!'

She rushed out the back door to stumble across the rockstrewn hillside in the dim wash of moonlight towards the building that housed some officers of the Madras Native Infantry with a detachment of sepoys. Their watch half-asleep despite the audible crash of the battering ram on her door. Dead to the world from hashish no doubt. She shook him, waking him with her shout 'bandits!' He struck the alarm gong loud enough to wake the dead. Men poured from their beds, muskets in hand. None of the spic and span of native tunics and turbans as on parade. More like hungry ghosts in their white underwear as they rushed up the hill towards her house, smoke already pouring ominously from a window. Holly, lagging behind, halted in anguish at the sight. Her house put to the torch already, the only home she had ever had. Robbers plainly looting it to judge by those emerging from it. Shots rang out from the sepoys. Two staggered but kept on towards their boat pulled up on shore below. One fell.

By the time she reached the front door another lay dying, blood pouring from his wound, beside the large wooden shield, faced with iron, used to batter it down. As she entered, an officer barred her way.

'You can't go in, Ma'am, till we clear the smoke bombs. Pots charged with gunpowder. Dangerous if you don't know where they are, and what to do. Meant blow you up if you should seize them. No doubt of it, Ma'am. Just as well you had a quick head on your shoulders, Ma'am. This one said they came from the walled city of Kowloon.' He prodded the fallen man, but he was beyond words now.

As Holly waited shivering in the still night air from shock and fright, Betty White appeared to take her arm. 'I'm so sorry, Holly. I hope you won't take it as a bad omen.'

'Why should I?'

'I saw a man go by with your wedding dress.'

Holly wept hysterically then - all the tears she had not wept for her father, for Jim, for Billy, for the losses of her life believing all through those tragedies the only way to live life on the Coast was, as these men had, with stoicism.

'Poor dear!' Hetty said to the distressed officer, 'getting married with none of her own folk around.'

'Ma'am,' he said, standing to attention, 'God bless you!'

The goodwill in the salutation from the half-dressed officer on the raw hillside in the dead of night recalled her to the fact that discipline was the cardinal virtue of these men, who survived hardship and calamity so well when far from home as she was. She must borrow that virtue from them. She straightened her back and led Hetty inside her house.

* * * * * *

Whom God has joined

The Reverend Lodge, newly arrived from Malacca with his wan wife, apologetically declined to marry Sean and Holly in the salon of Government House as Hong Kong had no church yet. 'I can only marry you on holy ground. In the chapel in Macao perhaps.'

Governor Davies assayed a joke about the devil's playground which fell flat. 'What's wrong with the Eugenia, Holly?'

'That's hardly holy. But not involved in the devil's work.'

Sean exclaimed, 'He's reminded us Tough Wagoner can do it.'

Holly threw her arms around Sean to a clucking from Governor Davies. 'You'll have a lifetime for that.'

She retorted, 'look how long I've waited. And he can take us to Canton for our honeymoon.'

'Canton?' Sean and Governor Davies asked in concerted dismay.

Not only Canton, but all the countryside around, had become more dangerous than they had ever been as Kaida had predicted. In Canton, discharged volunteers were refusing to yield their arms or return home. The gentry of ninety villages, and their patriotic associations, had published manifestos condemning the mandarins for giving the city up so easily when they had 'that rude clown', Forge, and all the redbeard dogmen on the run; and boasting General Gaunt had not dared to attack or enter the city once they were on the march in force. They swore they were not prepared to live under the same sky as the British rebels but would exterminate them off the face of the earth. The Petition Gate of the city was as closed to the foreign devils as it had ever been. As Captain Forge had so truly said, 'it is easier to get on than get in.'

'Canton seems the last place on earth you'd want for a honeymoon,' Governor Davies grimaced at the thought of this blasphemy, Canton being so famously a batchelor retreat. 'Surely you'd want some peaceful spot?'

'Where may I ask does one exist in China?' Sean enquired amused, his arms still around Holly as if he were afraid she would fly away if he let her go.

She looked up at him, and as he bent towards her in response, kissed him lightly on the cheek in assurance. 'Our first trip together was up the Pearl river,' she explained.

Governor Davies pursed his lips in reproof. He had never been inclined to romance at the best of times. 'The circumstances are much more hostile now.'

'More hostile in general. Less in particular. I don't have to steal up to the Factories in disguise like a criminal on the run. I can go by right of treaty.'

Governor Davies sighed. If only tolerance could be created so easily. 'Not by right of custom,' he warned her. Who knew Chinese better than he?

'Sean and I believe we can't make a final decision about the future until we've laid a few ghosts to rest.' She swung the little cricket cage she carried on her wrist to keep the devils away, as everyone in Chinatown did after the autumn Feast of Hungry Ghosts. 'Since I thought my future lay there when I came to China, I have to be certain it does not.'

Governor Davies could see the logic of that. Holly had seen none of the to and fro of the clashes and battles of the River for herself, none of the change. She had to be sure. But he tried to stop her going to Chinatown first to see Chung Tai Tai. Holly insisted she had to say goodbye to Kaida, however. He was sailing out of harm's way to Singapore to act for Chung Tai Tai there before he went to America.

Chung Tai Tai had also bought up rice paddies and swamplands in Shanghai for a song and stood to make a vast fortune there if the most significant gamble of her life, that it would be the emporium of the future, proved correct. She would yield the battlefield of the Hong Kong Triads to Ah Shan, the new gambling and pirate king, and turn her eyes to the future of the Eastern trade from Shanghai through Singapore to the west. This meant she would need all the ships she could lay her hands on. By offering to contract Holly's ships she had resolved the thorny question of Holly's independence. For Sean had signed a marriage contract conserving the proceeds for her exclusive use - at his insistence not hers - and sealed it with a kiss joking 'cheap at the price'.

'Now you won't have to worry about the Jarman tainted silver,' he had teased her, 'or that I might embezzle your well-gotten gains once we're married.'

He himself, when in Scotland, had canvassed the chance of running a new branch of Jarman Malleson's trade, diverging from their staples of tea, silk and opium into goods like china, sewing machines and other newer products of the industrial revolution. 'After all,' he had said, 'we've all talked long enough about the virgin market teeming with four hundred million souls panting for our products. Let me try!'

James Malleson had tried to discourage him. 'You can't expect so much profit.'

Sean responded, 'I don't want to build a castle.' This was a barbed reference to the fact Malleson was rearing a castle in Scotland, his equivalent of a great mandarin's garden.

The only one who seemed to approve entirely of their plans was Chung Tai Tai after they had made their way through the hostile stares of the sprawling shanty town, a glorified bumboat town on land, increasingly resentful of the arrogant behaviour of their new white rulers and the source of daily robberies, violence and instant riots.

Chung Tai Tai excused her house. 'I will build a mansion in Shanghai,' she promised, her hand delicately describing a flowing edifice.

Everyone, Sean thought, seemed to be building castles in the air except themselves. What and where they would build as yet written only in their stars. He only knew his castle was wherever Holly was, as Barron had known with Flora.

Holly offered the tiny gold cricket cage to Chung Tai Tai. Even as she intruded the gold splinter through the slender bars to tease the cricket to sound, it began a steady chirrup without prompting. 'That should frighten the very biggest devils away,' she laughed just as Kaida bowed his way into the room. No sign of his usual genial smile.

'What's wrong, Kaida?' He hesitated.

Chung Tai Tai answered for him. 'His brother, Geli, was arrested at the assembly this morning. He and sixteen others.'

'What assembly?' Sean asked sharply. No news of any assembly.

'Ah Shan plans a mass attack on Victoria in Hong Kong when the military and naval garrisons are depleted soon.'

Sean was outraged. 'Why would Ah Shan have such a madness of the brain to think he could seize Hong Kong after our parade of armament this past three years?'

Chung Tai Tai answered glumly. 'Because he's stupid. He thinks this is just another pirate war.'

'And now Geli is in prison. Denounced by someone. This time we could not bribe the gaol keeper,' Geli added sadly.

Holly's bewilderment turned into confusion. 'I thought Geli belonged to the old Triads.'

'That's exactly why he was there. To spy on the new Triads. Now he'll be branded with a tattoo under his arm as if he were one of them. Everyone will take him for one of Ah Shan's men.'

A tattoo seemed a mild punishment to Sean who was one of the few merchants to agree with Governor Davies the only way he could control the growing menace of the new Triads was to brand them, once identified. He had only drawn the line at branding on the cheeks which had been Governor Davies' first angry response.

They decided to intercede for Geli on one condition only, he leave Canton for good and go either to Shanghai or Singapore for he would no longer be safe in Kwantung.

Holly boarded the Eugenia without a backward glance at Hong Kong, no longer the cradle of all her hopes of security and happiness. It had proved a nursery of all bedevilment of the gods - Hong Kong fever, plague, cholera, typhoons, violence and now rebellions. As Governor Davies said the objects of the new Triads were incompatible with good order. She welcomed the haven of her own little kingdom. It was absolutely right to make their wedding vows to each other bfore the durable and gentle Tough Wagoner, his weatherworn dark face composed into uncommon gravity and to be given away by her mate, loyal through ten long years since that first timid adventure out of Salem.

She felt a serenity so long foreign to her as she stood side by side with Sean, arms entwined, bracing themselves against the stern rail as the ship bucked in a brisk wind. She remembered the girl she had been when she first crossed this stretch of water at the Bogue. How much had changed since then in her! She had found the adventure too easy, the romance too hard. She had made money as she hoped. She was independent, but had found independence nothing without love. Happiness and dependence were inextricable. Home was where the heart was. Here and now, it was in this man-made island of wood and creaking rope on the dancing waters of the Bogue.

How much had changed in China! She could sit openly on deck without fear of arrest as they came abreast of the Bogue. She could sail up Junk River from Whampoa openly and land at the Factories - admittedly not without a lot of stares and shouted remarks. When she reached 'Little Jerusalem' to stay with Seth Law, there would already be other wives there, Jenny Law and the ladies in the newly rebuilt New English.

On arrival they promptly told her they had not only been walking in the garden and on the Common but had been out and about in the suburbs in sedan chairs, unmolested but for one instance when forced to retreat from the Temple with the holy pigs on Honam Island by a hostile crowd.

How much had changed in the life of the Factories since David Malleson had bustled her up to 'Little Jerusalem.' David Malleson had turned his back on China for life as an advocate in Edinburgh long ago. Joshua Law had succumbed to the lethal environment of China as had Lord Nash and John Norris. Dr. Jarman, surviving all its hazards for many years, had died of cancer. The incorrigible Laird would torment them all no more. Howqua could no longer be tormented, only just surviving the torments of the opium war. James Malleson had gone home to build his castle. Mary Ann, Abby and Dr. Tom had vanished from her life. Billy, little Jason, Jim Peel and Tim Bird had all drowned. Colin Kingsman had returned home defeated by China. High Commissioner Lin was dead and Chishan in exile as Great Ambassador to Tibet. Captain Forge and Flora were rumoured to be in Texas where he was Charge d'Affaires. New merchants and missionaries were on the scene. Only the High Devil Maxwell Raine, Chinnery and John Davies endured, but Davies was unlikely to last much longer in his post as Governor.

When Sean took Holly in her arms she forgot all melancholy. If life was a sad tale of death it was also a joyous tale of resurrection. In love was the indestructible gift of renewal, each encounter holding the promise of future love and children to confirm that love. They held each other as if they feared the fates would part them yet once again. The cruelty of change no longer mattered. Sean was all the vigour, all the passion, all the sensitive adoration she could imaginably want.

'You're like a dream come true,' she whispered in his ear, brushing it with her lips.

'One that took far too long to come true,' he responded by burying his face in her shoulder, savouring the indefinable faint sweet of her skin. 'Don't ever abandon me again.'

For days, Sean and Holly were too lost in their own emotional quiescence, their daze of delight, to listen to rumours that agitators were holding meetings in principal halls, calling for loyal citizens to unite to oppose these foreign devils who planned to get extra land to take root with homes, families and garrisons. After all life in China was one long rumour and the mandarins generally managed to keep the wilder spirits in check.

Holly was saying exactly this to Jenny Law over tea while Sean was along at Number 1 Creek Hong 'tidying up loose ends' before they left Canton for ever, when they heard a turmoil of shouts boil up outside. Jenny clung to Holly in terror when she saw the raging mob seething below, shouting and brandishing fists like dervishes round the huge bonfire they had created round the British flagpole now too well alight for rescue.

'God, its like the Bastille,' Jenny groaned with memories of vivid engravings on enraged mobs of the Revolution.

Holly soothed her. 'Don't panic, Jenny. We're all veterans of these blow-ups.' Inwardly she panicked. How could Sean reach her through this pandemonium below?

Predictably the mob had begun to batter away at the wall and door of the New English, screaming Hongu or Red Beards. She rushed downstairs and into the inner garden with Jenny hard behind to find Seth Law lowering the Laws' treasure into the well. 'That bad, Seth?'

'You saw the fire,' he answered tersely, 'we'll all be next. We've got to get the women out.' He eased his back. ' you can't do that without disguise. Holly, there are Chinese robes and caps in my room.'

Holly reeled back in a fit of laughter until Jenny clutched her begging her. 'Please Holly don't have hysterics now. We all need you.'

Holly dried her eyes. 'Humour not hysterics, Jenny. To think I fooled myself I could move about Canton at long last dressed as a woman, and now Seth tells me I must dress up as a man to escape. It says everything about this God-forsaken country there is to say.'

Seth tapped her shoulder. 'Shake it up Holly. You must get out of here and go to Consoo House. You'll be safe there.'

They had barely assumed their disguise when Sean came bursting into the room, dirty and dishevelled after clambering over the intervening rooves and a plank thrown across the narrow Hog Lane that lay between the neighbouring factory and Little Jerusalem.

Holly threw her arms around him in ecstatic relief, 'my gallant knight to the rescue.'

'Only just. And more ridiculous than any Don Quixote! Over the rooves, my little cricket, just as you must to reach a point where there's a ladder down into 13 Factories Street.'

Jenny hung back in terror. ' Climb a ladder?'

'That or be burnt to death.'

There was no mistaking the urgency in his voice, the dense fire-laden smoke drifting past them now or the din as the mob assaulted their ears. There was no doubt the frenzy of this mob far surpassed any attack of past years fuelled, as they knew, by a new popular arrogance and hatred. This was indeed the day of the Bastille.

Holly clambered up the ladder with difficulty in the overlarge Chinese boots and long robe. Once on the roof they could see only too clearly the fierce glare of the fire raging in Number 1 Creek and adjoining Factories like a false dawn, its hot breath laden with sparks already a hazard to the buildings below them.

'Pity the Laird's not here to see Canton's revenge on him.' Sean muttered, hand on her elbow.

When they had struggled down the ladder into the frenzied crowd in 13 Factories Street, Mowqua Junior, with an eye to a bet each way as ever, had servants waiting to bustle them into Consoo House then hustle them through the streets to a quay removed from the Common and into a waiting boat.

As they pulled away from the shore, the burning Factories and the delirium of the armed mob looting the looters on the Common, seemed like a scene from Gustav Dore's Dantes Inferno. The fire, that seemed certain to spread to hundreds of nearby buildings, looked as if it would engulf not only the Factories but the lost souls caught up in their futile frenzies. The weird scene a fit study for a Fall of Gomorrah.

She turned away as if the Voice of the Lord had spoken. 'Look back and you too will be turned into salt.'

As Holly boarded the Eugenia at Whampoa, where the skeleton fleet of traders was a ghost of what it had been, she and Sean knew without a word exchanged between them that their journey would be much farther than Hong Kong Bay, all the way to the new home Holly had never seen, first to Scotland and then back to Shanghai.

'You'll find evergreen there, my little cricket,' Sean said.

'Where the elves live to bring me good luck.'

'Do you need elves, now, Holly?'

She tipped up her elfin face and wrinkled her nose at him as she squeezed his arm possessively. 'They've brought me all the luck in the world I need already.' She threw the faded twig into the Pearl River.'

They left Hong Kong knowing theirs was the path to freedom. Canton was now a prison, the streets to the Factories sealed off, no foreigners allowed out nor Chinese in.

Holly's last comment as she sailed away was, 'this being such a back the front country, I suppose they'll say now that we locked the Chinese out!' As indeed they did.

Postscript - The Abbe Huc talks to Chishan in Tibet

He summoned us several times to talk about politics. We were surprised how much he knew about European affairs. He asked us what has become of the Plenipotentiary? I told him he was recalled. Your dismissal caused his.

'A pity. He was a good man. Was he executed or dismissed?'

'Neither. In Europe we are not as extreme as you are in Beijing.'

'Yes true, your mandarins are luckier than we are. Our Emperor can't know everything yet he has to decide everything and no one ever dares criticise what he does. Our Emperor says 'that is white. We kowtow and say 'yes that is white'. Then he points to the same thing and says 'that is black'. We kowtow again and answer yes that is black.'

'But supposing you were to say that nothing can be both white and black?'

'The emperor might say 'you are right' to the bold man. Bu he would then have him strangled or beheaded.'

He told me that the Emperor summoned the eight Grand Councillors, who made up his Privy Council in 1839, and told them that adventurers from the Western Seas had committed rebellious acts in the south, and they must be captured and punished as a warning to any others who might be tempted to follow their example.

After expressing these opinions, he asked the Councillors for theirs. The four Manchu Councillors kowtowed and said 'yes, yes, yes, those are the Master's orders. The four Chinese Councillors kowtowed in their turn and said 'yes, yes, yes, it is the Heavenly gift of the Emperor. The Council was then dismissed.

Chishan, who was there, believed the Chinese could only stand up to the Europeans militarily if they changed their old habits and their weapons, but that he would take care never to tell the Emperor what he thought because it would not only be useless but might well cost him his life.

* * * * * *